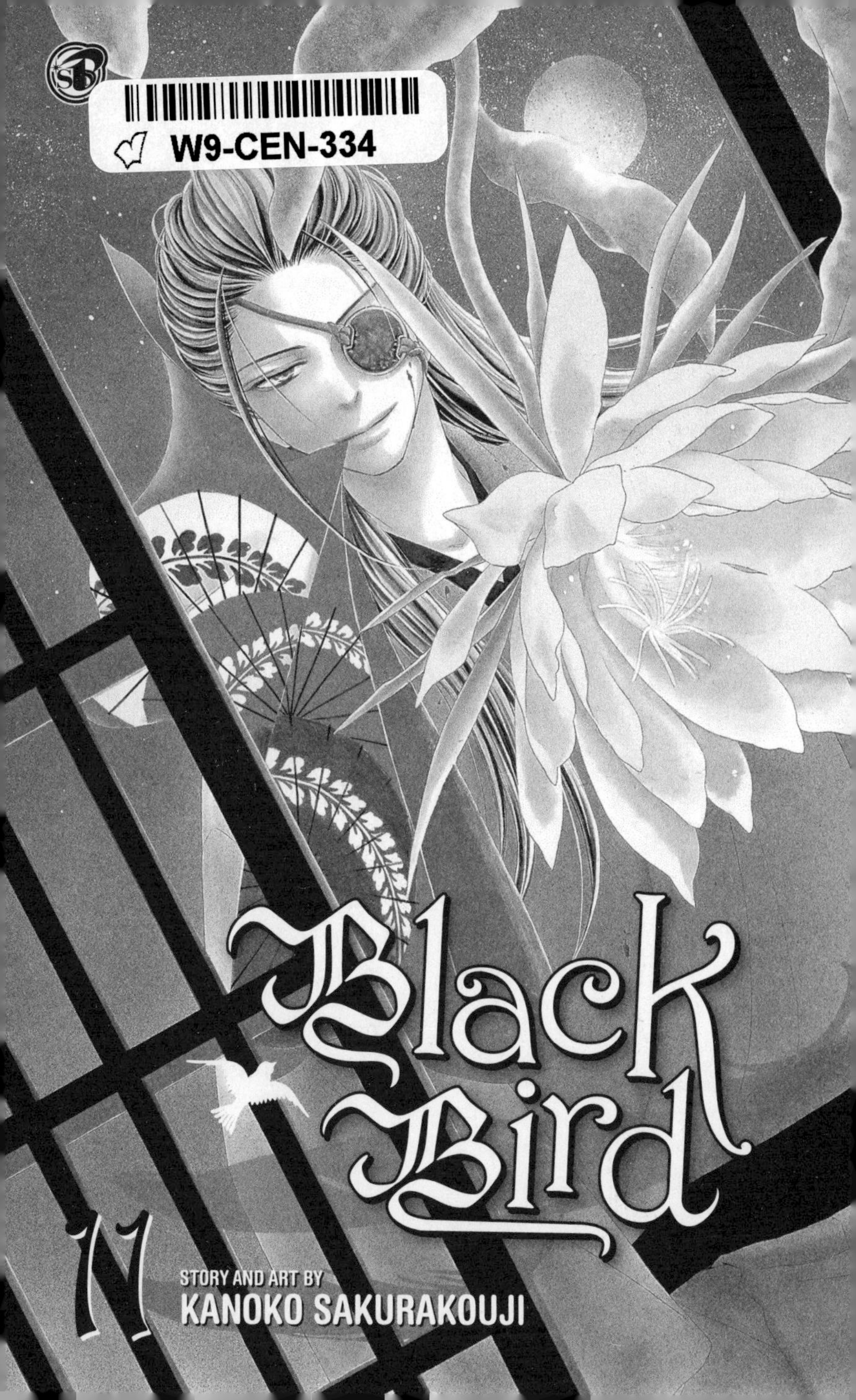
Black Bird
11
STORY AND ART BY
KANOKO SAKURAKOUJI

Black Bird

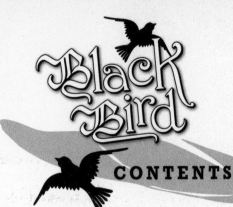

CONTENTS

CHARACTERS

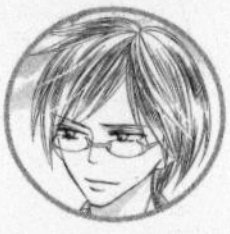

TADANOBU KUZUNOHA
Kyo's close friend since childhood. Current leader of the Kitsune clan.

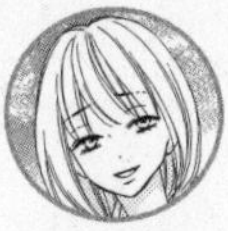

KAEDE
Her father Roh supported Sho's ambitions to seize the clan leadership. She is Sho's attendant.

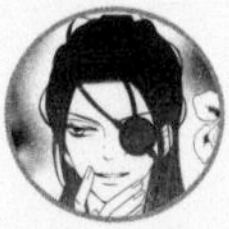

SHO USUI
Kyo's older brother and ex-member of the Eigh Daitengu. He is also know as Sojo. His attempted co failed and his whereabou are currently unknown.

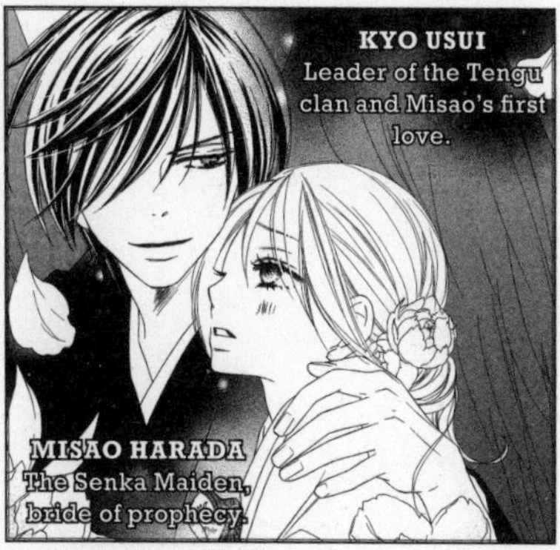
KYO USUI
Leader of the Tengu clan and Misao's first love.
MISAO HARADA
The Senka Maiden, bride of prophecy.

THE EIGHT DAITENGU
Kyo's bodyguards. Their names designate their official posts.

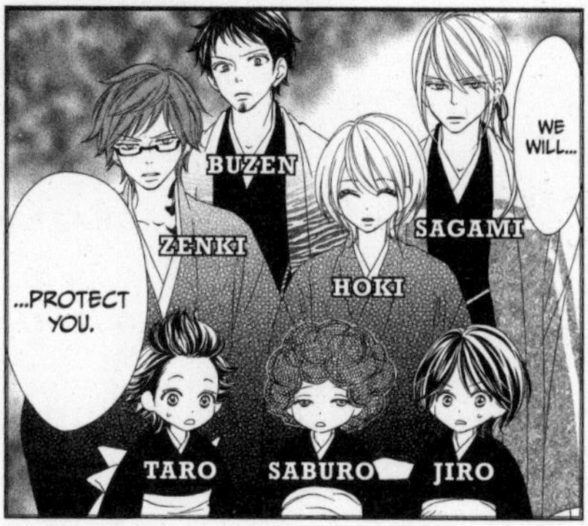
WE WILL...
...PROTECT YOU.
BUZEN
SAGAMI
ZENKI
HOKI
TARO
SABURO
JIRO

STORY THUS FAR
Misao can see spirits and demons, and her childhood sweetheart Kyo has been protecting her since she was little.

"Someday, I'll come for you, I promise."
Kyo reappears the day before Misao's 16th birthday to tell her, "Your 16th birthday marks 'open season' on you." She is the Senka Maiden, and if a demon drinks her blood, he is granted a long life. If he eats her flesh, he gains eternal youth. And if he makes her his bride, his clan will prosper...And Kyo is a *tengu*, a crow demon, with his sights firmly set on her.

So far, Kyo has avoided sleeping with Misao because he knows that sex with a demon is somehow dangerous for the Senka Maiden, but he finally gives in and takes Misao.

Now Kyo's powers have no equal, so other demon clans have begun a campaign of indiscriminate attacks on humans to pressure Kyo by working on Misao's sense of guilt.

One day Kyo's older brother Sho, who has been missing and presumed dead, suddenly shows up at the Tengu Village. Sho now possesses amazing powers, which puts Kyo on guard, but he is unable to ascertain Sho's plans. Furthermore, he discovers that Misao's new friend Kaede is the daughter of Roh, the man who supported Sho's bid to become clan leader...

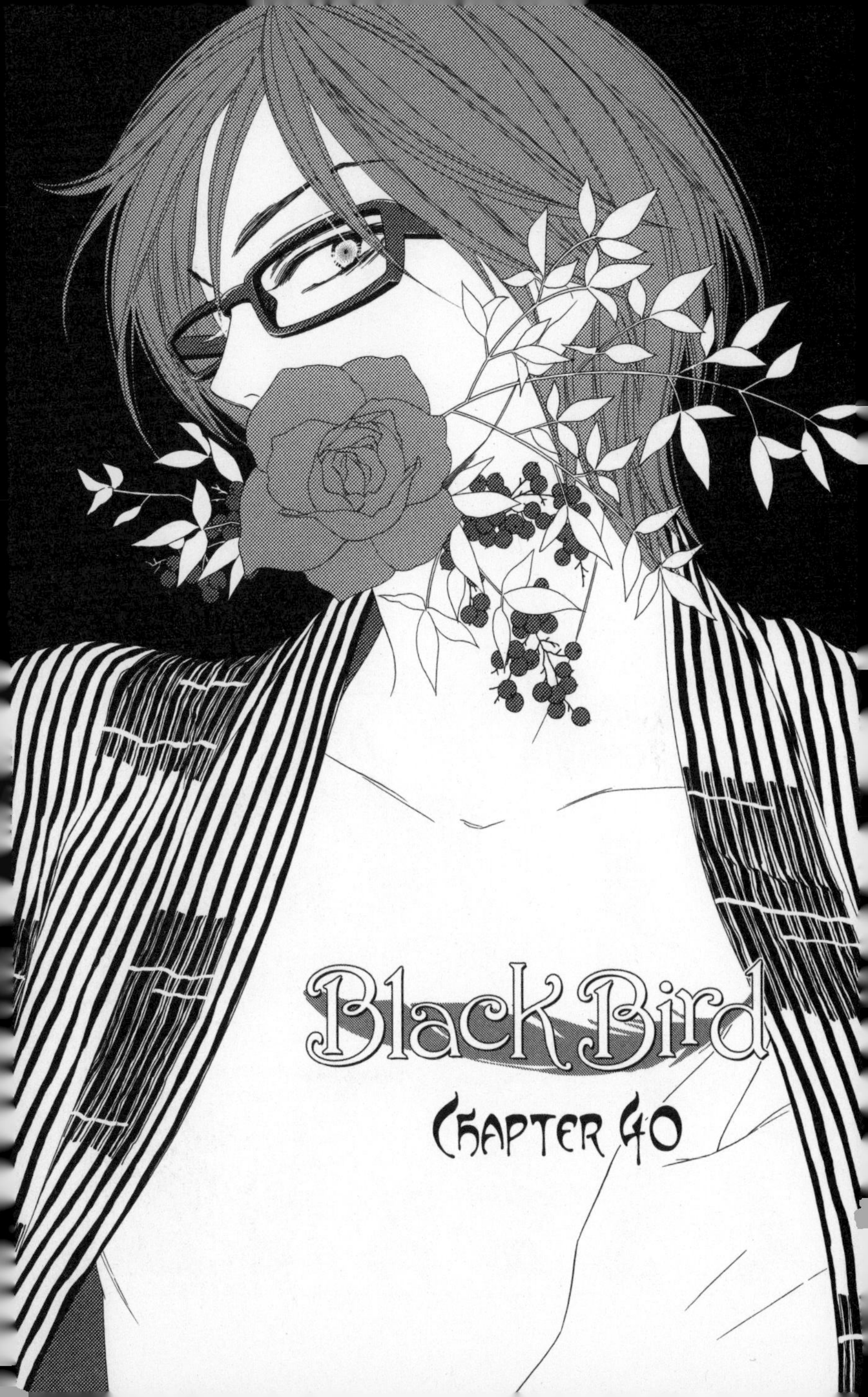
Black Bird
Chapter 40

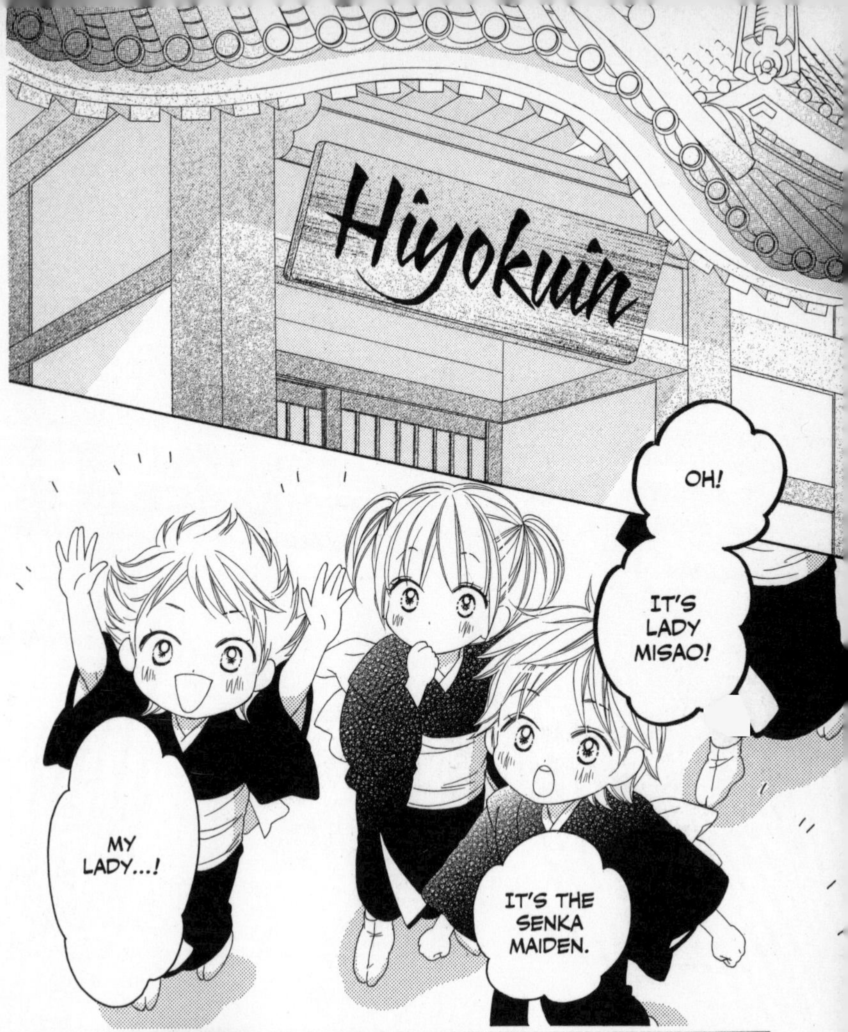
Hiyokuin
OH!
IT'S LADY MISAO!
IT'S THE SENKA MAIDEN.
MY LADY...!

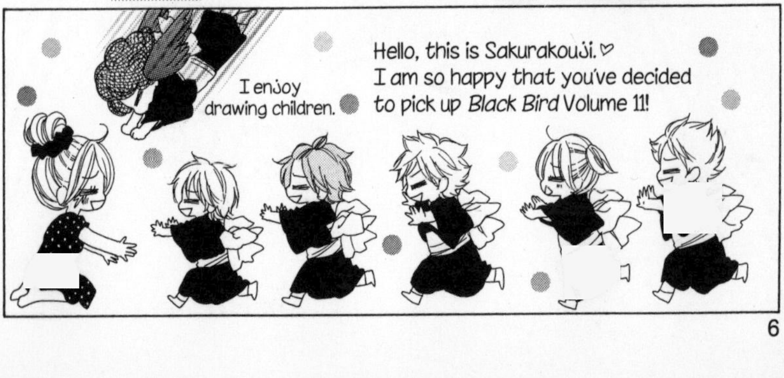
Hello, this is Sakurakouji.♡
I am so happy that you've decided to pick up *Black Bird* Volume 11!
I enjoy drawing children.

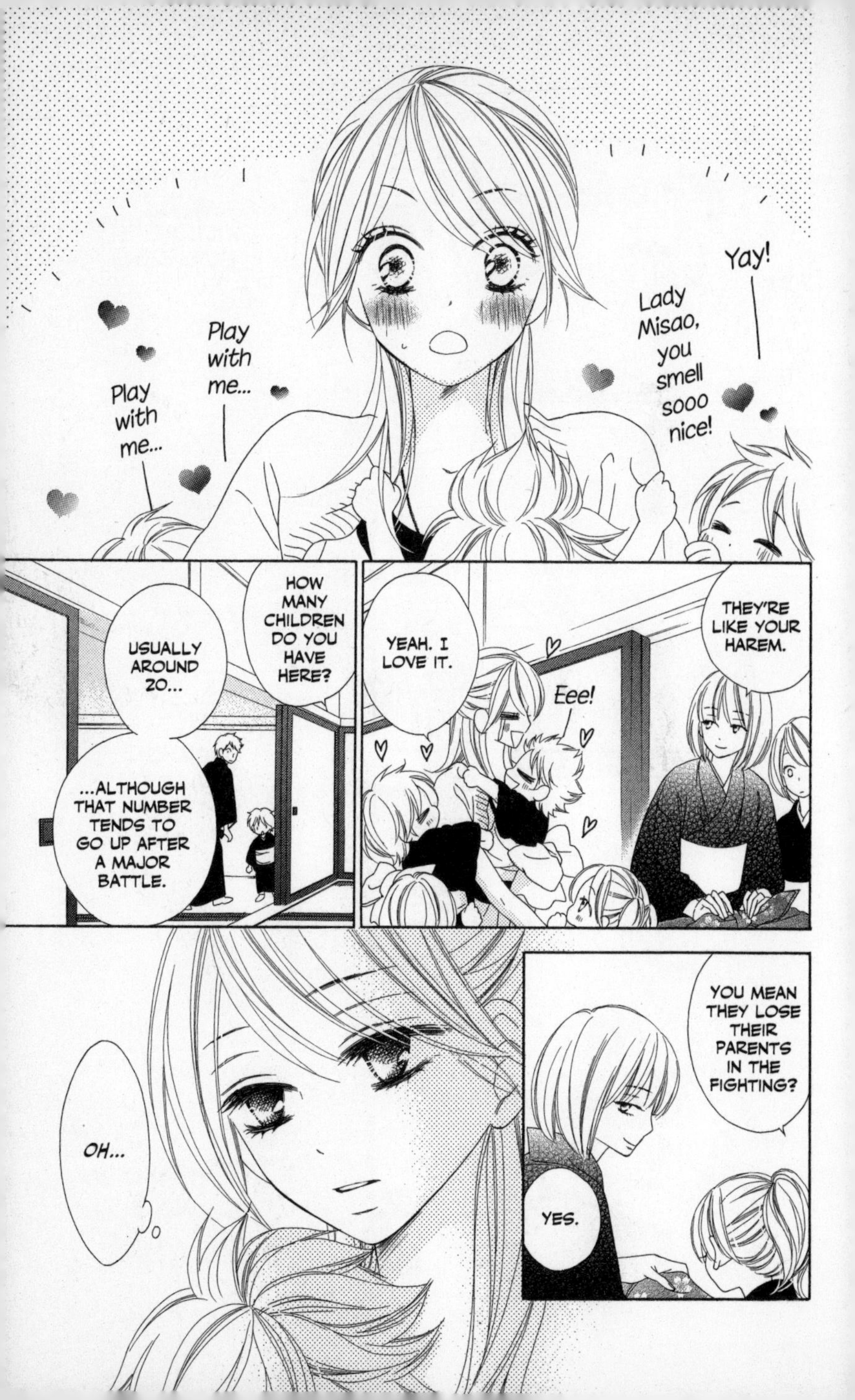
Yay!
Lady Misao, you smell sooo nice!
Play with me...
Play with me...
THEY'RE LIKE YOUR HAREM.
Eee!
YEAH. I LOVE IT.
HOW MANY CHILDREN DO YOU HAVE HERE?
USUALLY AROUND 20...
...ALTHOUGH THAT NUMBER TENDS TO GO UP AFTER A MAJOR BATTLE.
YOU MEAN THEY LOSE THEIR PARENTS IN THE FIGHTING?
YES.
OH...

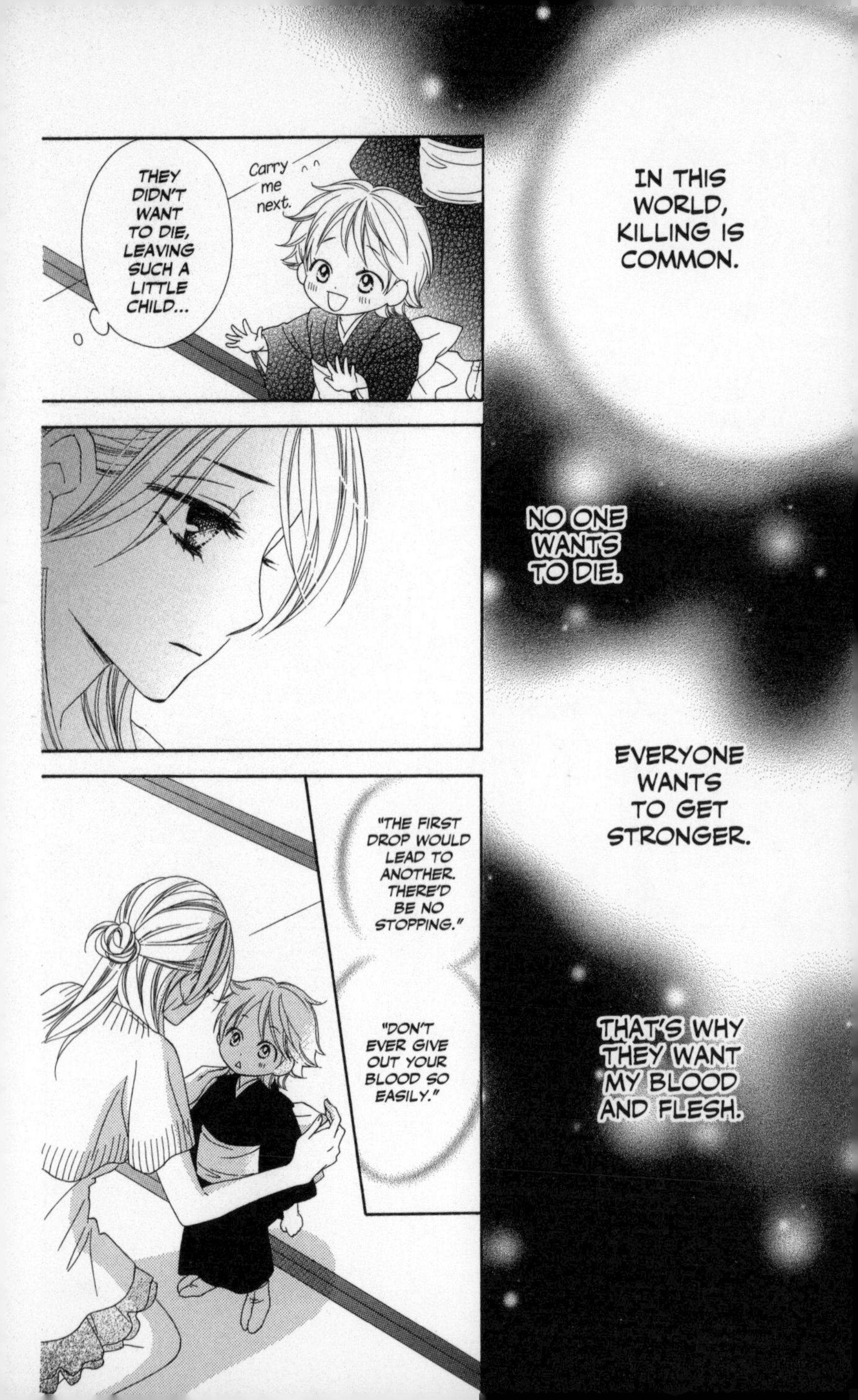
IN THIS WORLD, KILLING IS COMMON.
NO ONE WANTS TO DIE.
EVERYONE WANTS TO GET STRONGER.
THAT'S WHY THEY WANT MY BLOOD AND FLESH.
Carry me next.
THEY DIDN'T WANT TO DIE, LEAVING SUCH A LITTLE CHILD...
"THE FIRST DROP WOULD LEAD TO ANOTHER. THERE'D BE NO STOPPING."
"DON'T EVER GIVE OUT YOUR BLOOD SO EASILY."

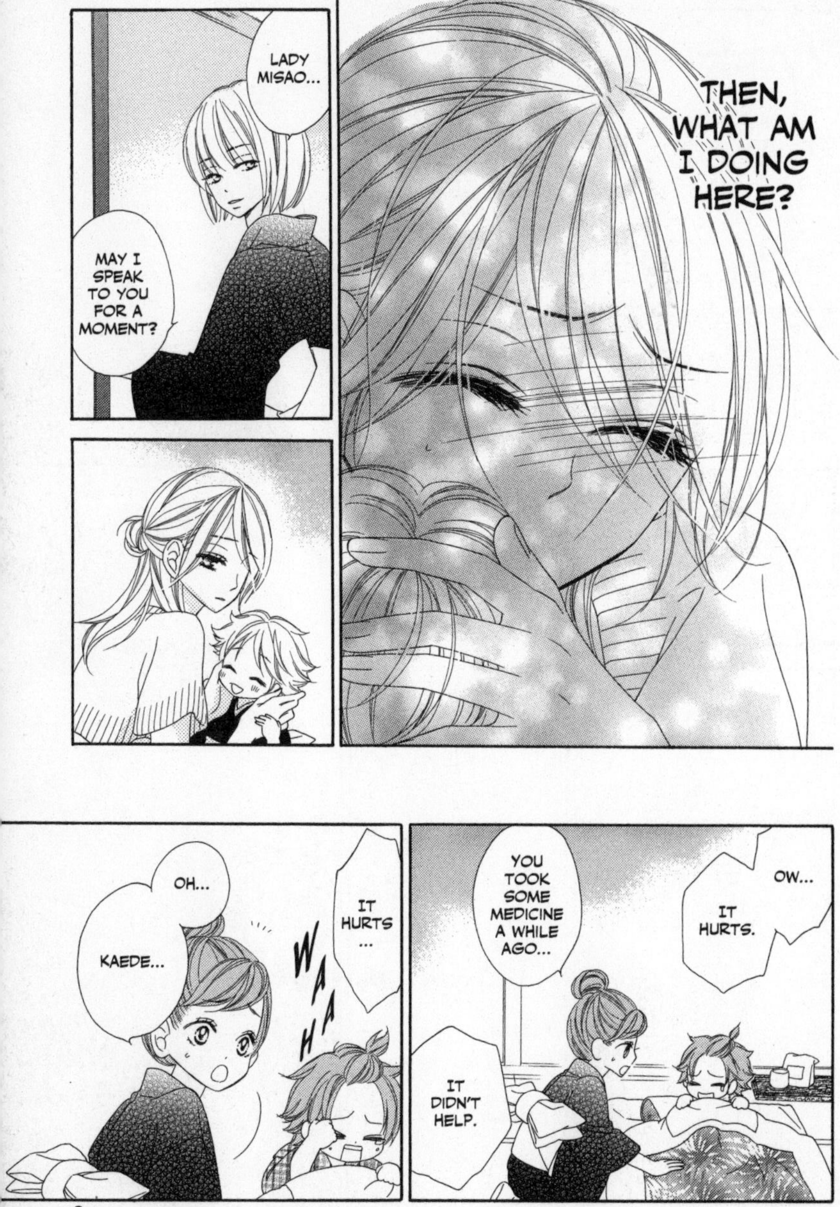
THEN, WHAT AM I DOING HERE?
LADY MISAO...
MAY I SPEAK TO YOU FOR A MOMENT?
OW...
IT HURTS.
YOU TOOK SOME MEDICINE A WHILE AGO...
IT DIDN'T HELP.
IT HURTS...
WAAH
OH...
KAEDE...

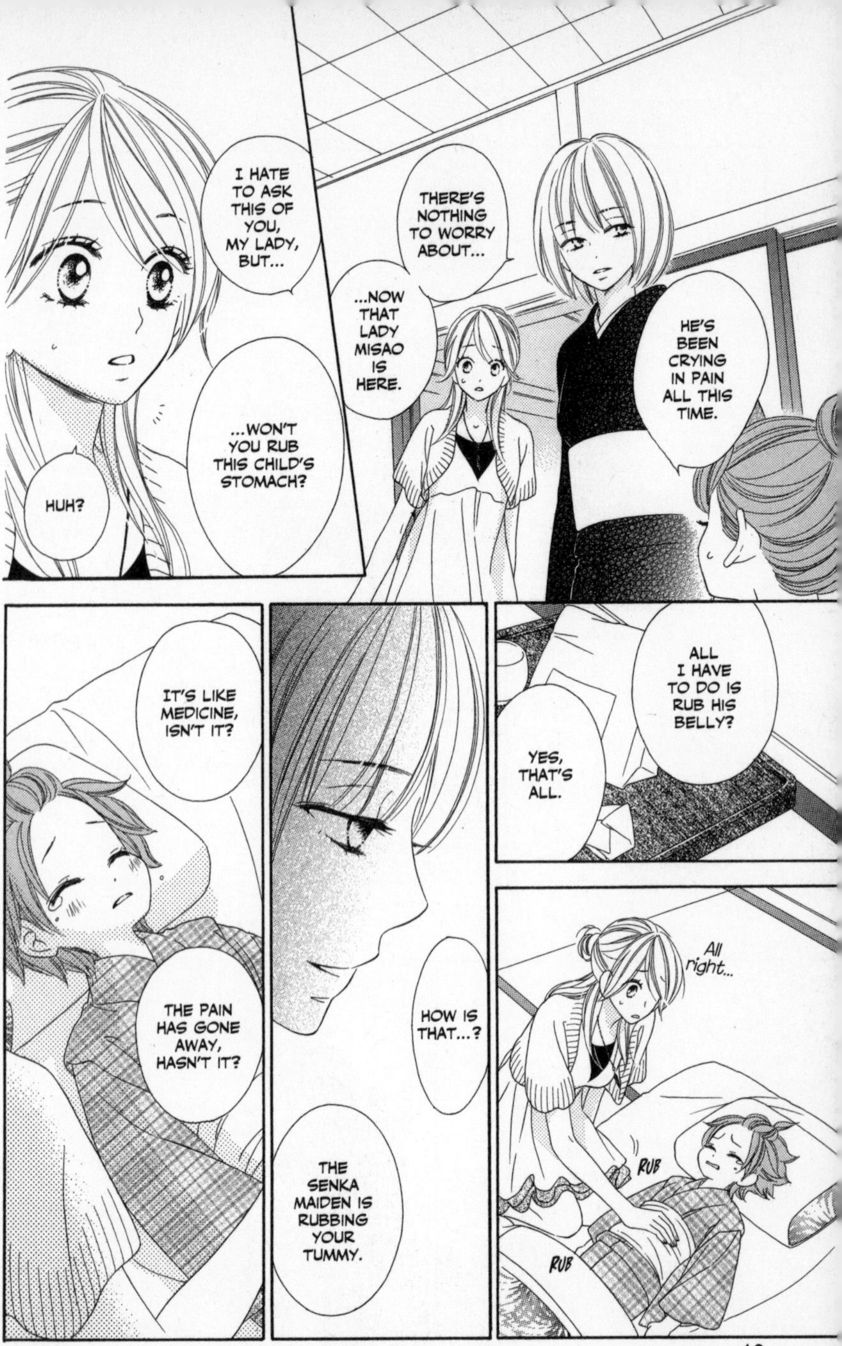
HE'S BEEN CRYING IN PAIN ALL THIS TIME.
THERE'S NOTHING TO WORRY ABOUT...
...NOW THAT LADY MISAO IS HERE.
I HATE TO ASK THIS OF YOU, MY LADY, BUT...
...WON'T YOU RUB THIS CHILD'S STOMACH?
HUH?
ALL I HAVE TO DO IS RUB HIS BELLY?
YES, THAT'S ALL.
All right...
RUB
RUB
HOW IS THAT...?
THE SENKA MAIDEN IS RUBBING YOUR TUMMY.
IT'S LIKE MEDICINE, ISN'T IT?
THE PAIN HAS GONE AWAY, HASN'T IT?

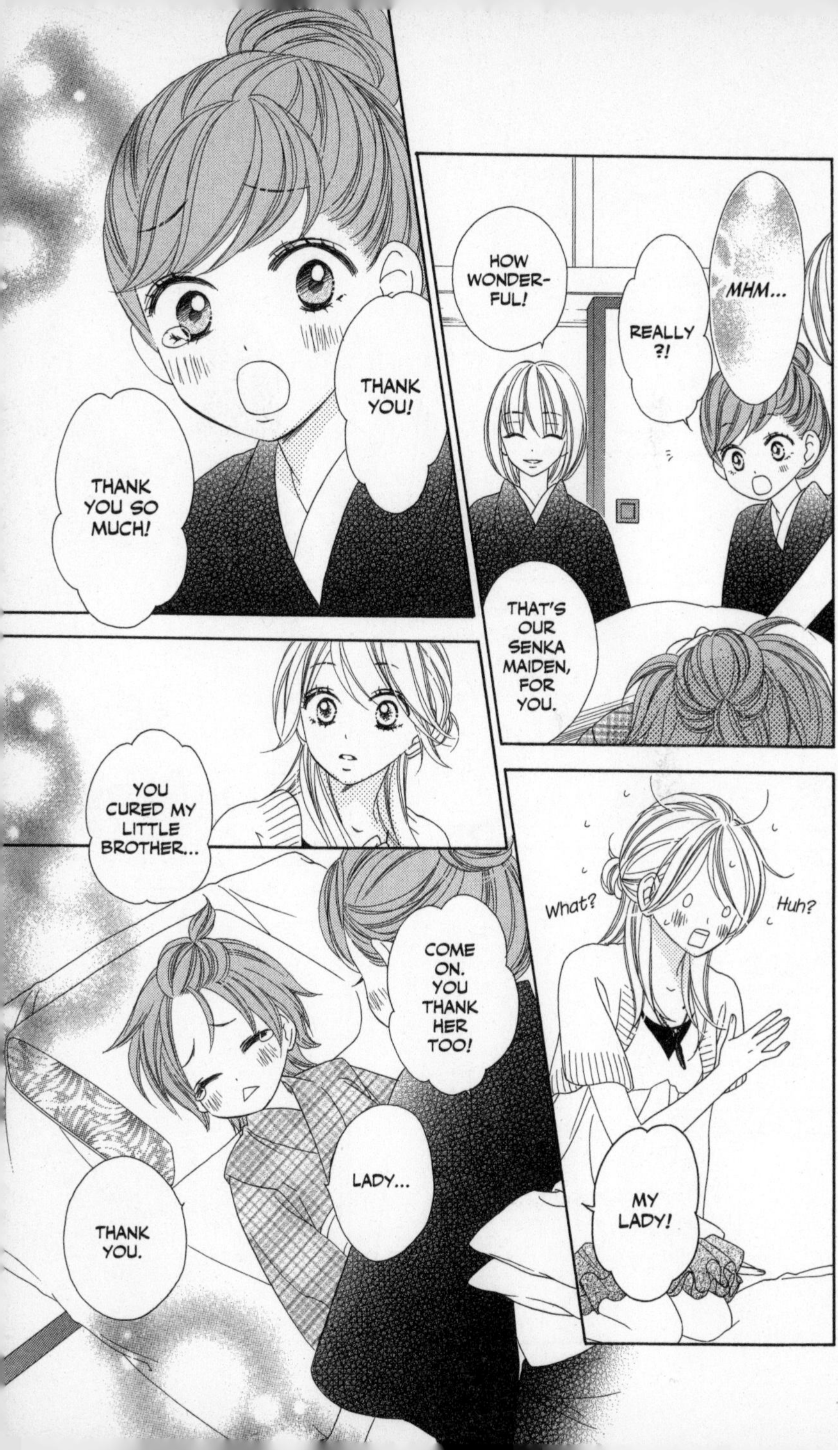
MHM...
REALLY?!
HOW WONDERFUL!
THAT'S OUR SENKA MAIDEN, FOR YOU.
THANK YOU!
THANK YOU SO MUCH!
YOU CURED MY LITTLE BROTHER...
COME ON. YOU THANK HER TOO!
LADY...
THANK YOU.
What?
Huh?
MY LADY!

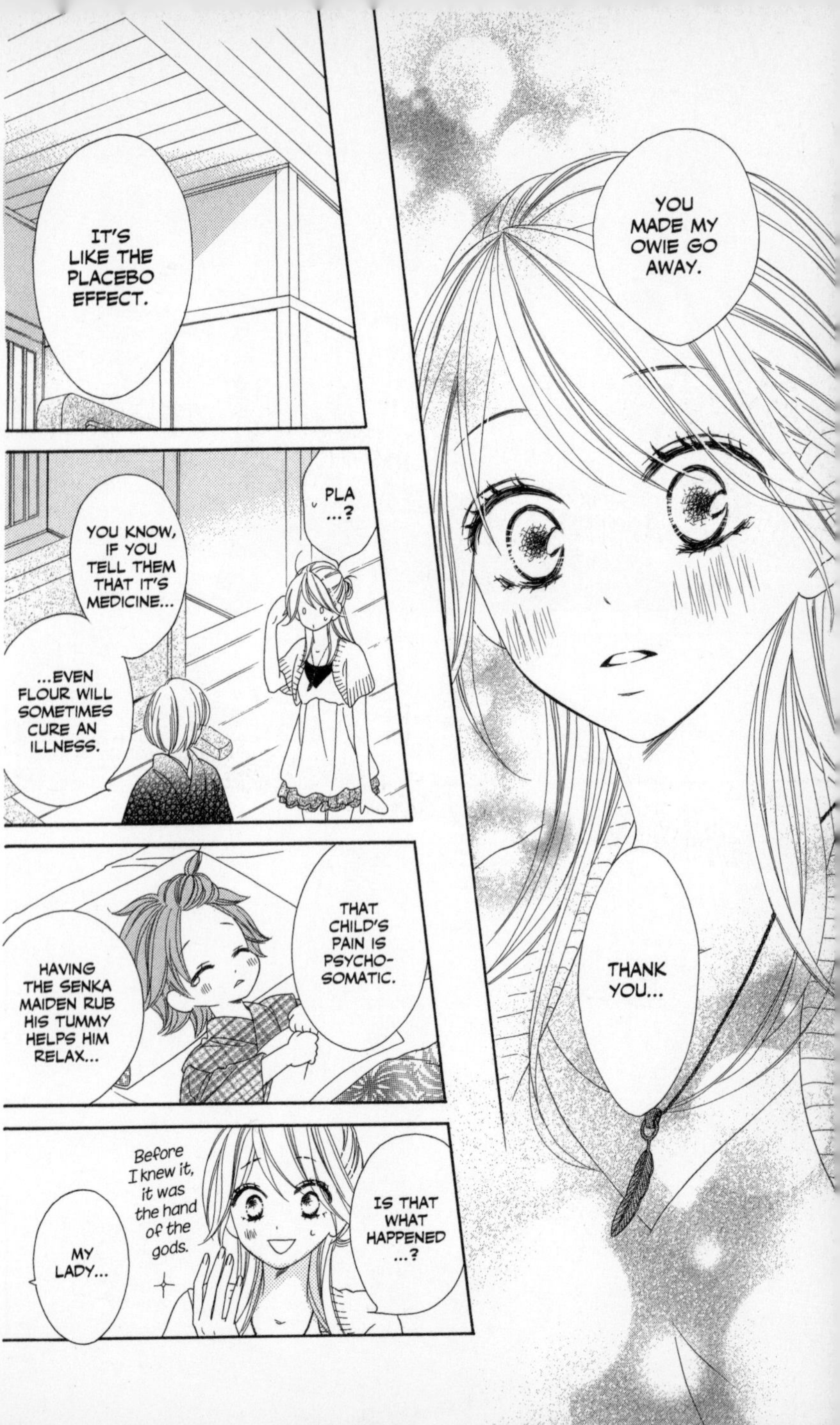
YOU MADE MY OWIE GO AWAY.
THANK YOU...
IT'S LIKE THE PLACEBO EFFECT.
PLA ...?
YOU KNOW, IF YOU TELL THEM THAT IT'S MEDICINE...
...EVEN FLOUR WILL SOMETIMES CURE AN ILLNESS.
THAT CHILD'S PAIN IS PSYCHO-SOMATIC.
HAVING THE SENKA MAIDEN RUB HIS TUMMY HELPS HIM RELAX...
IS THAT WHAT HAPPENED ...?
Before I knew it, it was the hand of the gods.
MY LADY...

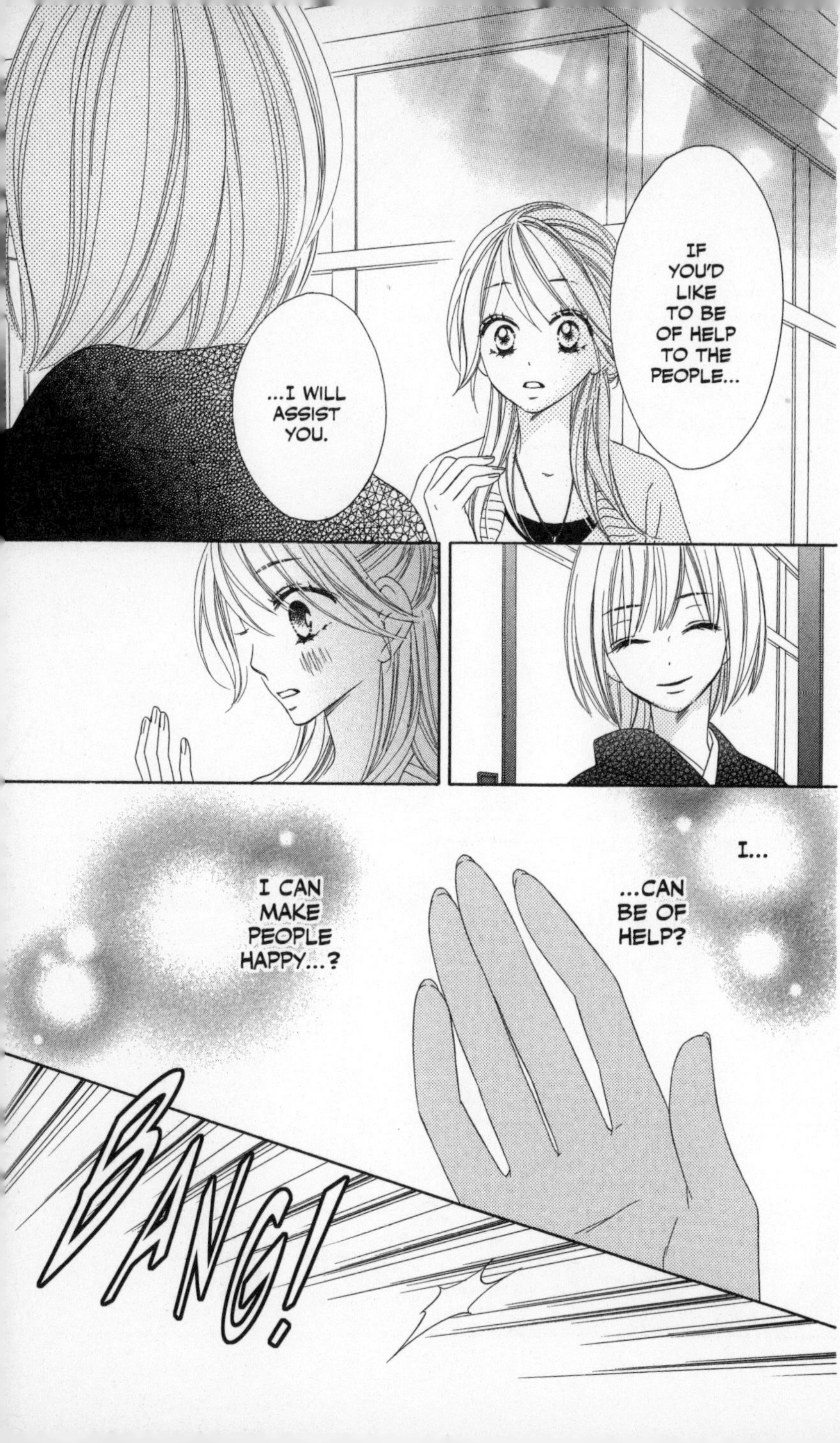
IF YOU'D LIKE TO BE OF HELP TO THE PEOPLE...
...I WILL ASSIST YOU.
I...
...CAN BE OF HELP?
I CAN MAKE PEOPLE HAPPY...?
BANG!

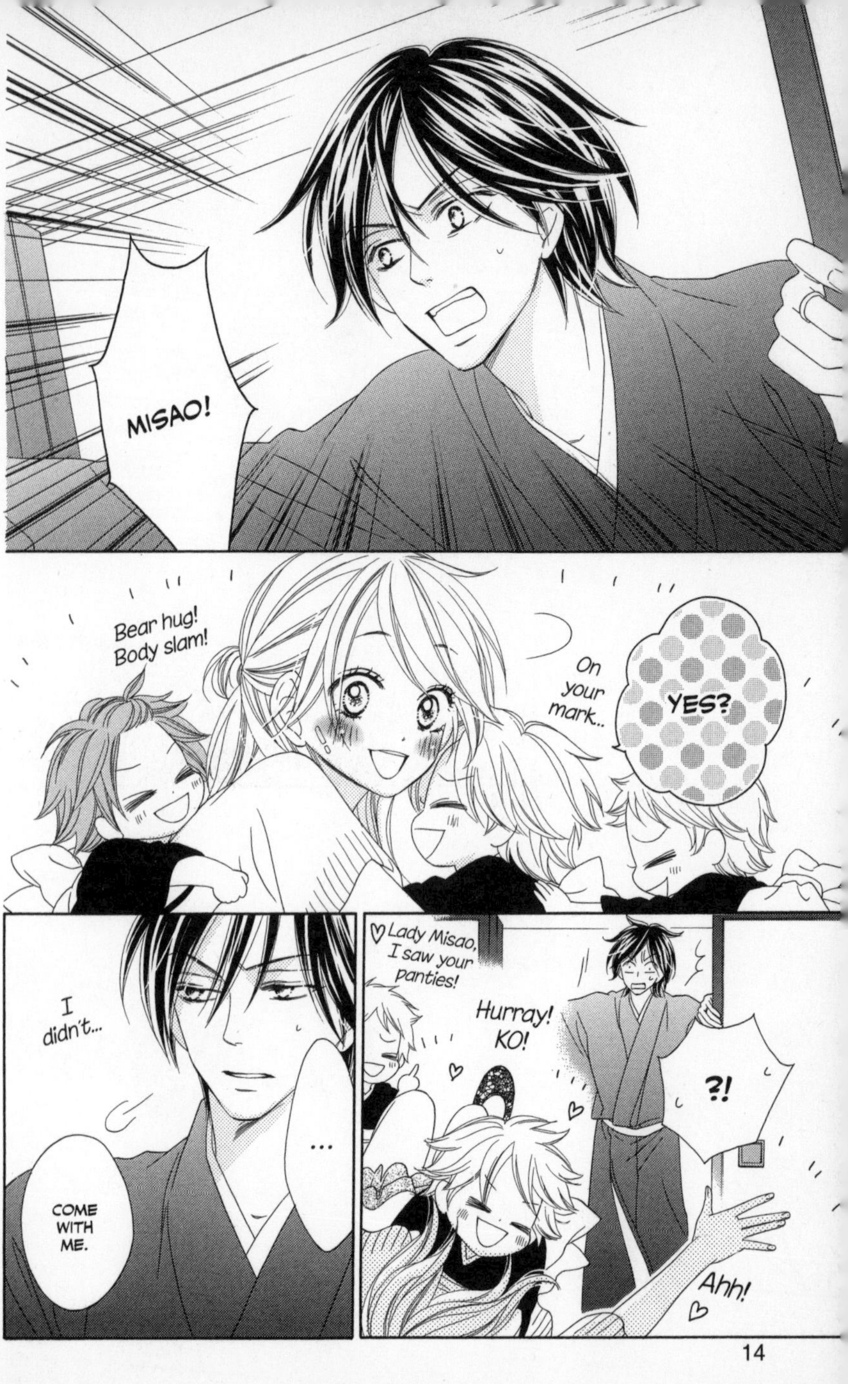
MISAO!
YES?
On your mark...
Bear hug! Body slam!
?!
Lady Misao, I saw your panties!
Hurray! KO!
Ahh!
I didn't...
...
COME WITH ME.

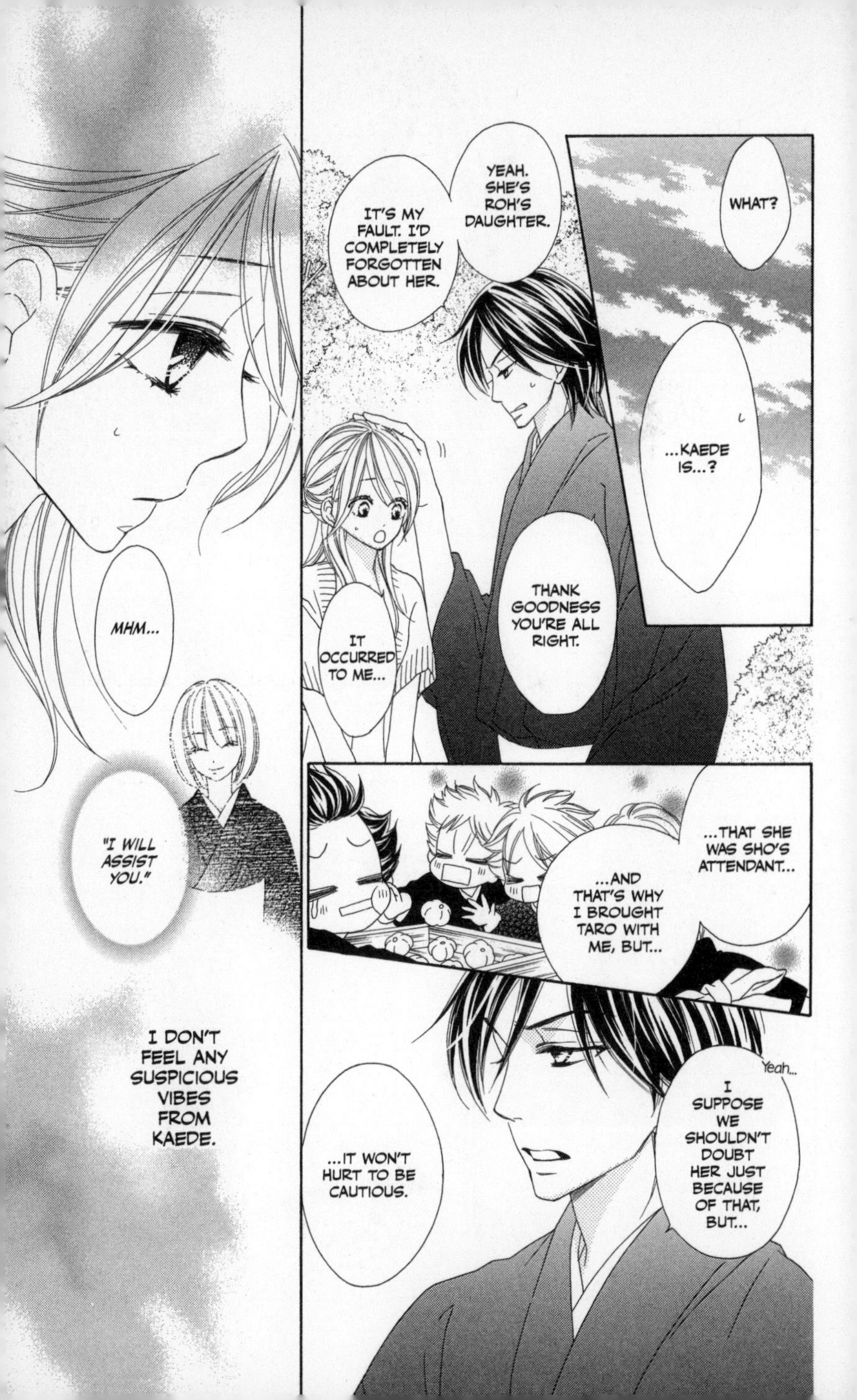
WHAT?
...KAEDE IS...?
YEAH. SHE'S ROH'S DAUGHTER.
IT'S MY FAULT. I'D COMPLETELY FORGOTTEN ABOUT HER.
THANK GOODNESS YOU'RE ALL RIGHT.
IT OCCURRED TO ME...
...THAT SHE WAS SHO'S ATTENDANT...
...AND THAT'S WHY I BROUGHT TARO WITH ME, BUT...
Yeah...
I SUPPOSE WE SHOULDN'T DOUBT HER JUST BECAUSE OF THAT, BUT...
...IT WON'T HURT TO BE CAUTIOUS.
MHM...
"I WILL ASSIST YOU."
I DON'T FEEL ANY SUSPICIOUS VIBES FROM KAEDE.

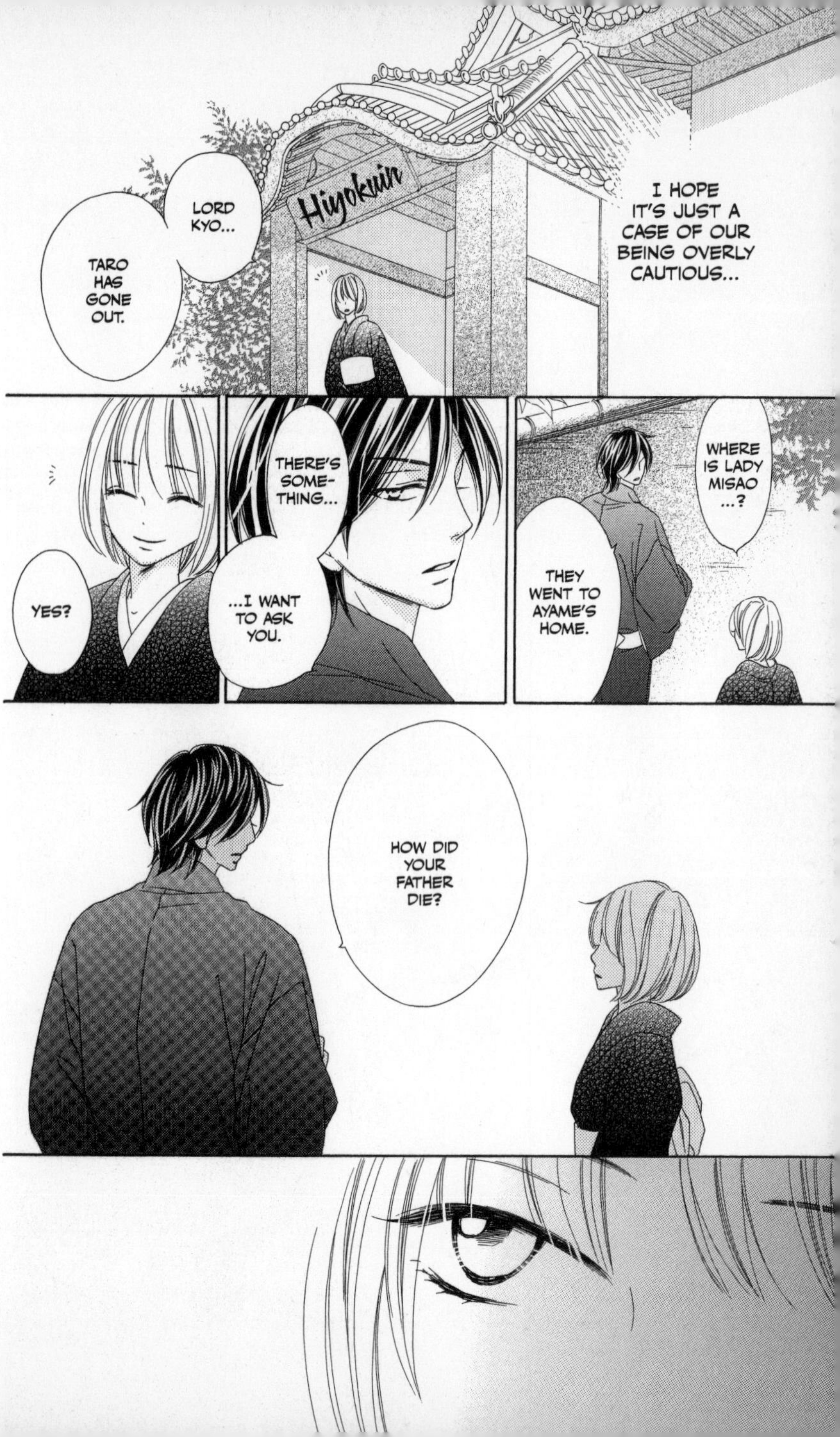
I HOPE IT'S JUST A CASE OF OUR BEING OVERLY CAUTIOUS...
Hiyokuin
LORD KYO...
TARO HAS GONE OUT.
WHERE IS LADY MISAO ...?
THEY WENT TO AYAME'S HOME.
THERE'S SOME-THING...
...I WANT TO ASK YOU.
YES?
HOW DID YOUR FATHER DIE?

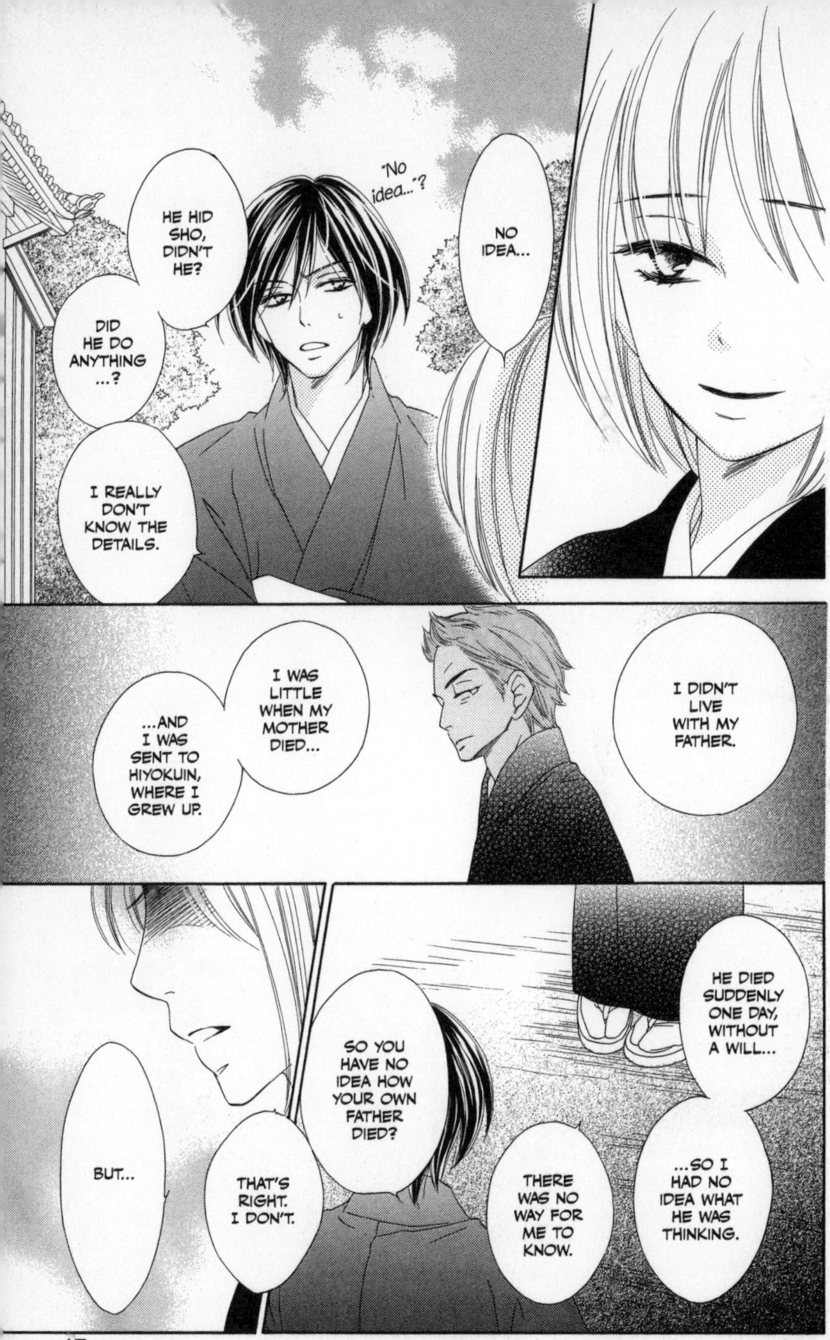
NO IDEA...
"No idea..."?
HE HID SHO, DIDN'T HE?
DID HE DO ANYTHING ...?
I REALLY DON'T KNOW THE DETAILS.
I DIDN'T LIVE WITH MY FATHER.
I WAS LITTLE WHEN MY MOTHER DIED...
...AND I WAS SENT TO HIYOKUIN, WHERE I GREW UP.
HE DIED SUDDENLY ONE DAY, WITHOUT A WILL...
...SO I HAD NO IDEA WHAT HE WAS THINKING.
THERE WAS NO WAY FOR ME TO KNOW.
SO YOU HAVE NO IDEA HOW YOUR OWN FATHER DIED?
THAT'S RIGHT. I DON'T.
BUT...

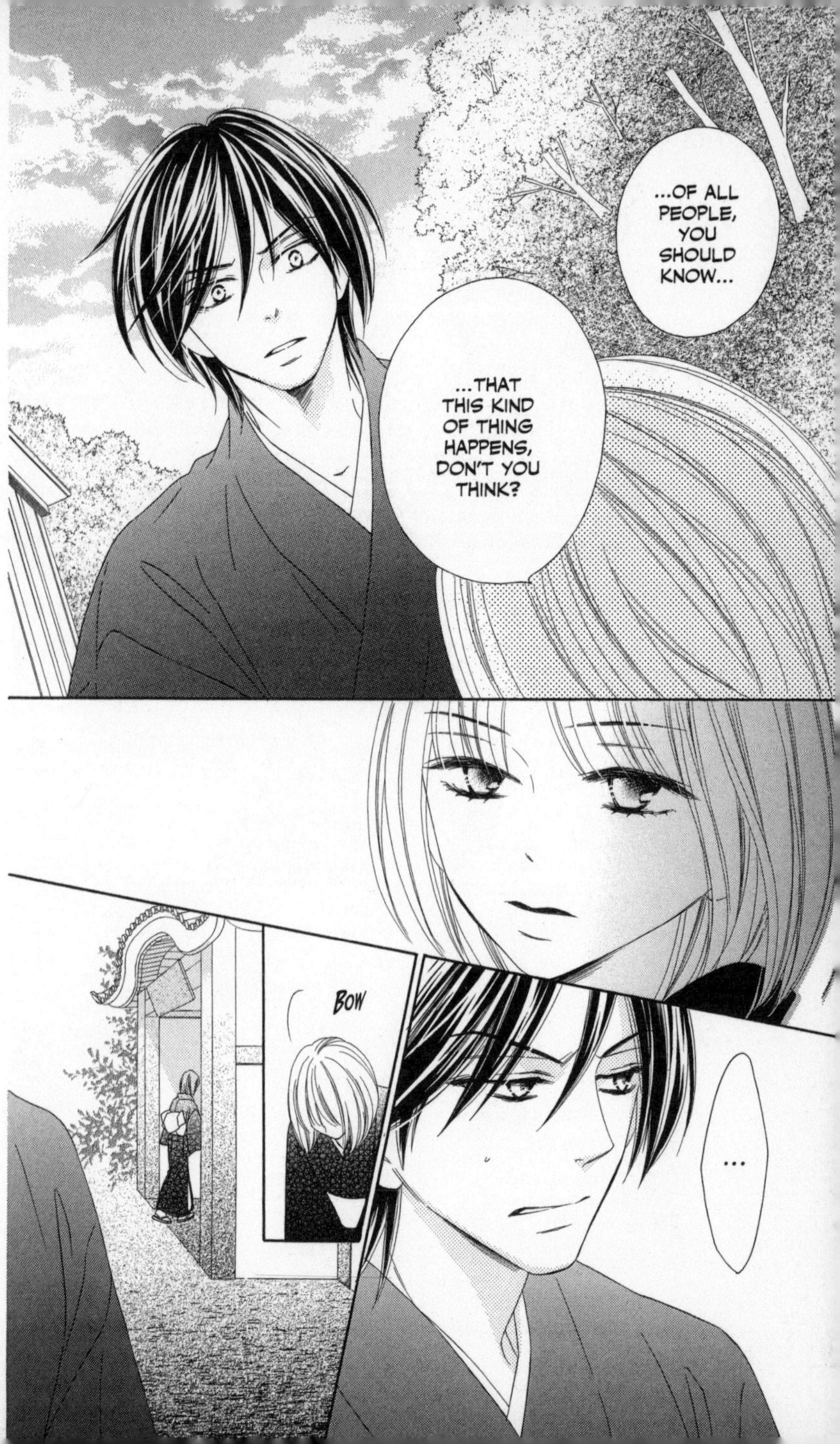
...OF ALL PEOPLE, YOU SHOULD KNOW...
...THAT THIS KIND OF THING HAPPENS, DON'T YOU THINK?
BOW
...

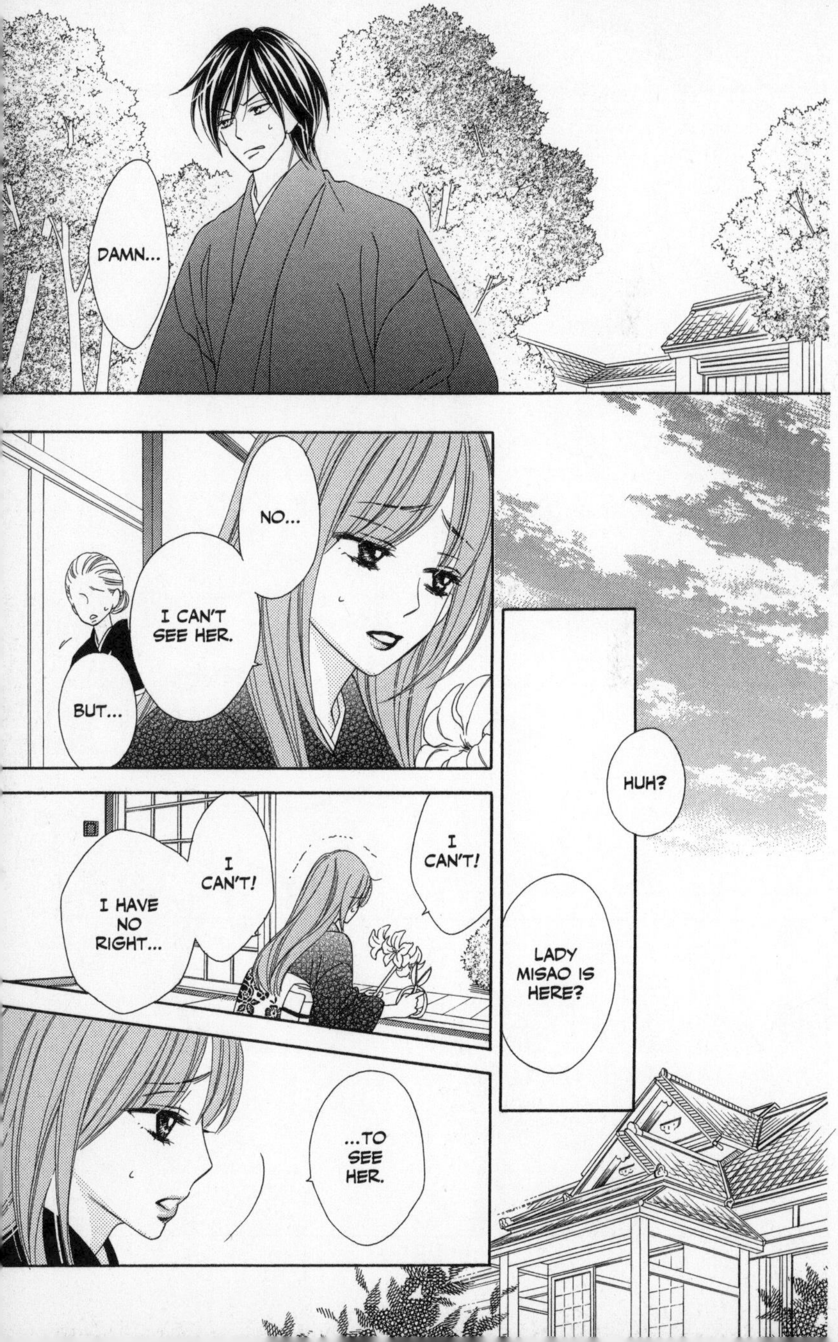
DAMN...
HUH?
LADY MISAO IS HERE?
NO...
I CAN'T SEE HER.
BUT...
I CAN'T!
I CAN'T!
I HAVE NO RIGHT...
...TO SEE HER.

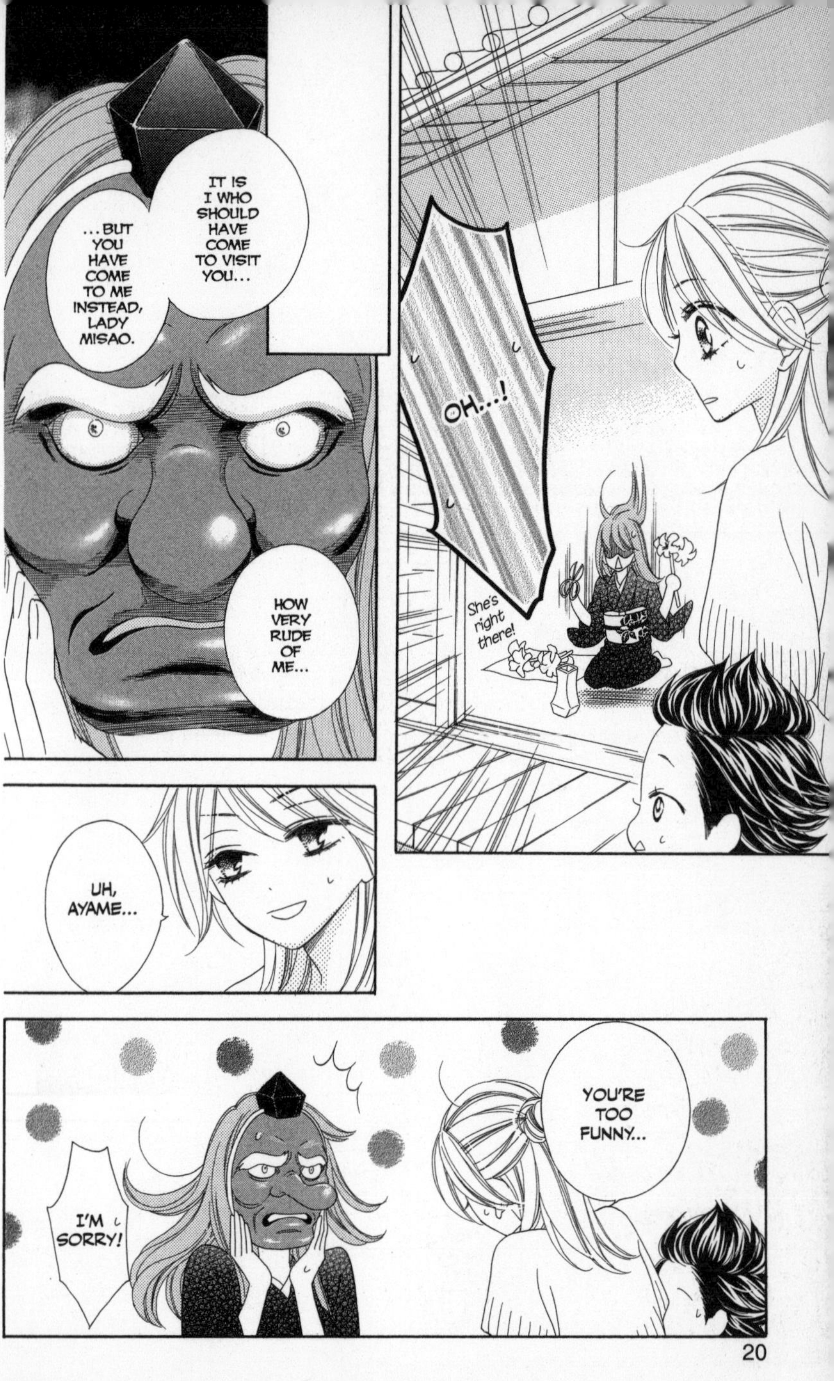
OH...!
She's right there!
IT IS I WHO SHOULD HAVE COME TO VISIT YOU...
...BUT YOU HAVE COME TO ME INSTEAD, LADY MISAO.
HOW VERY RUDE OF ME...
UH, AYAME...
YOU'RE TOO FUNNY...
I'M SORRY!

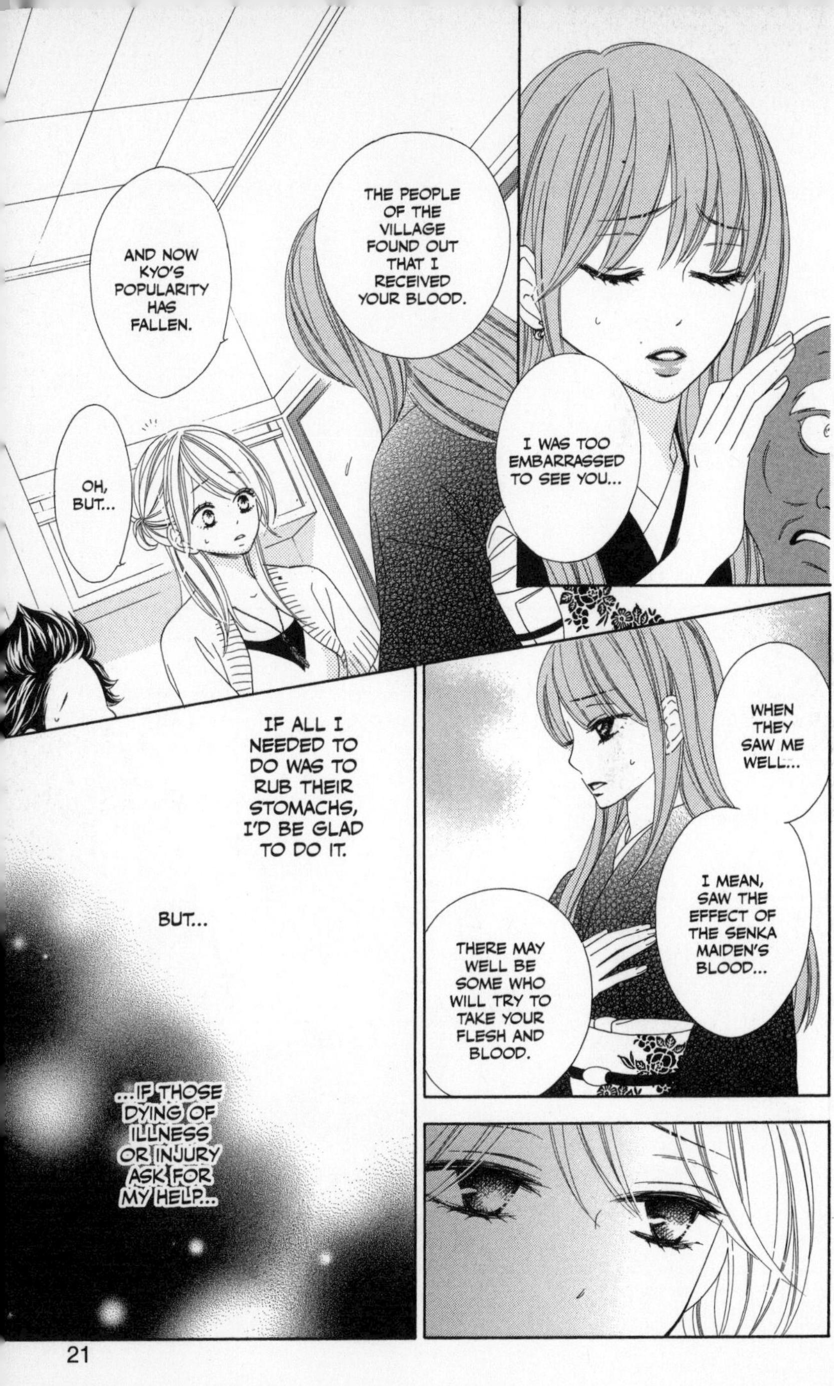
THE PEOPLE OF THE VILLAGE FOUND OUT THAT I RECEIVED YOUR BLOOD.
I WAS TOO EMBARRASSED TO SEE YOU...
AND NOW KYO'S POPULARITY HAS FALLEN.
OH, BUT...
WHEN THEY SAW ME WELL...
I MEAN, SAW THE EFFECT OF THE SENKA MAIDEN'S BLOOD...
THERE MAY WELL BE SOME WHO WILL TRY TO TAKE YOUR FLESH AND BLOOD.
IF ALL I NEEDED TO DO WAS TO RUB THEIR STOMACHS, I'D BE GLAD TO DO IT.
BUT...
...IF THOSE DYING OF ILLNESS OR INJURY ASK FOR MY HELP...

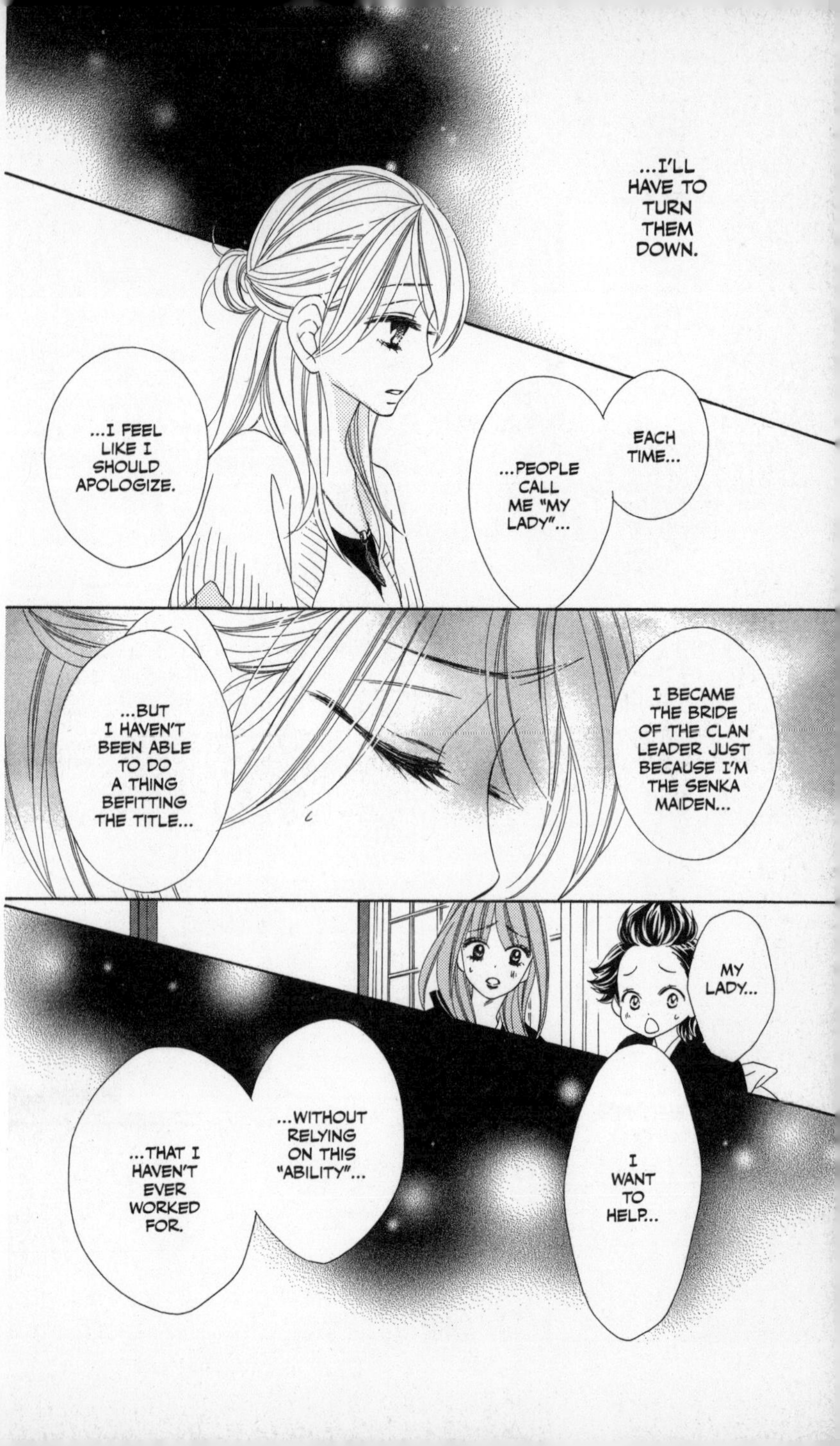
...I'LL HAVE TO TURN THEM DOWN.
EACH TIME...
...PEOPLE CALL ME "MY LADY"...
...I FEEL LIKE I SHOULD APOLOGIZE.
I BECAME THE BRIDE OF THE CLAN LEADER JUST BECAUSE I'M THE SENKA MAIDEN...
...BUT I HAVEN'T BEEN ABLE TO DO A THING BEFITTING THE TITLE...
MY LADY...
I WANT TO HELP...
...WITHOUT RELYING ON THIS "ABILITY"...
...THAT I HAVEN'T EVER WORKED FOR.

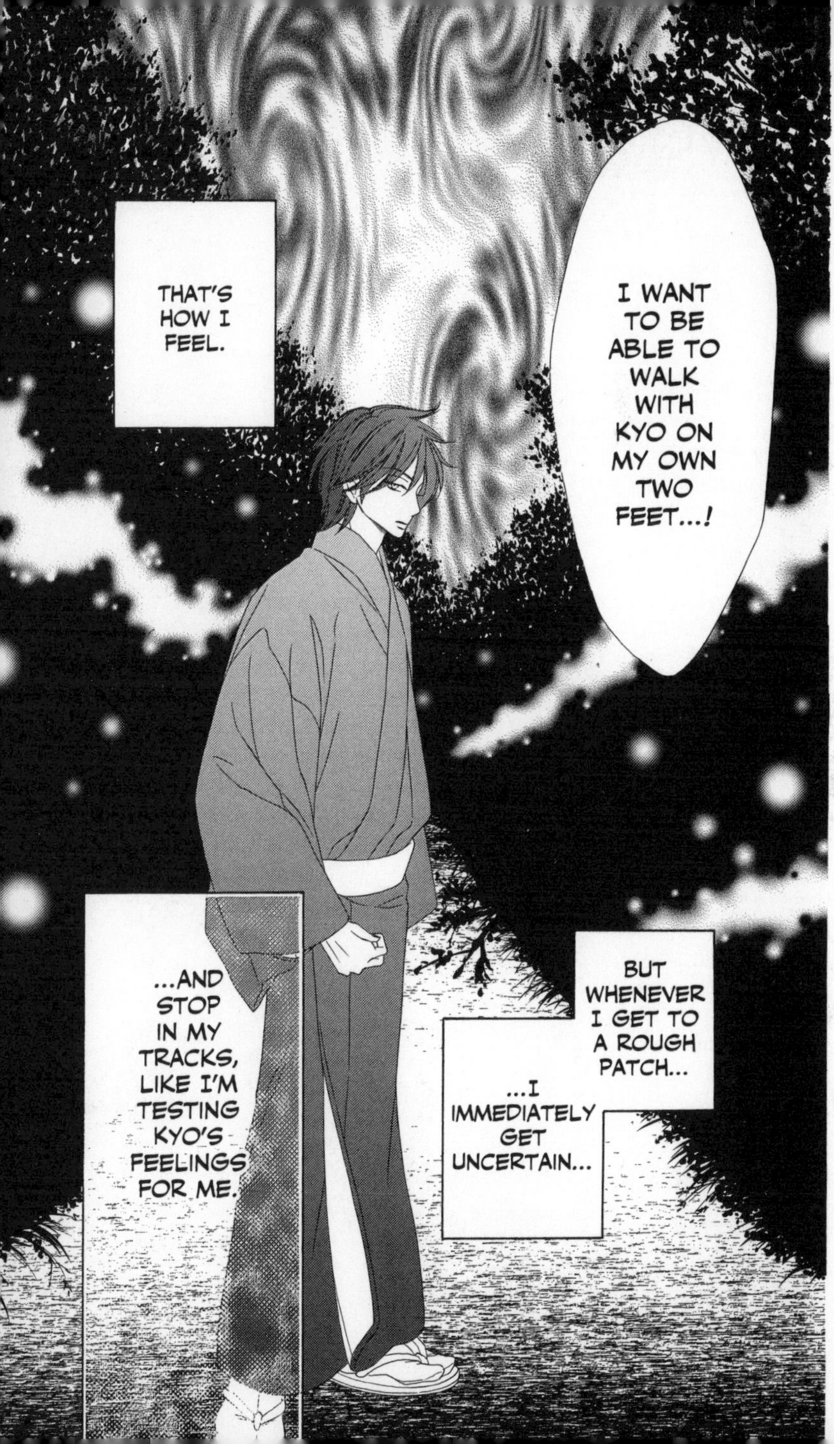
I WANT TO BE ABLE TO WALK WITH KYO ON MY OWN TWO FEET...!
THAT'S HOW I FEEL.
BUT WHENEVER I GET TO A ROUGH PATCH...
...I IMMEDIATELY GET UNCERTAIN...
...AND STOP IN MY TRACKS, LIKE I'M TESTING KYO'S FEELINGS FOR ME.

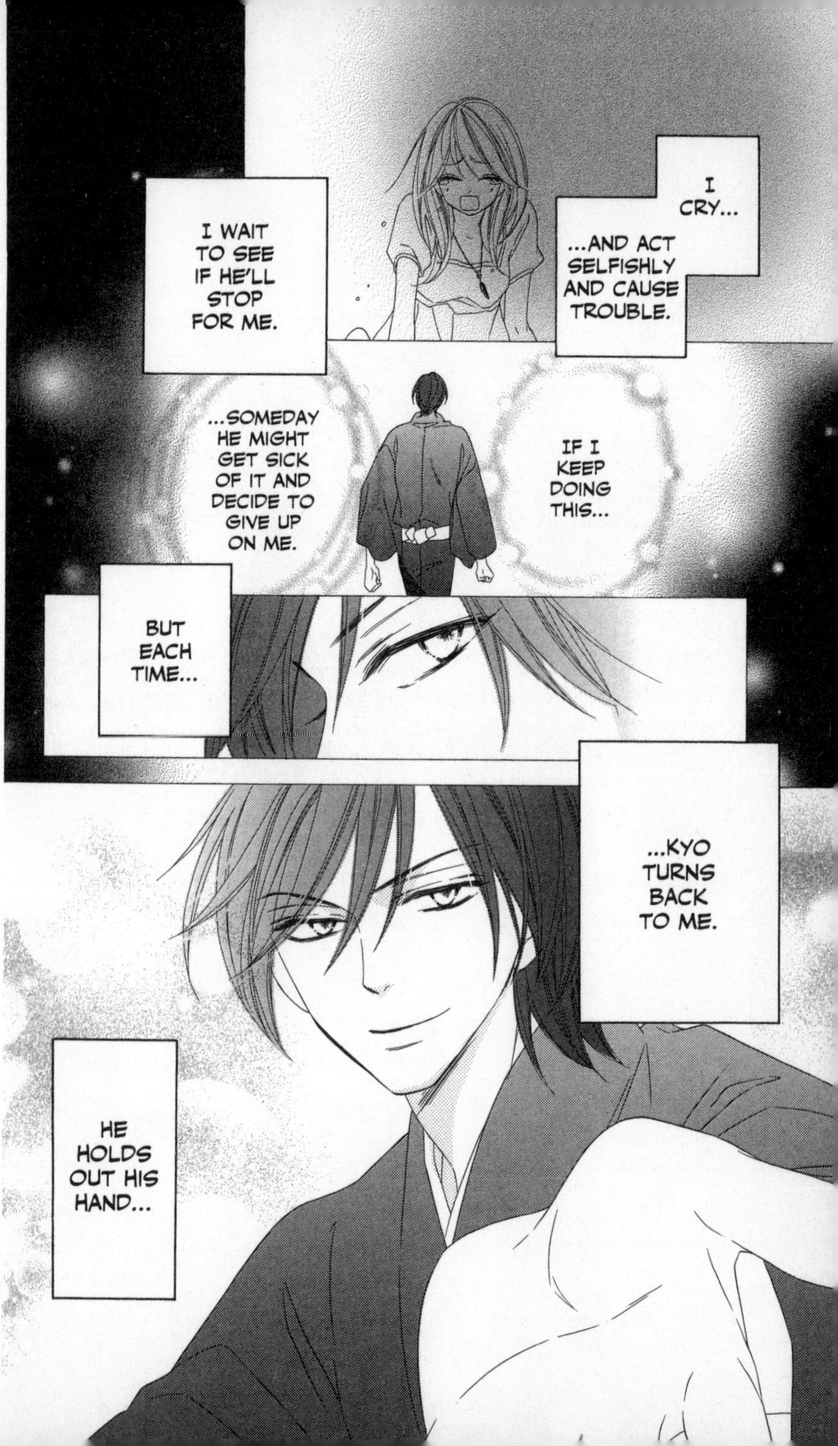
I CRY...
...AND ACT SELFISHLY AND CAUSE TROUBLE.
I WAIT TO SEE IF HE'LL STOP FOR ME.
IF I KEEP DOING THIS...
...SOMEDAY HE MIGHT GET SICK OF IT AND DECIDE TO GIVE UP ON ME.
BUT EACH TIME...
...KYO TURNS BACK TO ME.
HE HOLDS OUT HIS HAND...

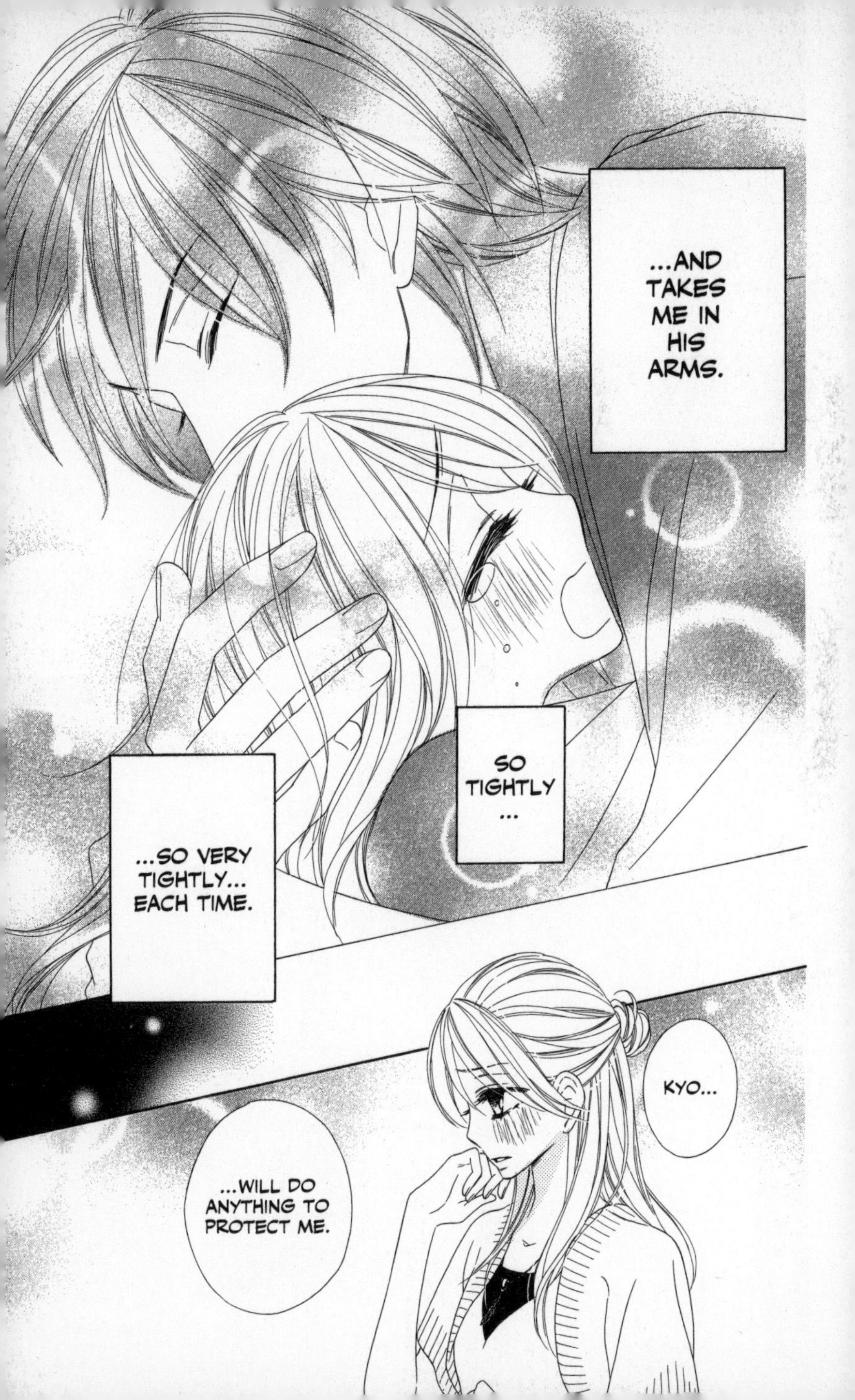
...AND TAKES ME IN HIS ARMS.
SO TIGHTLY...
...SO VERY TIGHTLY... EACH TIME.
KYO...
...WILL DO ANYTHING TO PROTECT ME.

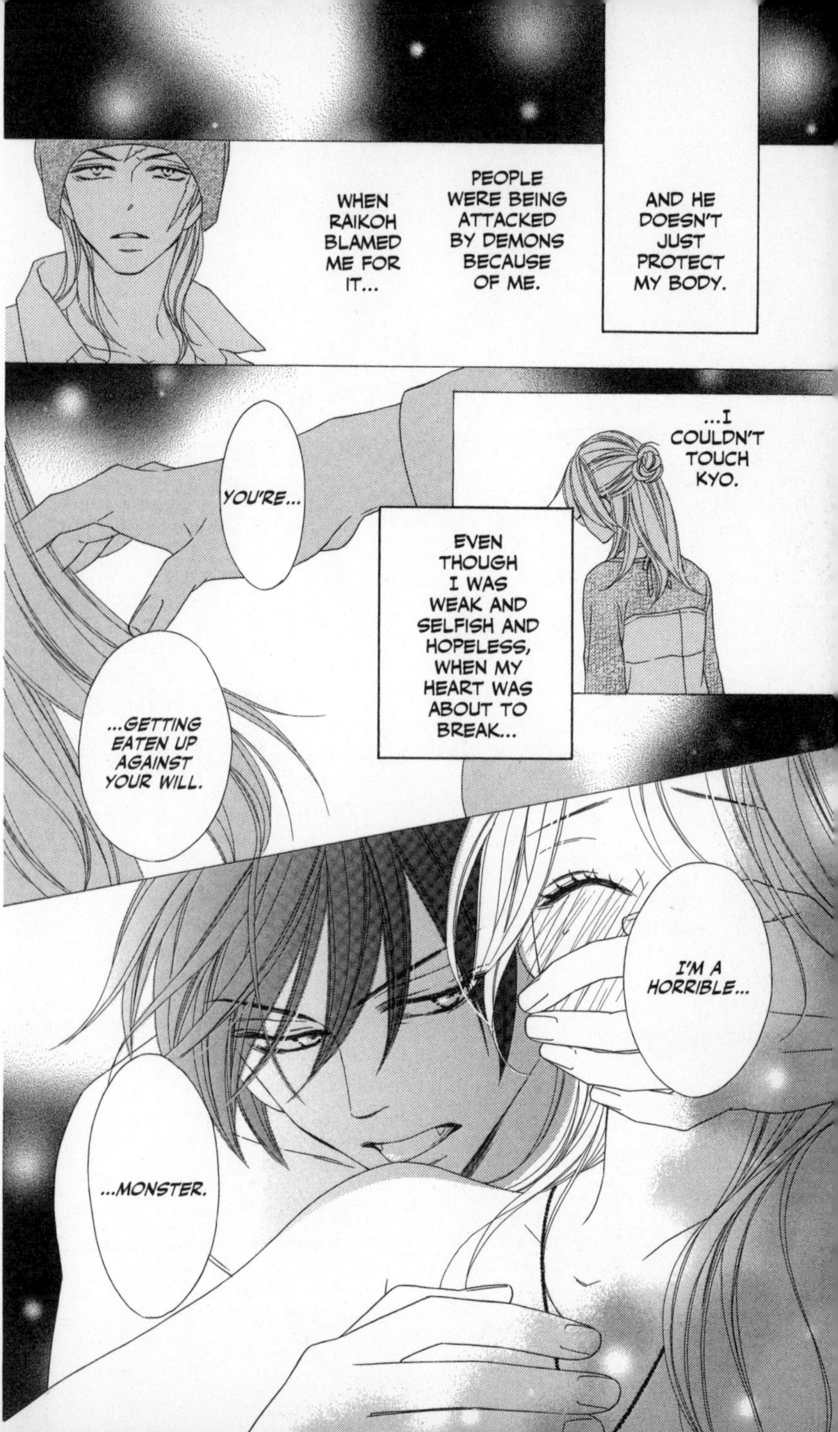
AND HE DOESN'T JUST PROTECT MY BODY.
PEOPLE WERE BEING ATTACKED BY DEMONS BECAUSE OF ME.
WHEN RAIKOH BLAMED ME FOR IT...
...I COULDN'T TOUCH KYO.
EVEN THOUGH I WAS WEAK AND SELFISH AND HOPELESS, WHEN MY HEART WAS ABOUT TO BREAK...
YOU'RE...
...GETTING EATEN UP AGAINST YOUR WILL.
I'M A HORRIBLE...
...MONSTER.

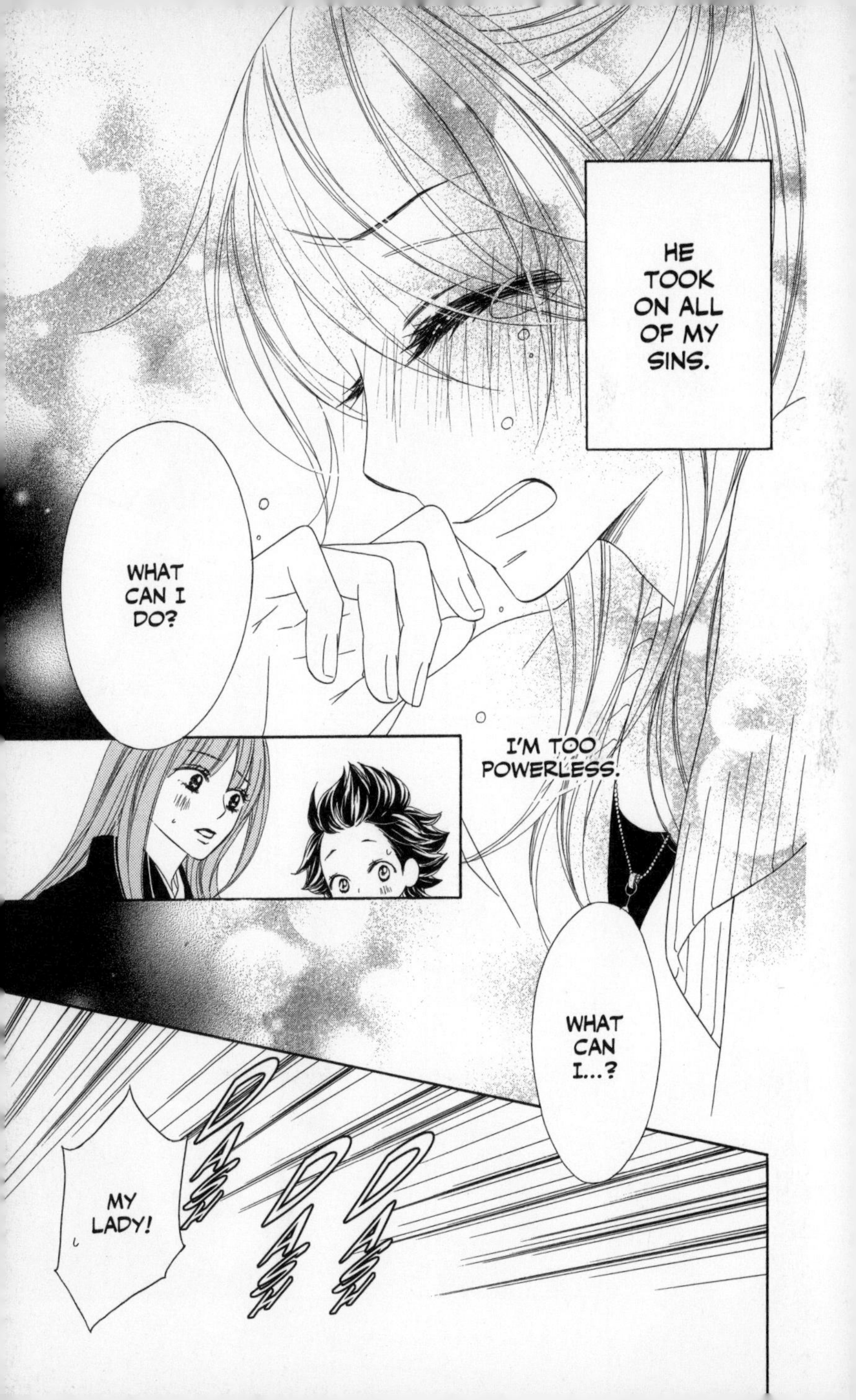
HE TOOK ON ALL OF MY SINS.
WHAT CAN I DO?
I'M TOO POWERLESS.
WHAT CAN I...?
MY LADY!

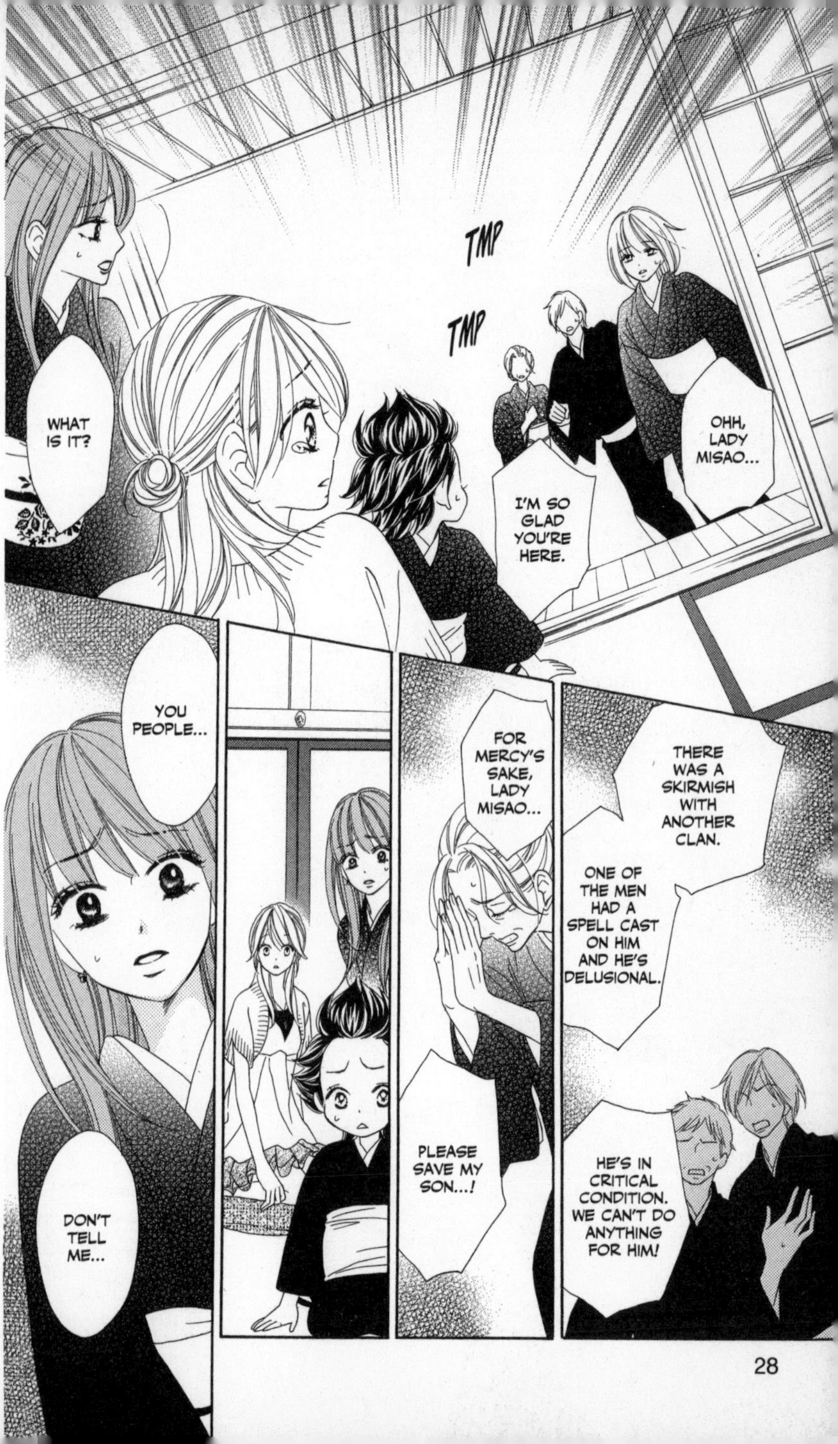
TMP
TMP
OHH, LADY MISAO...
I'M SO GLAD YOU'RE HERE.
WHAT IS IT?
THERE WAS A SKIRMISH WITH ANOTHER CLAN.
ONE OF THE MEN HAD A SPELL CAST ON HIM AND HE'S DELUSIONAL.
HE'S IN CRITICAL CONDITION. WE CAN'T DO ANYTHING FOR HIM!
FOR MERCY'S SAKE, LADY MISAO...
PLEASE SAVE MY SON...!
YOU PEOPLE...
DON'T TELL ME...

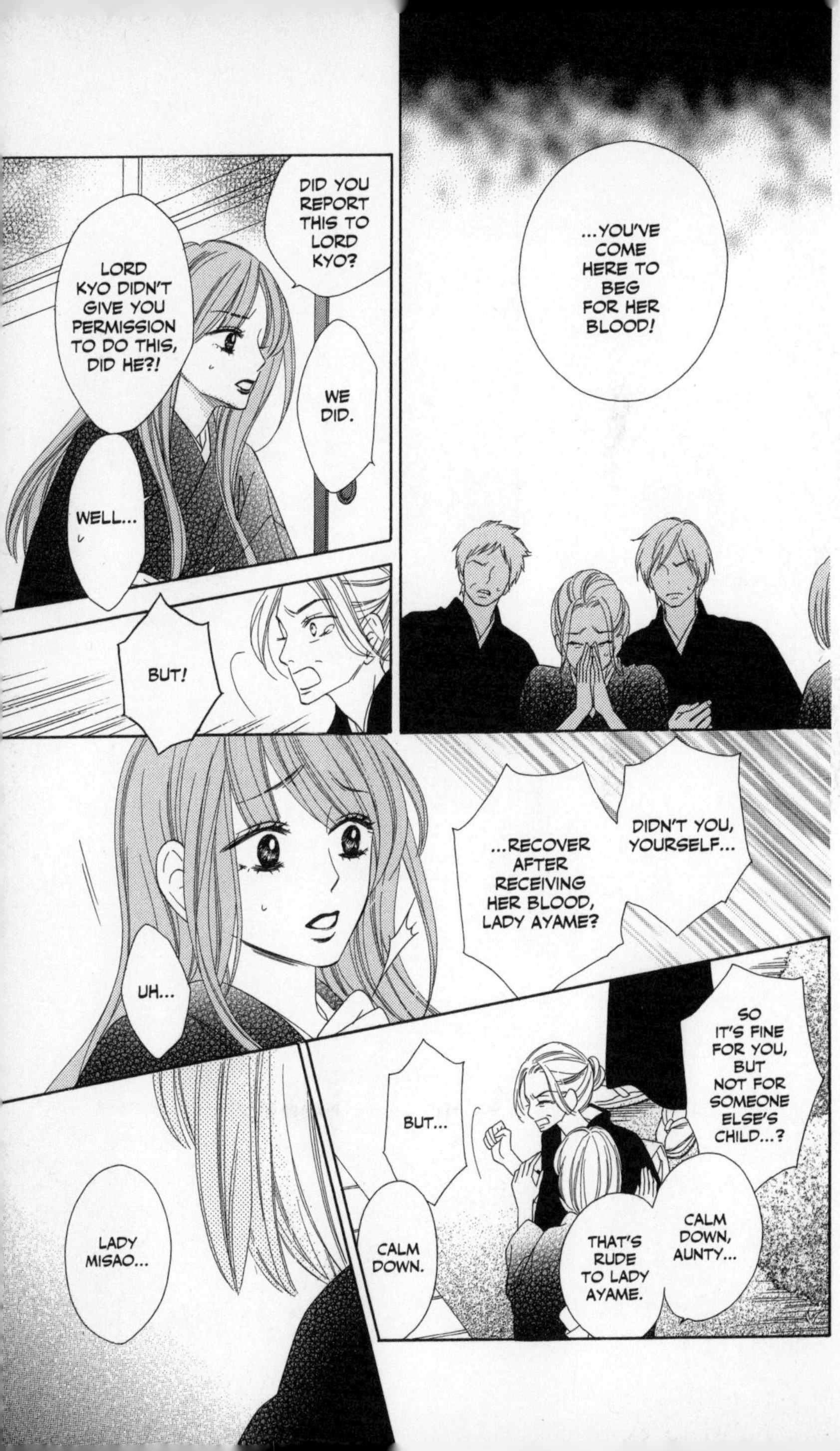
...YOU'VE COME HERE TO BEG FOR HER BLOOD!
DID YOU REPORT THIS TO LORD KYO?
WE DID.
LORD KYO DIDN'T GIVE YOU PERMISSION TO DO THIS, DID HE?!
WELL...
BUT!
DIDN'T YOU, YOURSELF...
...RECOVER AFTER RECEIVING HER BLOOD, LADY AYAME?
UH...
SO IT'S FINE FOR YOU, BUT NOT FOR SOMEONE ELSE'S CHILD...?
CALM DOWN, AUNTY...
THAT'S RUDE TO LADY AYAME.
BUT...
CALM DOWN.
LADY MISAO...

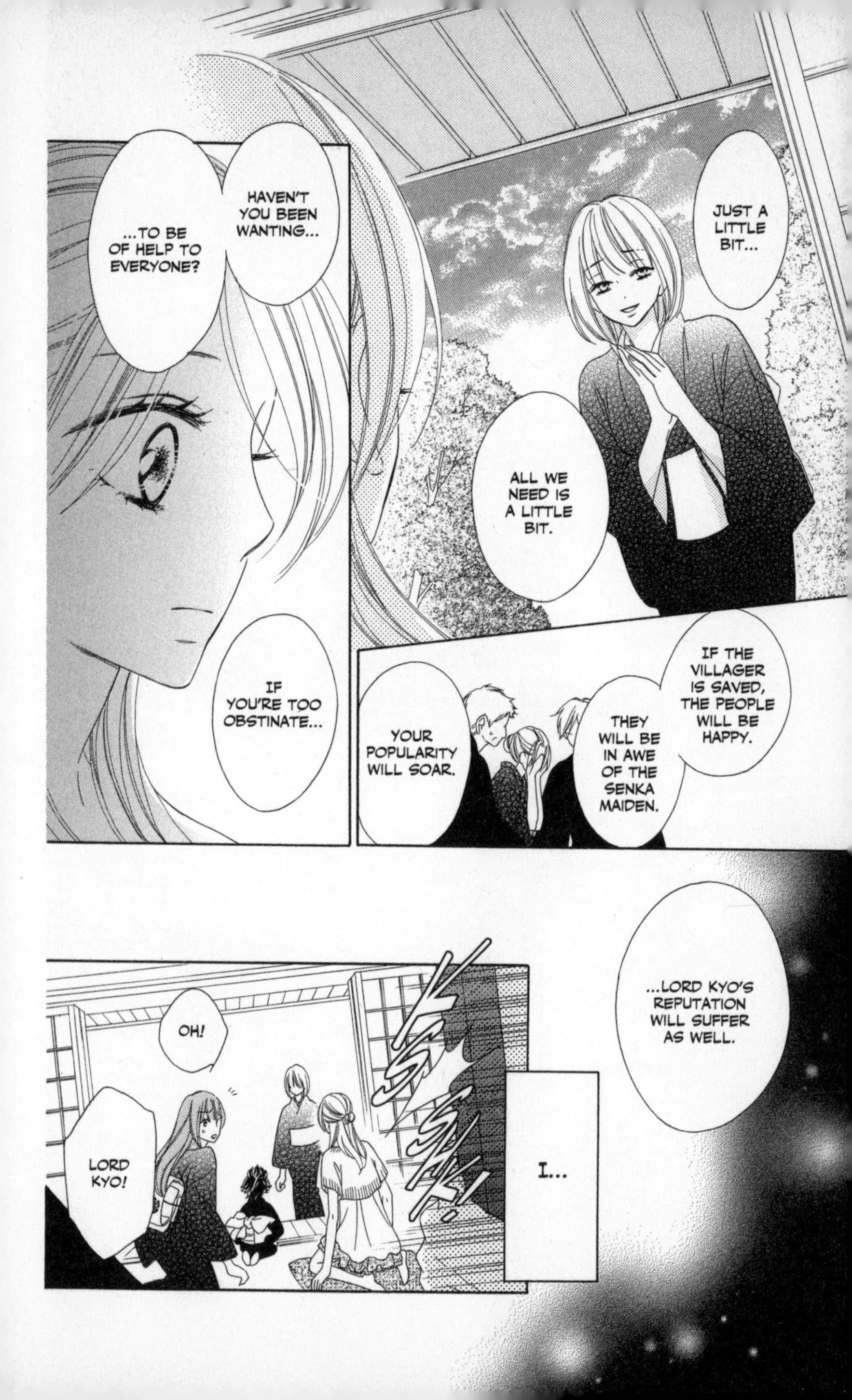
JUST A LITTLE BIT...
ALL WE NEED IS A LITTLE BIT.
IF THE VILLAGER IS SAVED, THE PEOPLE WILL BE HAPPY.
THEY WILL BE IN AWE OF THE SENKA MAIDEN.
YOUR POPULARITY WILL SOAR.
HAVEN'T YOU BEEN WANTING...
...TO BE OF HELP TO EVERYONE?
IF YOU'RE TOO OBSTINATE...
...LORD KYO'S REPUTATION WILL SUFFER AS WELL.
I...
OH!
LORD KYO!

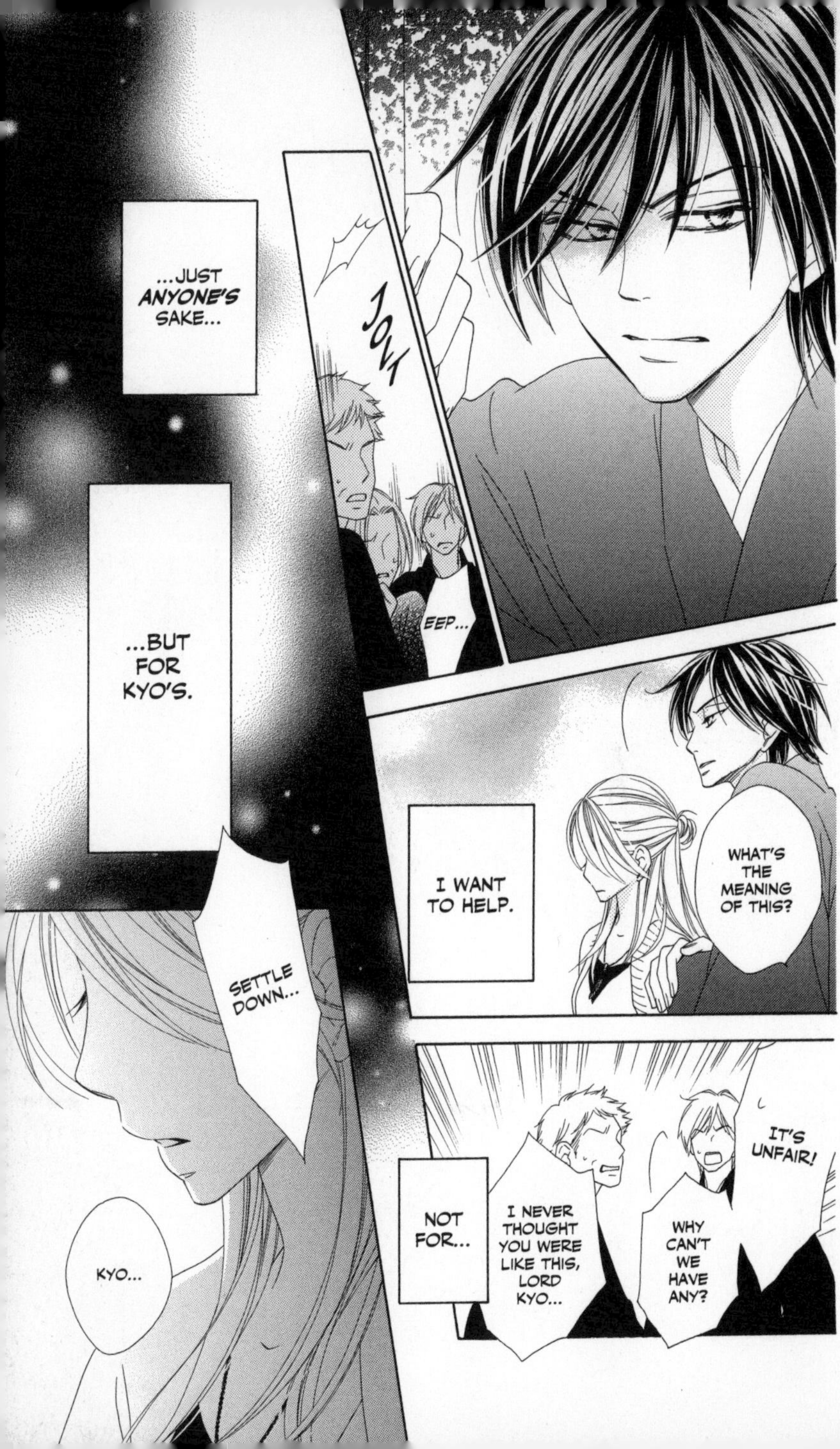

JOLT
EEP...
WHAT'S THE MEANING OF THIS?
I WANT TO HELP.
IT'S UNFAIR!
WHY CAN'T WE HAVE ANY?
I NEVER THOUGHT YOU WERE LIKE THIS, LORD KYO...
NOT FOR...
...JUST ANYONE'S SAKE...
...BUT FOR KYO'S.
SETTLE DOWN...
KYO...

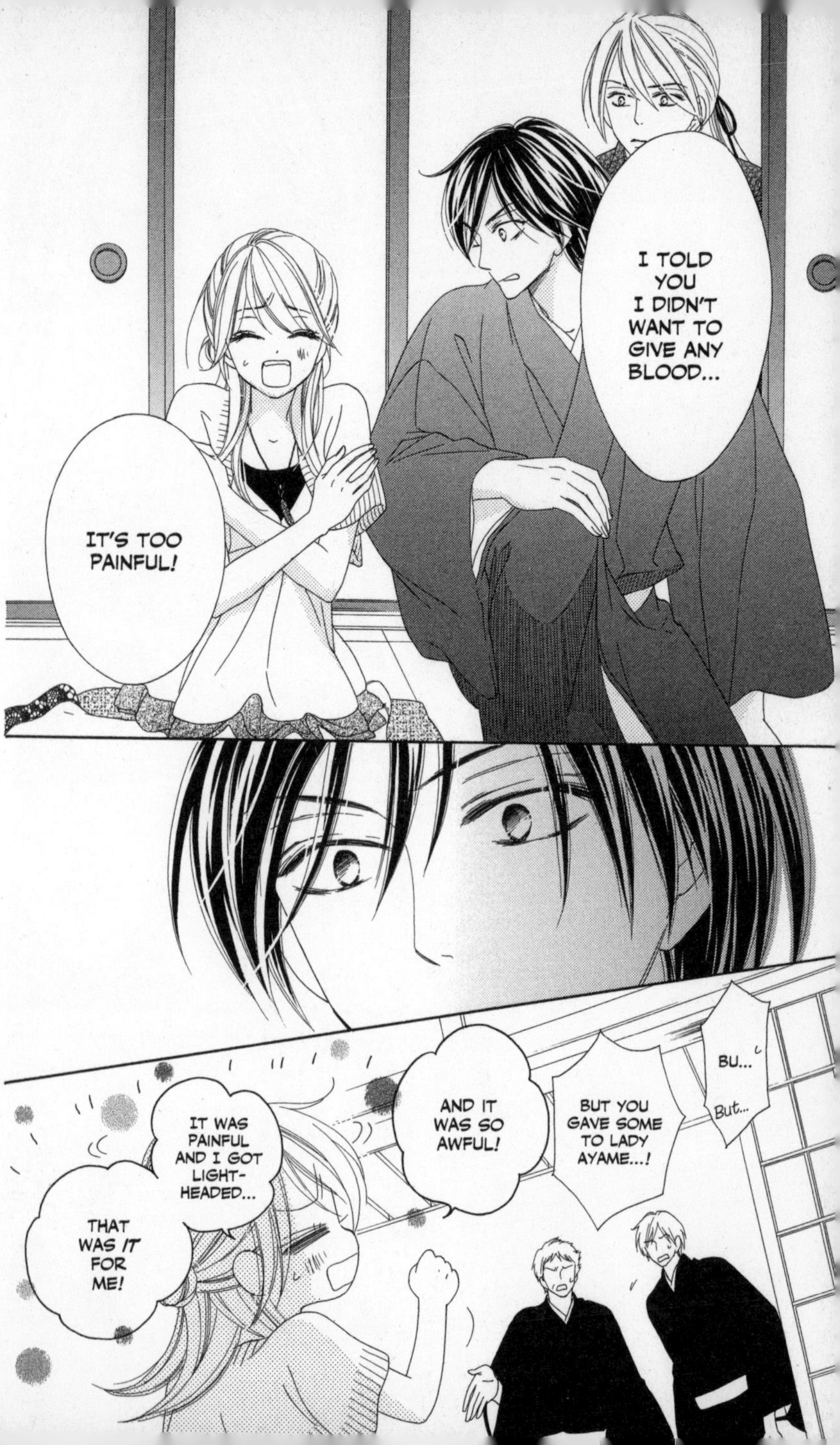
I TOLD YOU I DIDN'T WANT TO GIVE ANY BLOOD...
IT'S TOO PAINFUL!
BU...
But...
BUT YOU GAVE SOME TO LADY AYAME...!
AND IT WAS SO AWFUL!
IT WAS PAINFUL AND I GOT LIGHT-HEADED...
THAT WAS *IT* FOR ME!

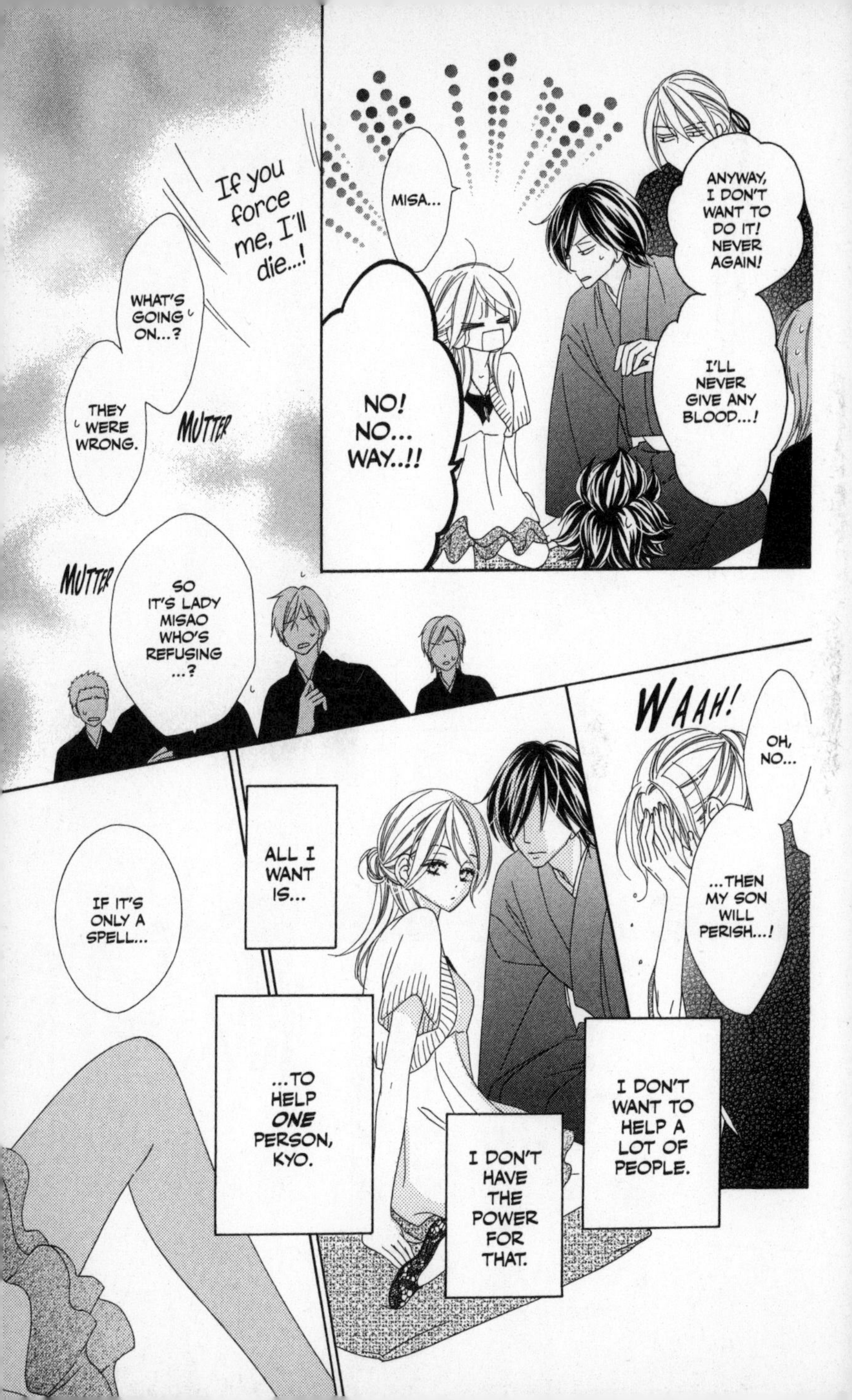
ANYWAY, I DON'T WANT TO DO IT! NEVER AGAIN!
I'LL NEVER GIVE ANY BLOOD...!
MISA...
NO! NO... WAY..!!
If you force me, I'll die...!
WHAT'S GOING ON...?
THEY WERE WRONG.
MUTTER
SO IT'S LADY MISAO WHO'S REFUSING...?
MUTTER
WAAH!
OH, NO...
...THEN MY SON WILL PERISH...!
I DON'T WANT TO HELP A LOT OF PEOPLE.
I DON'T HAVE THE POWER FOR THAT.
ALL I WANT IS...
...TO HELP *ONE* PERSON, KYO.
IF IT'S ONLY A SPELL...

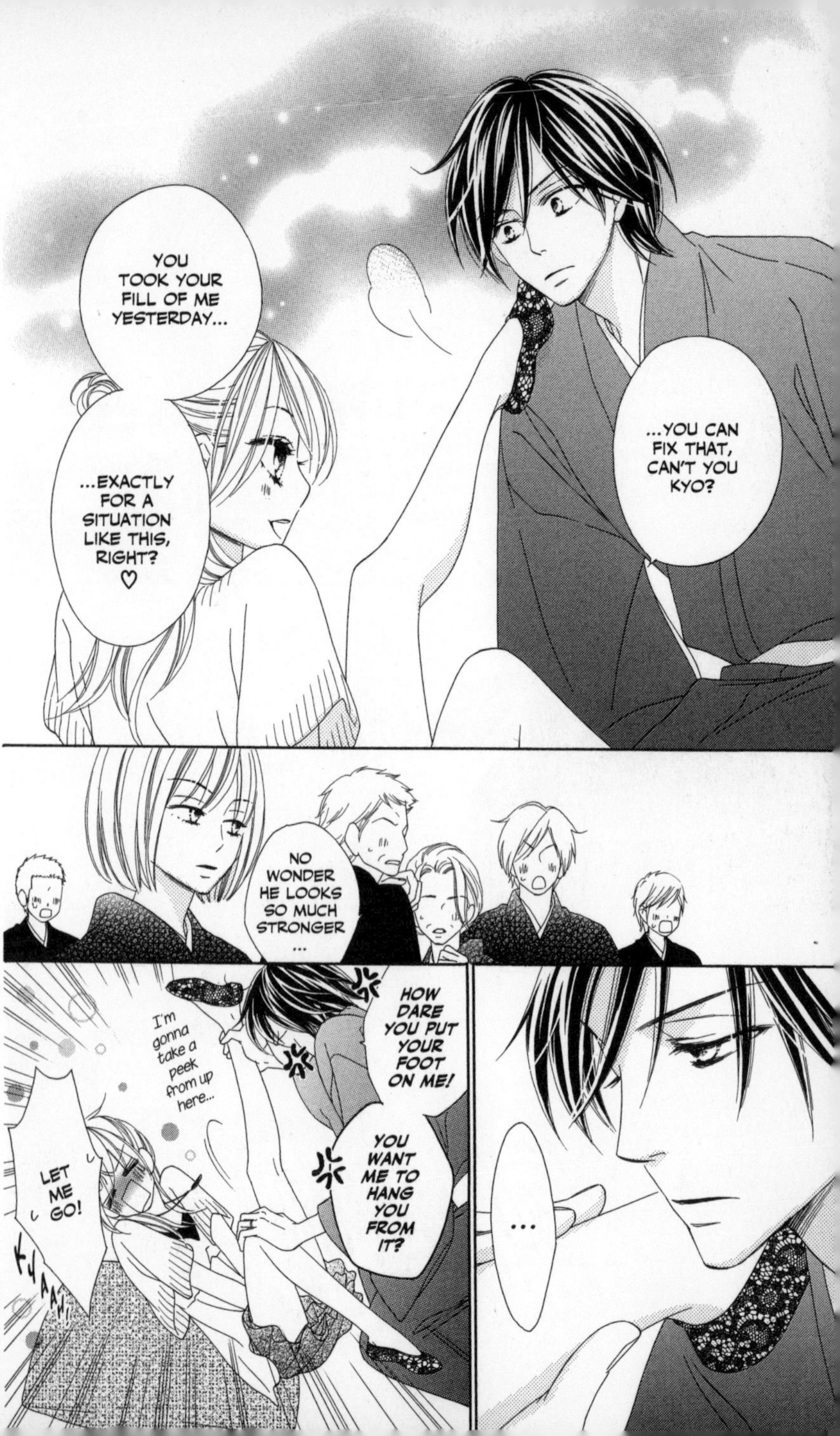
...YOU CAN FIX THAT, CAN'T YOU KYO?
YOU TOOK YOUR FILL OF ME YESTERDAY...
...EXACTLY FOR A SITUATION LIKE THIS, RIGHT? ♡
NO WONDER HE LOOKS SO MUCH STRONGER...
...
HOW DARE YOU PUT YOUR FOOT ON ME!
YOU WANT ME TO HANG YOU FROM IT?
I'm gonna take a peek from up here...
LET ME GO!
KYAAAH!

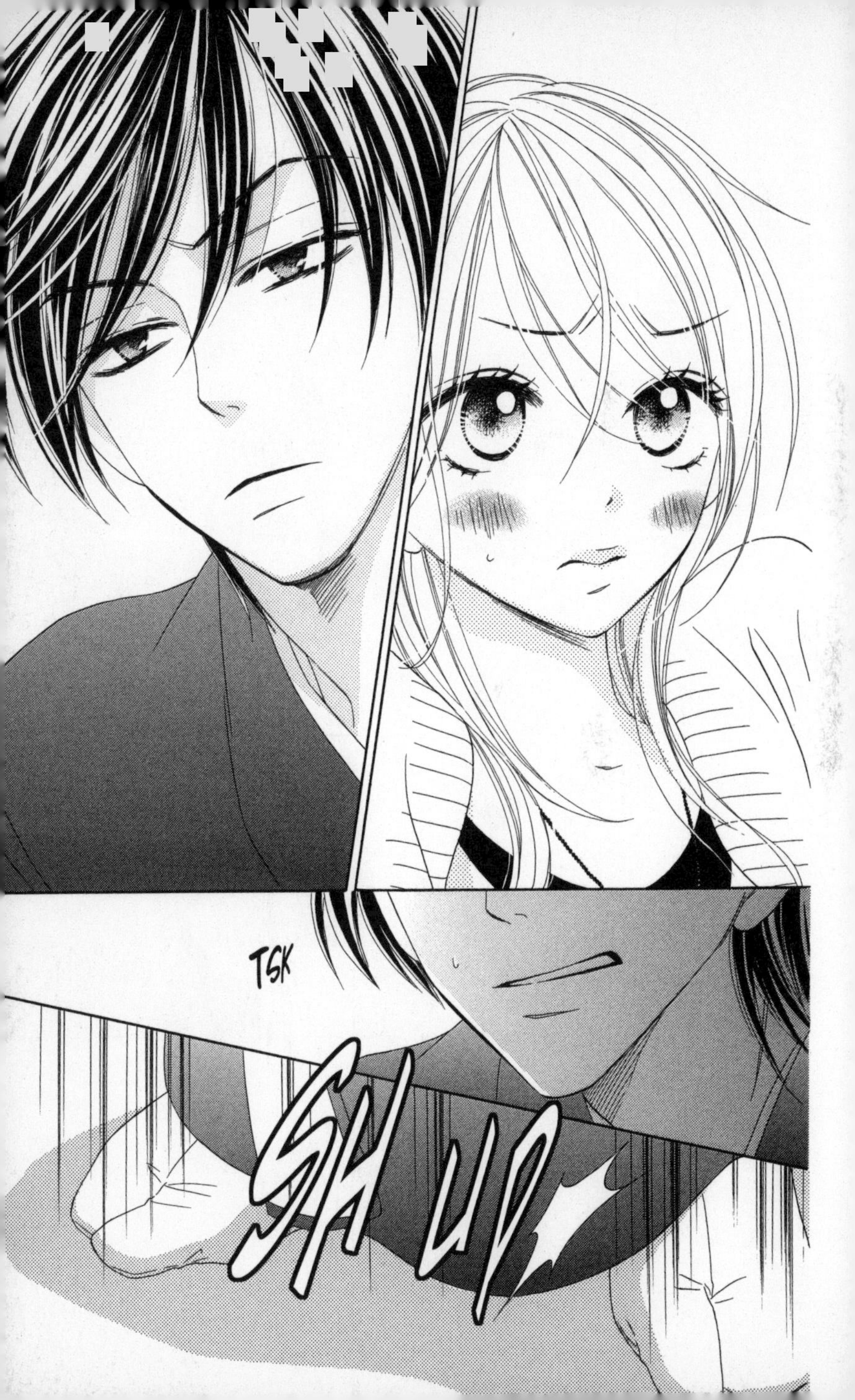
TSK
SHUP

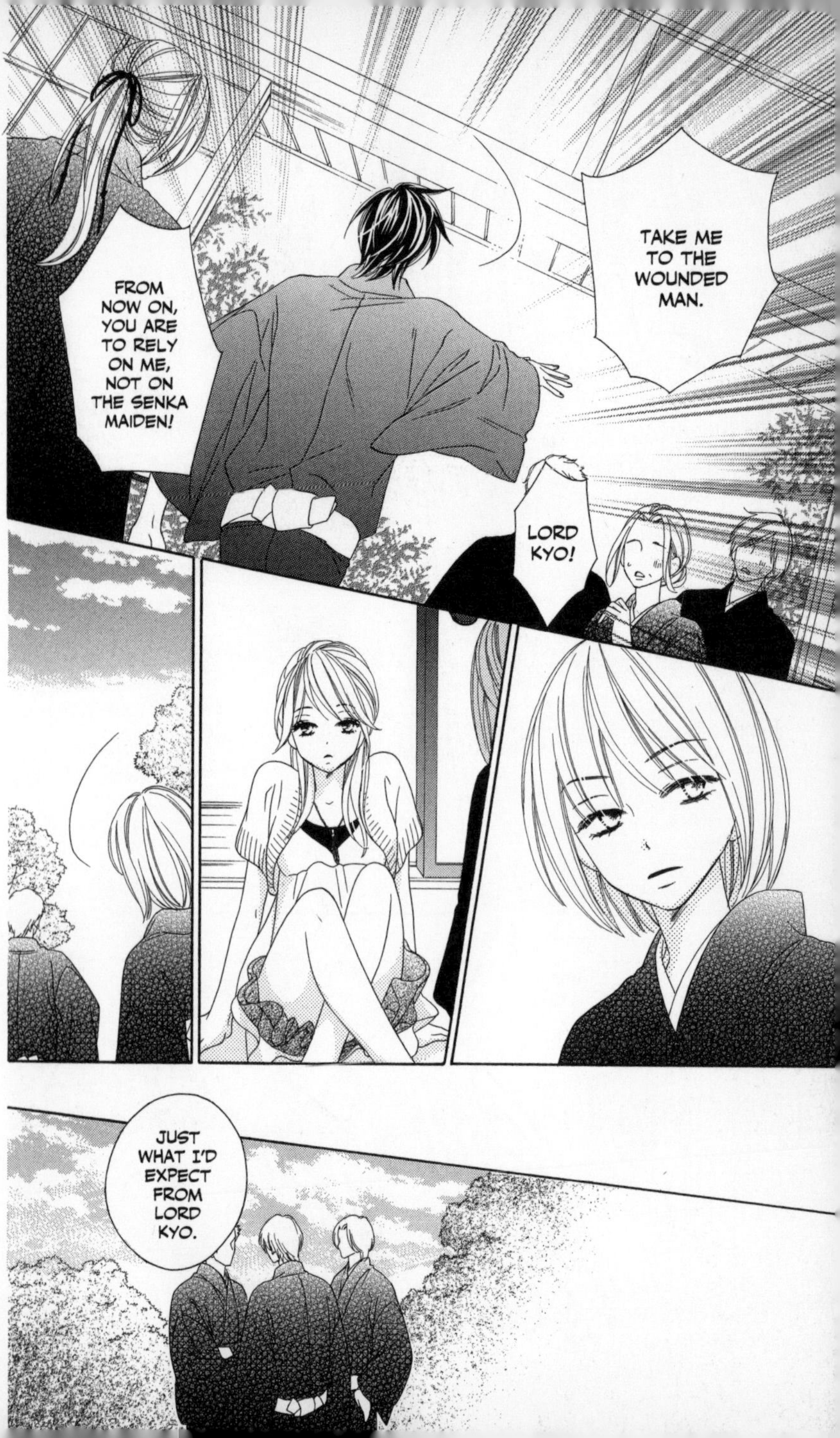
TAKE ME TO THE WOUNDED MAN.
FROM NOW ON, YOU ARE TO RELY ON ME, NOT ON THE SENKA MAIDEN!
LORD KYO!
JUST WHAT I'D EXPECT FROM LORD KYO.

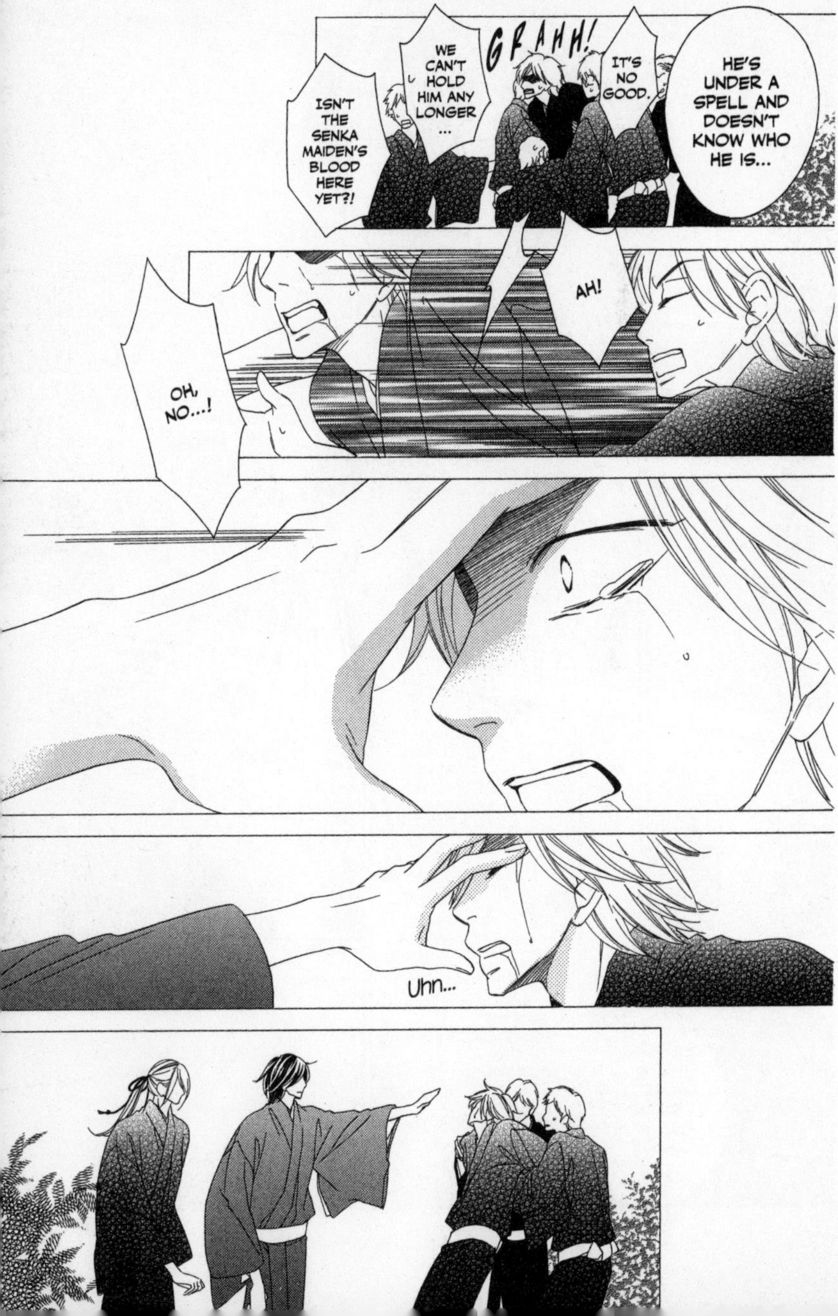
HE'S UNDER A SPELL AND DOESN'T KNOW WHO HE IS...
IT'S NO GOOD.
GRAHH!
WE CAN'T HOLD HIM ANY LONGER...
ISN'T THE SENKA MAIDEN'S BLOOD HERE YET?!
AH!
OH, NO...!
Uhn...

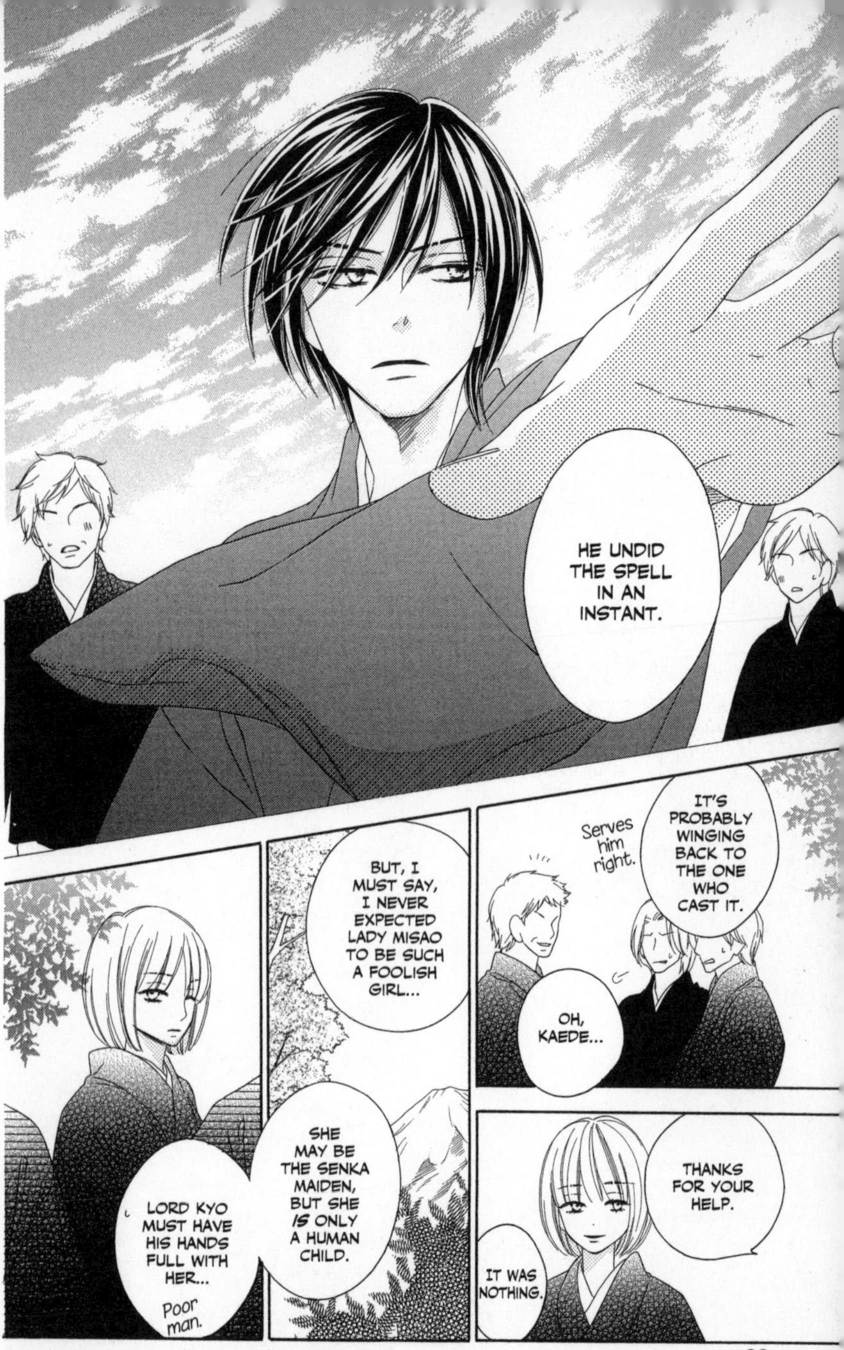
HE UNDID THE SPELL IN AN INSTANT.
IT'S PROBABLY WINGING BACK TO THE ONE WHO CAST IT.
Serves him right.
OH, KAEDE...
THANKS FOR YOUR HELP.
IT WAS NOTHING.
BUT, I MUST SAY, I NEVER EXPECTED LADY MISAO TO BE SUCH A FOOLISH GIRL...
SHE MAY BE THE SENKA MAIDEN, BUT SHE *IS* ONLY A HUMAN CHILD.
LORD KYO MUST HAVE HIS HANDS FULL WITH HER...
Poor man.

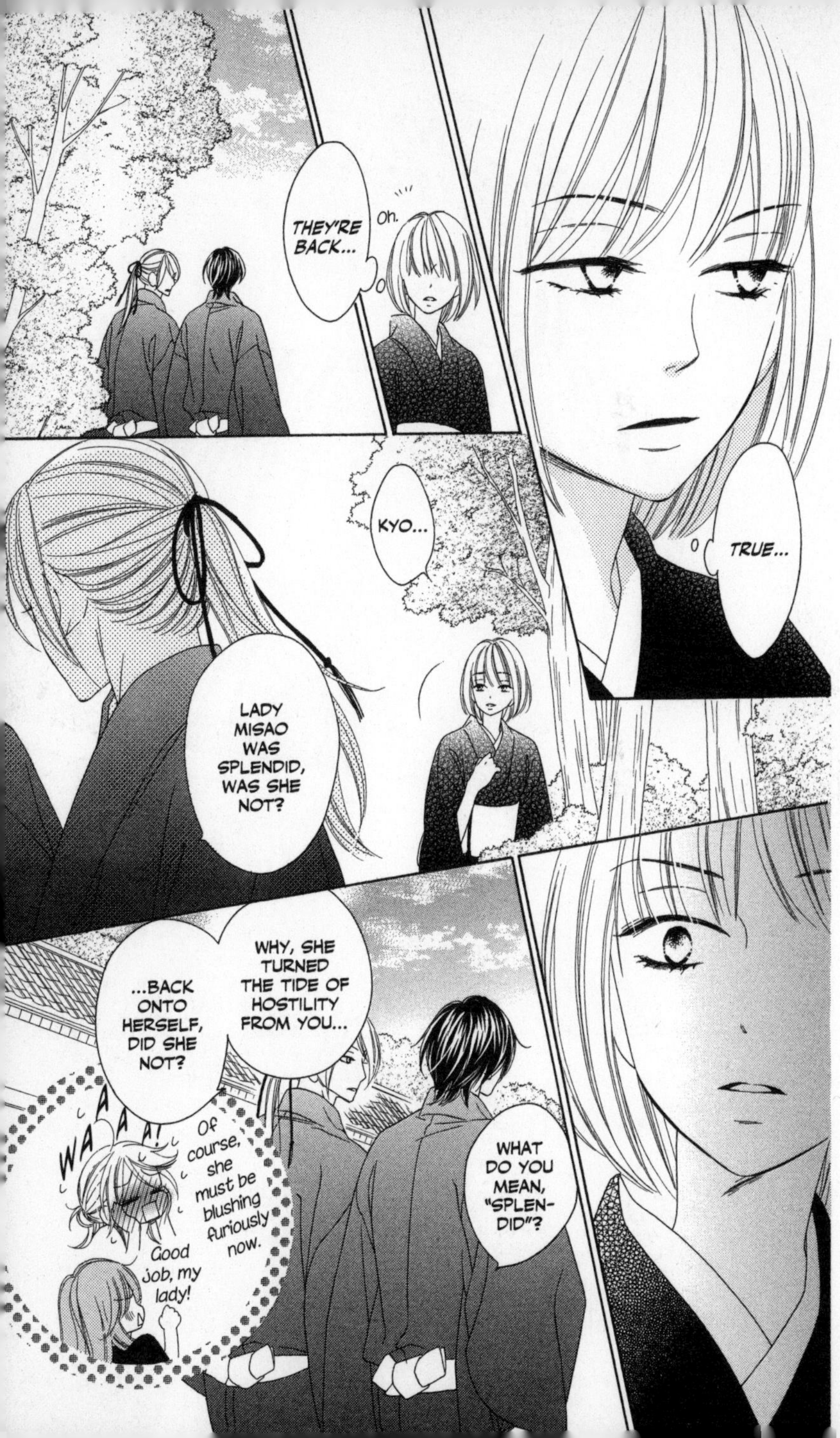
TRUE...
Oh.
THEY'RE BACK...
KYO...
LADY MISAO WAS SPLENDID, WAS SHE NOT?
WHAT DO YOU MEAN, "SPLEN-DID"?
WHY, SHE TURNED THE TIDE OF HOSTILITY FROM YOU...
...BACK ONTO HERSELF, DID SHE NOT?
WAAAA!
Of course, she must be blushing furiously now.
Good job, my lady!

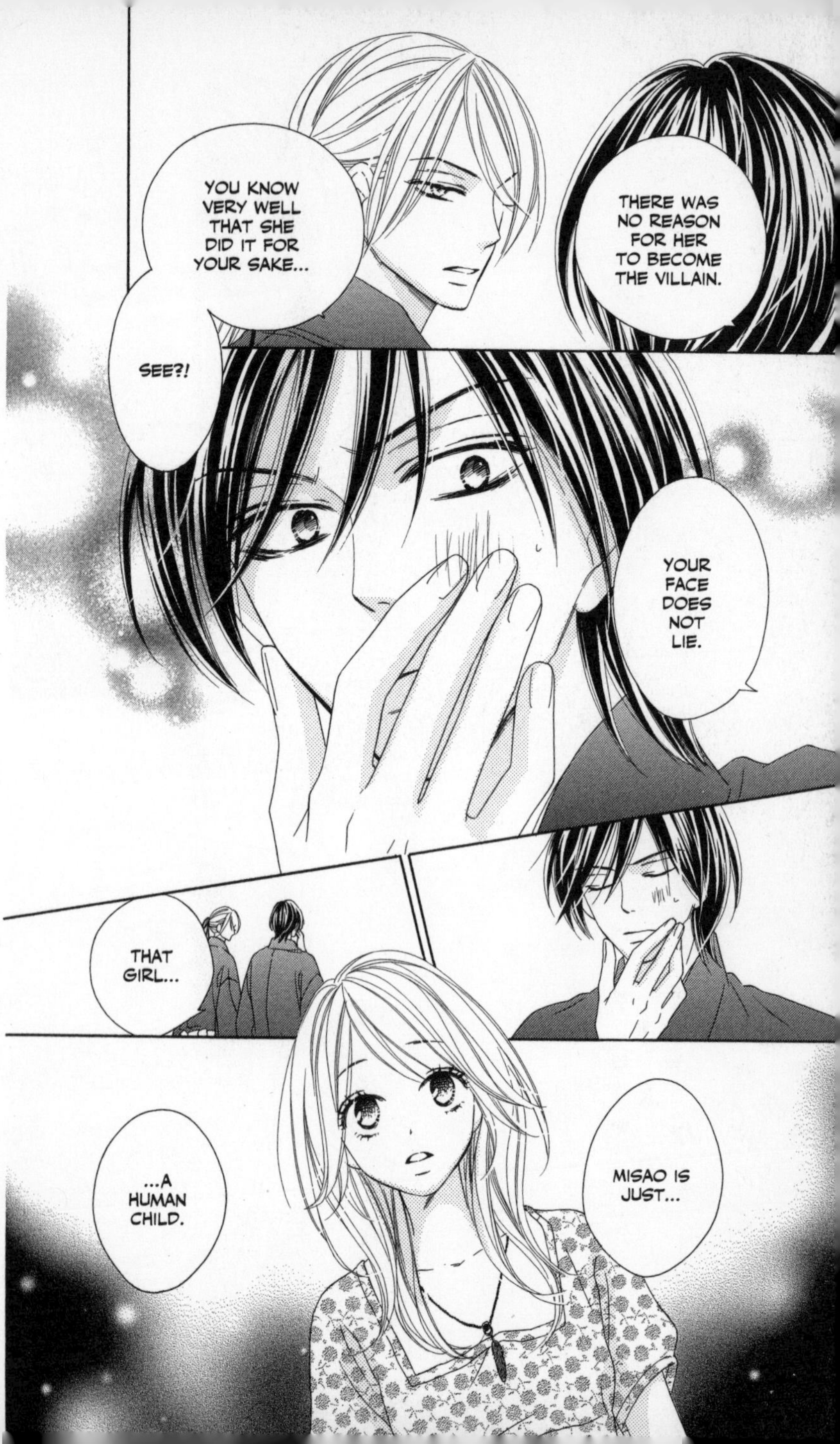
THERE WAS NO REASON FOR HER TO BECOME THE VILLAIN.
YOU KNOW VERY WELL THAT SHE DID IT FOR YOUR SAKE...
SEE?!
YOUR FACE DOES NOT LIE.
THAT GIRL...
MISAO IS JUST...
...A HUMAN CHILD.

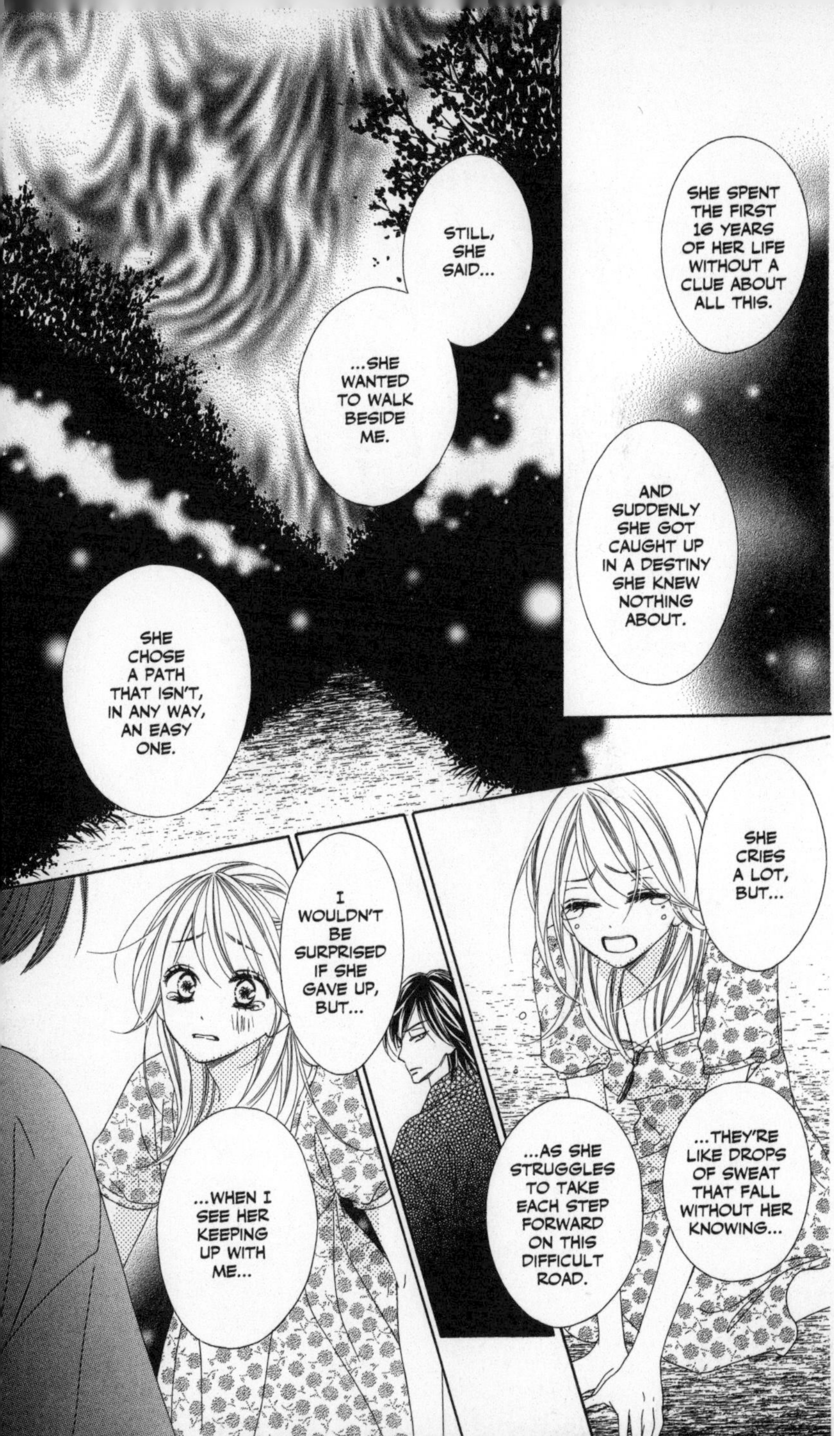
SHE SPENT THE FIRST 16 YEARS OF HER LIFE WITHOUT A CLUE ABOUT ALL THIS.
AND SUDDENLY SHE GOT CAUGHT UP IN A DESTINY SHE KNEW NOTHING ABOUT.
STILL, SHE SAID...
...SHE WANTED TO WALK BESIDE ME.
SHE CHOSE A PATH THAT ISN'T, IN ANY WAY, AN EASY ONE.
SHE CRIES A LOT, BUT...
...THEY'RE LIKE DROPS OF SWEAT THAT FALL WITHOUT HER KNOWING...
...AS SHE STRUGGLES TO TAKE EACH STEP FORWARD ON THIS DIFFICULT ROAD.
I WOULDN'T BE SURPRISED IF SHE GAVE UP, BUT...
...WHEN I SEE HER KEEPING UP WITH ME...

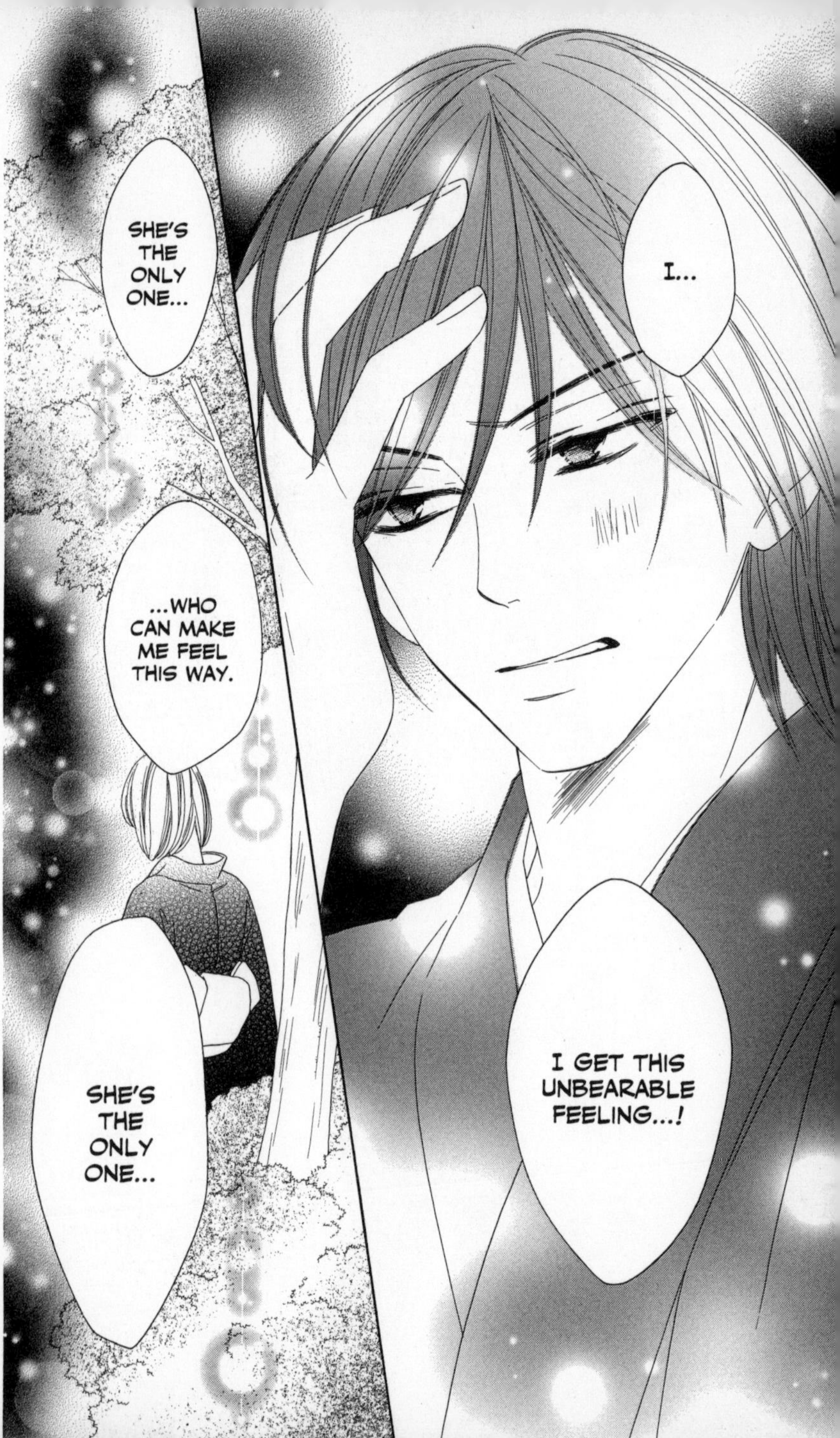
I...
I GET THIS UNBEARABLE FEELING...!
SHE'S THE ONLY ONE...
...WHO CAN MAKE ME FEEL THIS WAY.
SHE'S THE ONLY ONE...

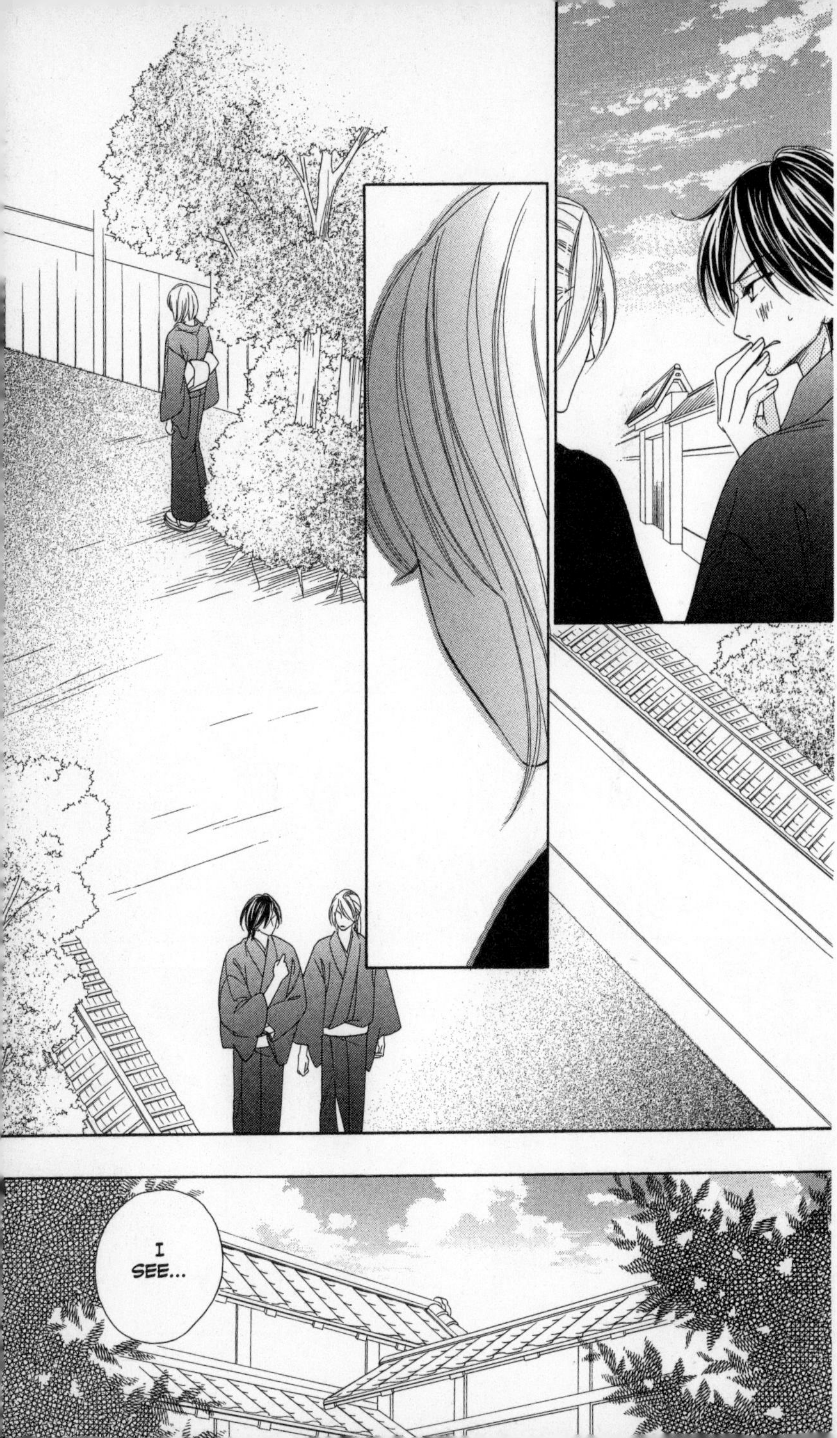
I SEE...

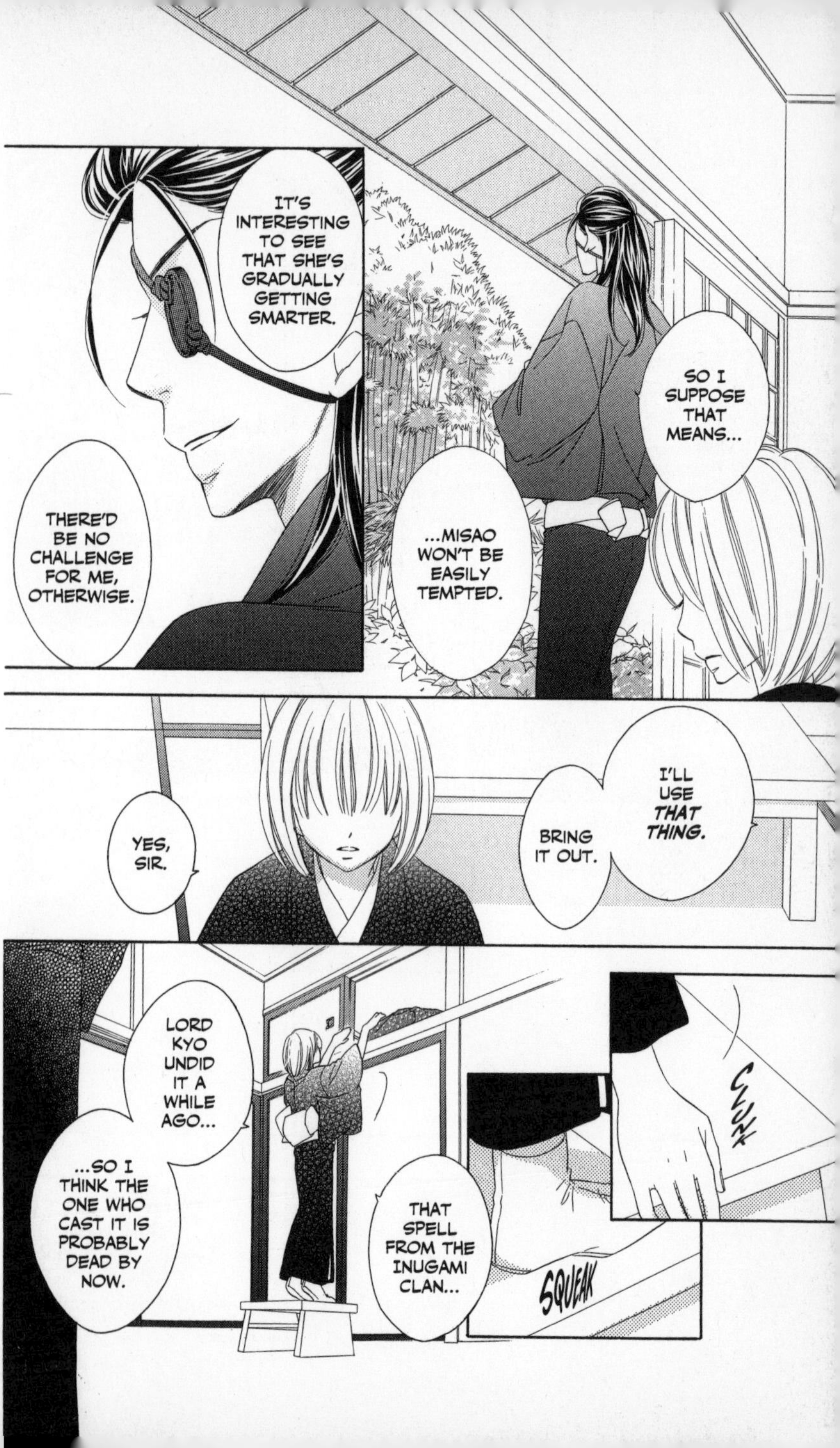
SO I SUPPOSE THAT MEANS...
...MISAO WON'T BE EASILY TEMPTED.
IT'S INTERESTING TO SEE THAT SHE'S GRADUALLY GETTING SMARTER.
THERE'D BE NO CHALLENGE FOR ME, OTHERWISE.
I'LL USE *THAT THING.*
BRING IT OUT.
YES, SIR.
CLUNK
SQUEAK
THAT SPELL FROM THE INUGAMI CLAN...
LORD KYO UNDID IT A WHILE AGO...
...SO I THINK THE ONE WHO CAST IT IS PROBABLY DEAD BY NOW.

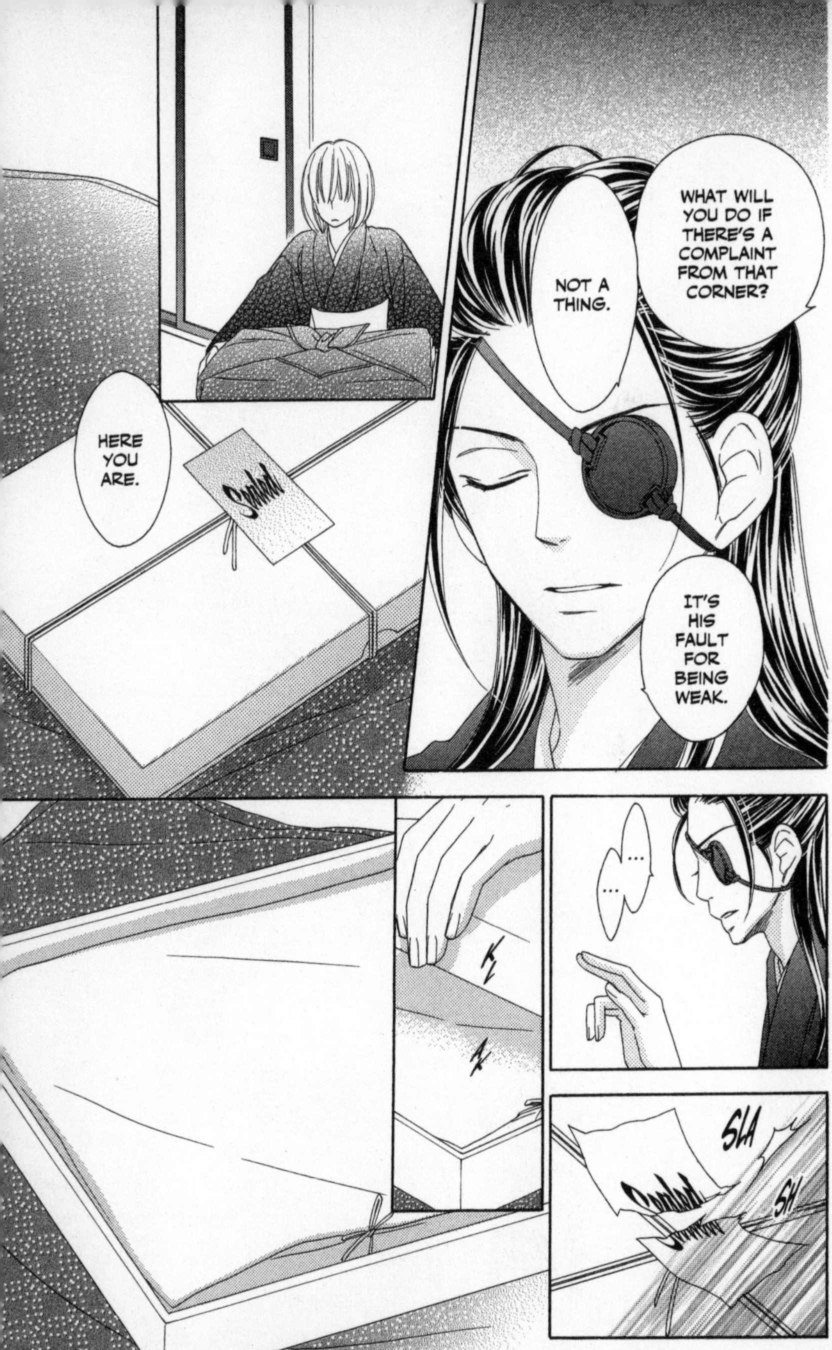
WHAT WILL YOU DO IF THERE'S A COMPLAINT FROM THAT CORNER?
NOT A THING.
IT'S HIS FAULT FOR BEING WEAK.
HERE YOU ARE.
......
SLA
SH

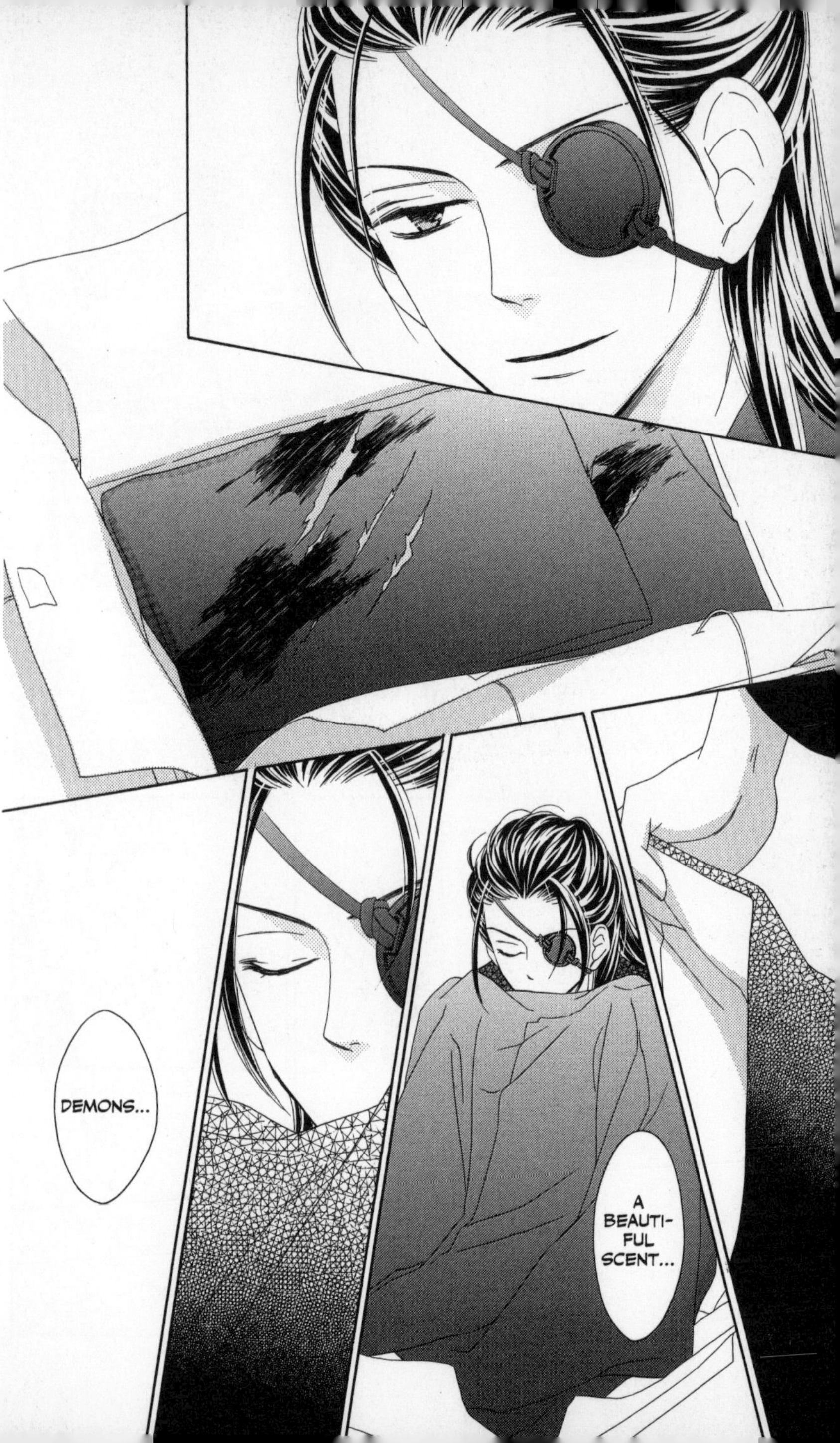
A BEAUTI-FUL SCENT...
DEMONS...

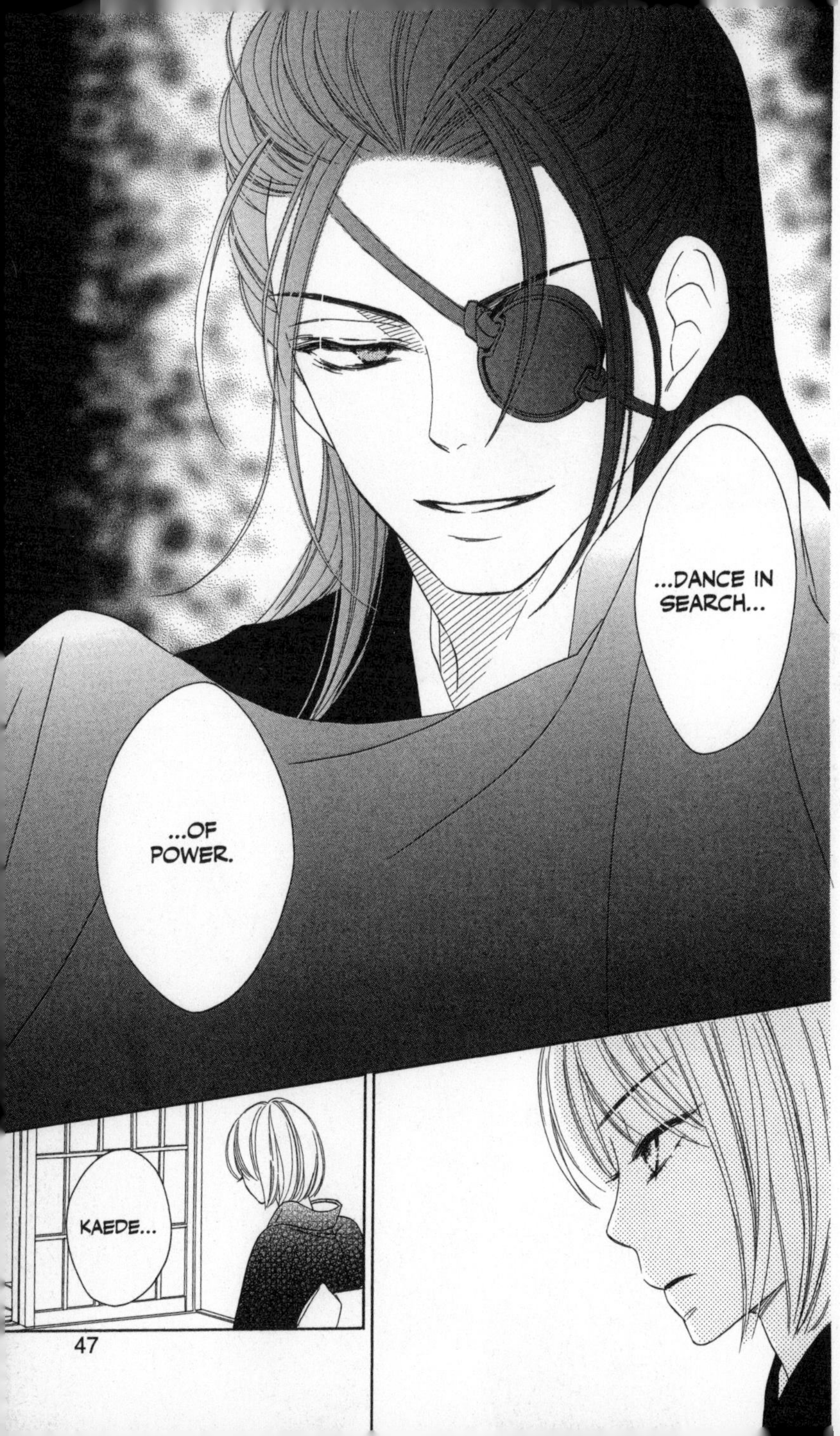
...DANCE IN SEARCH...
...OF POWER.
KAEDE...

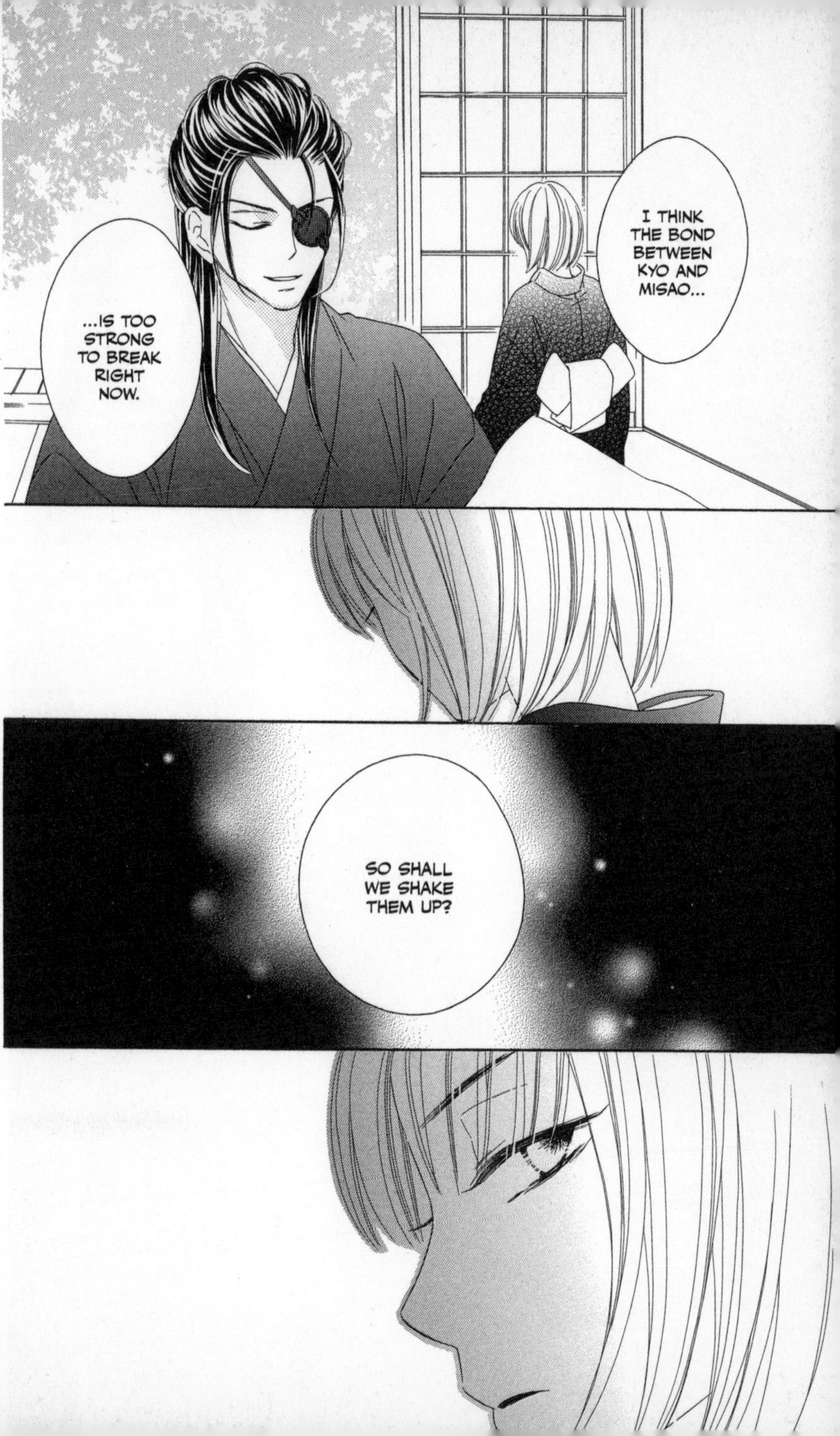
I THINK THE BOND BETWEEN KYO AND MISAO...
...IS TOO STRONG TO BREAK RIGHT NOW.
SO SHALL WE SHAKE THEM UP?

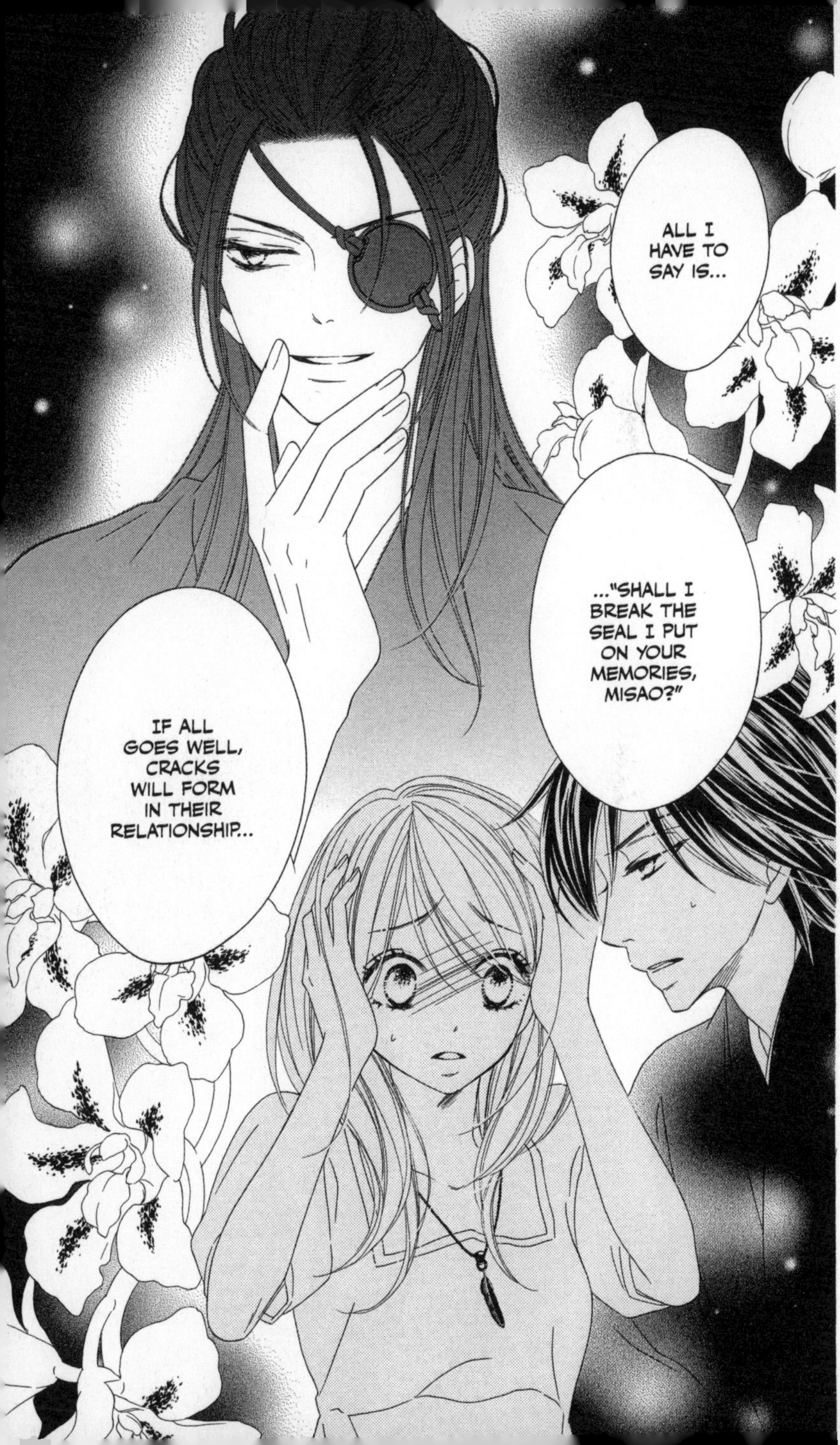
ALL I HAVE TO SAY IS...
..."SHALL I BREAK THE SEAL I PUT ON YOUR MEMORIES, MISAO?"
IF ALL GOES WELL, CRACKS WILL FORM IN THEIR RELATIONSHIP...

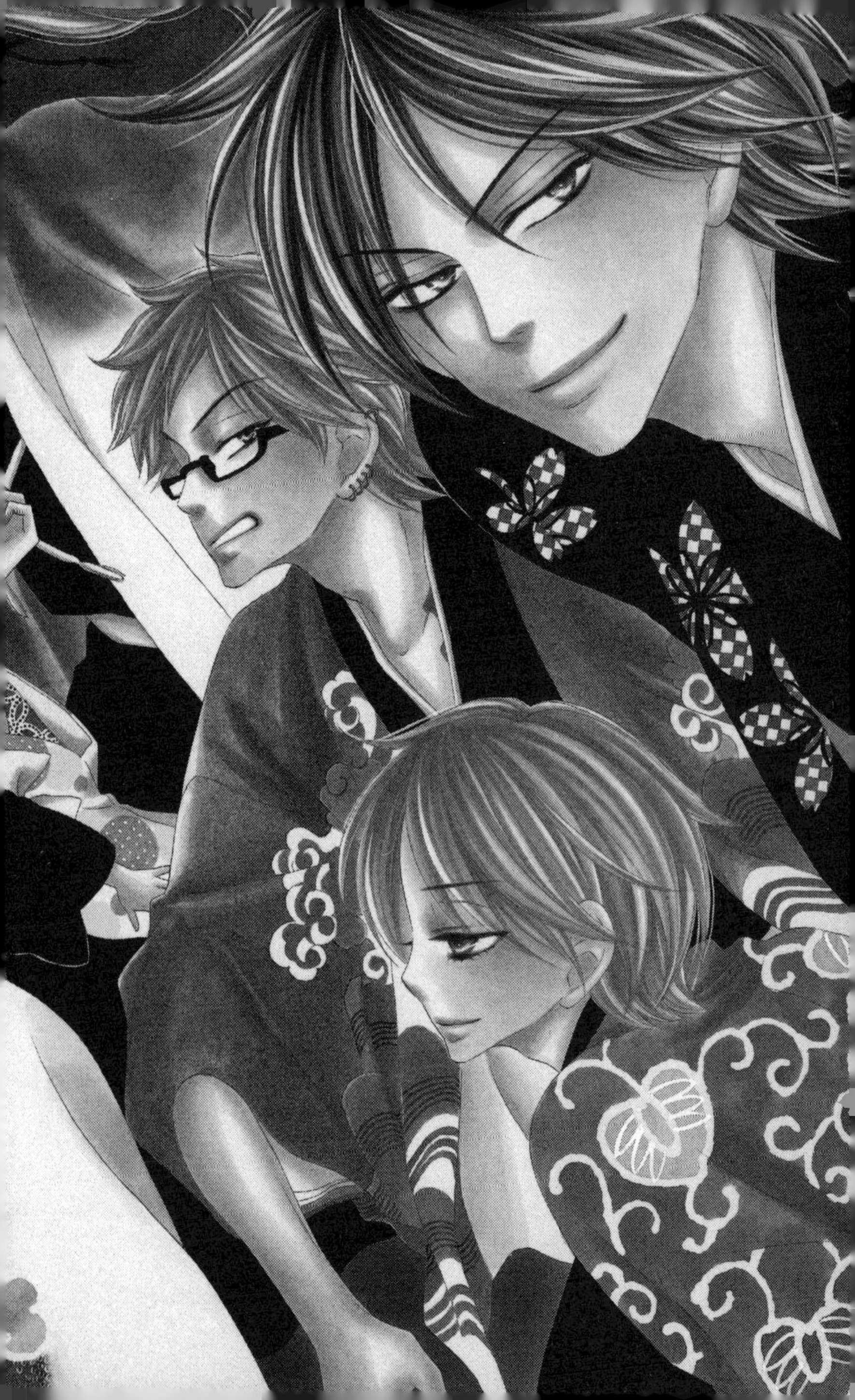

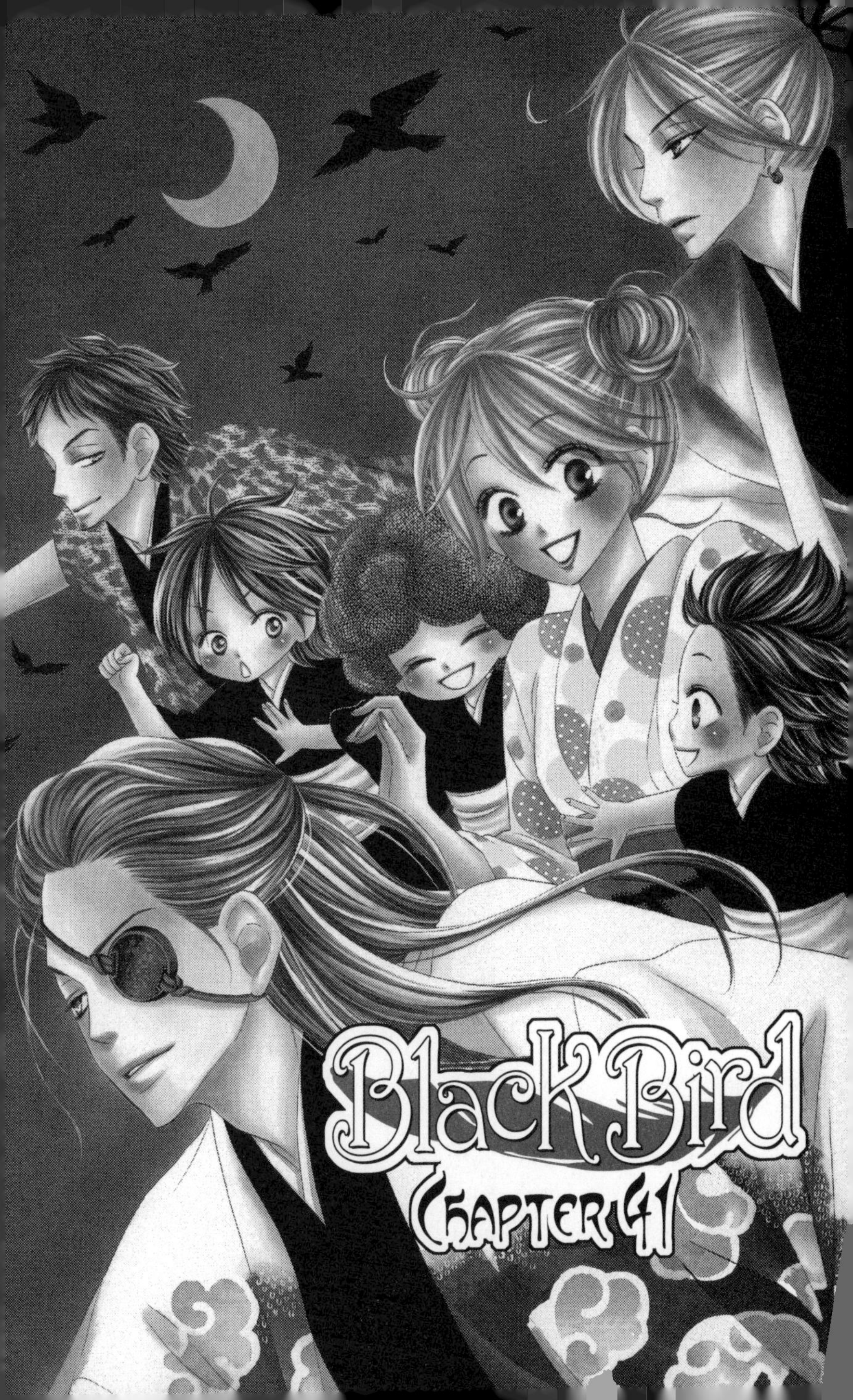
Black Bird
Chapter 41

*KIDO: MAGICAL BARRIER

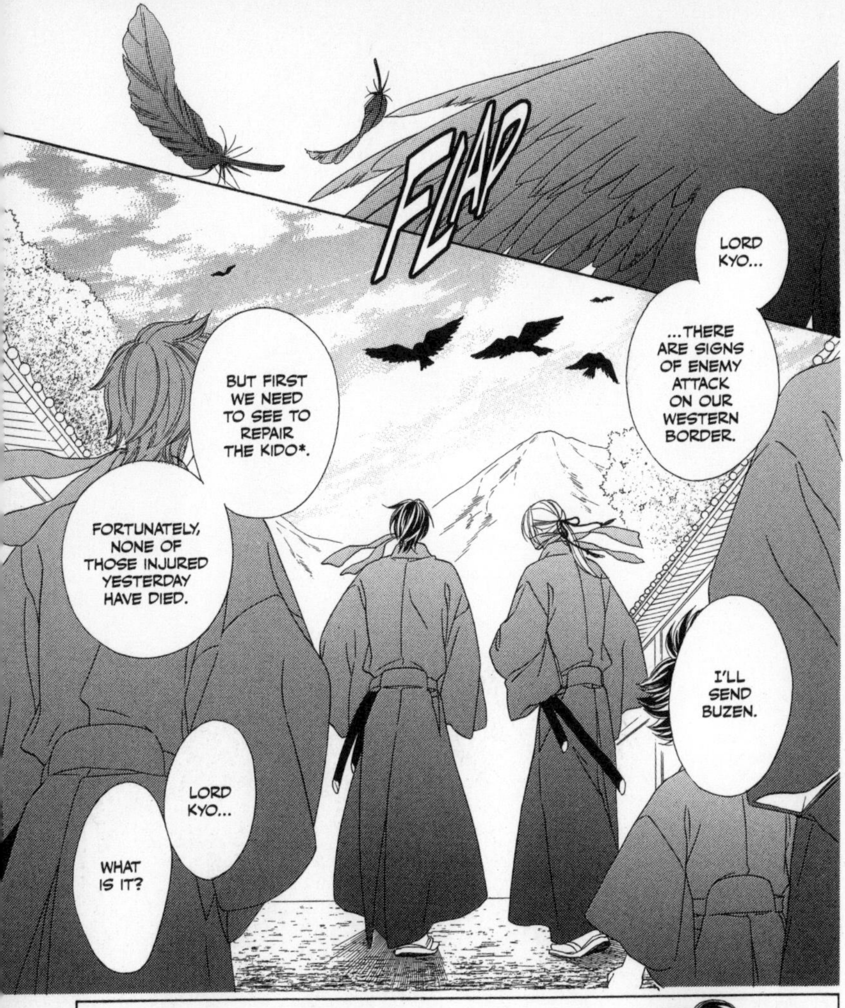
FLAP
LORD KYO...
...THERE ARE SIGNS OF ENEMY ATTACK ON OUR WESTERN BORDER.
BUT FIRST WE NEED TO SEE TO REPAIR THE KIDO*.
FORTUNATELY, NONE OF THOSE INJURED YESTERDAY HAVE DIED.
I'LL SEND BUZEN.
LORD KYO...
WHAT IS IT?

● Character Introduction ●

烏水 楊 age: 51
Yoh Usui height: 6′

I actually had a model for this character (two of them, in fact) but the longer I spent drawing him, the less he looked like them, so I won't tell you who they were... He is a very easy character to draw.

Yuri was supposed to be an exquisite beauty, but... I have just arrived at the limit of my artistic skills.

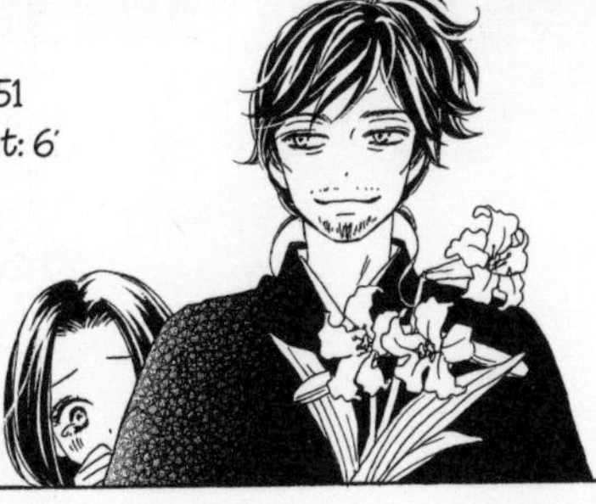

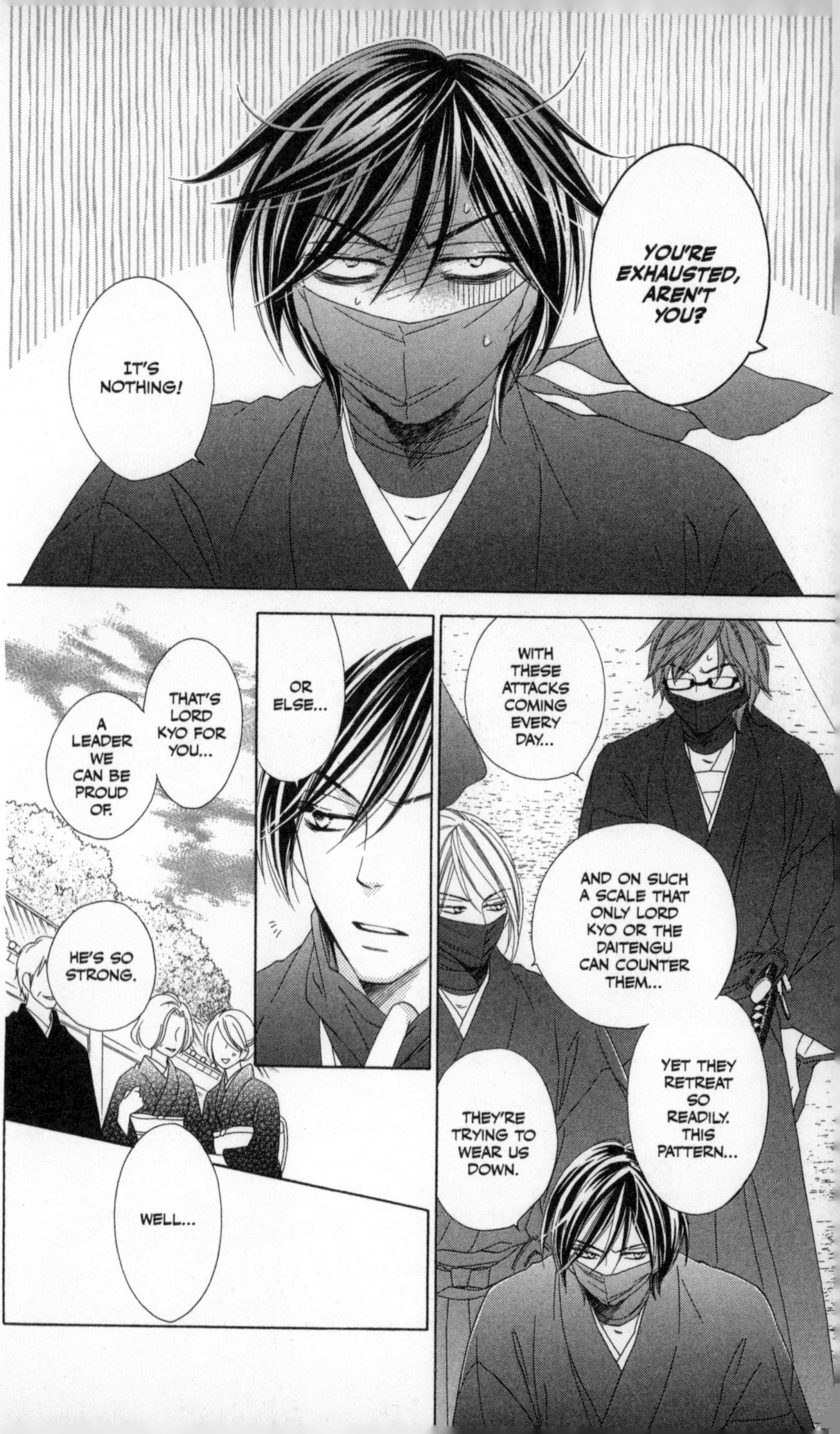
YOU'RE EXHAUSTED, AREN'T YOU?
IT'S NOTHING!
WITH THESE ATTACKS COMING EVERY DAY...
AND ON SUCH A SCALE THAT ONLY LORD KYO OR THE DAITENGU CAN COUNTER THEM...
YET THEY RETREAT SO READILY. THIS PATTERN...
THEY'RE TRYING TO WEAR US DOWN.
OR ELSE...
THAT'S LORD KYO FOR YOU...
A LEADER WE CAN BE PROUD OF.
HE'S SO STRONG.
WELL...

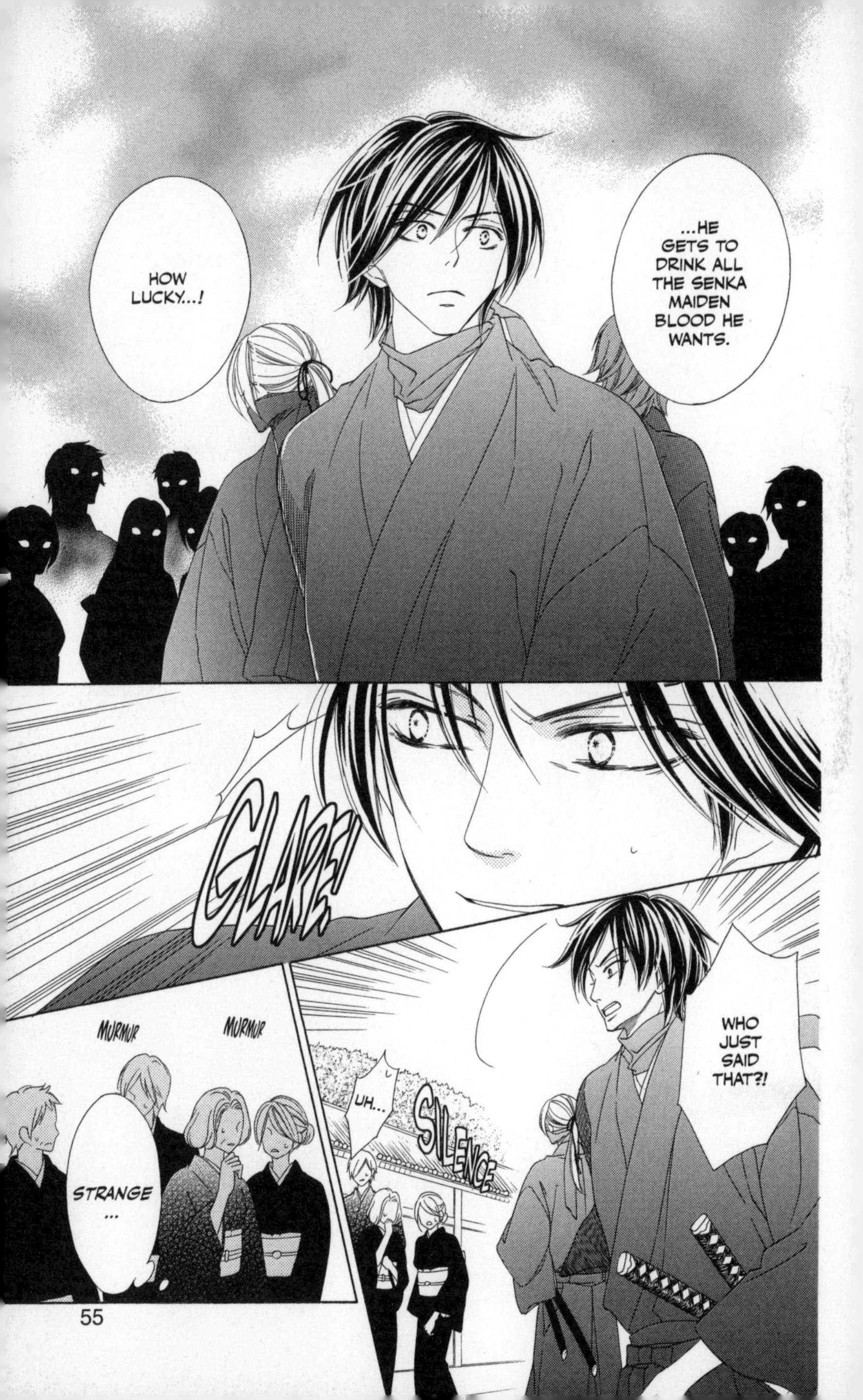
...HE GETS TO DRINK ALL THE SENKA MAIDEN BLOOD HE WANTS.
HOW LUCKY...!
GLARE!
WHO JUST SAID THAT?!
SILENCE
UH...
MURMUR
MURMUR
STRANGE ...

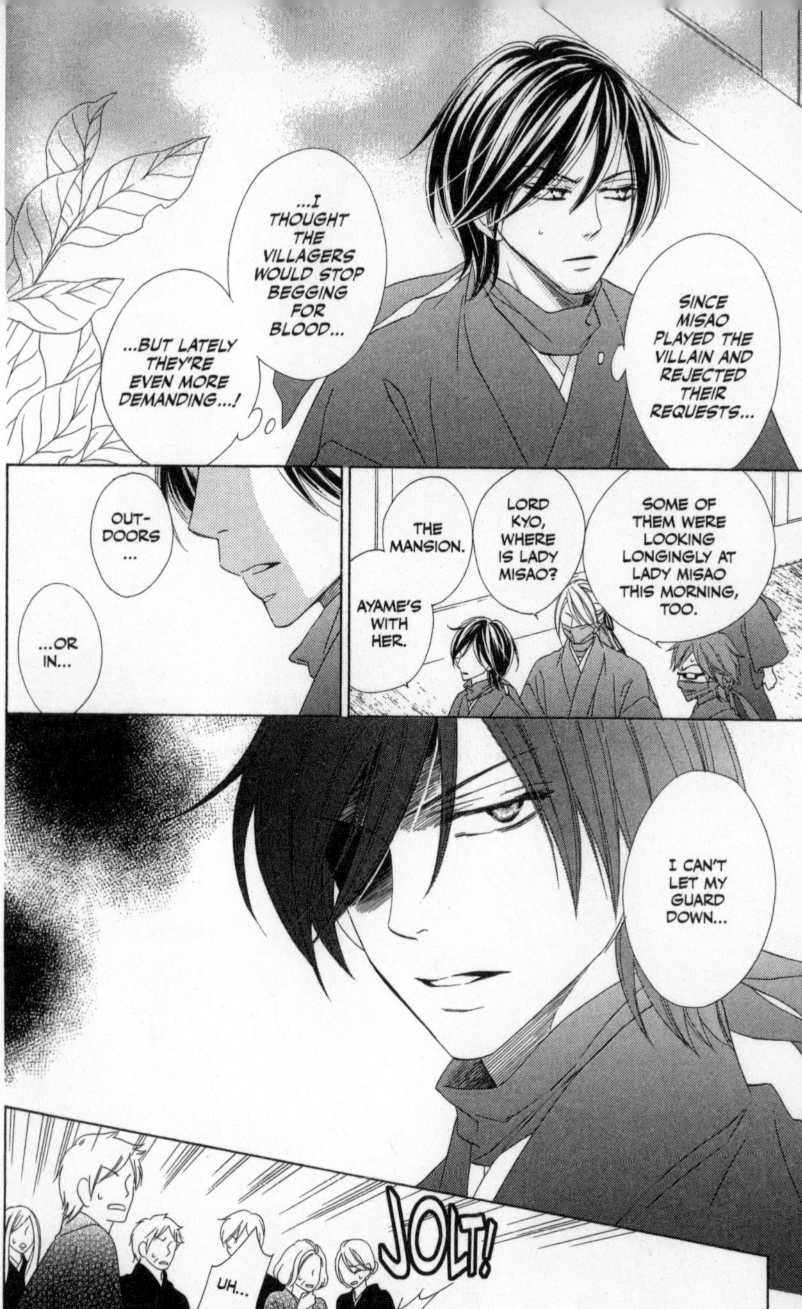
SINCE MISAO PLAYED THE VILLAIN AND REJECTED THEIR REQUESTS...
...I THOUGHT THE VILLAGERS WOULD STOP BEGGING FOR BLOOD...
...BUT LATELY THEY'RE EVEN MORE DEMANDING...!
SOME OF THEM WERE LOOKING LONGINGLY AT LADY MISAO THIS MORNING, TOO.
LORD KYO, WHERE IS LADY MISAO?
THE MANSION.
AYAME'S WITH HER.
OUT-DOORS...
...OR IN...
I CAN'T LET MY GUARD DOWN...
JOLT!
UH...

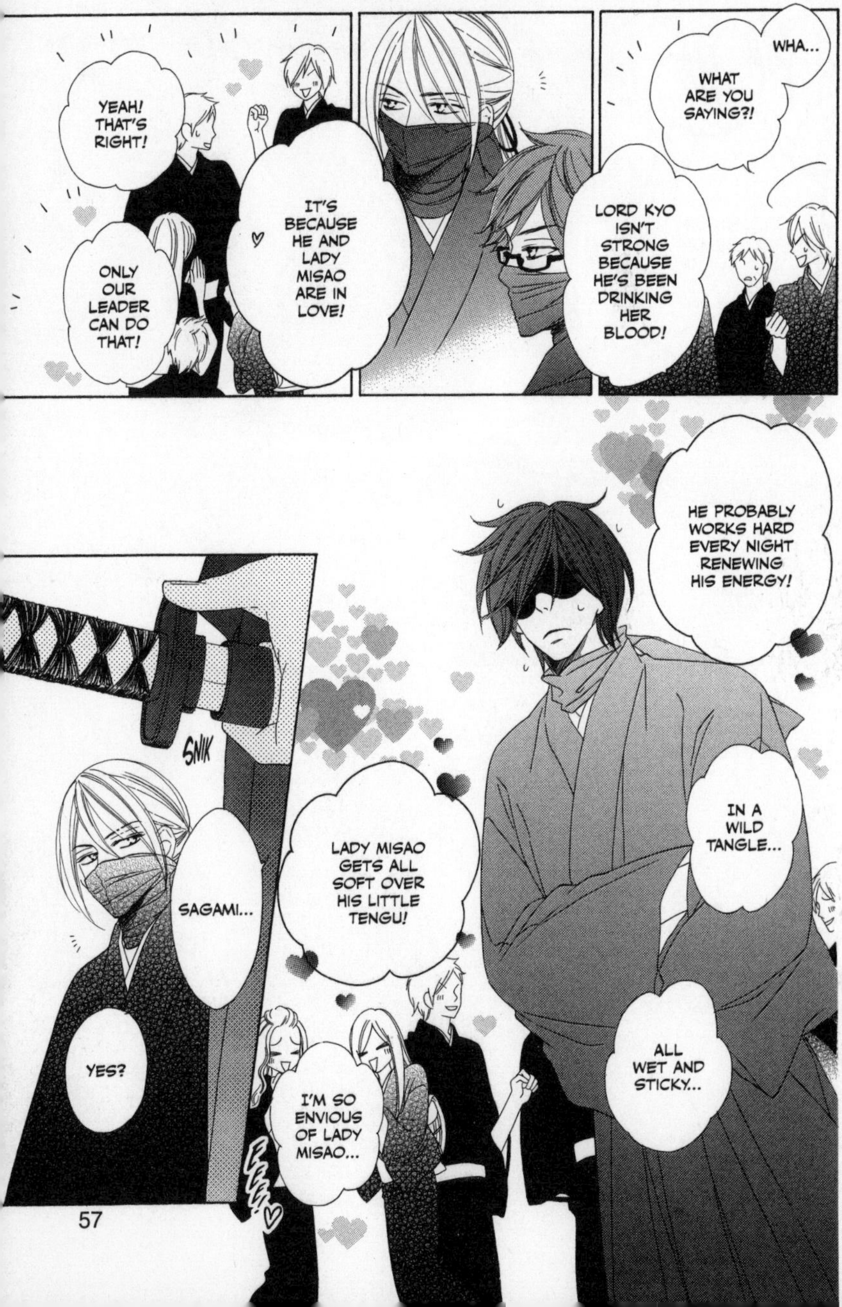
WHA...
WHAT ARE YOU SAYING?!
LORD KYO ISN'T STRONG BECAUSE HE'S BEEN DRINKING HER BLOOD!
IT'S BECAUSE HE AND LADY MISAO ARE IN LOVE!
YEAH! THAT'S RIGHT!
ONLY OUR LEADER CAN DO THAT!
HE PROBABLY WORKS HARD EVERY NIGHT RENEWING HIS ENERGY!
IN A WILD TANGLE...
ALL WET AND STICKY...
LADY MISAO GETS ALL SOFT OVER HIS LITTLE TENGU!
I'M SO ENVIOUS OF LADY MISAO...
EEEE
SNIK
SAGAMI...
YES?

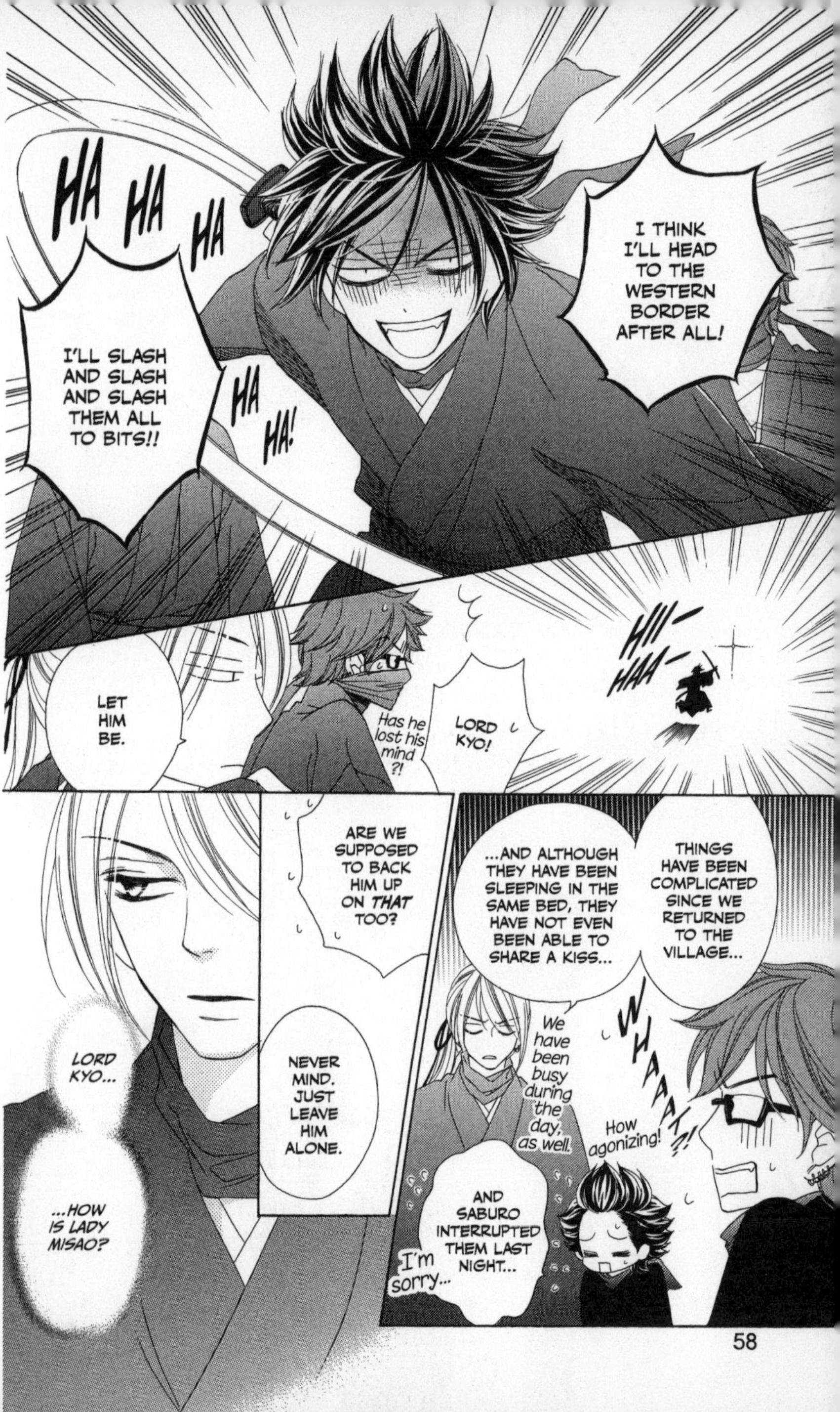
I THINK I'LL HEAD TO THE WESTERN BORDER AFTER ALL!
HA HA HA
I'LL SLASH AND SLASH AND SLASH THEM ALL TO BITS!!
HA HA!
HII-HAA
LORD KYO!
Has he lost his mind?!
LET HIM BE.
THINGS HAVE BEEN COMPLICATED SINCE WE RETURNED TO THE VILLAGE...
...AND ALTHOUGH THEY HAVE BEEN SLEEPING IN THE SAME BED, THEY HAVE NOT EVEN BEEN ABLE TO SHARE A KISS...
WHAAAAA!
We have been busy during the day, as well.
How agonizing!
AND SABURO INTERRUPTED THEM LAST NIGHT...
I'm sorry...
ARE WE SUPPOSED TO BACK HIM UP ON THAT TOO?
NEVER MIND. JUST LEAVE HIM ALONE.
LORD KYO...
...HOW IS LADY MISAO?

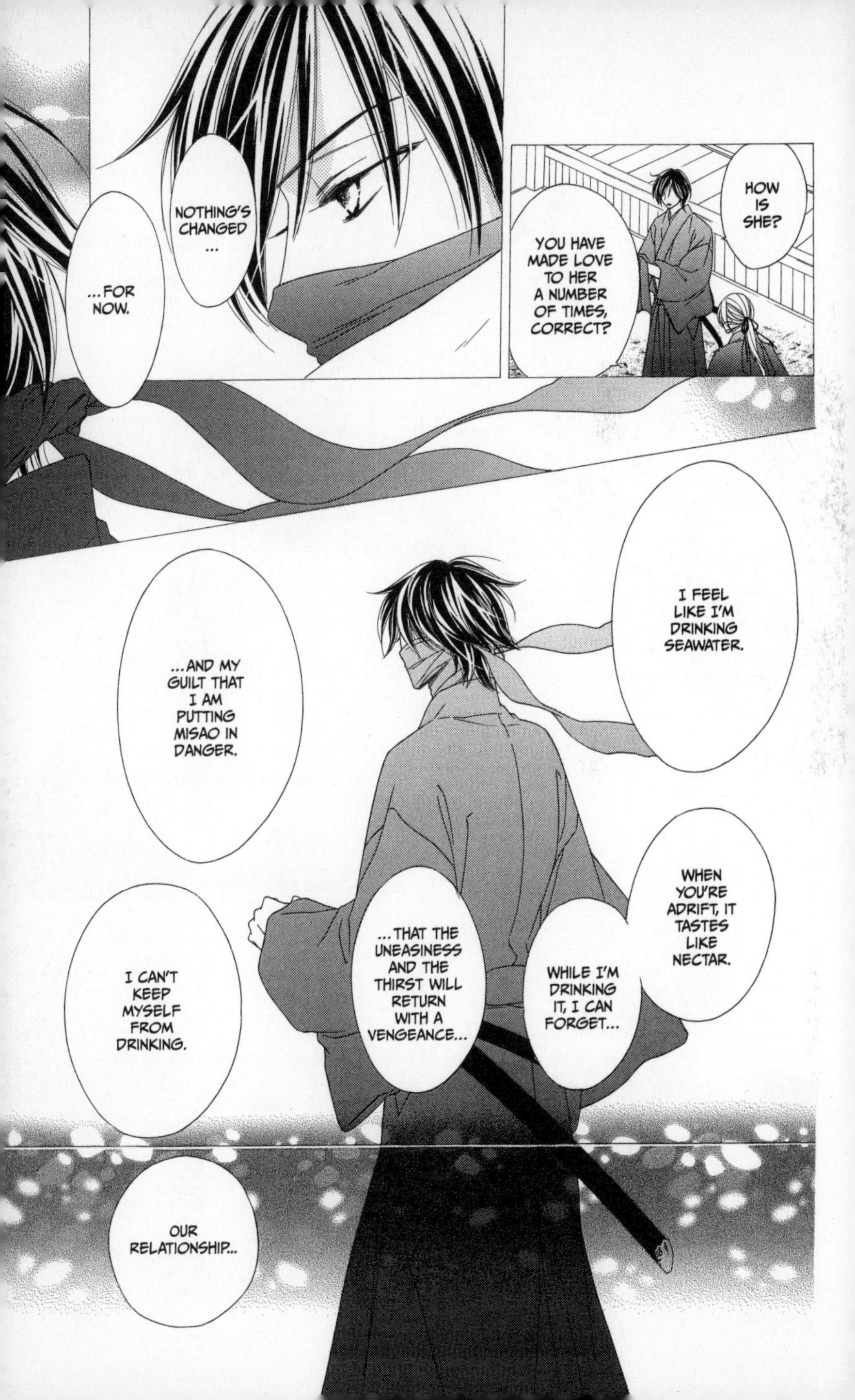
HOW IS SHE?
YOU HAVE MADE LOVE TO HER A NUMBER OF TIMES, CORRECT?
NOTHING'S CHANGED ...
...FOR NOW.
I FEEL LIKE I'M DRINKING SEAWATER.
WHEN YOU'RE ADRIFT, IT TASTES LIKE NECTAR.
WHILE I'M DRINKING IT, I CAN FORGET...
...THAT THE UNEASINESS AND THE THIRST WILL RETURN WITH A VENGEANCE...
...AND MY GUILT THAT I AM PUTTING MISAO IN DANGER.
I CAN'T KEEP MYSELF FROM DRINKING.
OUR RELATIONSHIP...

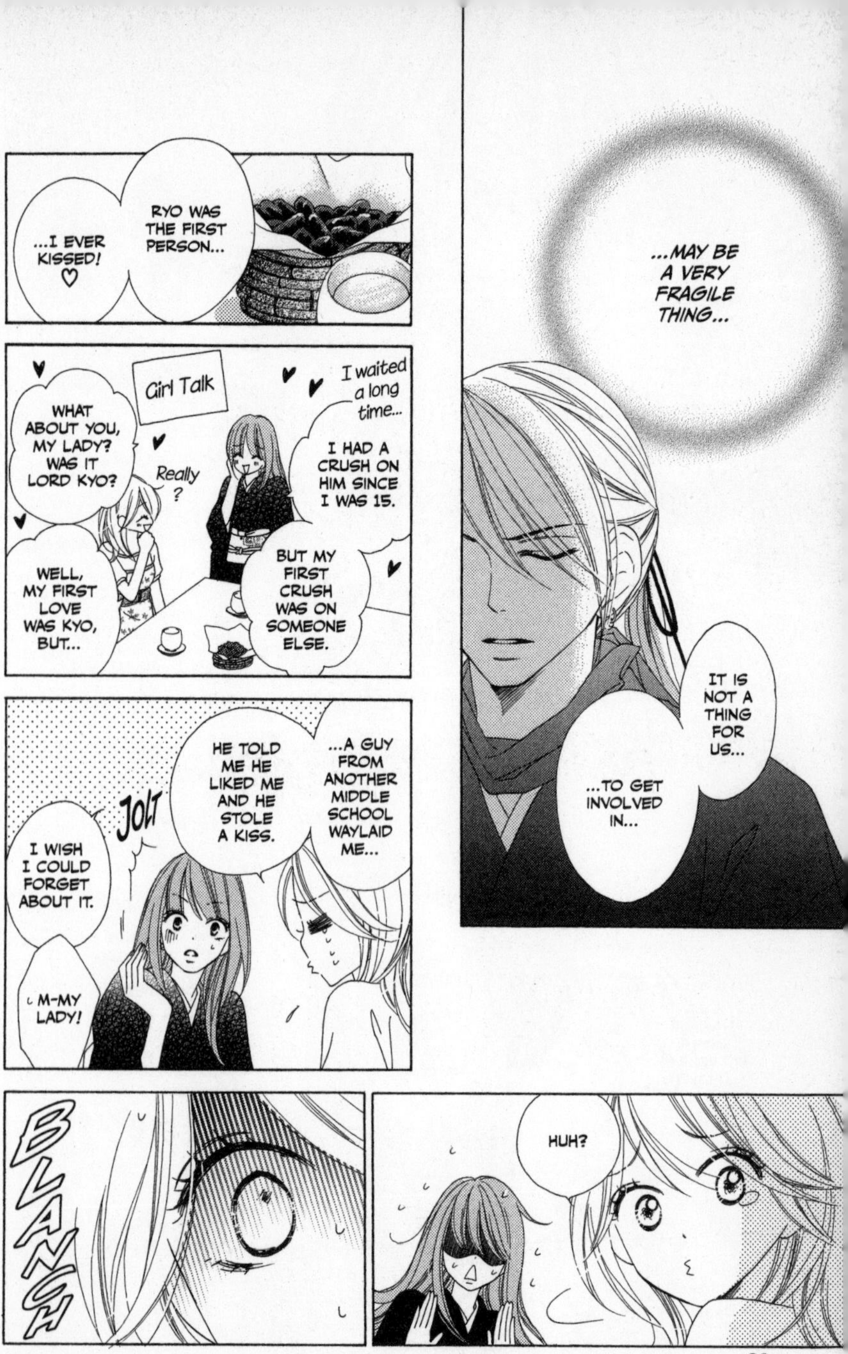
...MAY BE A VERY FRAGILE THING...
IT IS NOT A THING FOR US...
...TO GET INVOLVED IN...
RYO WAS THE FIRST PERSON...
...I EVER KISSED! ♡
Girl Talk
I waited a long time...
I HAD A CRUSH ON HIM SINCE I WAS 15.
WHAT ABOUT YOU, MY LADY? WAS IT LORD KYO?
Really?
WELL, MY FIRST LOVE WAS KYO, BUT...
BUT MY FIRST CRUSH WAS ON SOMEONE ELSE.
...A GUY FROM ANOTHER MIDDLE SCHOOL WAYLAID ME...
HE TOLD ME HE LIKED ME AND HE STOLE A KISS.
JOLT
I WISH I COULD FORGET ABOUT IT.
M-MY LADY!
HUH?
BLANCH

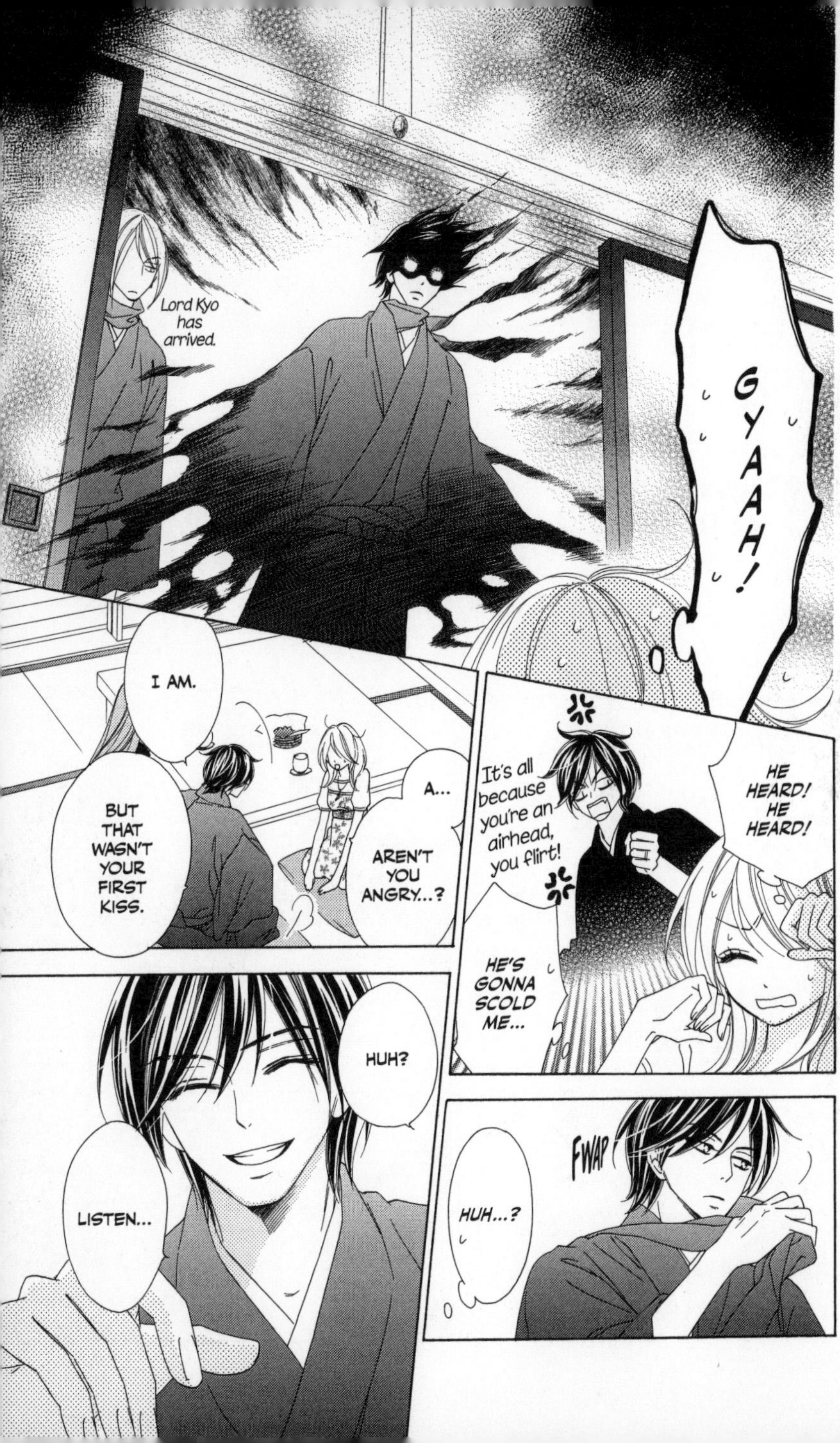
GYAAH!
Lord Kyo has arrived.
HE HEARD! HE HEARD!
It's all because you're an airhead, you flirt!
HE'S GONNA SCOLD ME...
A...
AREN'T YOU ANGRY...?
I AM.
BUT THAT WASN'T YOUR FIRST KISS.
FWAP
HUH...?
HUH?
LISTEN...

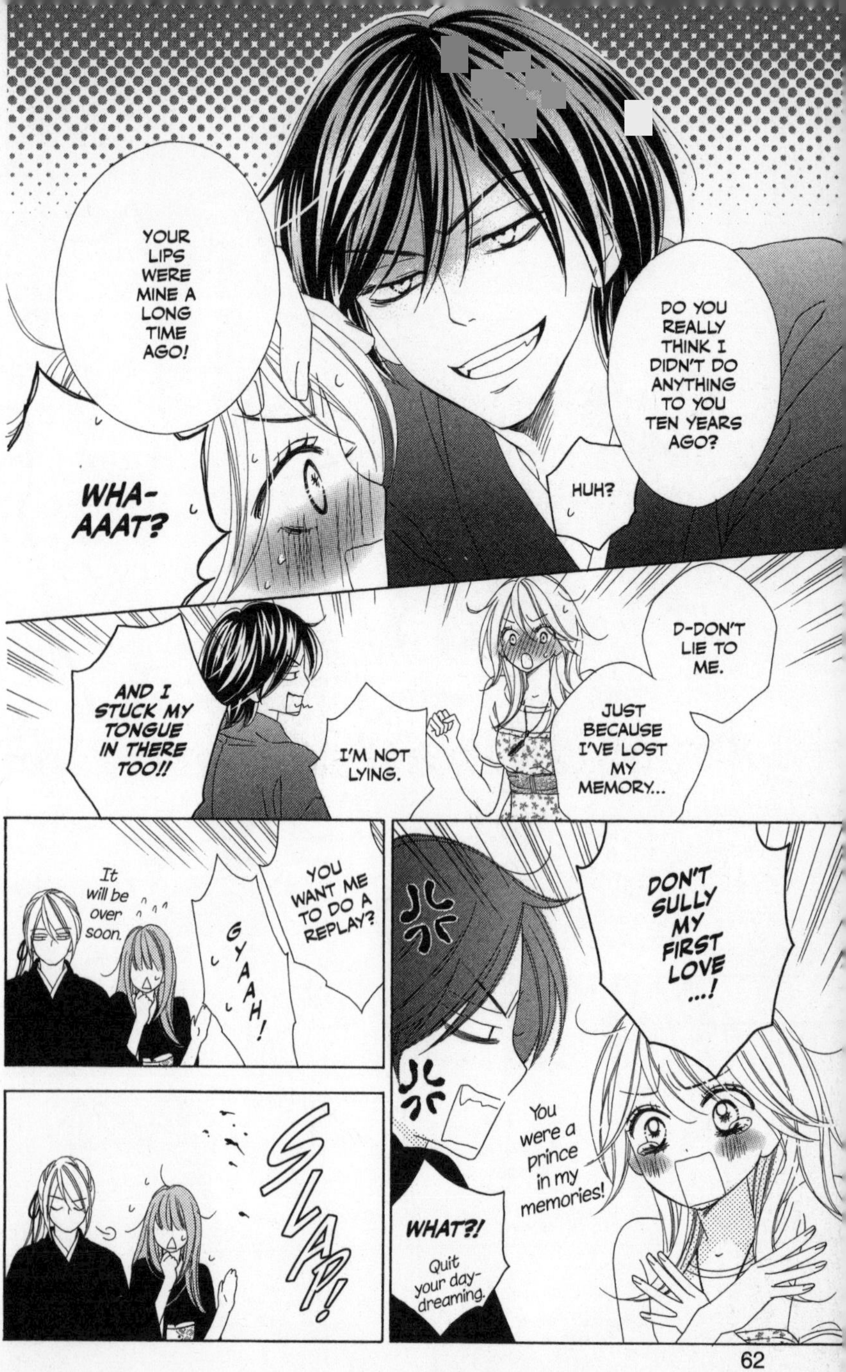
DO YOU REALLY THINK I DIDN'T DO ANYTHING TO YOU TEN YEARS AGO?
HUH?
YOUR LIPS WERE MINE A LONG TIME AGO!
WHA-AAAT?
D-DON'T LIE TO ME.
JUST BECAUSE I'VE LOST MY MEMORY...
I'M NOT LYING.
AND I STUCK MY TONGUE IN THERE TOO!!
DON'T SULLY MY FIRST LOVE ...!
You were a prince in my memories!
WHAT?!
Quit your day-dreaming.
YOU WANT ME TO DO A REPLAY?
GYAAAH!
It will be over soon.
SLAP!

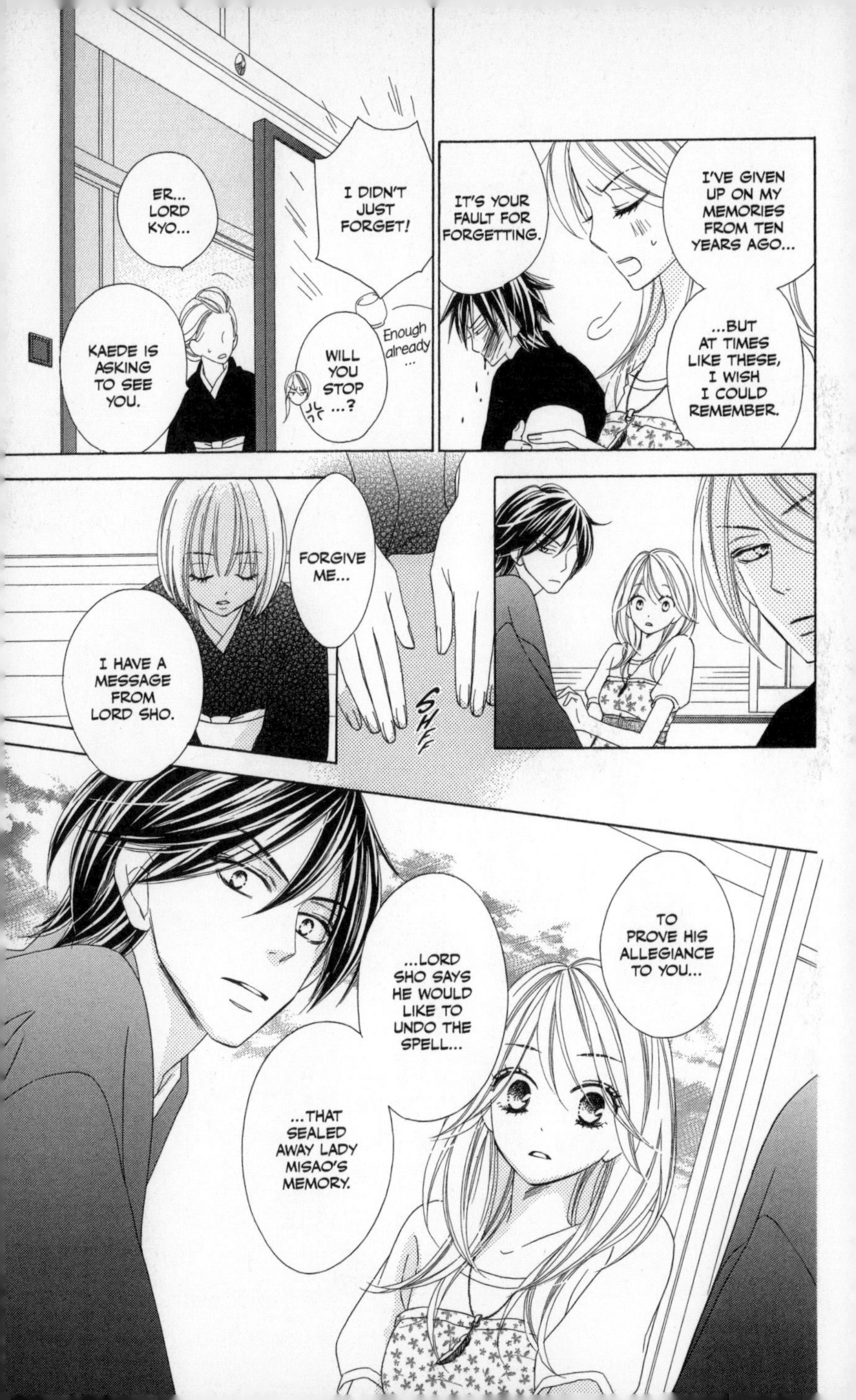
I'VE GIVEN UP ON MY MEMORIES FROM TEN YEARS AGO...
...BUT AT TIMES LIKE THESE, I WISH I COULD REMEMBER.
IT'S YOUR FAULT FOR FORGETTING.
I DIDN'T JUST FORGET!
Enough already...
WILL YOU STOP ...?
ER... LORD KYO...
KAEDE IS ASKING TO SEE YOU.
FORGIVE ME...
SHFF
I HAVE A MESSAGE FROM LORD SHO.
TO PROVE HIS ALLEGIANCE TO YOU...
...LORD SHO SAYS HE WOULD LIKE TO UNDO THE SPELL...
...THAT SEALED AWAY LADY MISAO'S MEMORY.

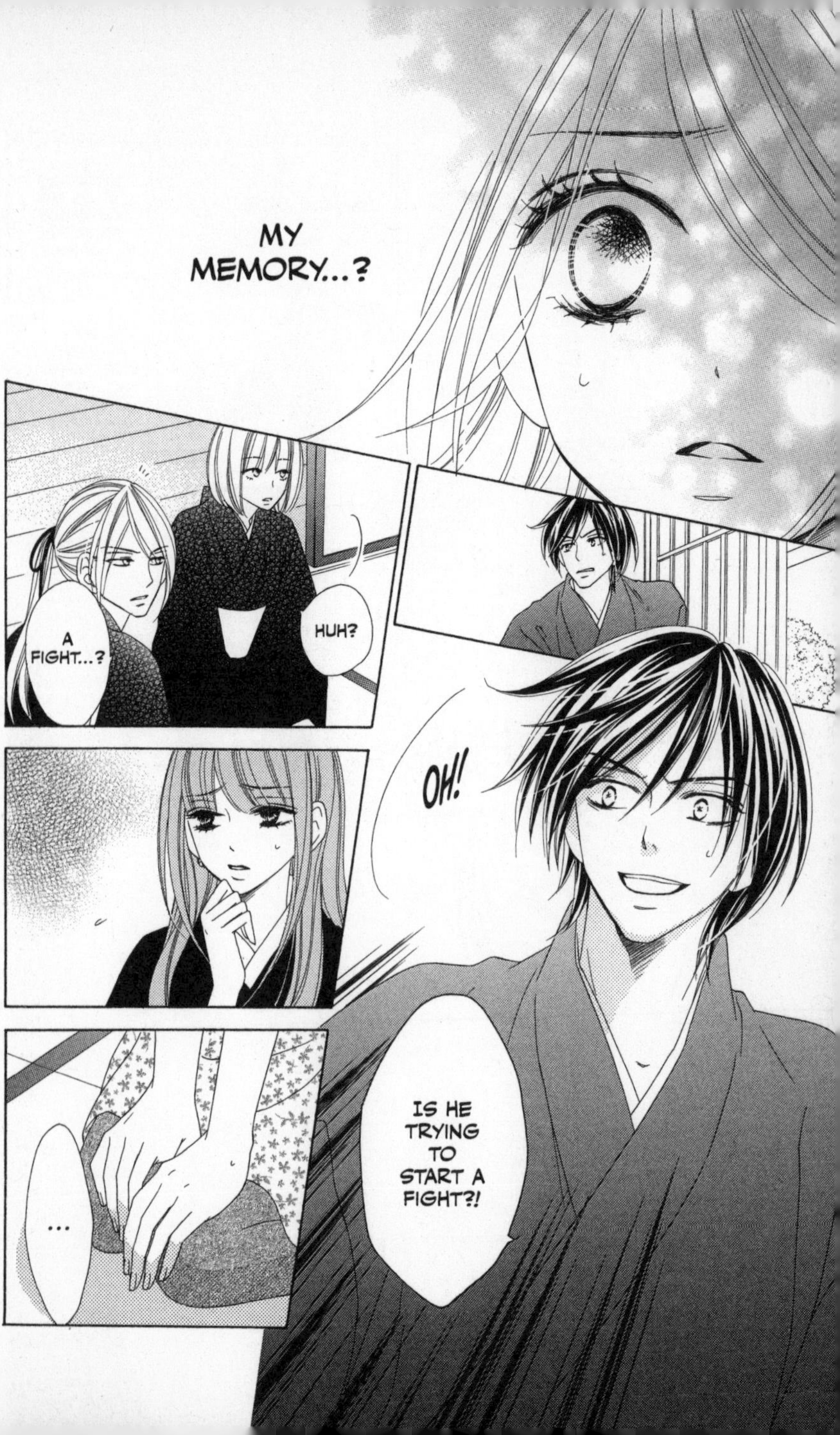
MY MEMORY...?
HUH?
A FIGHT...?
OH!
IS HE TRYING TO START A FIGHT?!
...

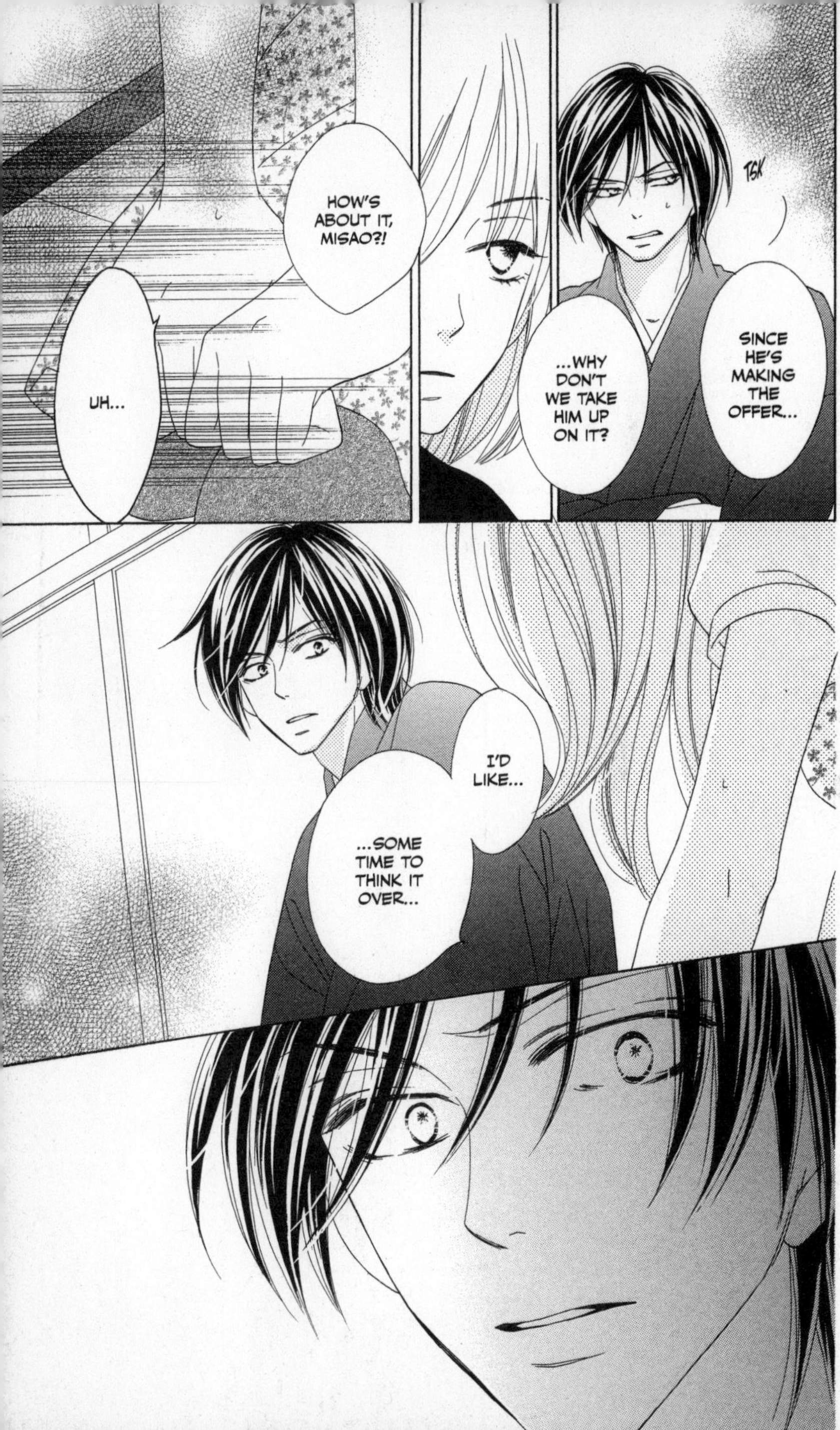
TSK
SINCE HE'S MAKING THE OFFER...
...WHY DON'T WE TAKE HIM UP ON IT?
HOW'S ABOUT IT, MISAO?!
UH...
I'D LIKE...
...SOME TIME TO THINK IT OVER...

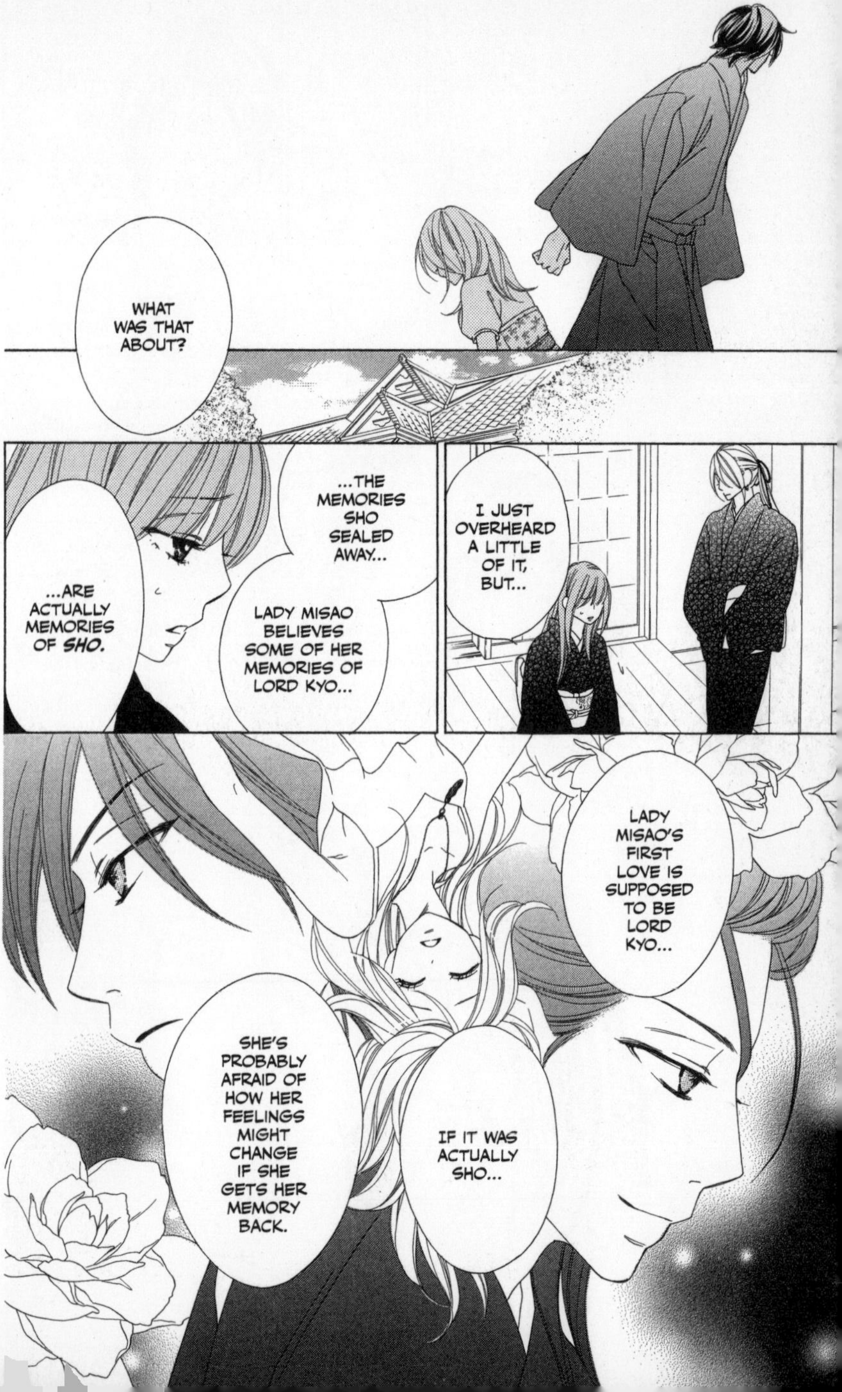
WHAT WAS THAT ABOUT?
I JUST OVERHEARD A LITTLE OF IT, BUT...
...THE MEMORIES SHO SEALED AWAY...
LADY MISAO BELIEVES SOME OF HER MEMORIES OF LORD KYO...
...ARE ACTUALLY MEMORIES OF SHO.
LADY MISAO'S FIRST LOVE IS SUPPOSED TO BE LORD KYO...
IF IT WAS ACTUALLY SHO...
SHE'S PROBABLY AFRAID OF HOW HER FEELINGS MIGHT CHANGE IF SHE GETS HER MEMORY BACK.

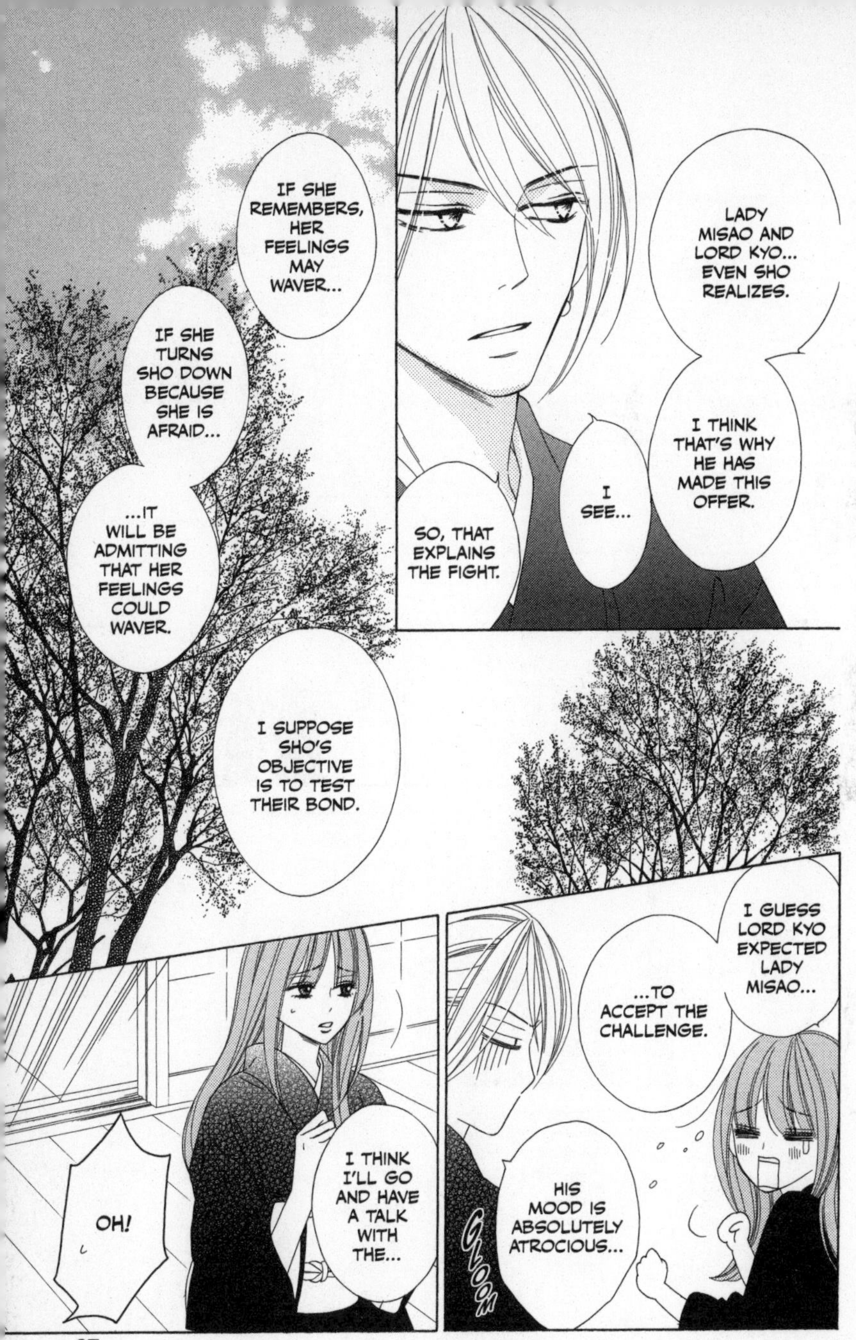
LADY MISAO AND LORD KYO... EVEN SHO REALIZES.
I THINK THAT'S WHY HE HAS MADE THIS OFFER.
I SEE...
SO, THAT EXPLAINS THE FIGHT.
IF SHE REMEMBERS, HER FEELINGS MAY WAVER...
IF SHE TURNS SHO DOWN BECAUSE SHE IS AFRAID...
...IT WILL BE ADMITTING THAT HER FEELINGS COULD WAVER.
I SUPPOSE SHO'S OBJECTIVE IS TO TEST THEIR BOND.
I GUESS LORD KYO EXPECTED LADY MISAO...
...TO ACCEPT THE CHALLENGE.
HIS MOOD IS ABSOLUTELY ATROCIOUS...
GLOOM
I THINK I'LL GO AND HAVE A TALK WITH THE...
OH!

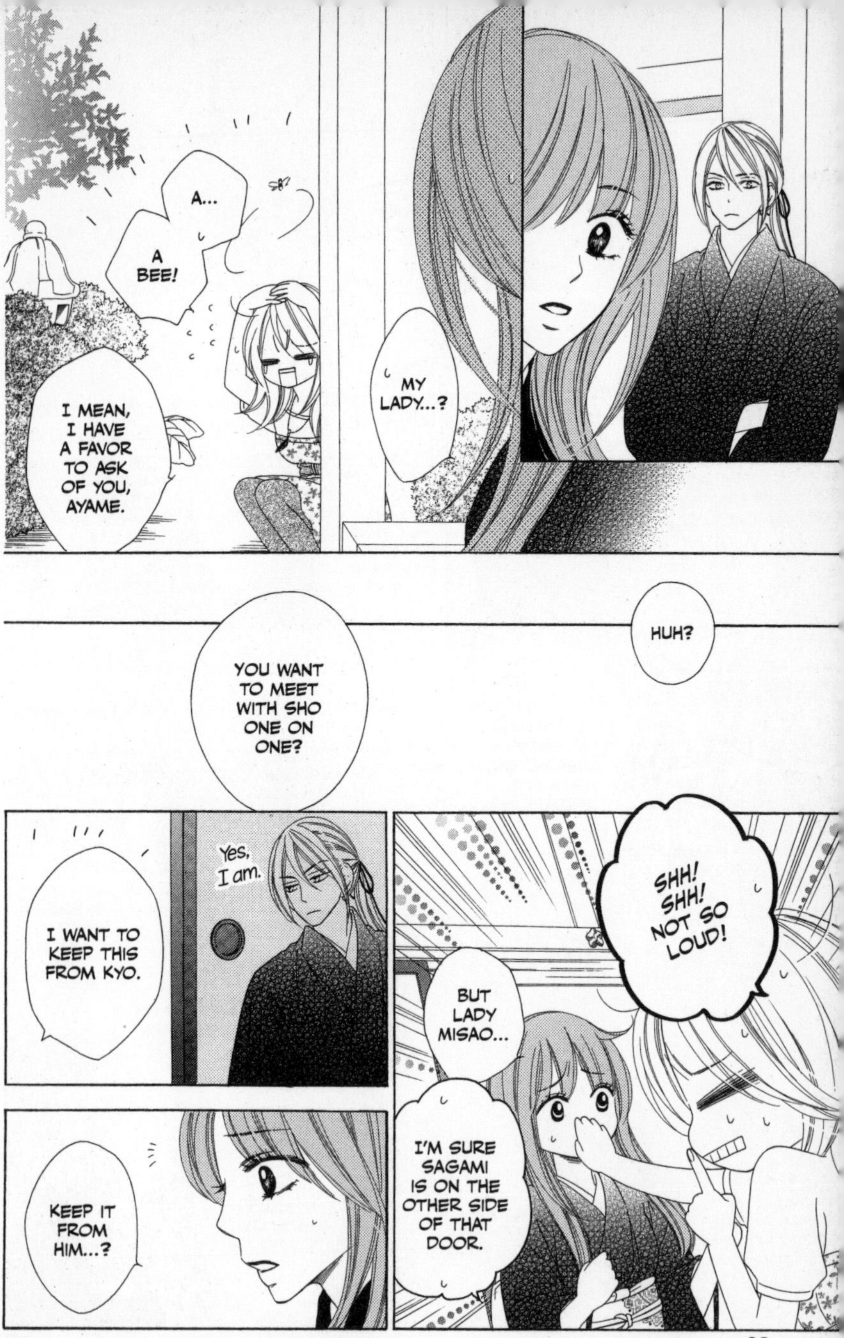
MY LADY...?
A...
A BEE!
I MEAN, I HAVE A FAVOR TO ASK OF YOU, AYAME.
HUH?
YOU WANT TO MEET WITH SHO ONE ON ONE?
SHH! SHH! NOT SO LOUD!
BUT LADY MISAO...
I'M SURE SAGAMI IS ON THE OTHER SIDE OF THAT DOOR.
Yes, I am.
I WANT TO KEEP THIS FROM KYO.
KEEP IT FROM HIM...?

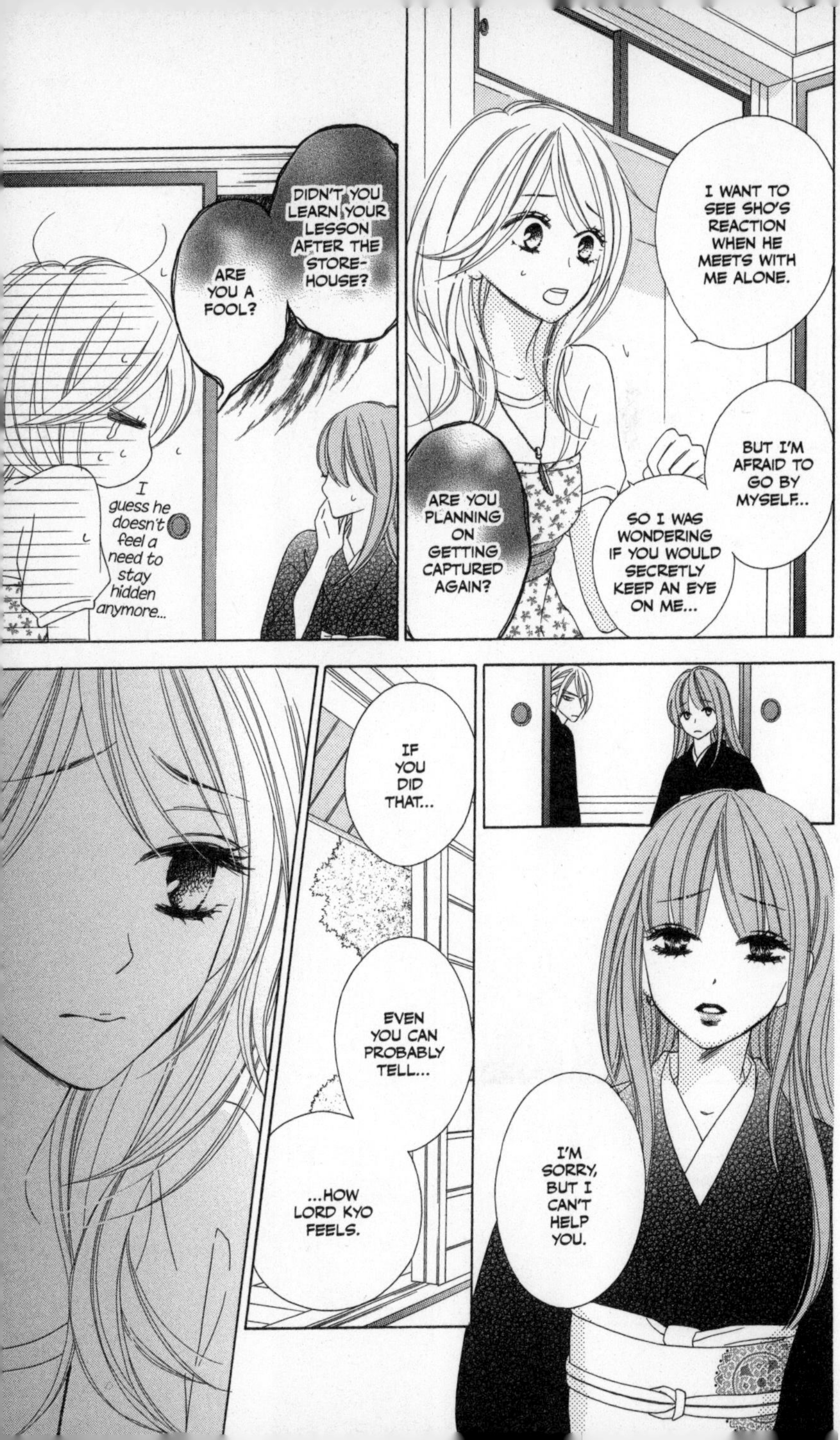
I WANT TO SEE SHO'S REACTION WHEN HE MEETS WITH ME ALONE.
BUT I'M AFRAID TO GO BY MYSELF...
SO I WAS WONDERING IF YOU WOULD SECRETLY KEEP AN EYE ON ME...
ARE YOU PLANNING ON GETTING CAPTURED AGAIN?
DIDN'T YOU LEARN YOUR LESSON AFTER THE STORE-HOUSE?
ARE YOU A FOOL?
I guess he doesn't feel a need to stay hidden anymore...
I'M SORRY, BUT I CAN'T HELP YOU.
IF YOU DID THAT...
EVEN YOU CAN PROBABLY TELL...
...HOW LORD KYO FEELS.

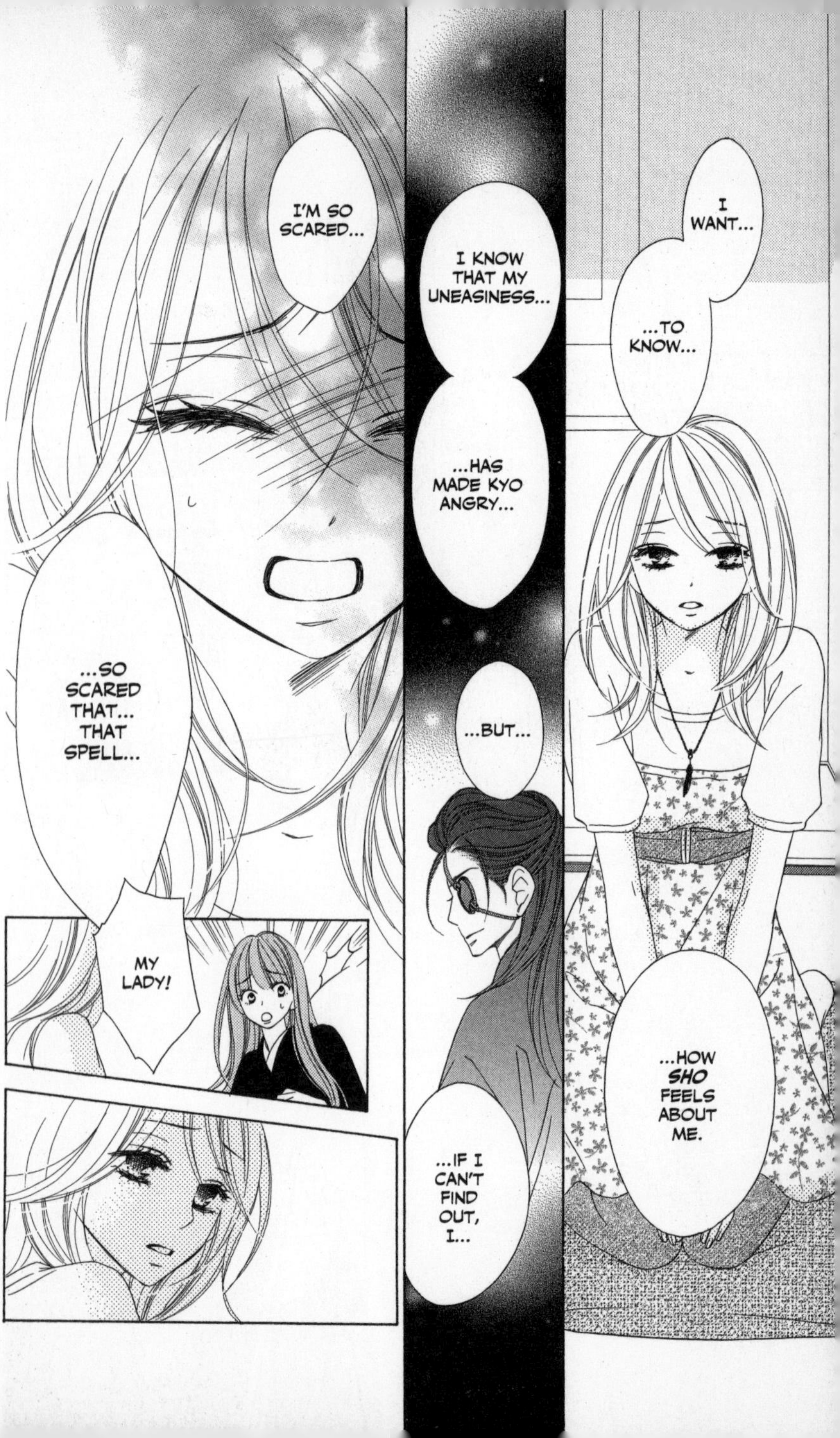
I WANT...
...TO KNOW...
...HOW SHO FEELS ABOUT ME.
I KNOW THAT MY UNEASINESS...
...HAS MADE KYO ANGRY...
...BUT...
...IF I CAN'T FIND OUT, I...
I'M SO SCARED...
...SO SCARED THAT... THAT SPELL...
MY LADY!

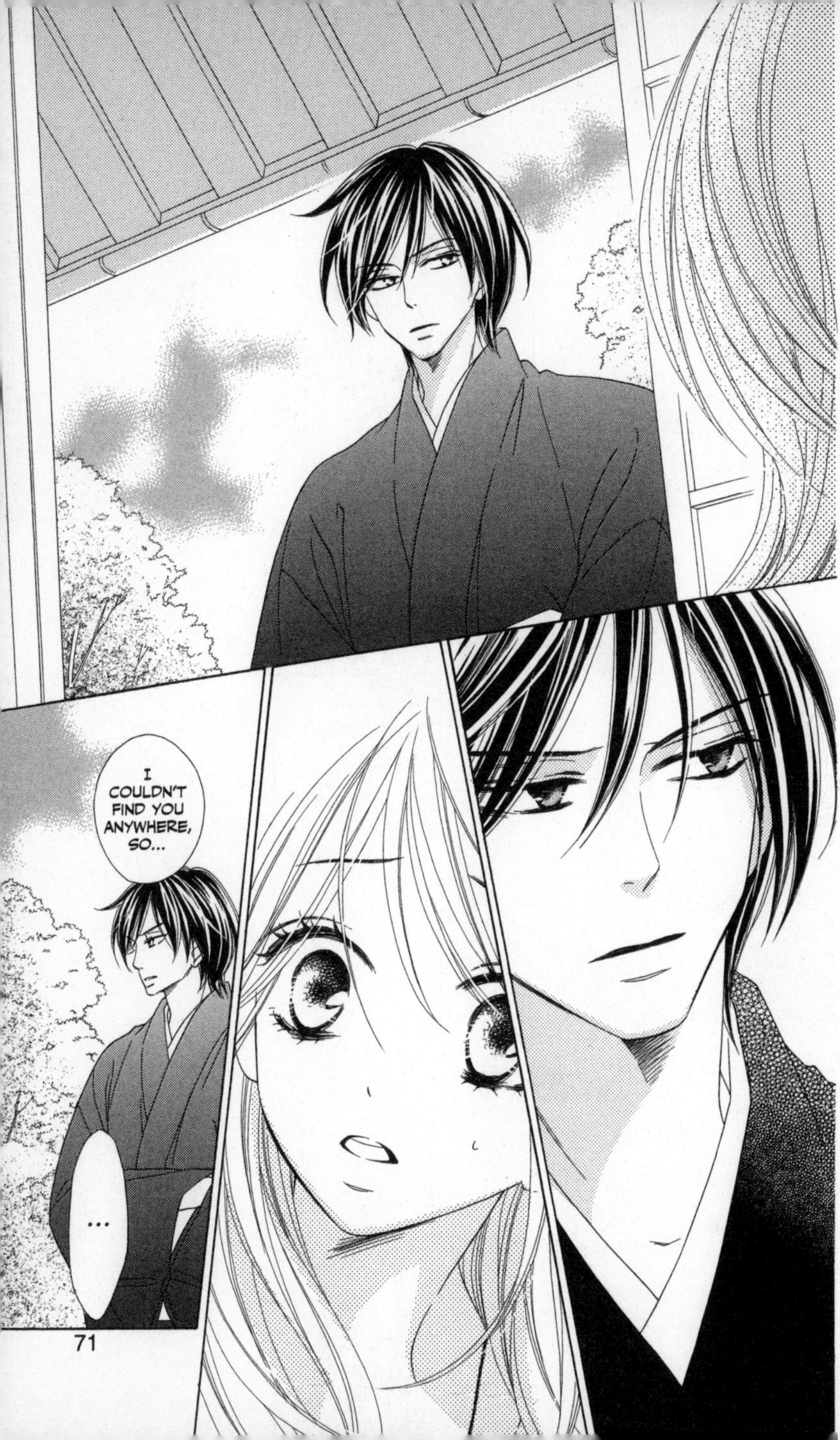
I COULDN'T FIND YOU ANYWHERE, SO...
...

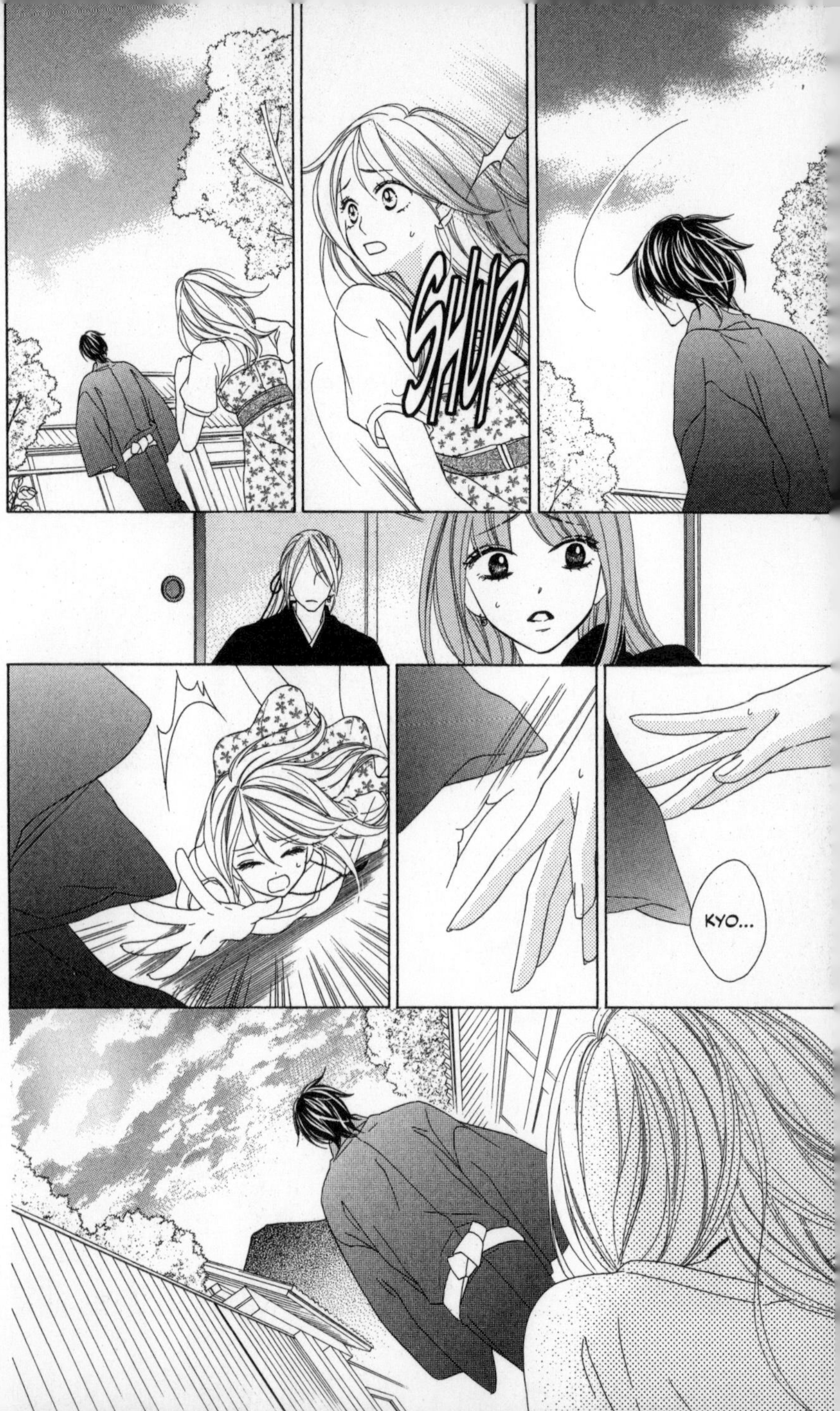
SHUP
KYO...

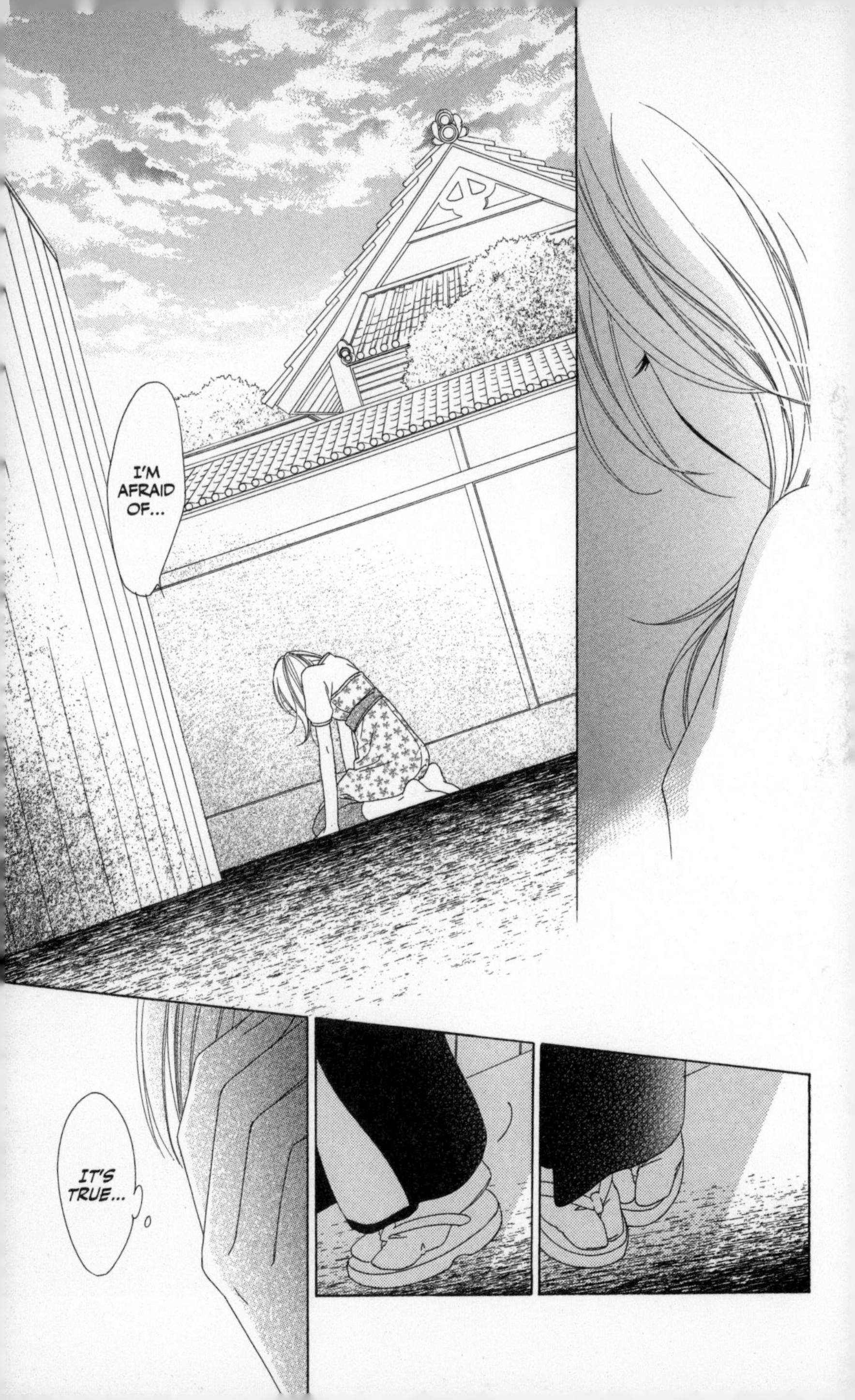
I'M AFRAID OF...
IT'S TRUE...

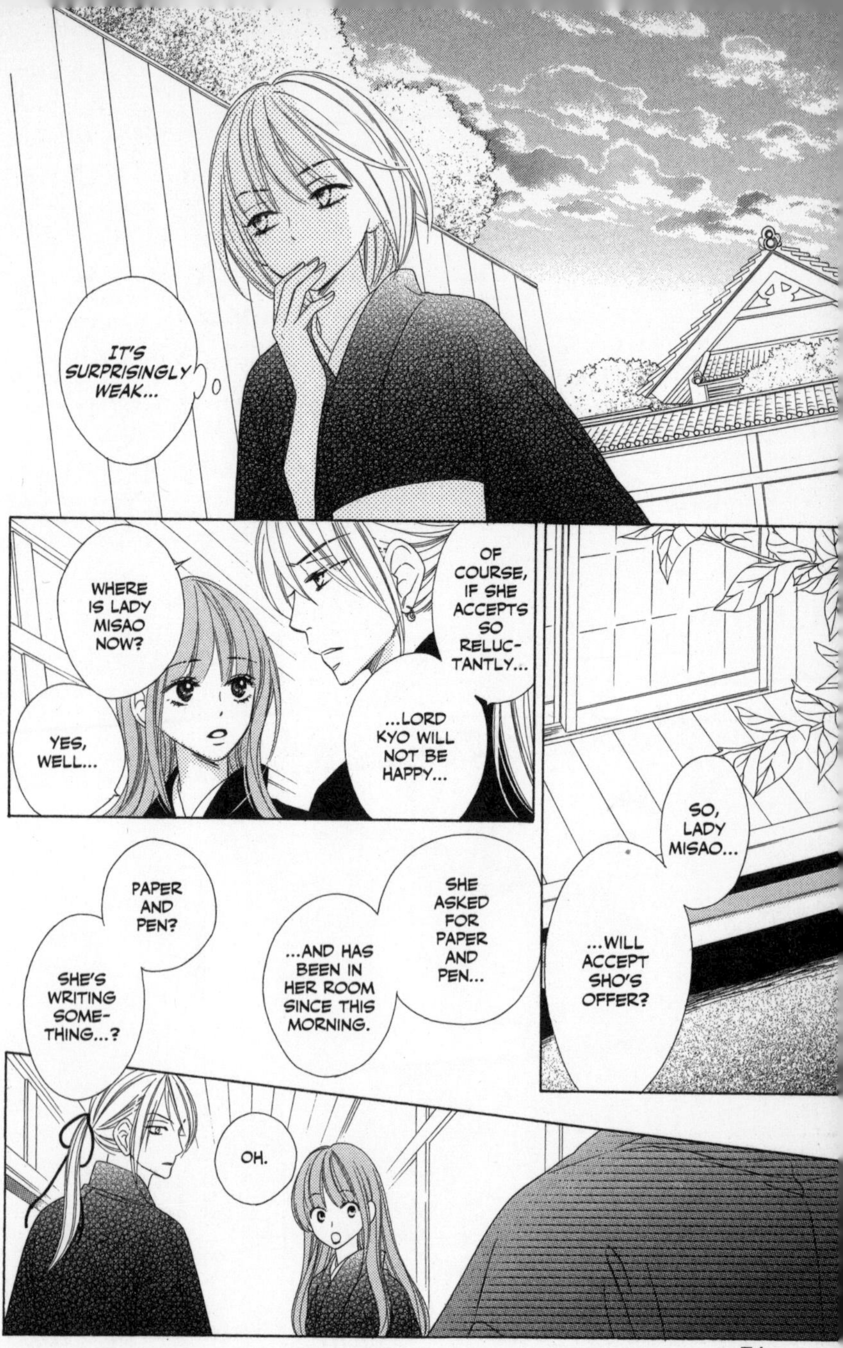
IT'S SURPRISINGLY WEAK...
SO, LADY MISAO...
...WILL ACCEPT SHO'S OFFER?
OF COURSE, IF SHE ACCEPTS SO RELUC-TANTLY...
...LORD KYO WILL NOT BE HAPPY...
WHERE IS LADY MISAO NOW?
YES, WELL...
SHE ASKED FOR PAPER AND PEN...
...AND HAS BEEN IN HER ROOM SINCE THIS MORNING.
PAPER AND PEN?
SHE'S WRITING SOME-THING...?
OH.

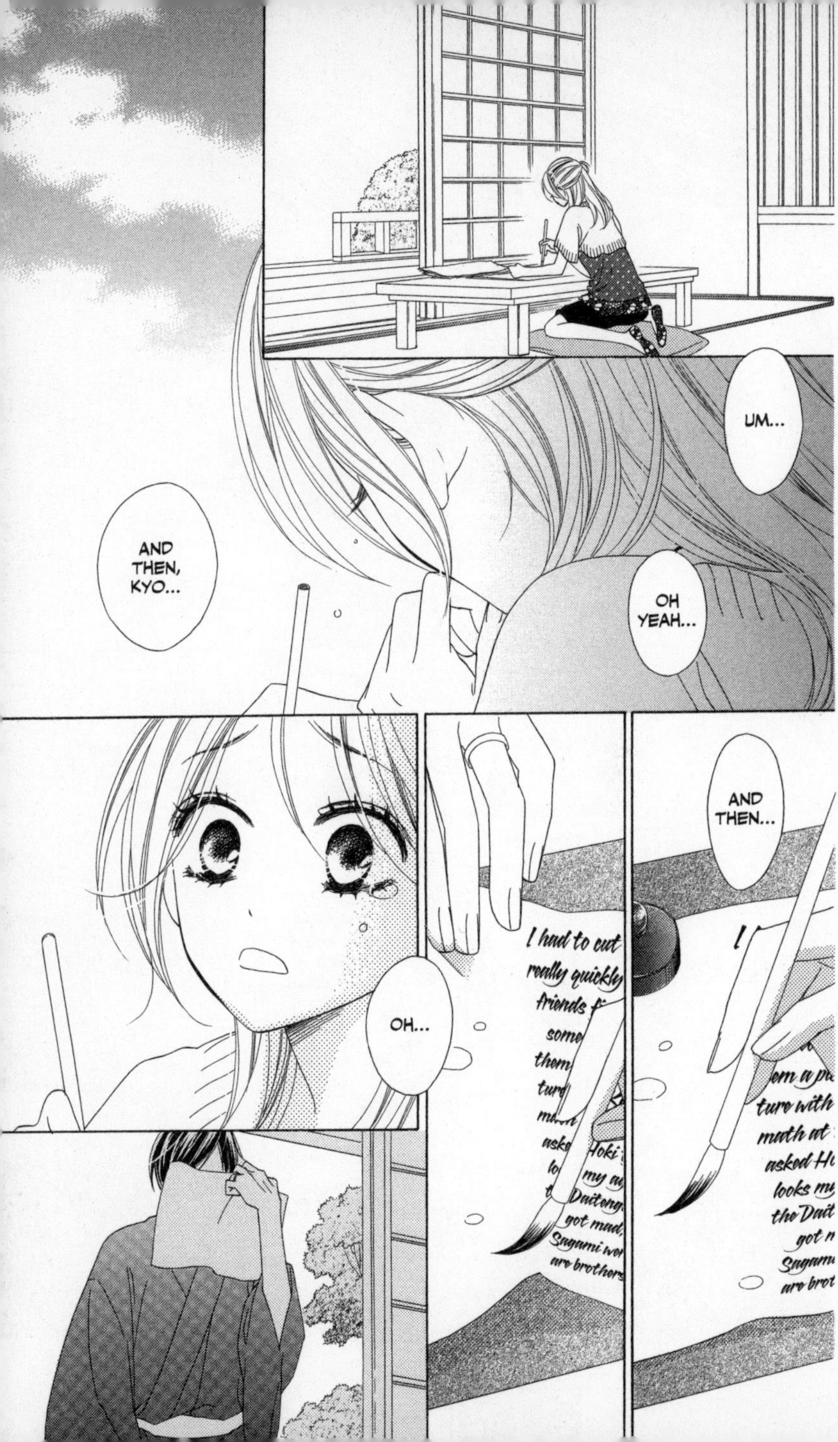
UM...
OH YEAH...
AND THEN, KYO...
AND THEN...
OH...

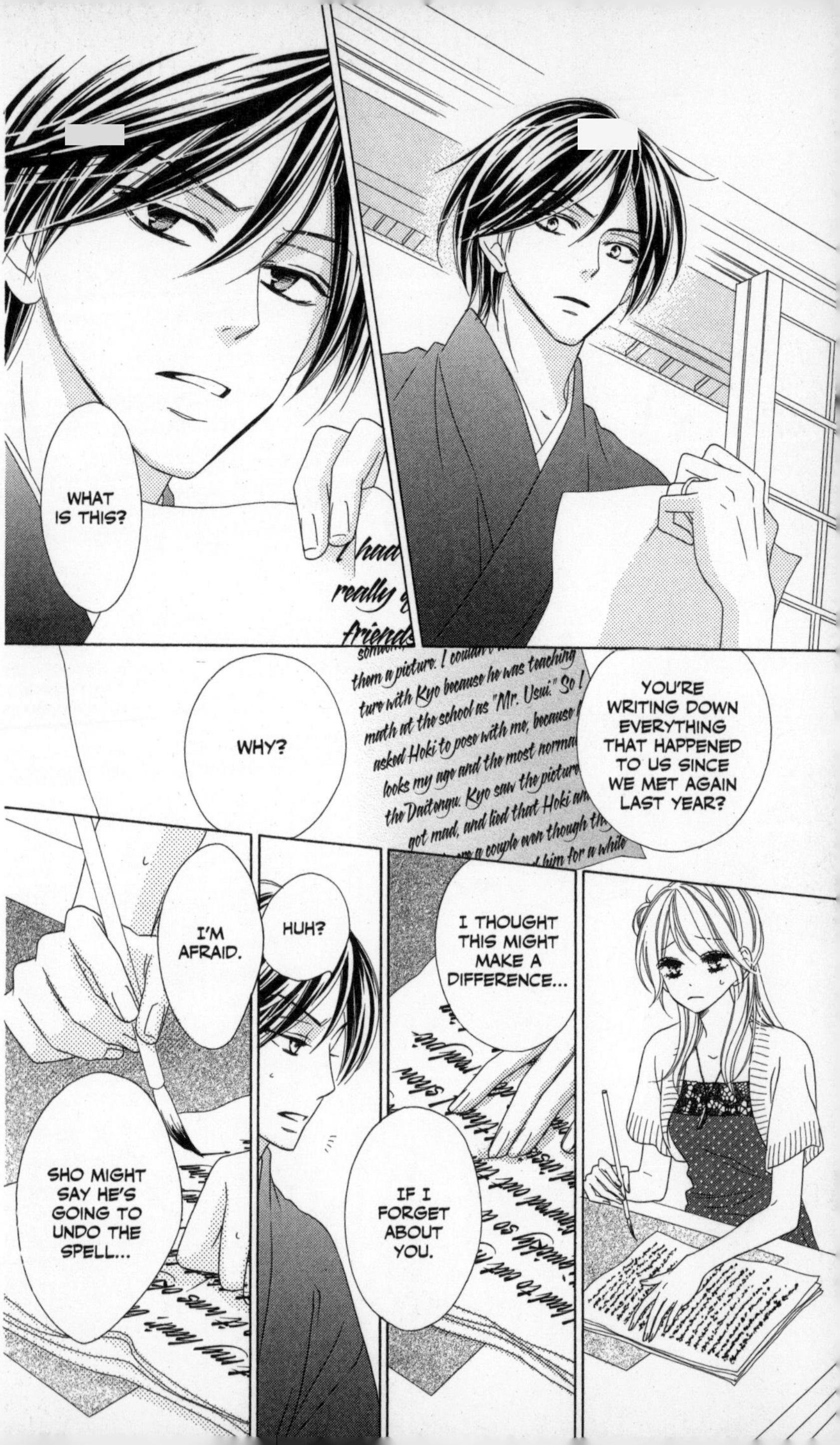
WHAT IS THIS?
YOU'RE WRITING DOWN EVERYTHING THAT HAPPENED TO US SINCE WE MET AGAIN LAST YEAR?
WHY?
I THOUGHT THIS MIGHT MAKE A DIFFERENCE...
IF I FORGET ABOUT YOU.
HUH?
I'M AFRAID.
SHO MIGHT SAY HE'S GOING TO UNDO THE SPELL...

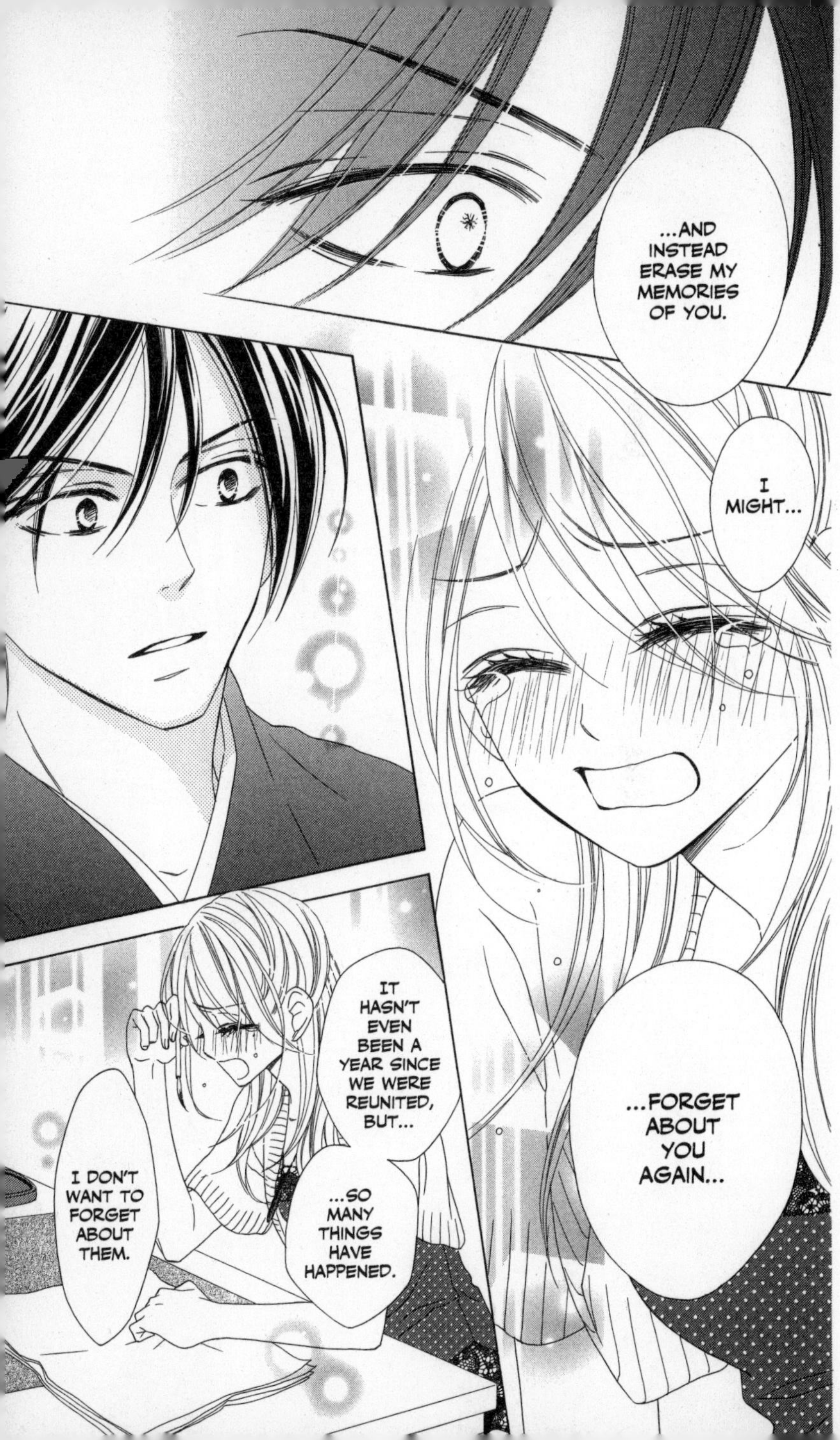
...AND INSTEAD ERASE MY MEMORIES OF YOU.
I MIGHT...
...FORGET ABOUT YOU AGAIN...
IT HASN'T EVEN BEEN A YEAR SINCE WE WERE REUNITED, BUT...
...SO MANY THINGS HAVE HAPPENED.
I DON'T WANT TO FORGET ABOUT THEM.

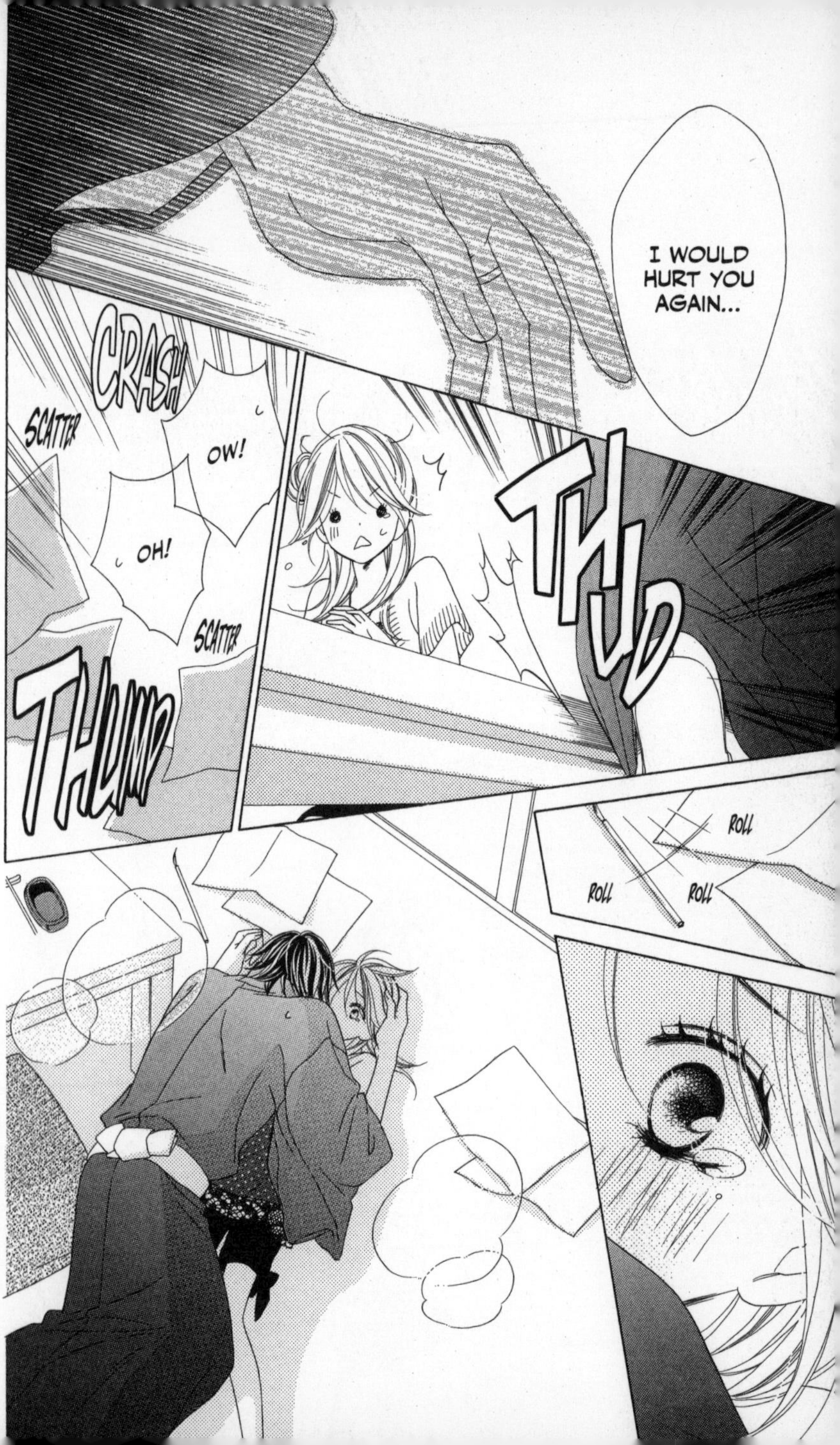
I WOULD HURT YOU AGAIN...
THUD
OW!
CRASH
SCATTER
OH!
SCATTER
THUMP
ROLL
ROLL
ROLL

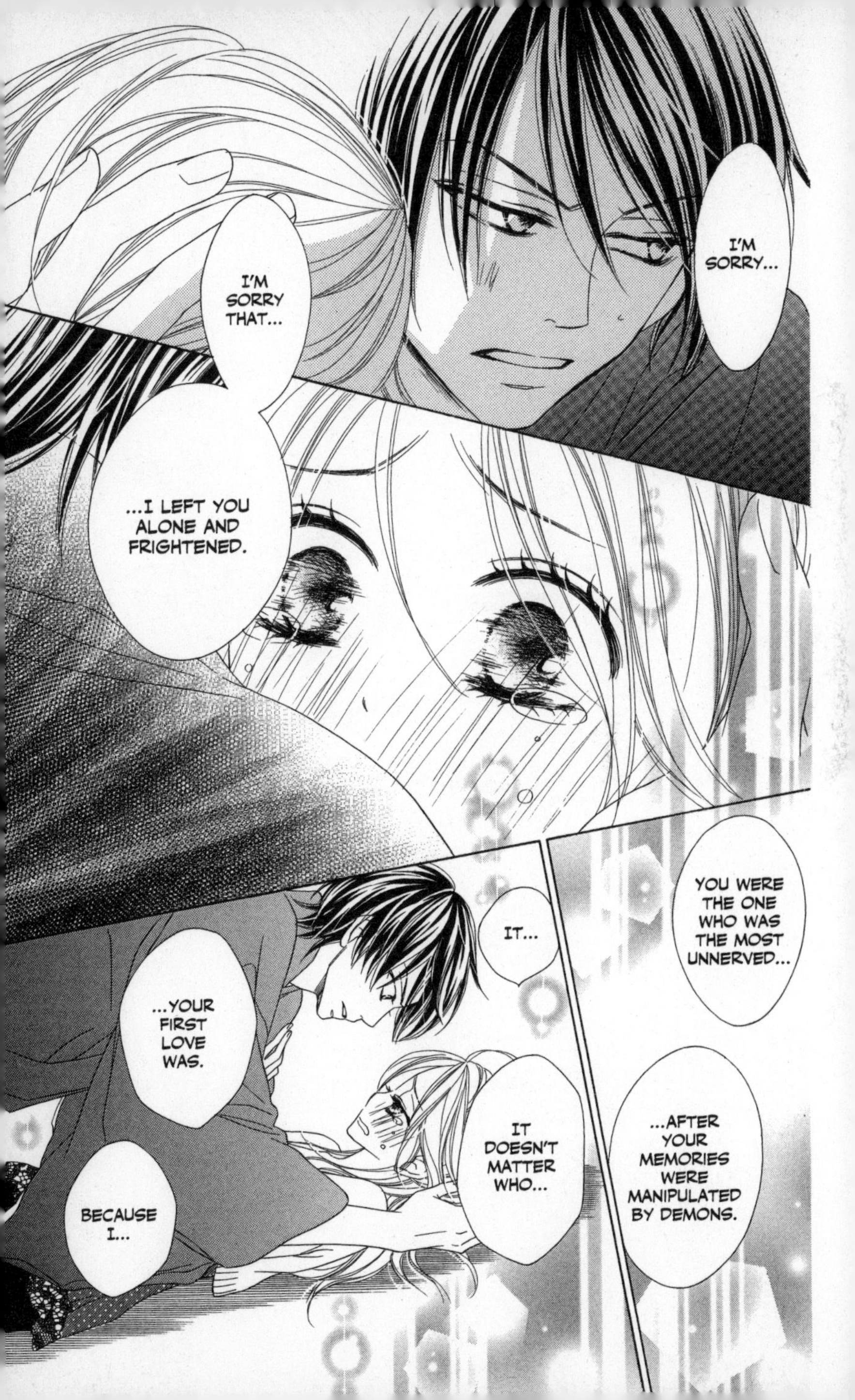
I'M SORRY...
I'M SORRY THAT...
...I LEFT YOU ALONE AND FRIGHTENED.
YOU WERE THE ONE WHO WAS THE MOST UNNERVED...
...AFTER YOUR MEMORIES WERE MANIPULATED BY DEMONS.
IT...
IT DOESN'T MATTER WHO...
...YOUR FIRST LOVE WAS.
BECAUSE I...

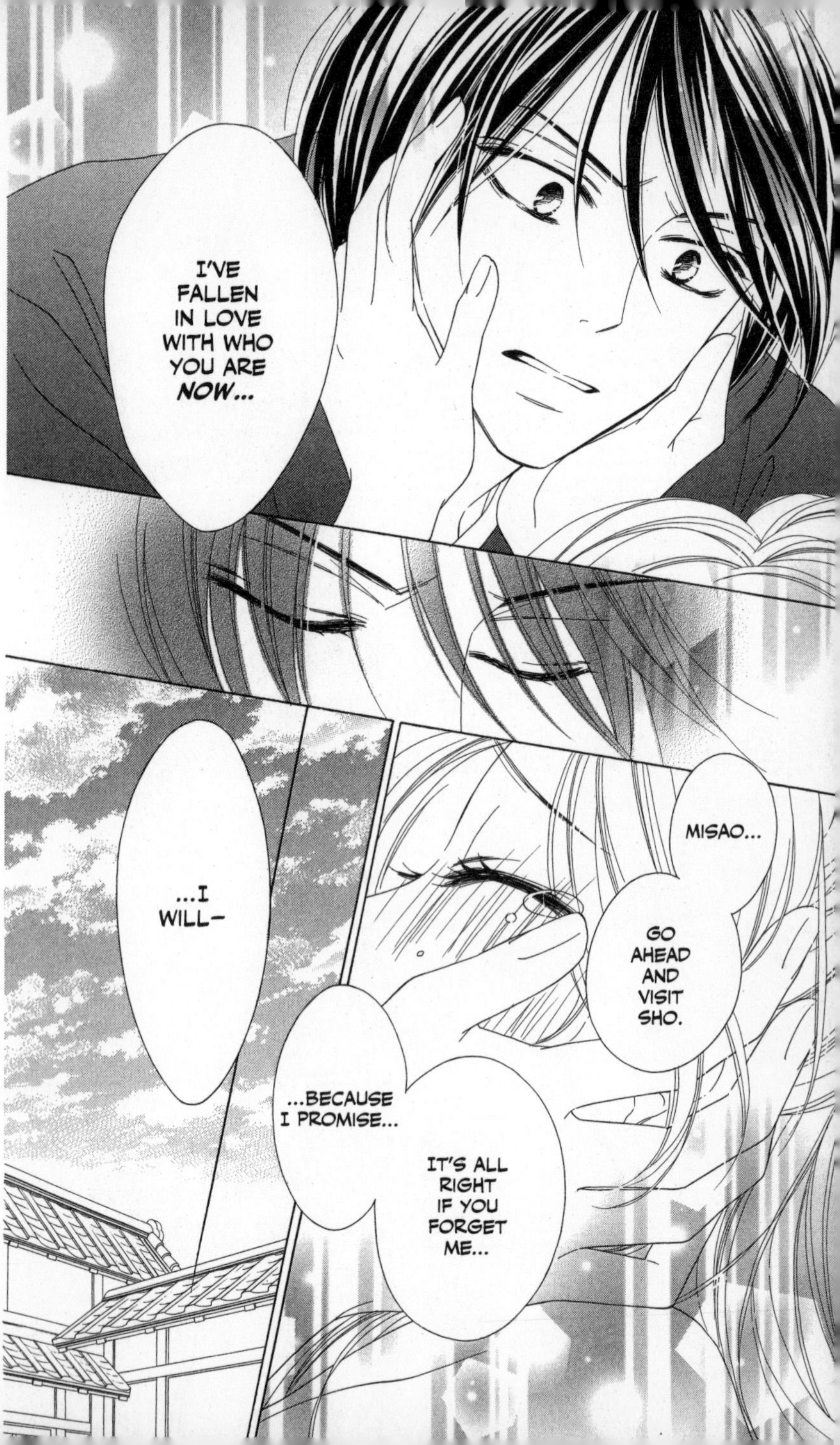
I'VE FALLEN IN LOVE WITH WHO YOU ARE NOW...
MISAO...
GO AHEAD AND VISIT SHO.
IT'S ALL RIGHT IF YOU FORGET ME...
...BECAUSE I PROMISE...
...I WILL–

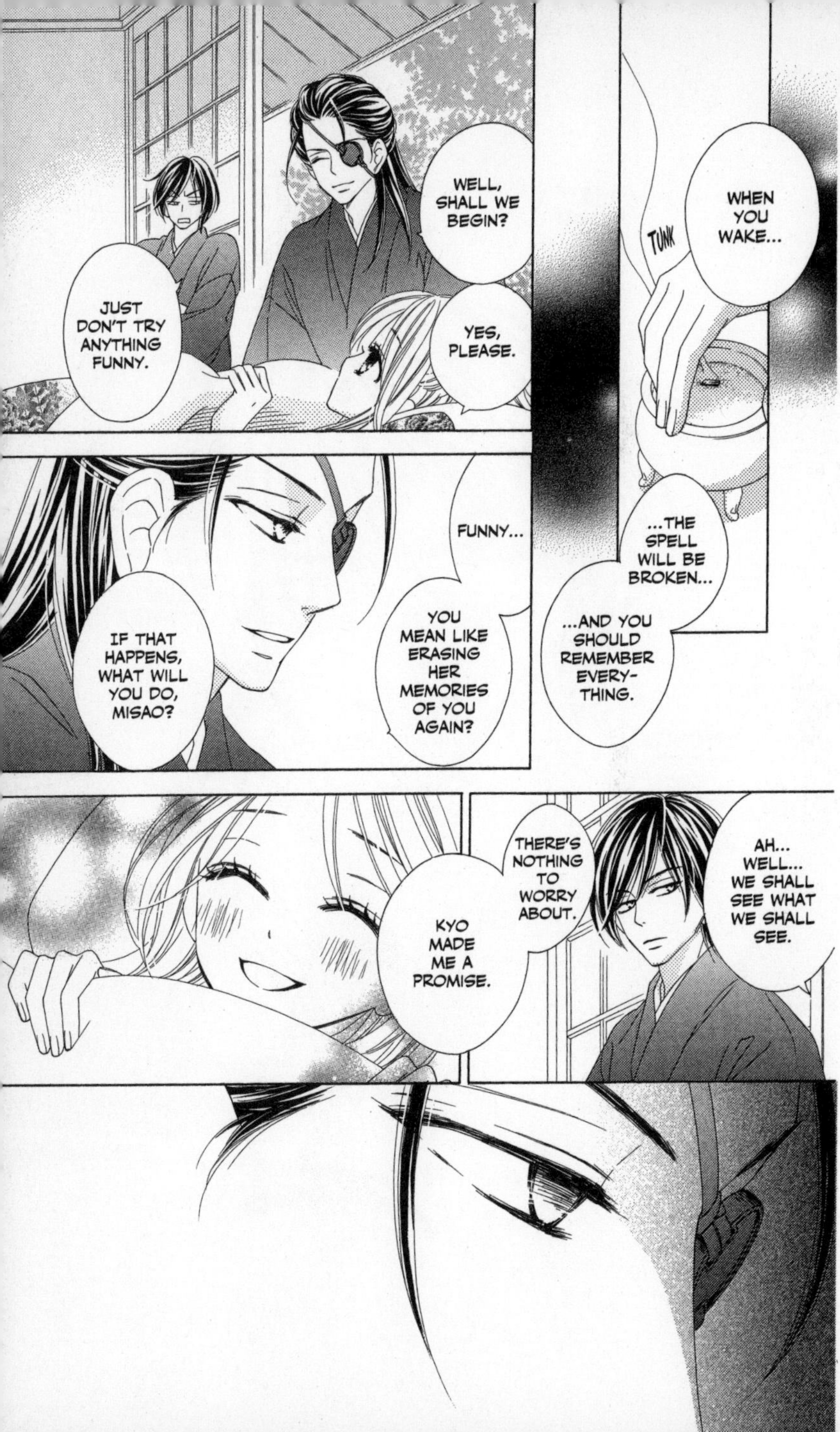
WHEN YOU WAKE...
TUNK
...THE SPELL WILL BE BROKEN...
...AND YOU SHOULD REMEMBER EVERY-THING.
WELL, SHALL WE BEGIN?
YES, PLEASE.
JUST DON'T TRY ANYTHING FUNNY.
FUNNY...
YOU MEAN LIKE ERASING HER MEMORIES OF YOU AGAIN?
IF THAT HAPPENS, WHAT WILL YOU DO, MISAO?
THERE'S NOTHING TO WORRY ABOUT.
KYO MADE ME A PROMISE.
AH... WELL... WE SHALL SEE WHAT WE SHALL SEE.

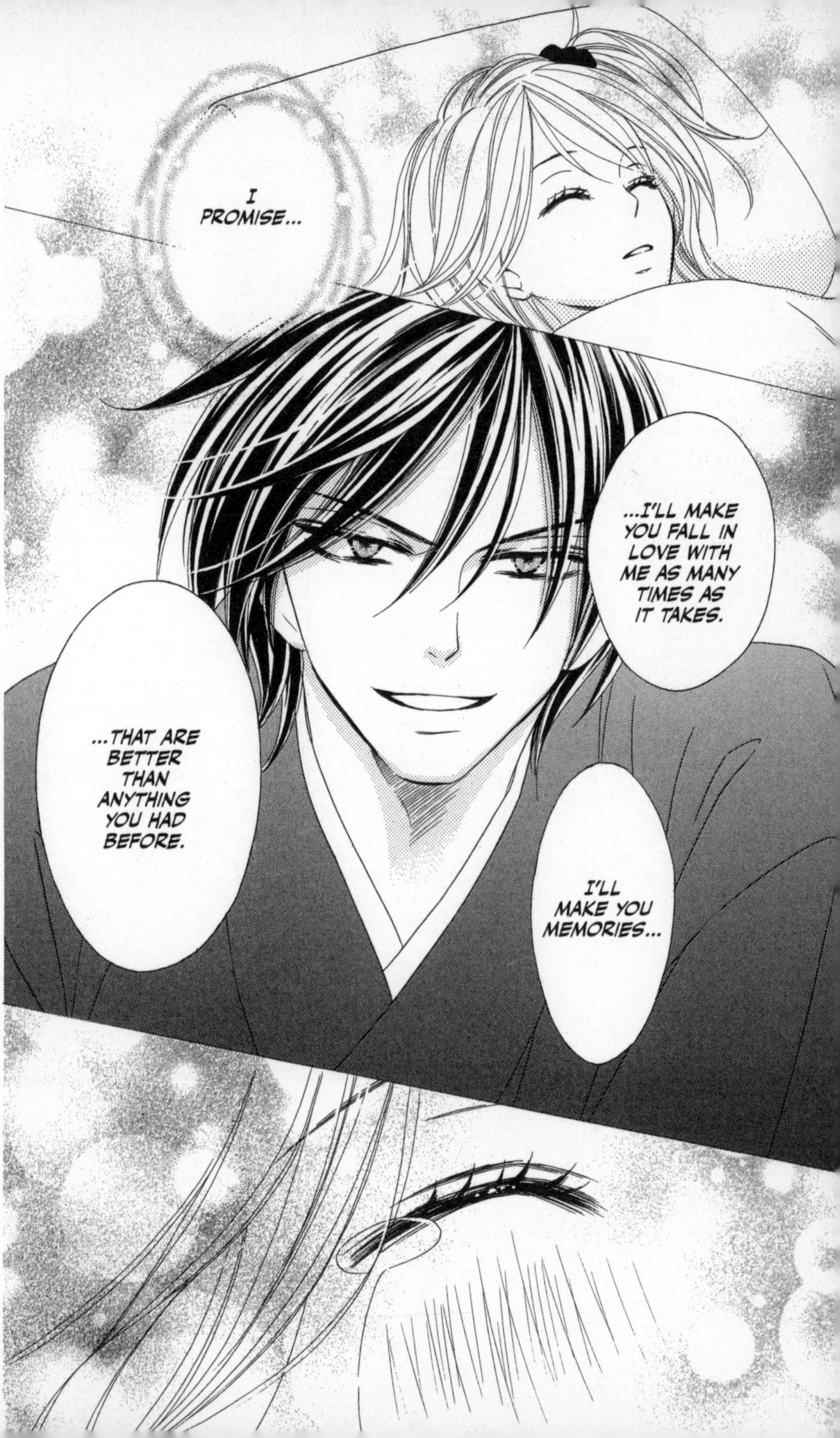
I PROMISE...
...I'LL MAKE YOU FALL IN LOVE WITH ME AS MANY TIMES AS IT TAKES.
I'LL MAKE YOU MEMORIES...
...THAT ARE BETTER THAN ANYTHING YOU HAD BEFORE.

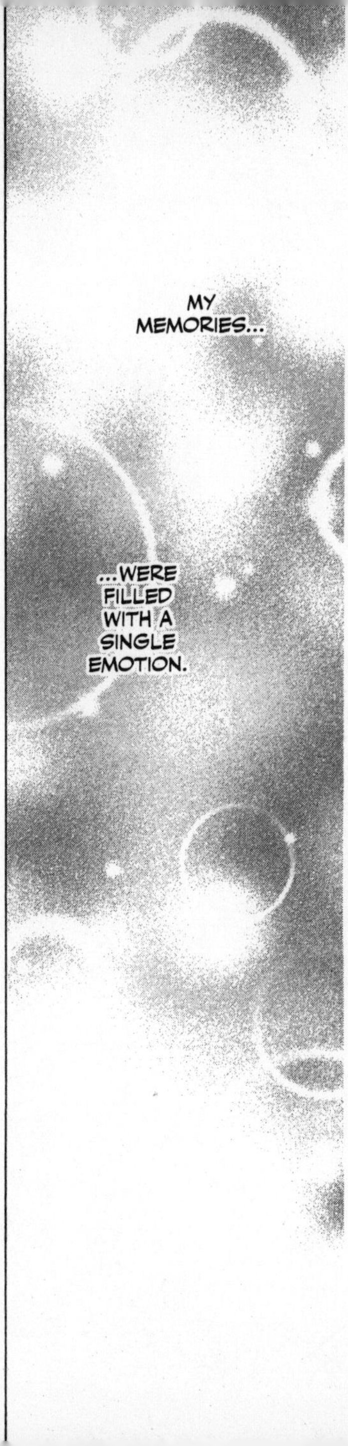
MY MEMORIES...
...WERE FILLED WITH A SINGLE EMOTION.

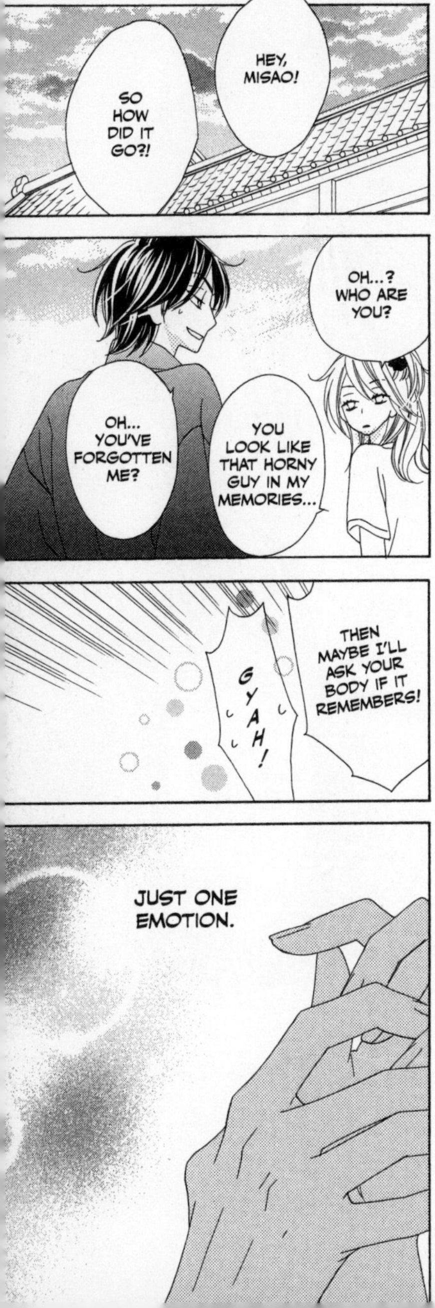
HEY, MISAO!
SO HOW DID IT GO?!
OH...? WHO ARE YOU?
YOU LOOK LIKE THAT HORNY GUY IN MY MEMORIES...
OH... YOU'VE FORGOTTEN ME?
THEN MAYBE I'LL ASK YOUR BODY IF IT REMEMBERS!
GYAH!
JUST ONE EMOTION.

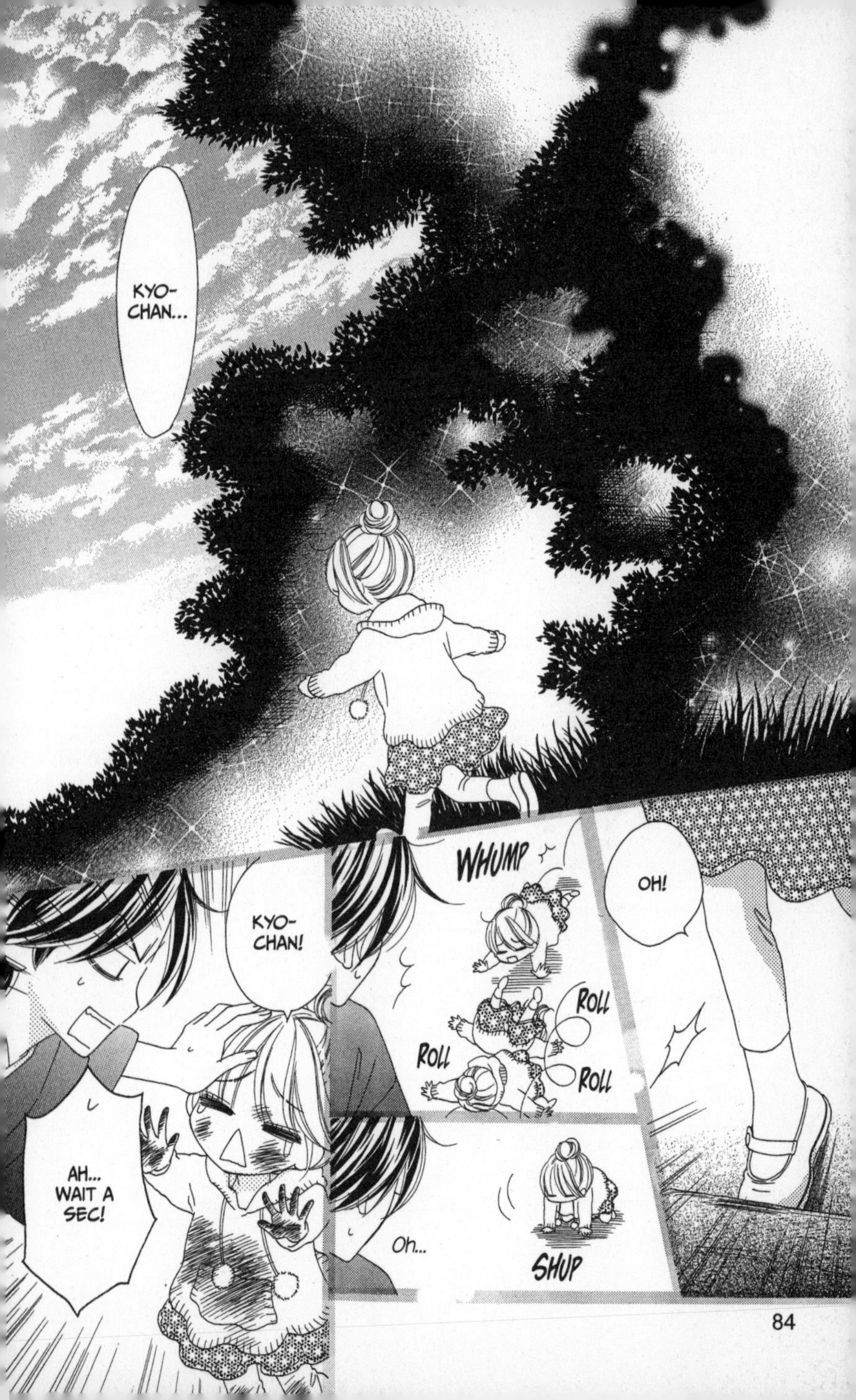
KYO-CHAN...
OH!
WHUMP
ROLL
ROLL
ROLL
SHUP
Oh...
KYO-CHAN!
AH... WAIT A SEC!

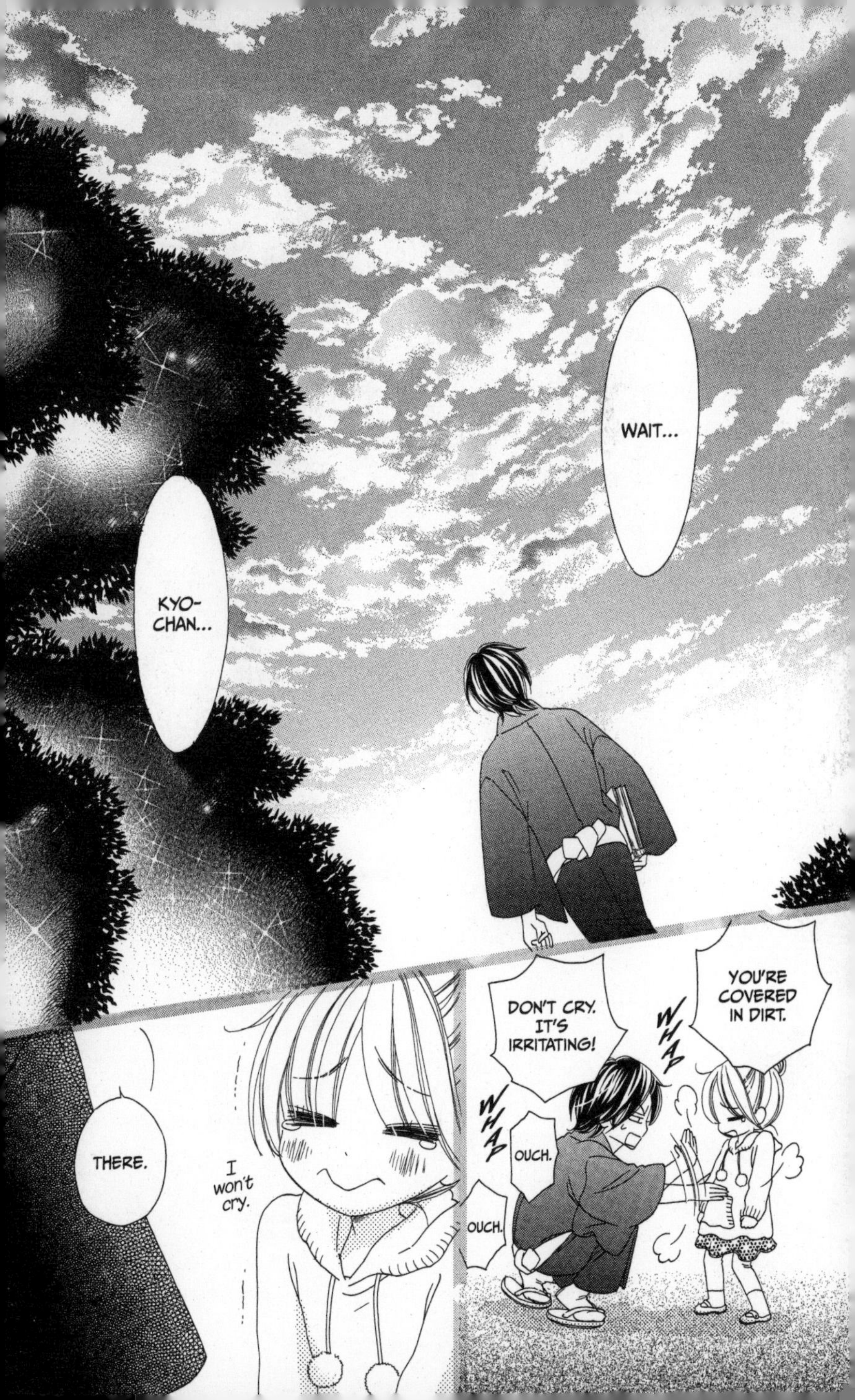
WAIT...
KYO-CHAN...
YOU'RE COVERED IN DIRT.
DON'T CRY. IT'S IRRITATING!
WHAP
WHAP
OUCH.
OUCH.
I won't cry.
THERE.

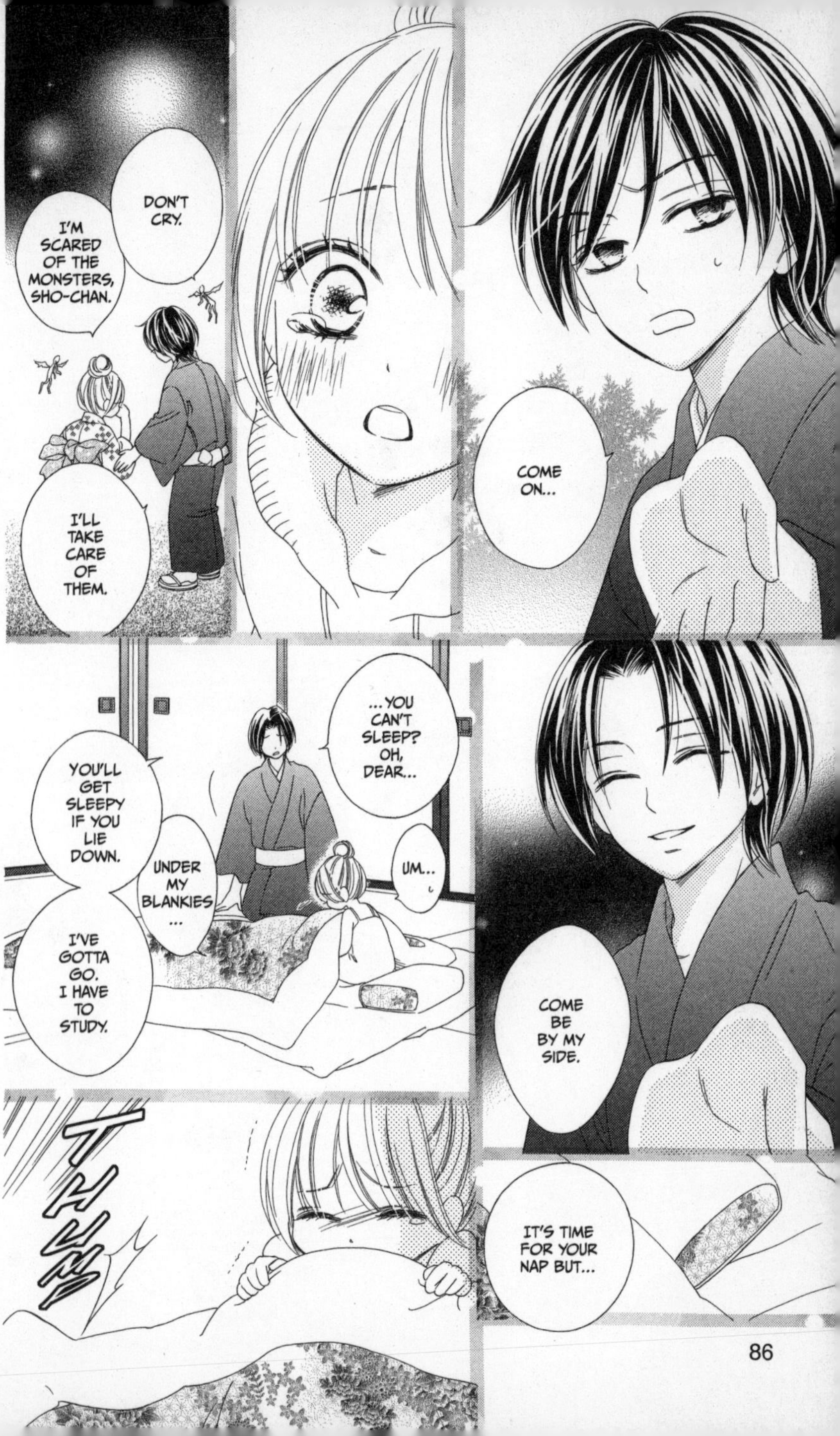
COME ON...
DON'T CRY.
I'M SCARED OF THE MONSTERS, SHO-CHAN.
I'LL TAKE CARE OF THEM.
COME BE BY MY SIDE.
IT'S TIME FOR YOUR NAP BUT...
...YOU CAN'T SLEEP? OH, DEAR...
UM...
YOU'LL GET SLEEPY IF YOU LIE DOWN.
UNDER MY BLANKIES...
I'VE GOTTA GO. I HAVE TO STUDY.
THUMP

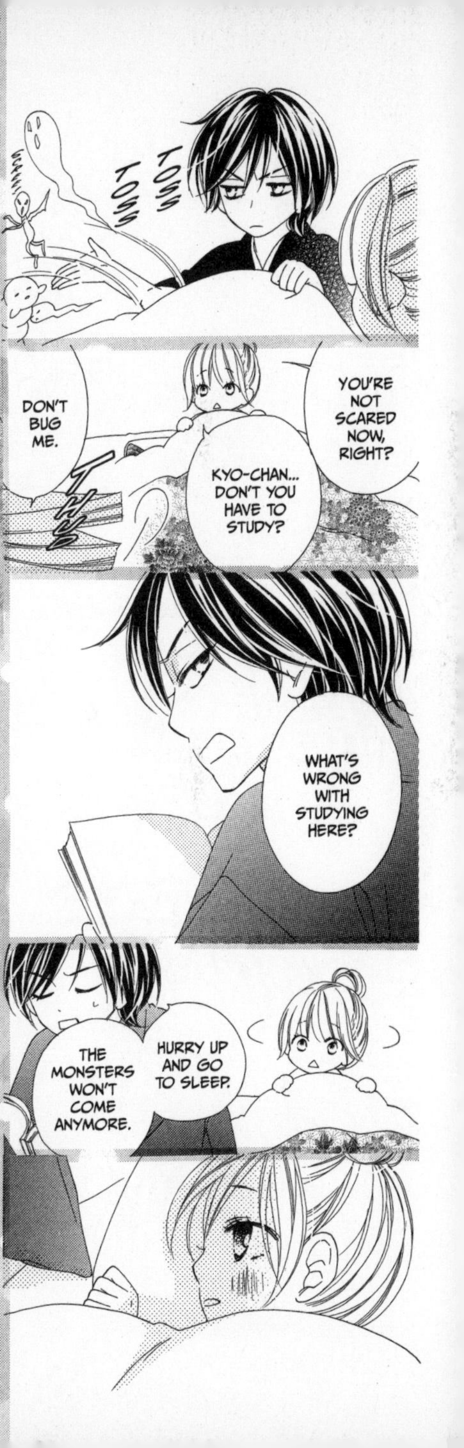
TOSS TOSS
YOU'RE NOT SCARED NOW, RIGHT?
KYO-CHAN... DON'T YOU HAVE TO STUDY?
DON'T BUG ME.
WHAT'S WRONG WITH STUDYING HERE?
HURRY UP AND GO TO SLEEP.
THE MONSTERS WON'T COME ANYMORE.

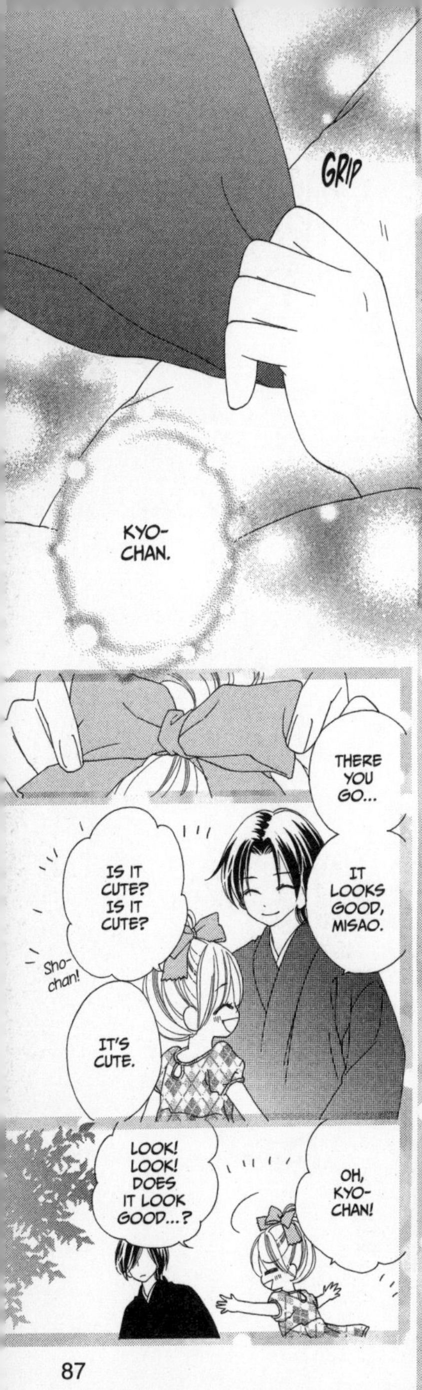
GRIP
KYO-CHAN.
THERE YOU GO...
IT LOOKS GOOD, MISAO.
IS IT CUTE? IS IT CUTE?
Sho-chan!
IT'S CUTE.
OH, KYO-CHAN!
LOOK! LOOK! DOES IT LOOK GOOD...?

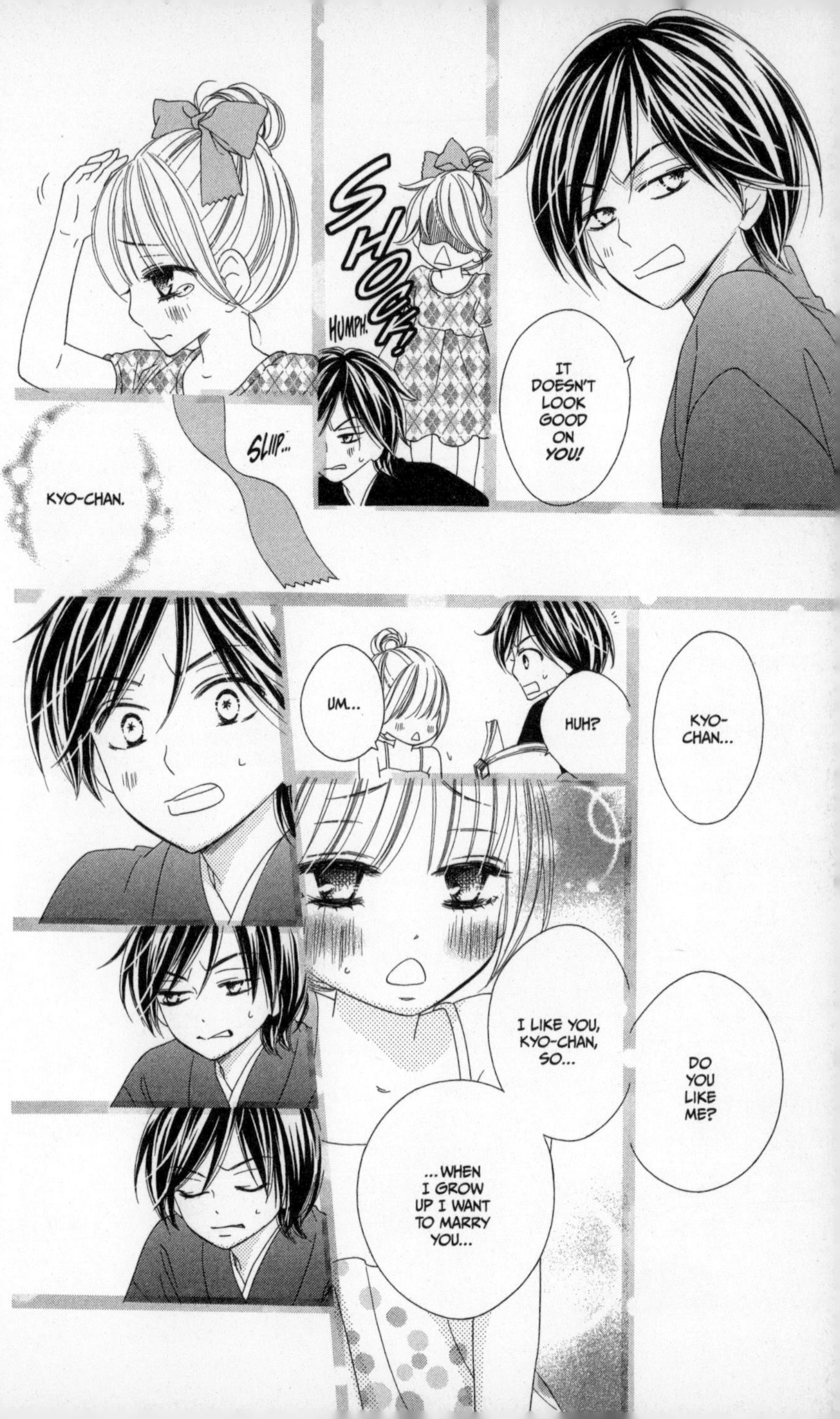
IT DOESN'T LOOK GOOD ON YOU!
SHOCK!
HUMPH.
SLIP...
KYO-CHAN.
KYO-CHAN...
HUH?
UM...
DO YOU LIKE ME?
I LIKE YOU, KYO-CHAN, SO...
...WHEN I GROW UP I WANT TO MARRY YOU...

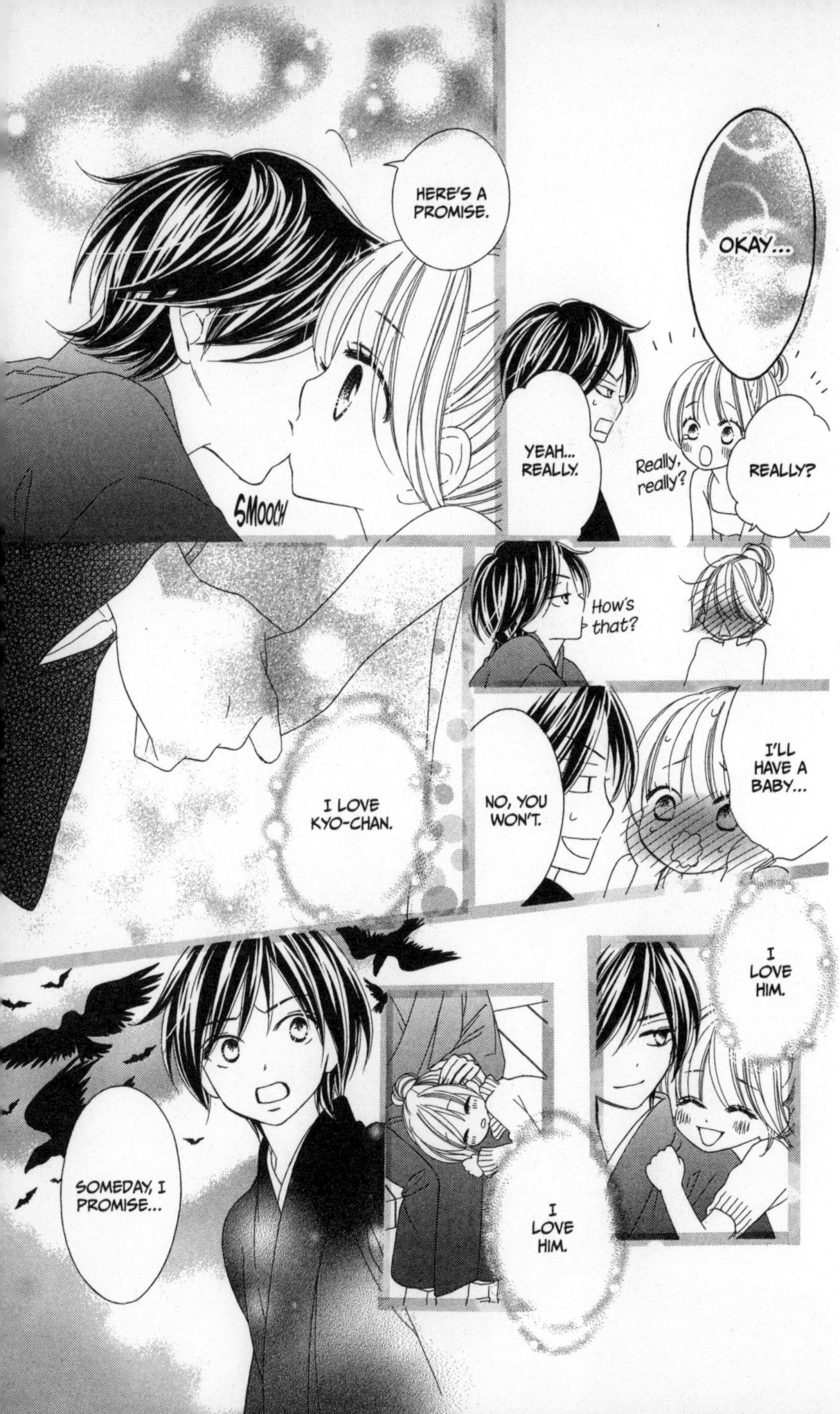
OKAY...
REALLY?
Really, really?
YEAH... REALLY.
HERE'S A PROMISE.
SMOOCH
How's that?
I'LL HAVE A BABY...
NO, YOU WON'T.
I LOVE KYO-CHAN.
I LOVE HIM.
I LOVE HIM.
SOMEDAY, I PROMISE...

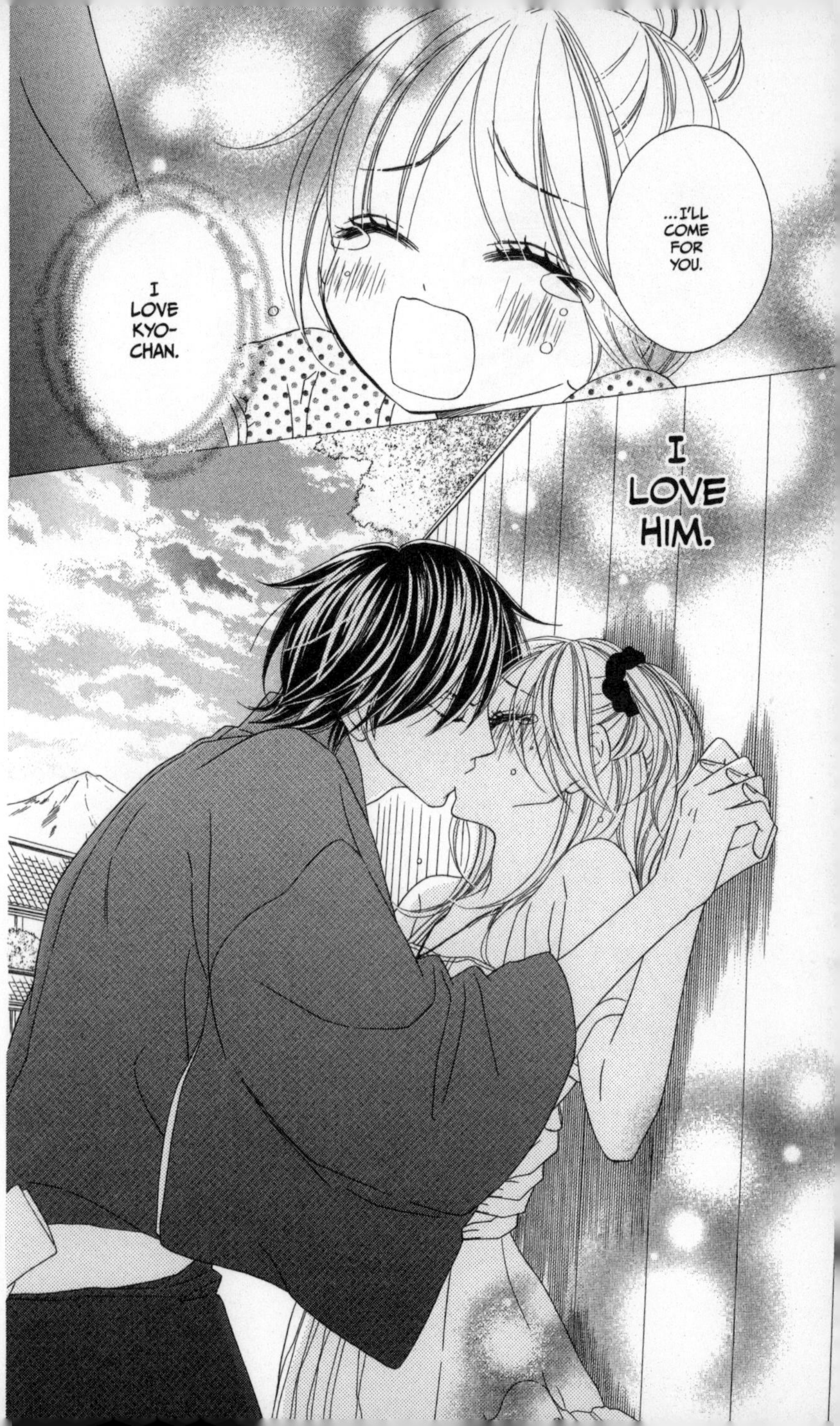
...I'LL COME FOR YOU.
I LOVE KYO-CHAN.
I LOVE HIM.

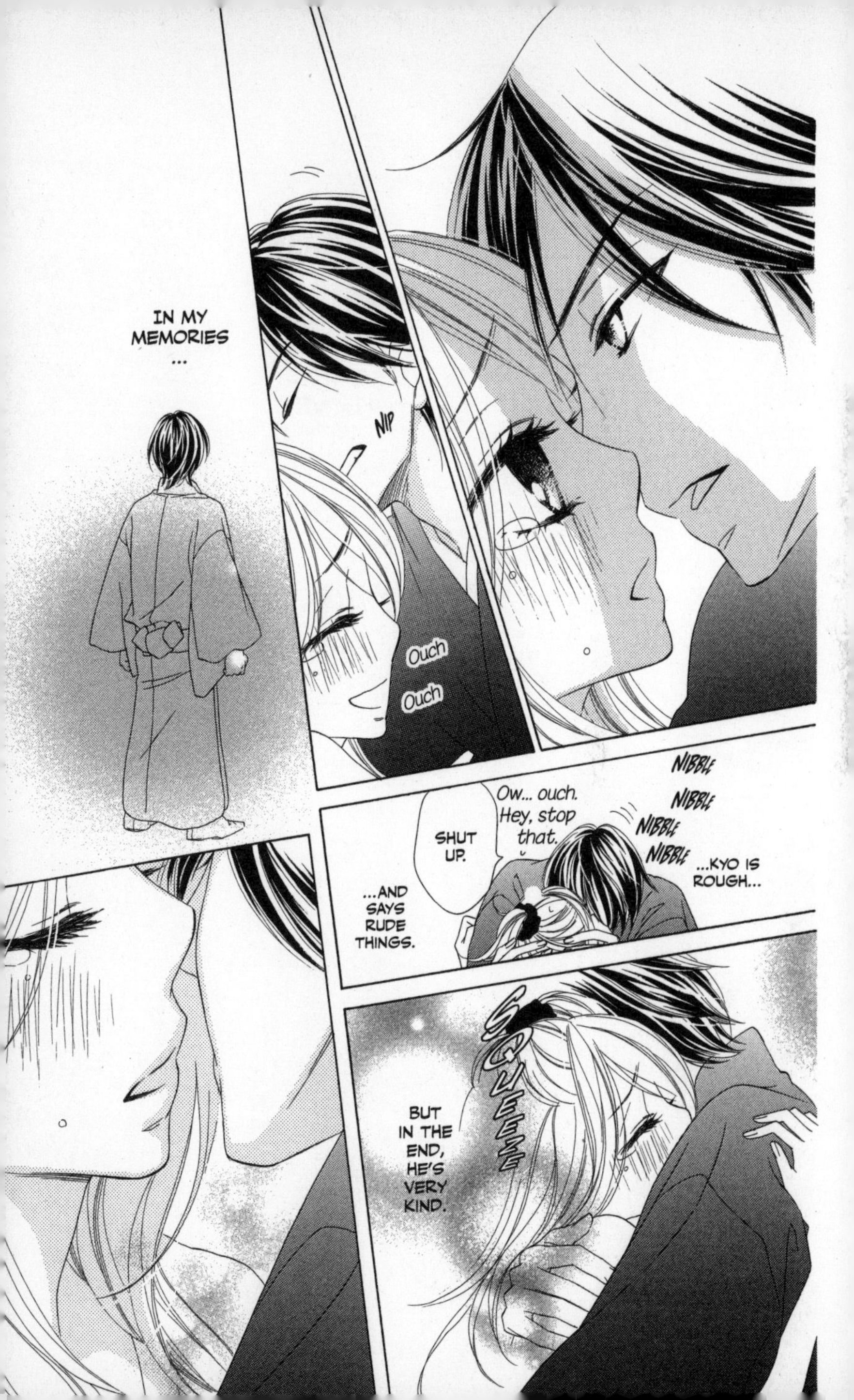
NIP
Ouch
Ouch
IN MY MEMORIES...
NIBBLE
NIBBLE
NIBBLE
NIBBLE
...KYO IS ROUGH...
Ow... ouch. Hey, stop that.
SHUT UP.
...AND SAYS RUDE THINGS.
SQUEEZE
BUT IN THE END, HE'S VERY KIND.

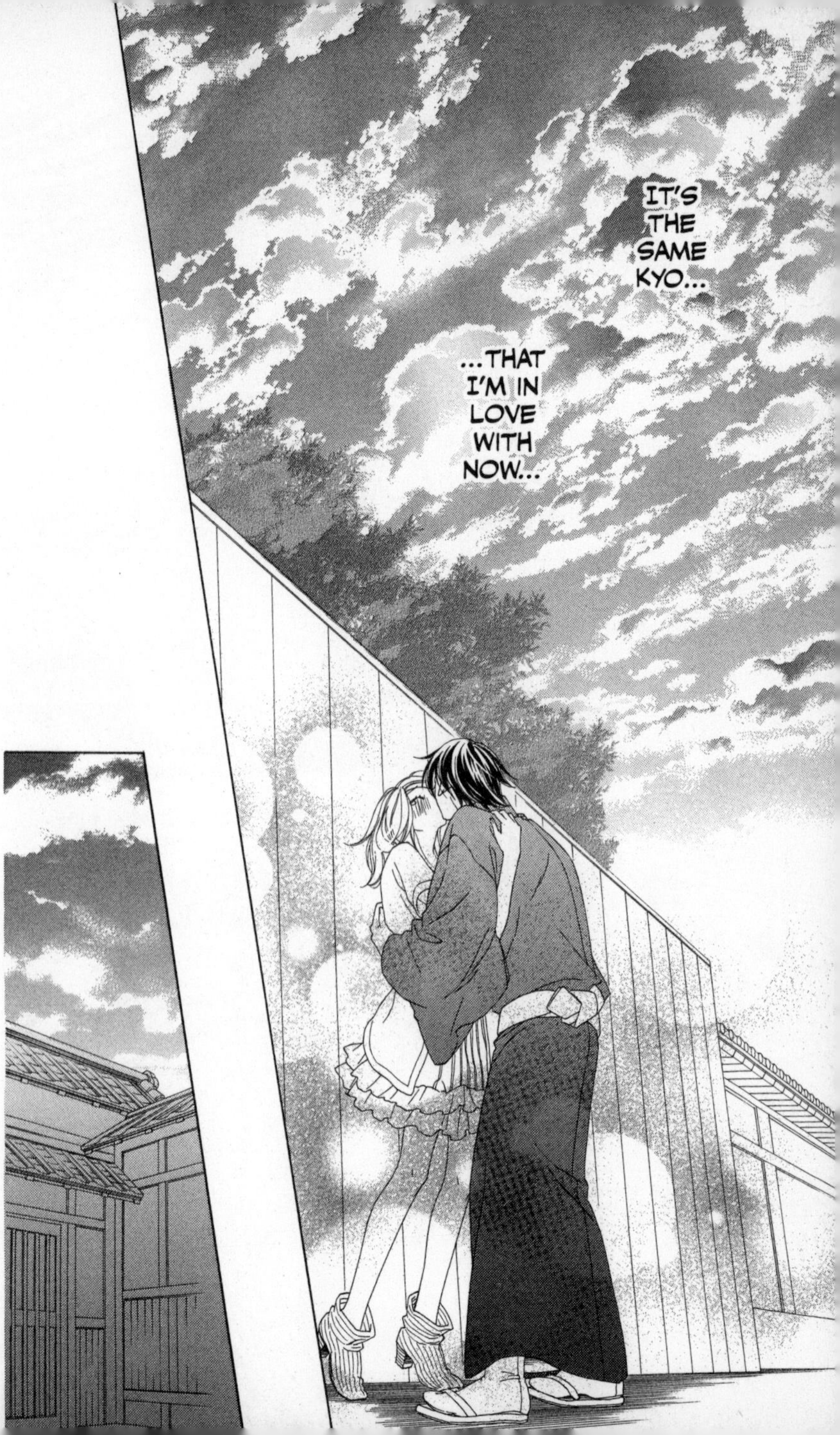
IT'S THE SAME KYO...
...THAT I'M IN LOVE WITH NOW...

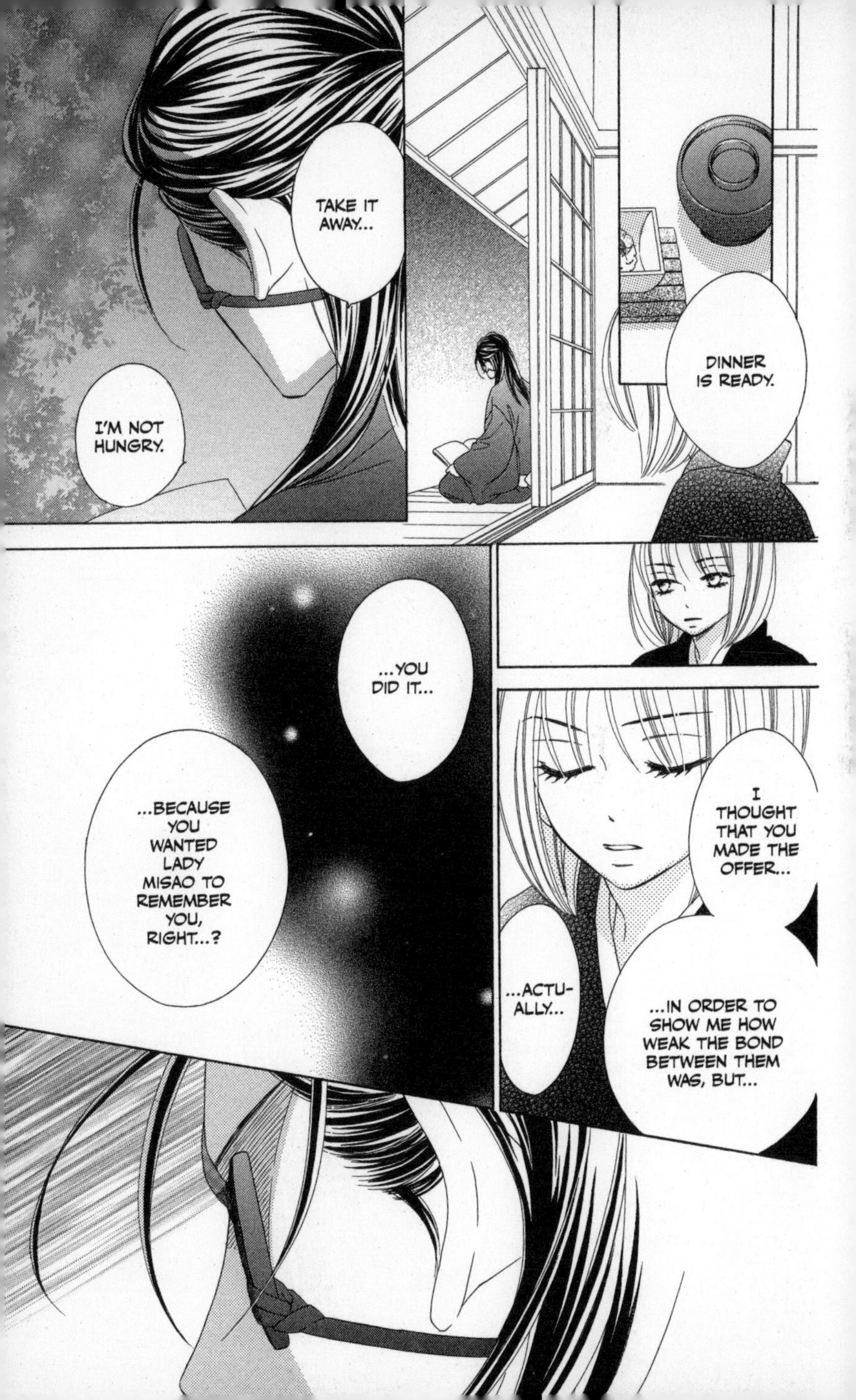
DINNER IS READY.
TAKE IT AWAY...
I'M NOT HUNGRY.
I THOUGHT THAT YOU MADE THE OFFER...
...IN ORDER TO SHOW ME HOW WEAK THE BOND BETWEEN THEM WAS, BUT...
...ACTU-ALLY...
...YOU DID IT...
...BECAUSE YOU WANTED LADY MISAO TO REMEMBER YOU, RIGHT...?

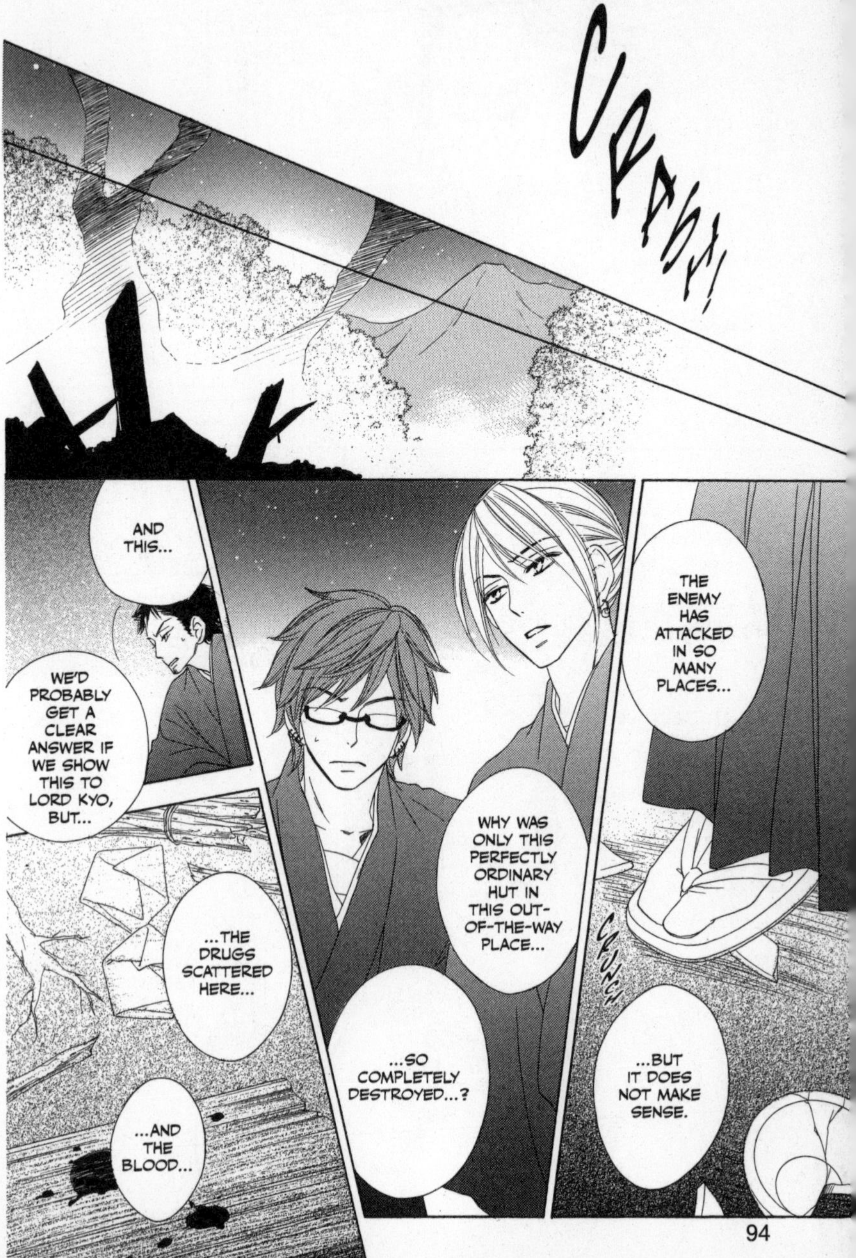
CRASH!!
THE ENEMY HAS ATTACKED IN SO MANY PLACES...
CRUNCH
...BUT IT DOES NOT MAKE SENSE.
WHY WAS ONLY THIS PERFECTLY ORDINARY HUT IN THIS OUT-OF-THE-WAY PLACE...
...SO COMPLETELY DESTROYED...?
AND THIS...
WE'D PROBABLY GET A CLEAR ANSWER IF WE SHOW THIS TO LORD KYO, BUT...
...THE DRUGS SCATTERED HERE...
...AND THE BLOOD...

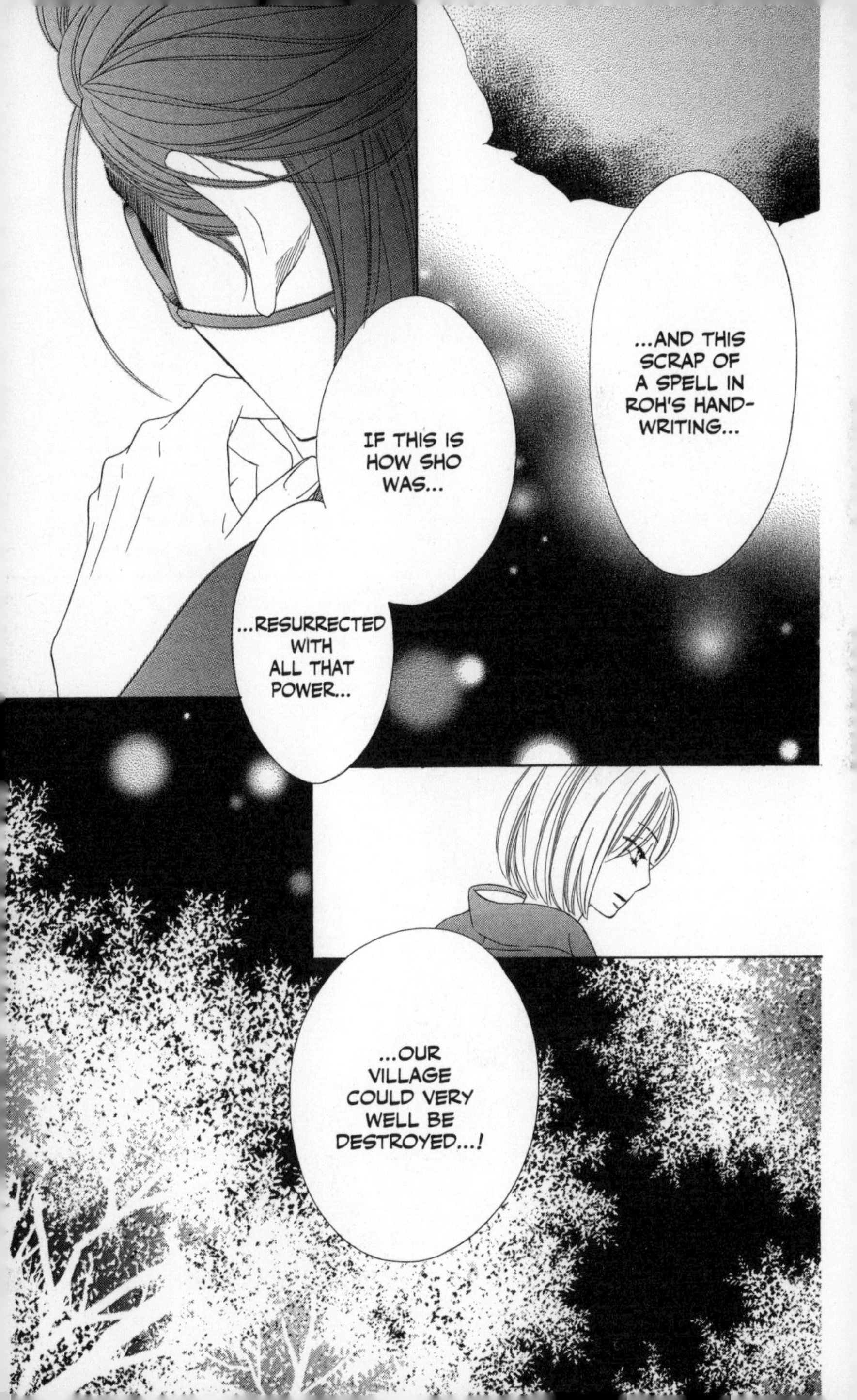
...AND THIS SCRAP OF A SPELL IN ROH'S HAND-WRITING...
IF THIS IS HOW SHO WAS...
...RESURRECTED WITH ALL THAT POWER...
...OUR VILLAGE COULD VERY WELL BE DESTROYED...!

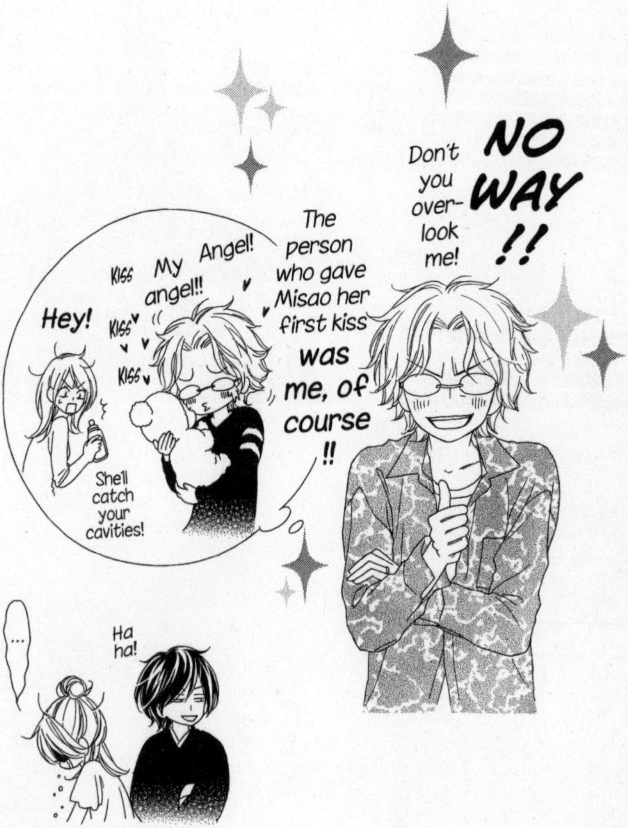
NO WAY!!
Don't you over-look me!
The person who gave Misao her first kiss was me, of course!!
Angel!
My angel!!
KISS
KISS
KISS
Hey!
She'll catch your cavities!
Ha ha!
...

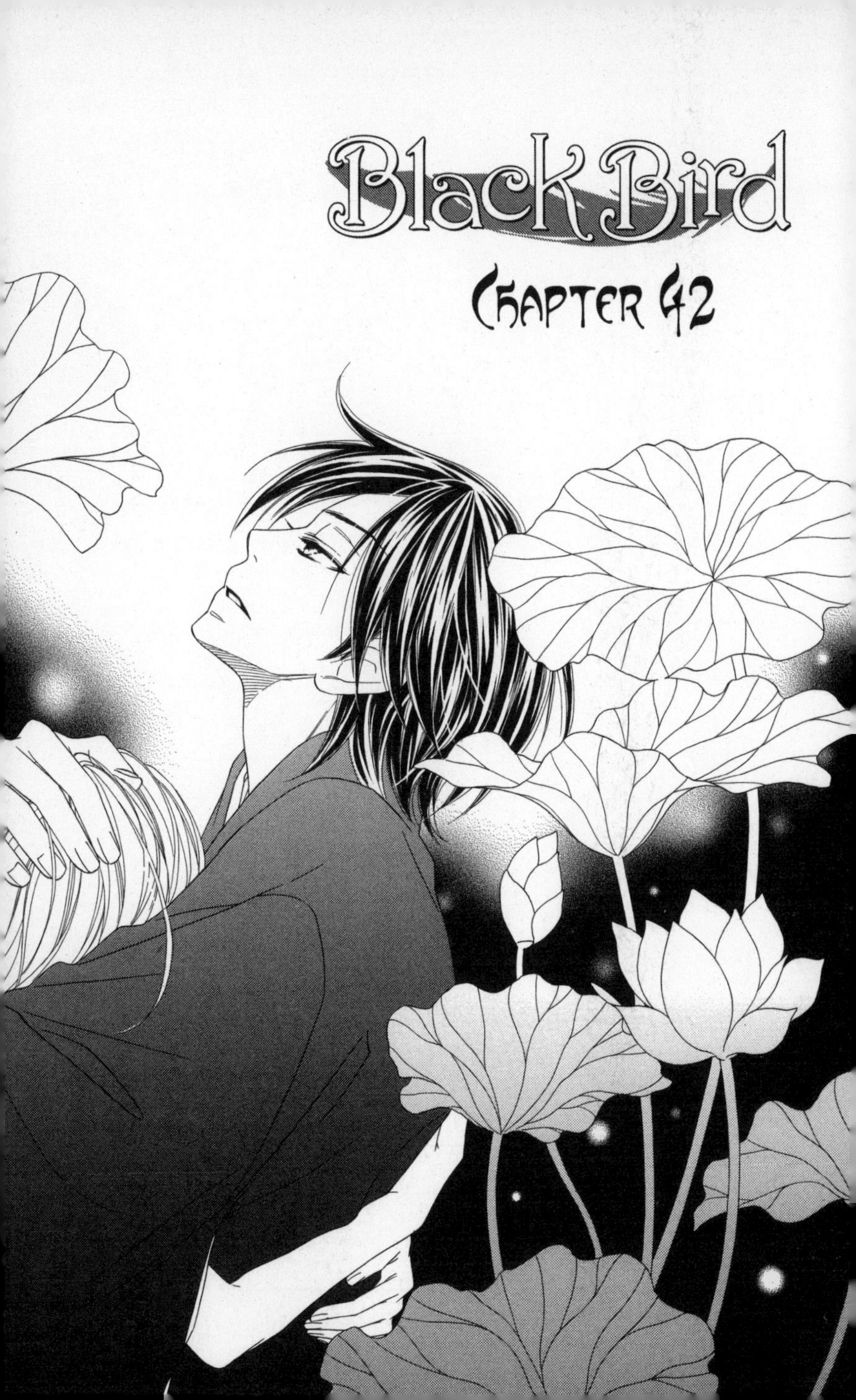
Black Bird
Chapter 42

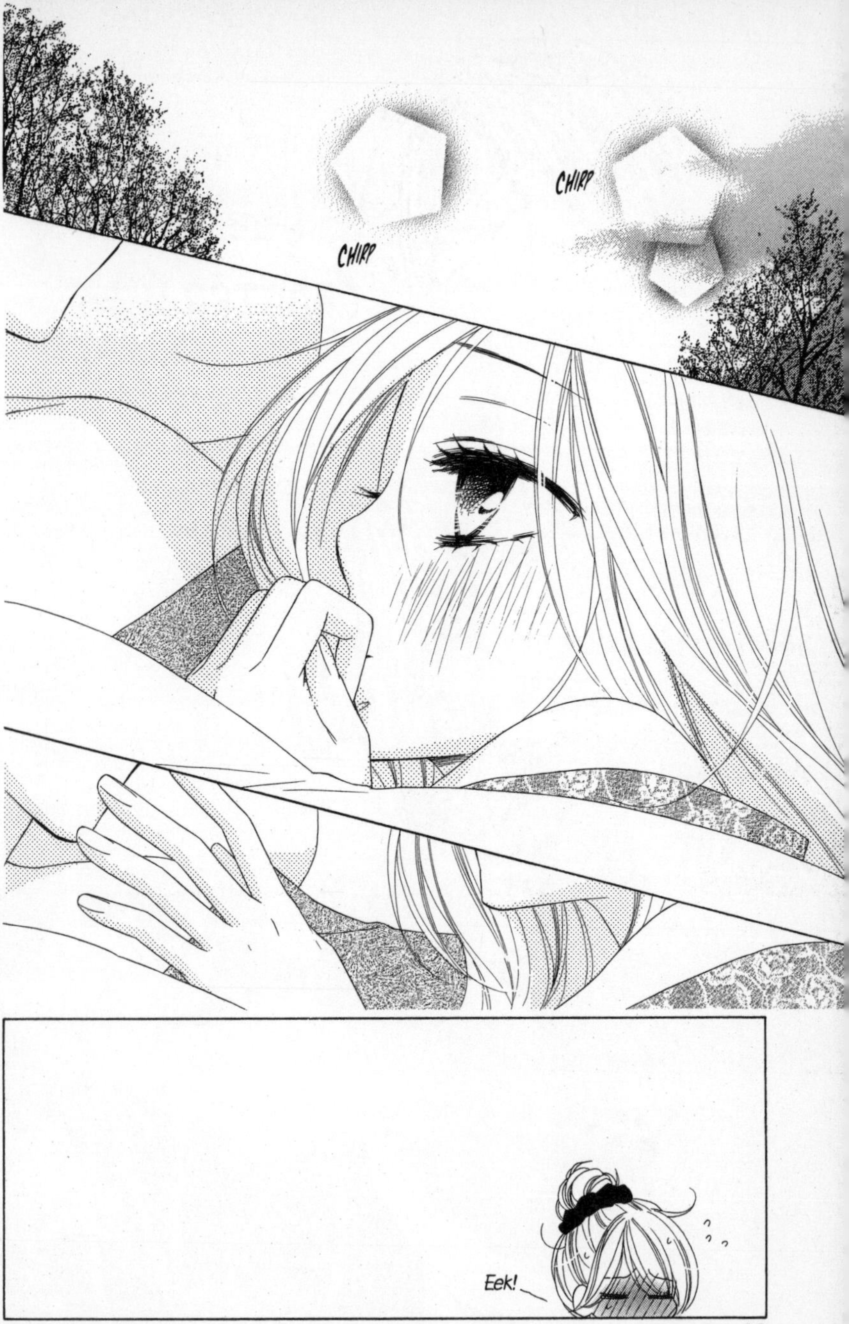
CHIRP
CHIRP
Eek!

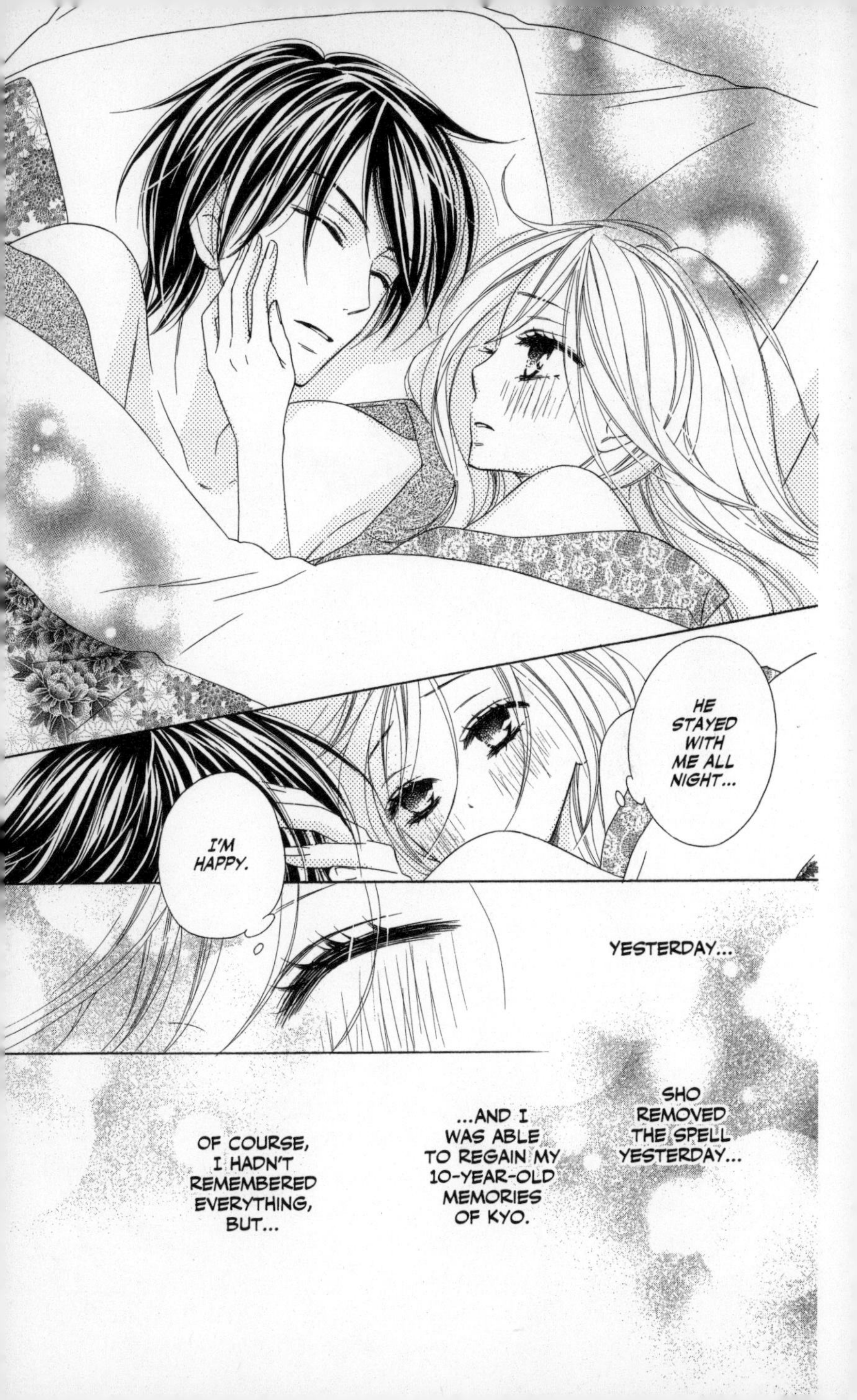
HE STAYED WITH ME ALL NIGHT...
I'M HAPPY.
YESTERDAY...
SHO REMOVED THE SPELL YESTERDAY...
...AND I WAS ABLE TO REGAIN MY 10-YEAR-OLD MEMORIES OF KYO.
OF COURSE, I HADN'T REMEMBERED EVERYTHING, BUT...

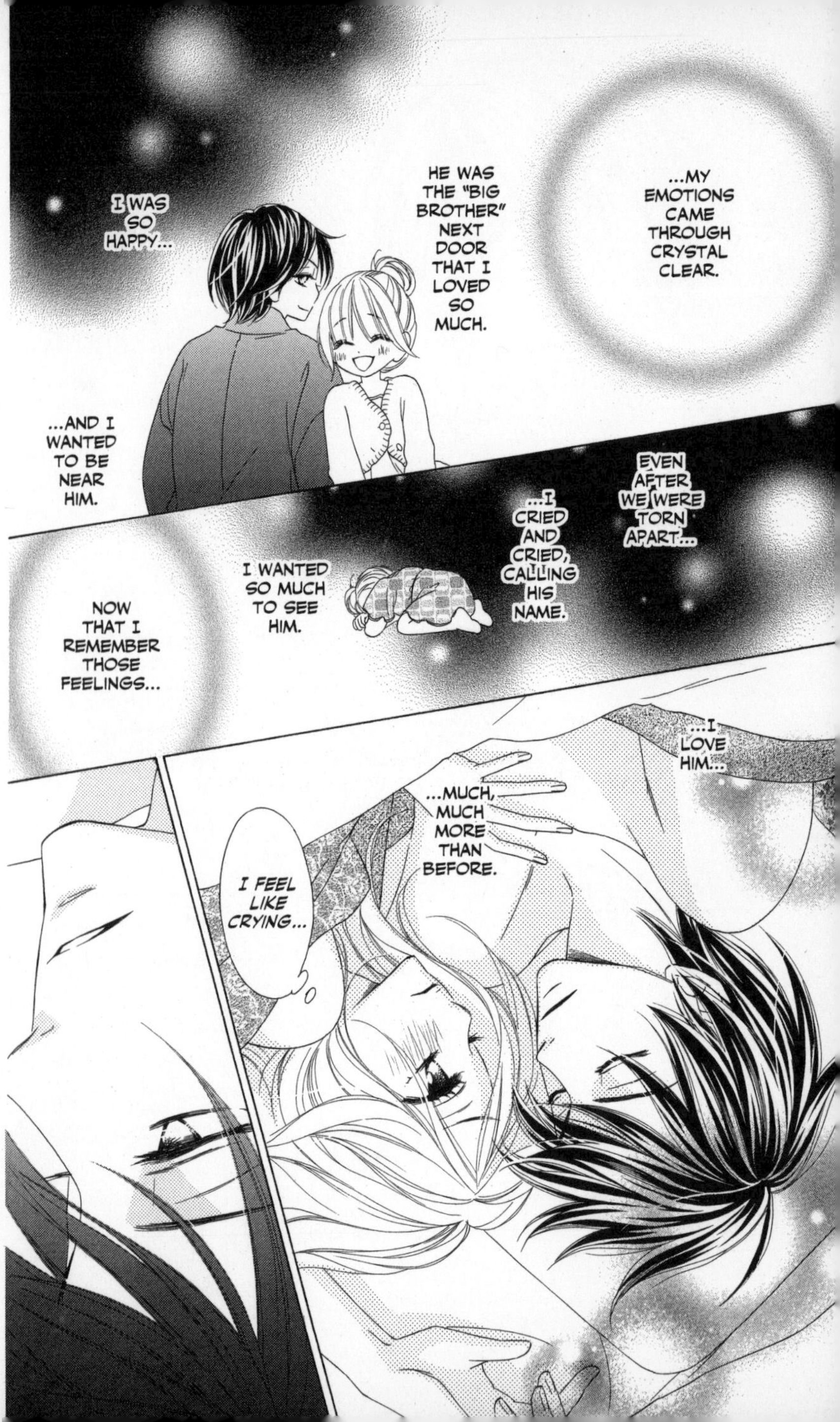
...MY EMOTIONS CAME THROUGH CRYSTAL CLEAR.
HE WAS THE "BIG BROTHER" NEXT DOOR THAT I LOVED SO MUCH.
I WAS SO HAPPY...
...AND I WANTED TO BE NEAR HIM.
EVEN AFTER WE WERE TORN APART...
...I CRIED AND CRIED, CALLING HIS NAME.
I WANTED SO MUCH TO SEE HIM.
NOW THAT I REMEMBER THOSE FEELINGS...
...I LOVE HIM...
...MUCH, MUCH MORE THAN BEFORE.
I FEEL LIKE CRYING...

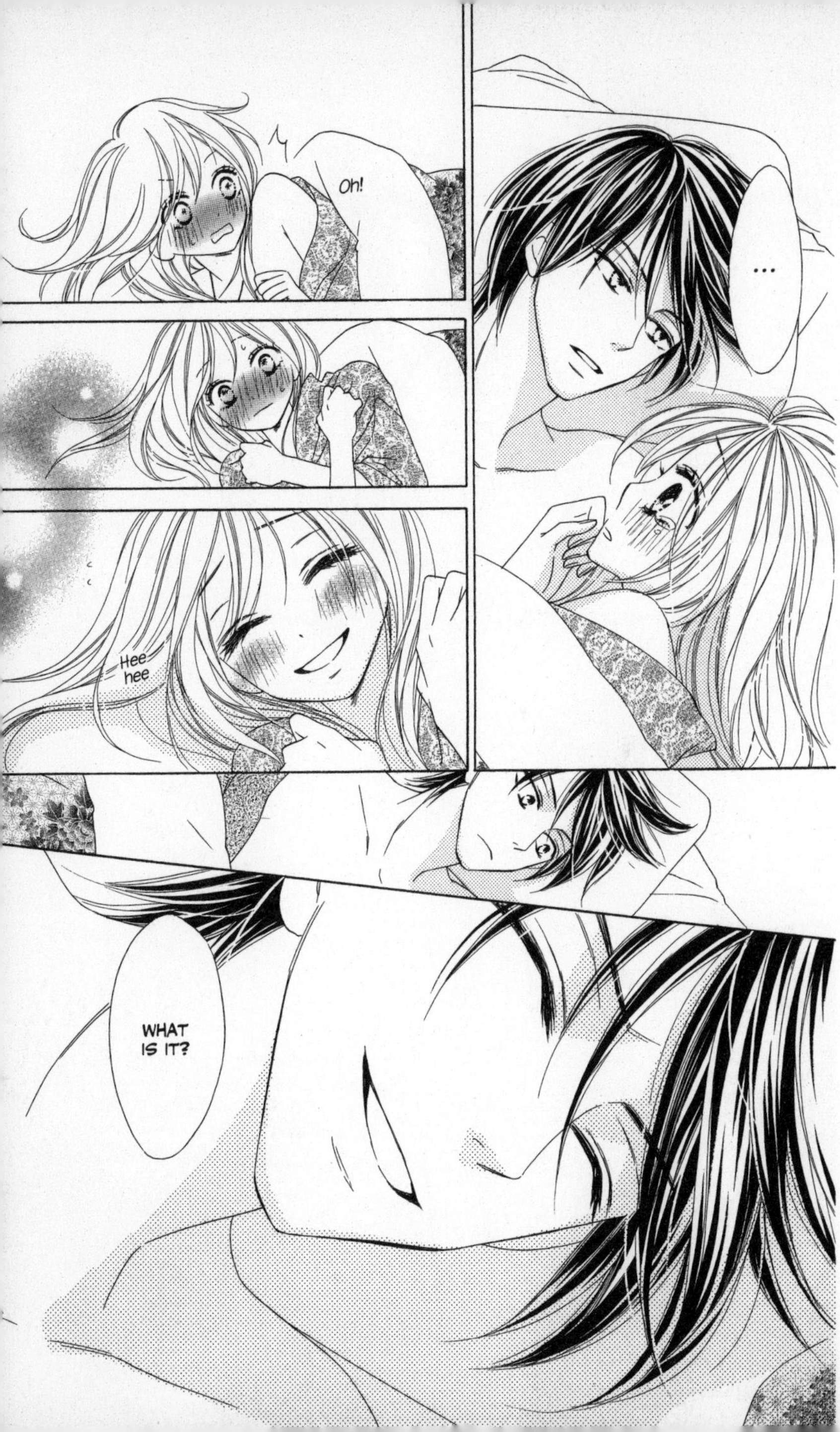
...
Oh!
Hee hee
WHAT IS IT?

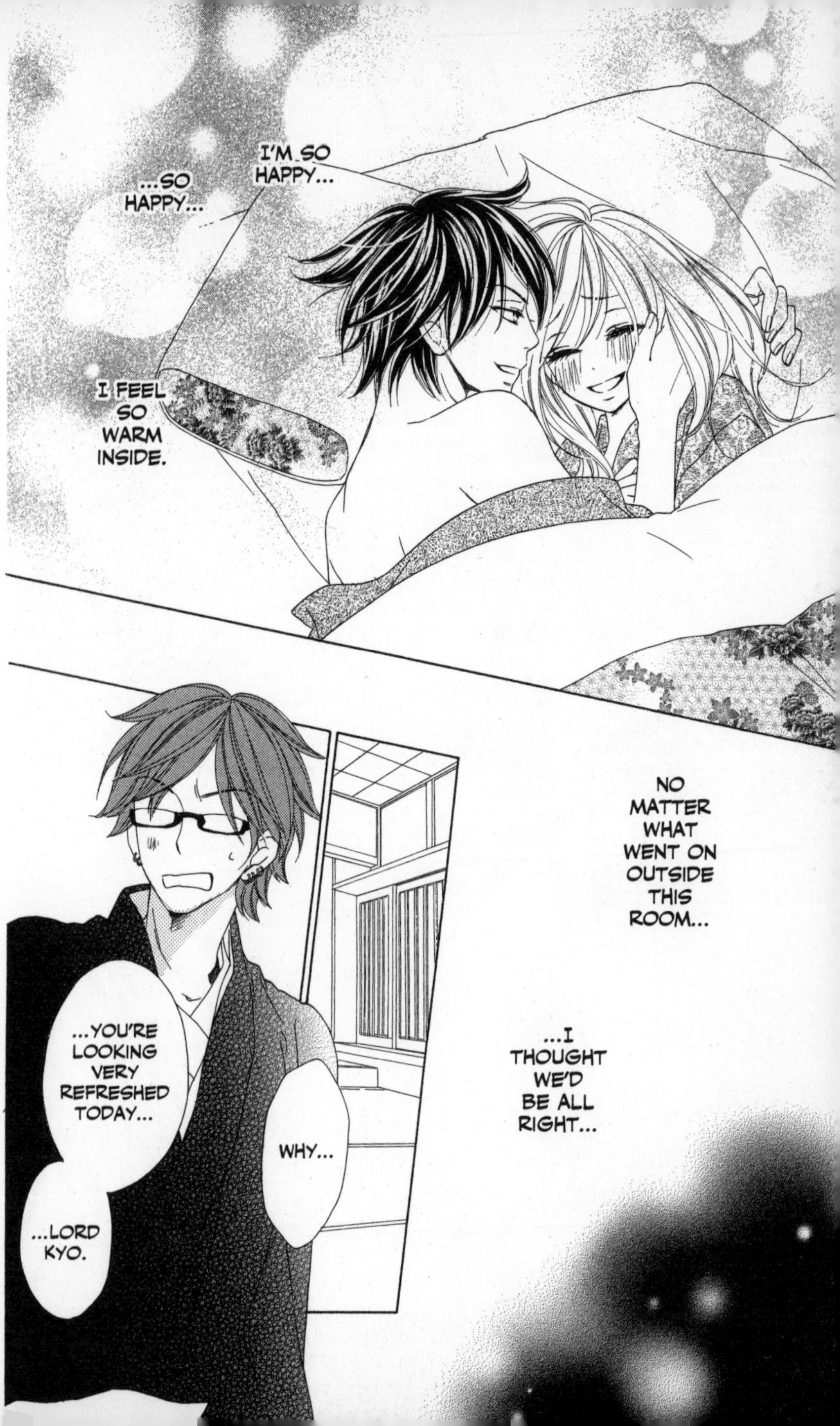
I'M SO HAPPY...
...SO HAPPY...
I FEEL SO WARM INSIDE.
NO MATTER WHAT WENT ON OUTSIDE THIS ROOM...
...I THOUGHT WE'D BE ALL RIGHT...
WHY...
...YOU'RE LOOKING VERY REFRESHED TODAY...
...LORD KYO.

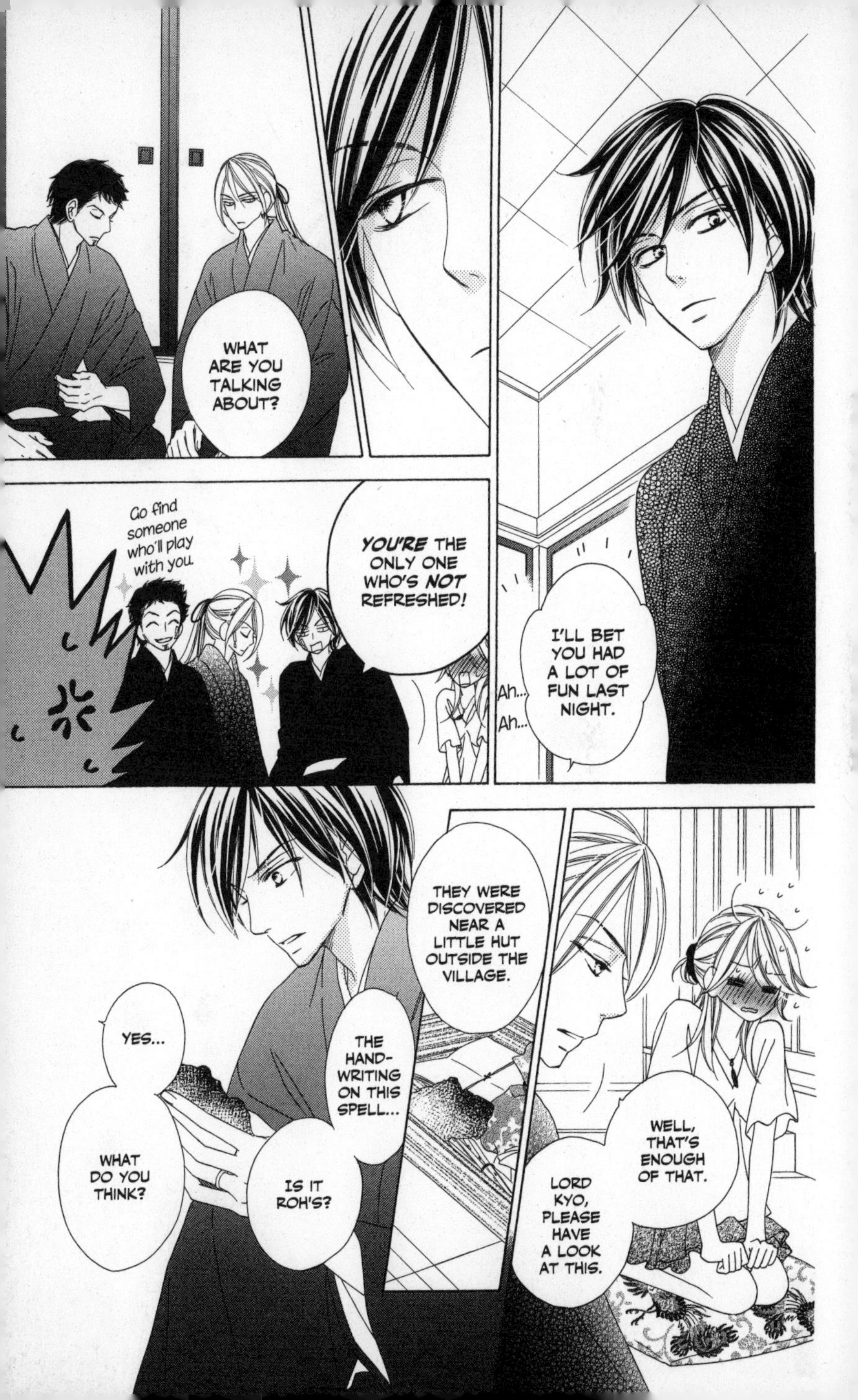
Ah...
Ah...
I'LL BET YOU HAD A LOT OF FUN LAST NIGHT.
WHAT ARE YOU TALKING ABOUT?
YOU'RE THE ONLY ONE WHO'S *NOT* REFRESHED!
Go find someone who'll play with you.
WELL, THAT'S ENOUGH OF THAT.
LORD KYO, PLEASE HAVE A LOOK AT THIS.
THEY WERE DISCOVERED NEAR A LITTLE HUT OUTSIDE THE VILLAGE.
THE HAND-WRITING ON THIS SPELL...
IS IT ROH'S?
YES...
WHAT DO YOU THINK?

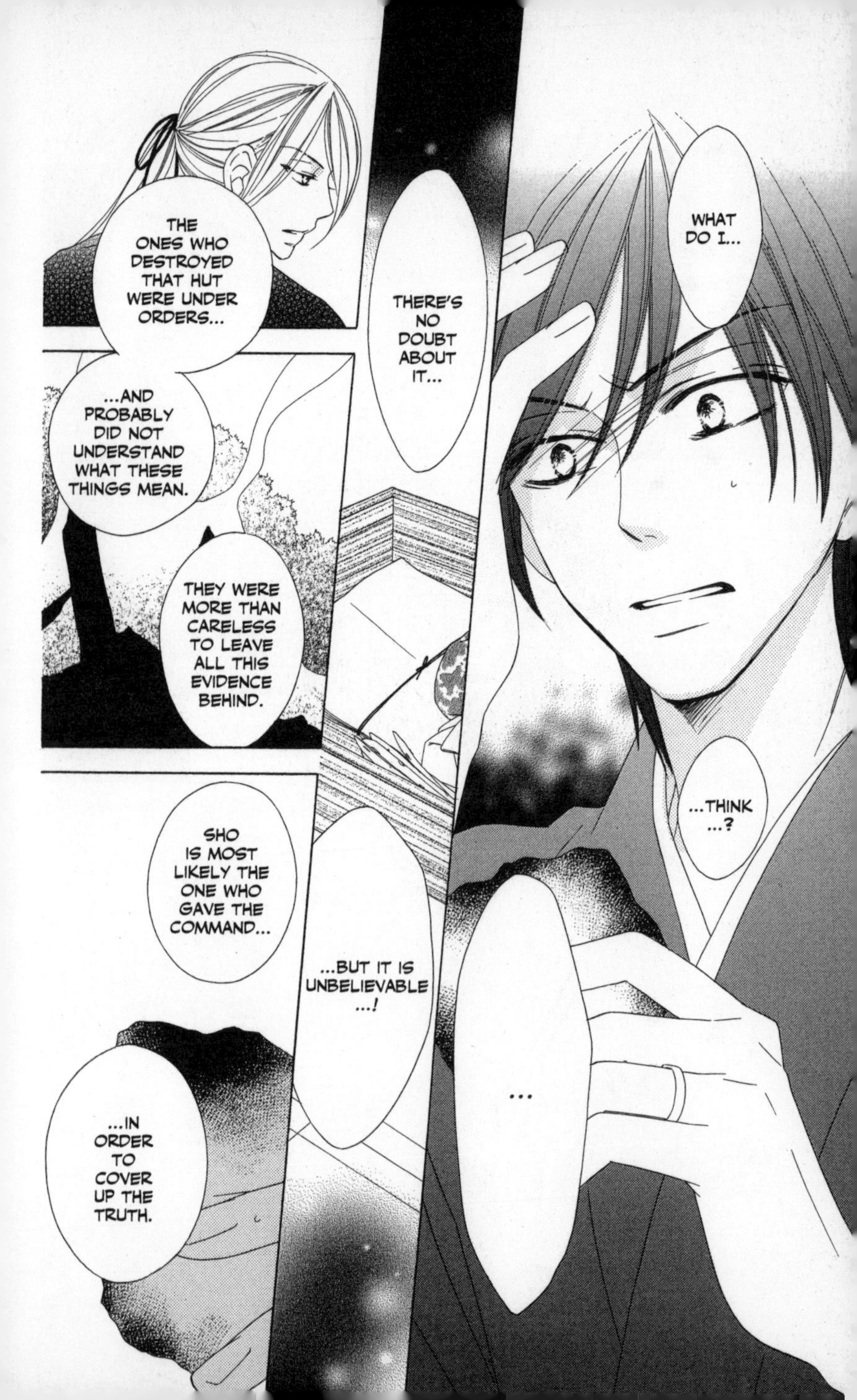
WHAT DO I...
...THINK ...?
...
THERE'S NO DOUBT ABOUT IT...
...BUT IT IS UNBELIEVABLE ...!
THE ONES WHO DESTROYED THAT HUT WERE UNDER ORDERS...
...AND PROBABLY DID NOT UNDERSTAND WHAT THESE THINGS MEAN.
THEY WERE MORE THAN CARELESS TO LEAVE ALL THIS EVIDENCE BEHIND.
SHO IS MOST LIKELY THE ONE WHO GAVE THE COMMAND...
...IN ORDER TO COVER UP THE TRUTH.

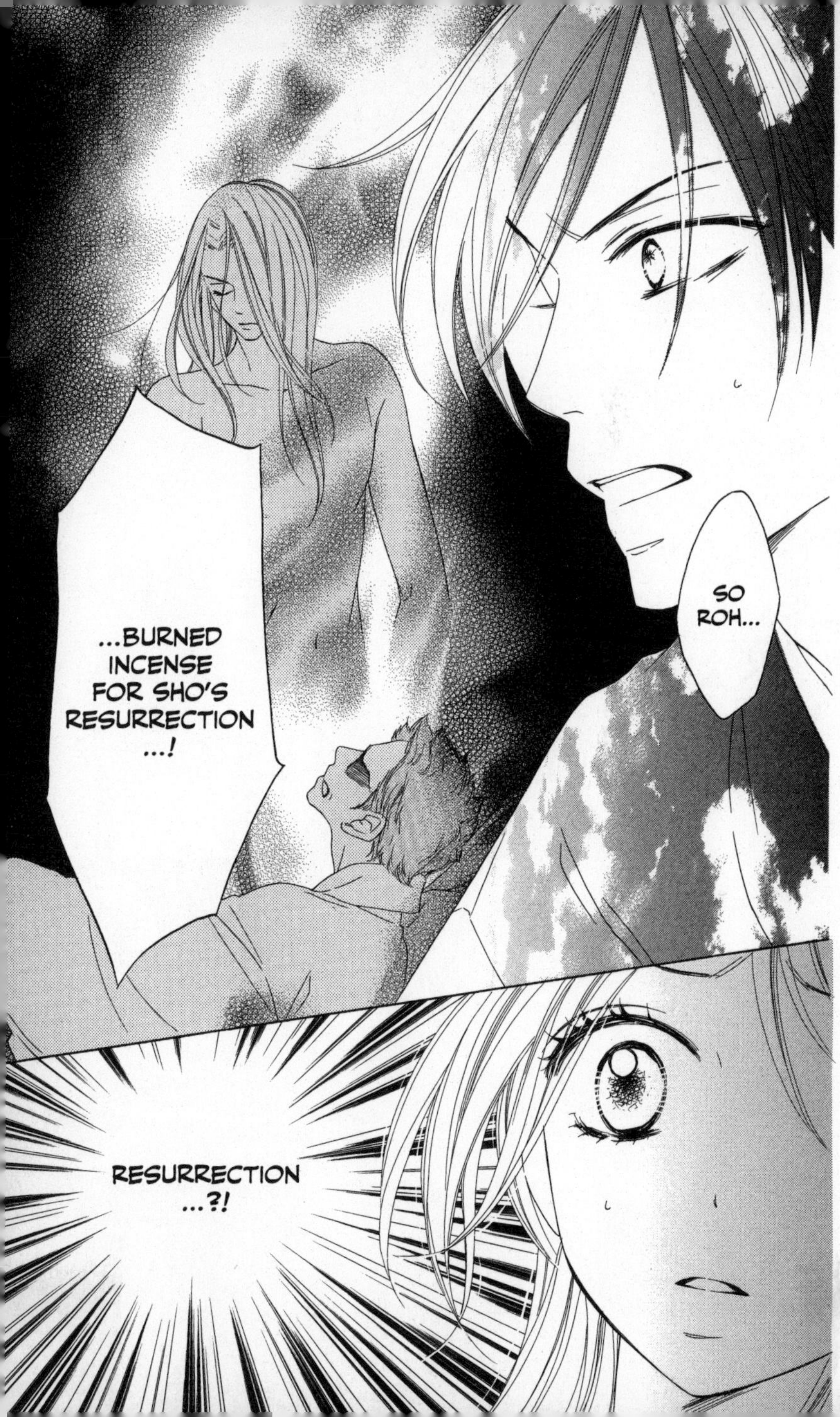
SO ROH...
...BURNED INCENSE FOR SHO'S RESURRECTION ...!
RESURRECTION ...?!

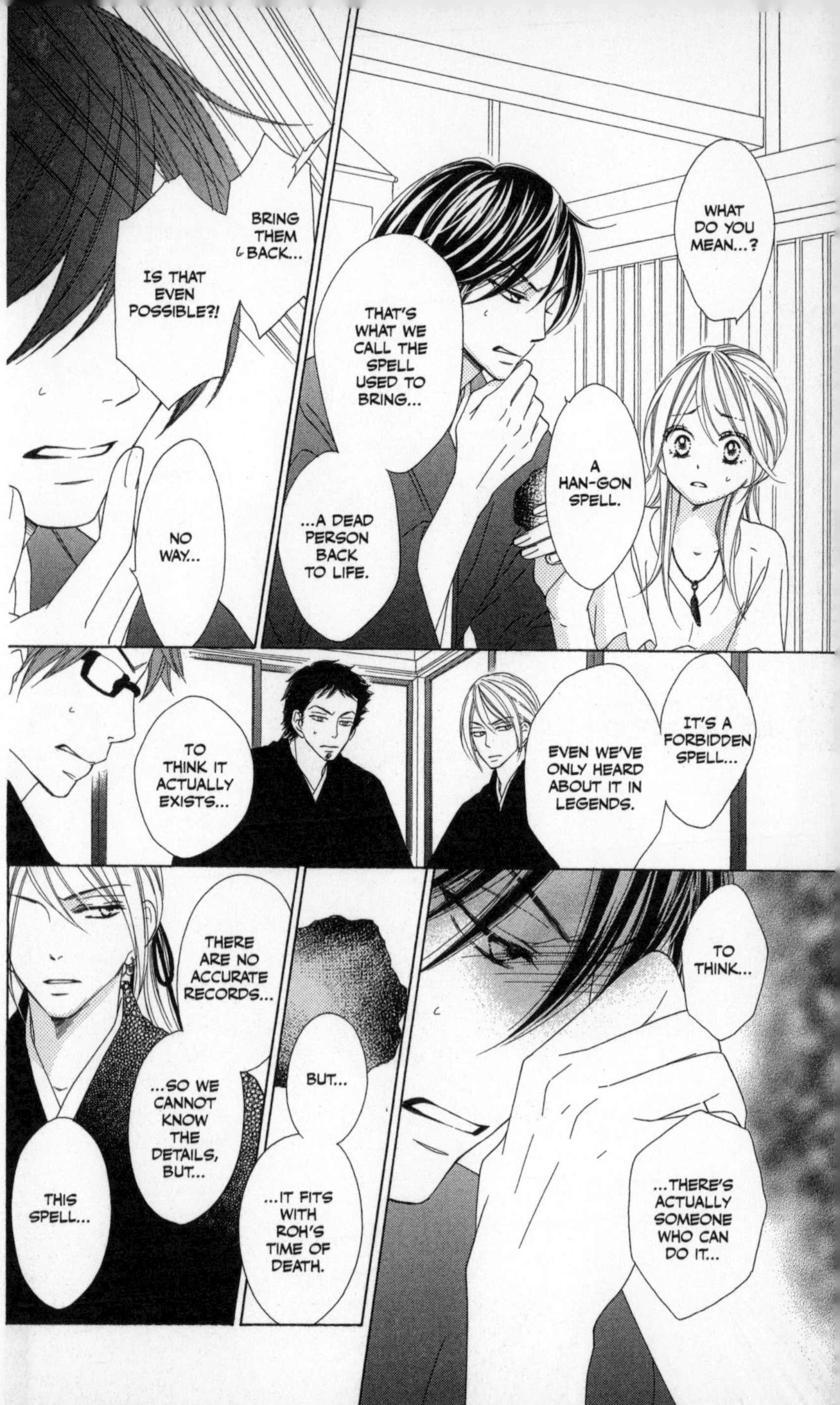
WHAT DO YOU MEAN...?
A HAN-GON SPELL.
THAT'S WHAT WE CALL THE SPELL USED TO BRING...
...A DEAD PERSON BACK TO LIFE.
BRING THEM BACK...
IS THAT EVEN POSSIBLE?!
NO WAY...
IT'S A FORBIDDEN SPELL...
EVEN WE'VE ONLY HEARD ABOUT IT IN LEGENDS.
TO THINK IT ACTUALLY EXISTS...
TO THINK...
...THERE'S ACTUALLY SOMEONE WHO CAN DO IT...
BUT...
...IT FITS WITH ROH'S TIME OF DEATH.
THERE ARE NO ACCURATE RECORDS...
...SO WE CANNOT KNOW THE DETAILS, BUT...
THIS SPELL...

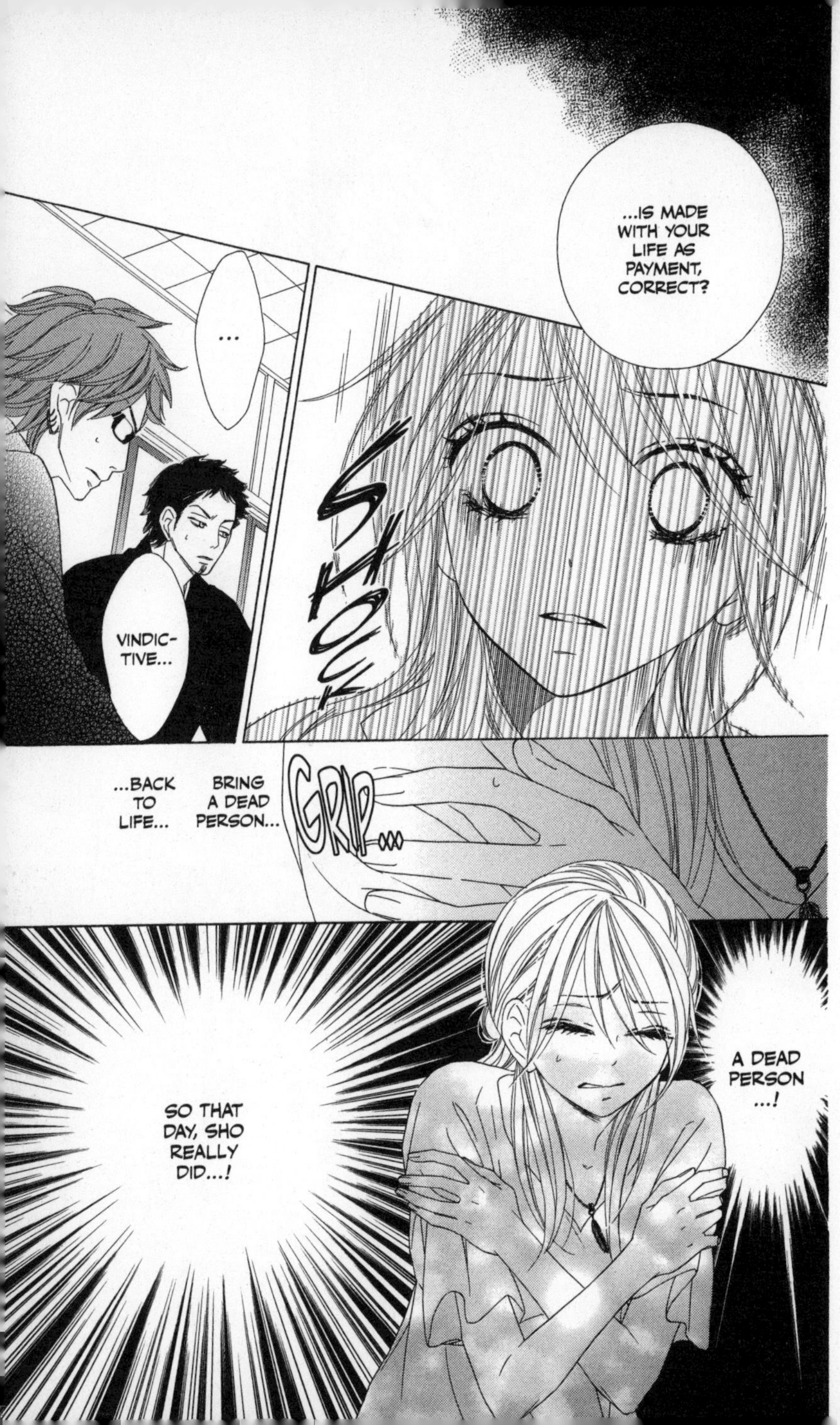
...IS MADE WITH YOUR LIFE AS PAYMENT, CORRECT?
SHOCK
...
VINDIC-TIVE...
GRIP...
BRING A DEAD PERSON...
...BACK TO LIFE...
A DEAD PERSON ...!
SO THAT DAY, SHO REALLY DID...!

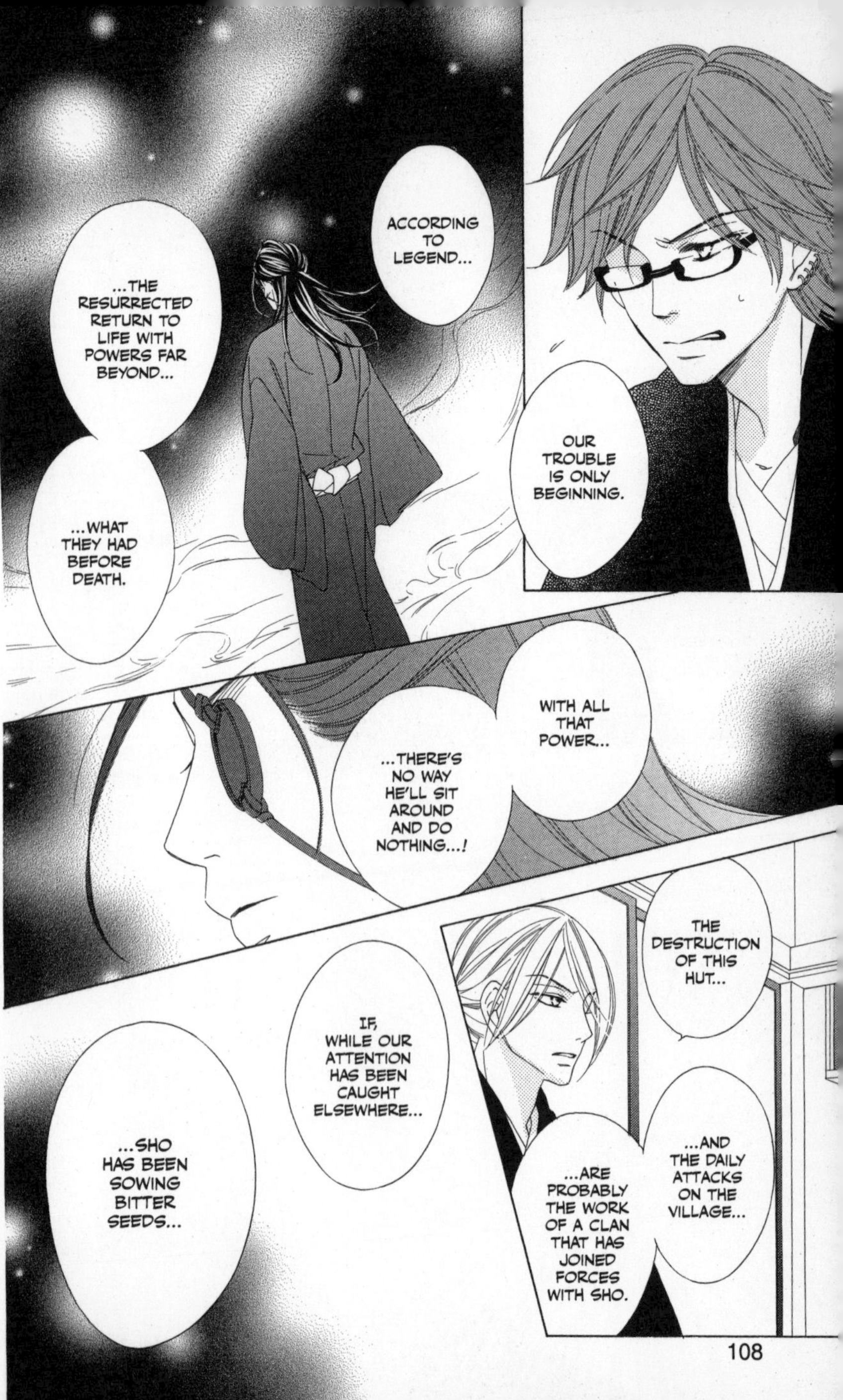
OUR TROUBLE IS ONLY BEGINNING.
ACCORDING TO LEGEND...
...THE RESURRECTED RETURN TO LIFE WITH POWERS FAR BEYOND...
...WHAT THEY HAD BEFORE DEATH.
WITH ALL THAT POWER...
...THERE'S NO WAY HE'LL SIT AROUND AND DO NOTHING...!
THE DESTRUCTION OF THIS HUT...
...AND THE DAILY ATTACKS ON THE VILLAGE...
...ARE PROBABLY THE WORK OF A CLAN THAT HAS JOINED FORCES WITH SHO.
IF, WHILE OUR ATTENTION HAS BEEN CAUGHT ELSEWHERE...
...SHO HAS BEEN SOWING BITTER SEEDS...

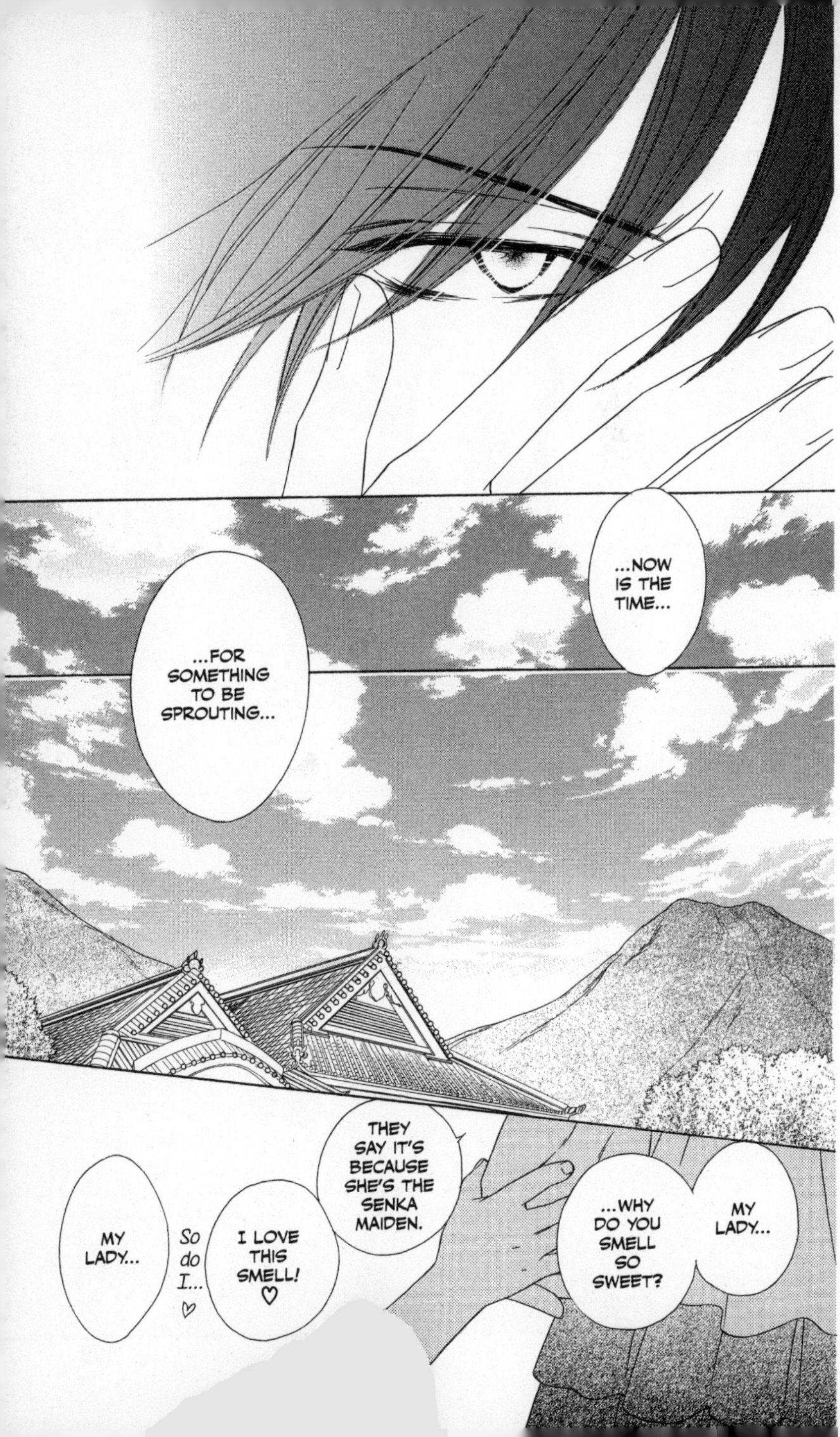
...NOW IS THE TIME...
...FOR SOMETHING TO BE SPROUTING...
MY LADY...
...WHY DO YOU SMELL SO SWEET?
THEY SAY IT'S BECAUSE SHE'S THE SENKA MAIDEN.
I LOVE THIS SMELL! ♡
So do I... ♡
MY LADY...

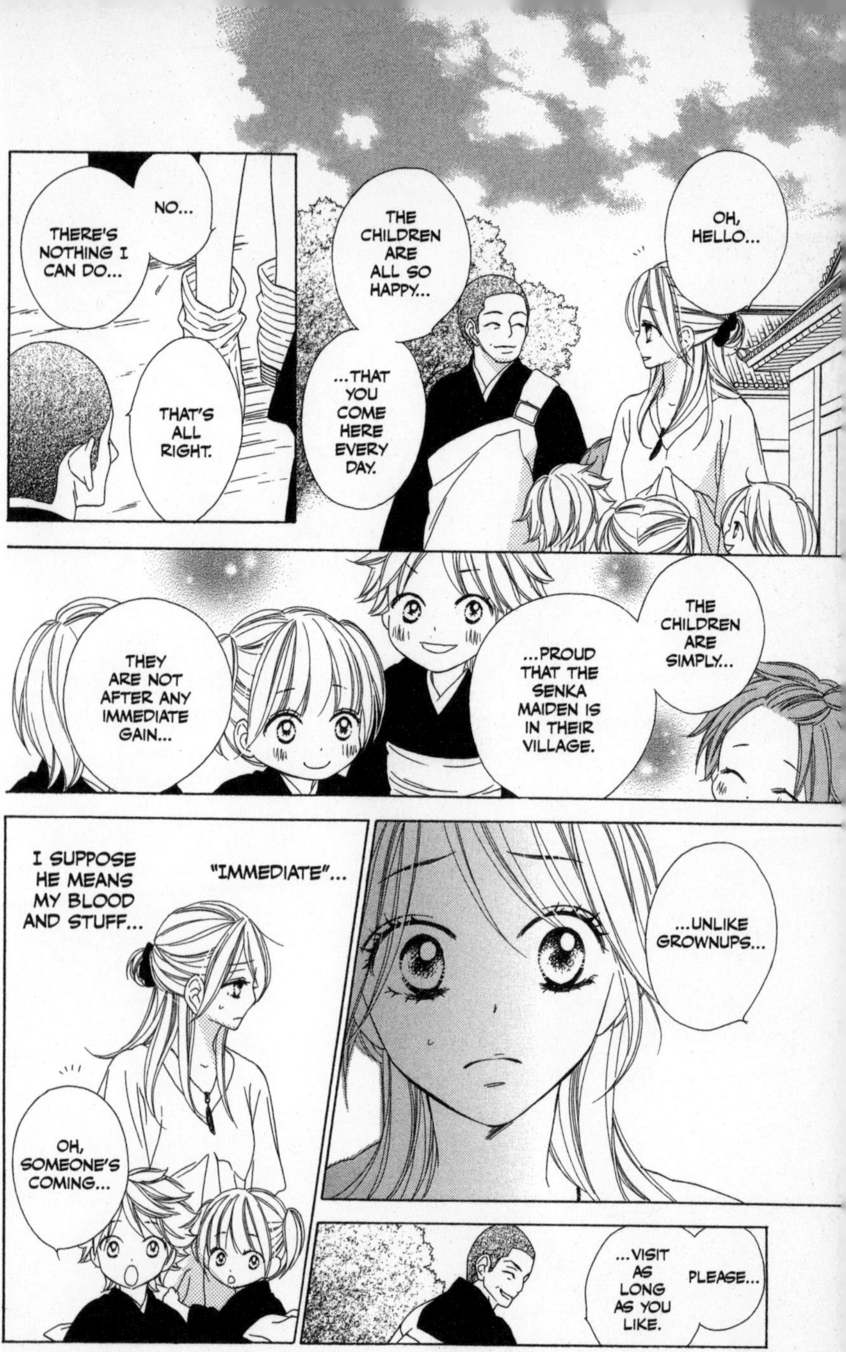
OH, HELLO...
THE CHILDREN ARE ALL SO HAPPY...
...THAT YOU COME HERE EVERY DAY.
NO...
THERE'S NOTHING I CAN DO...
THAT'S ALL RIGHT.
THE CHILDREN ARE SIMPLY...
...PROUD THAT THE SENKA MAIDEN IS IN THEIR VILLAGE.
THEY ARE NOT AFTER ANY IMMEDIATE GAIN...
...UNLIKE GROWNUPS...
PLEASE...
...VISIT AS LONG AS YOU LIKE.
"IMMEDIATE"...
I SUPPOSE HE MEANS MY BLOOD AND STUFF...
OH, SOMEONE'S COMING...

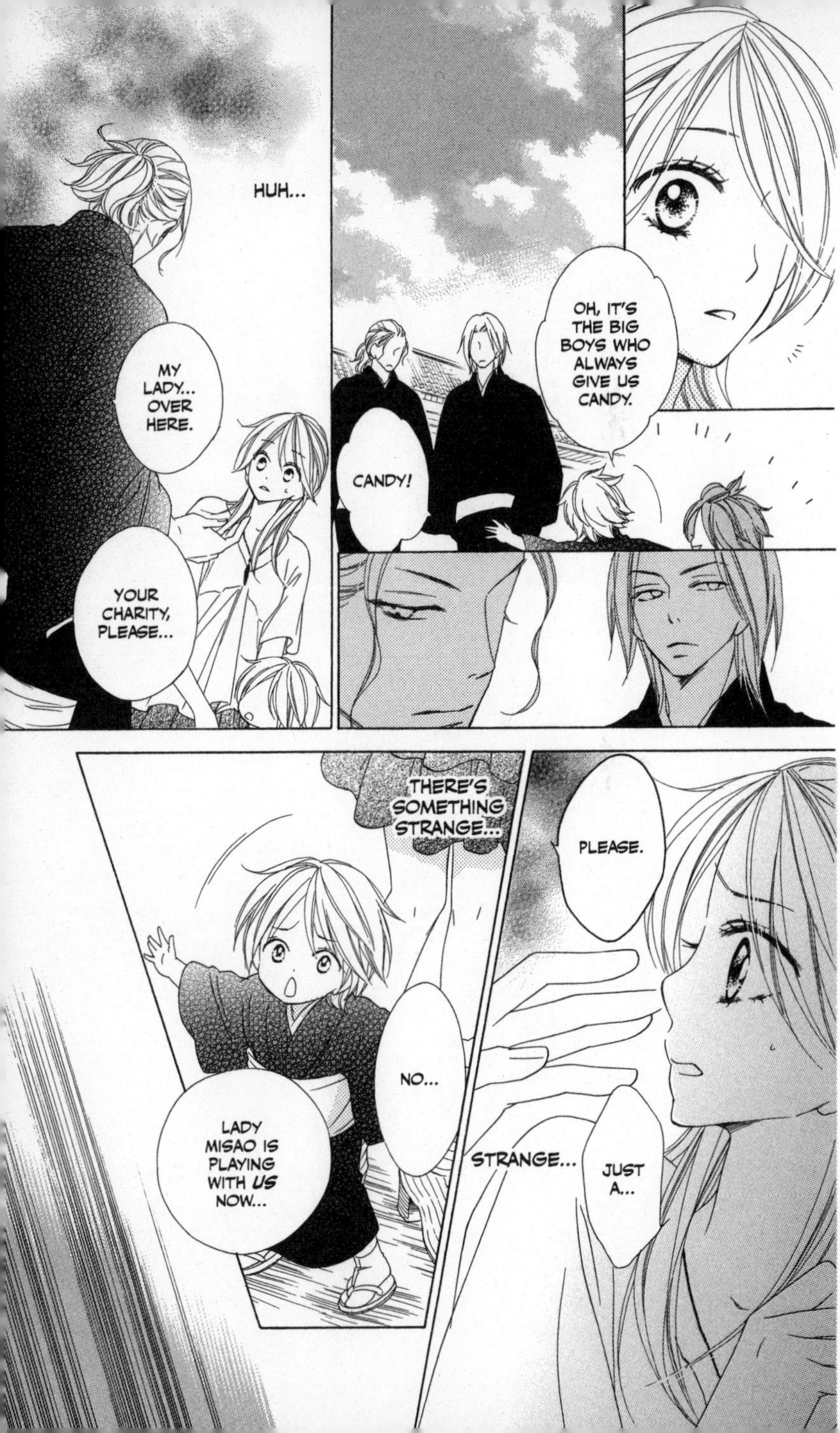
OH, IT'S THE BIG BOYS WHO ALWAYS GIVE US CANDY.
CANDY!
HUH...
MY LADY... OVER HERE.
YOUR CHARITY, PLEASE...
PLEASE.
JUST A...
STRANGE...
THERE'S SOMETHING STRANGE...
NO...
LADY MISAO IS PLAYING WITH *US* NOW...

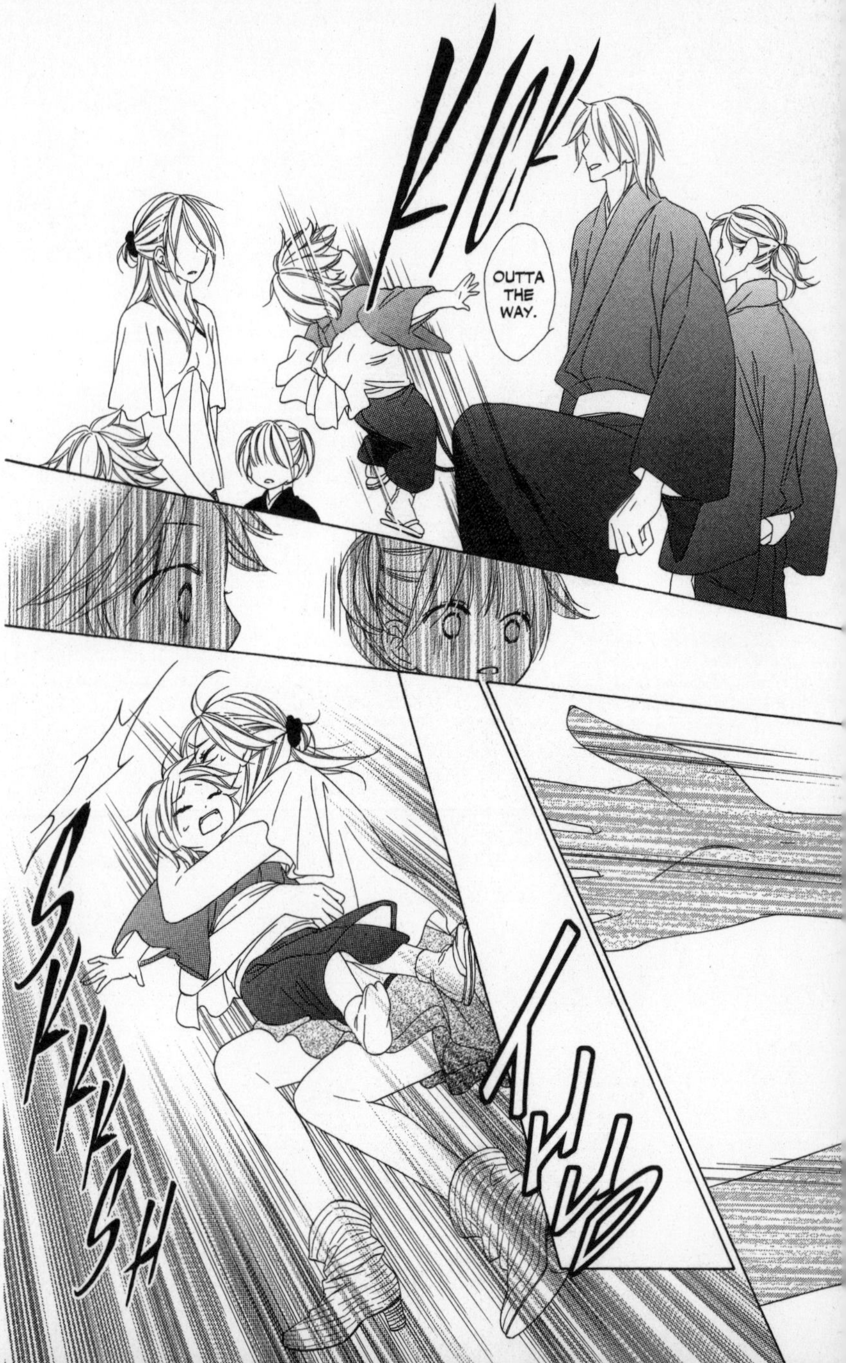
KICK
OUTTA THE WAY.
SKKKSH

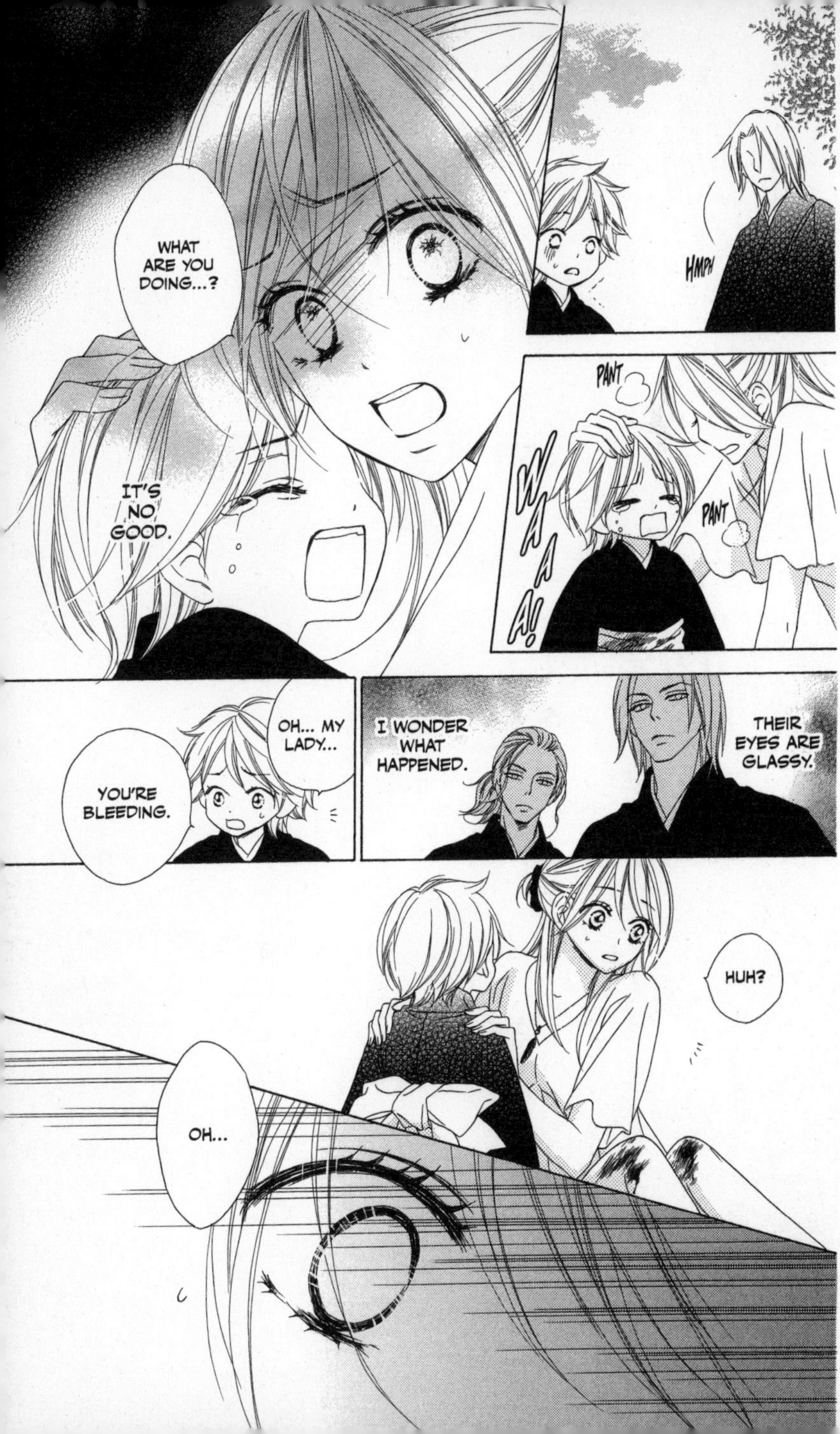
HMPH
PANT
WAAAA!
PANT
WHAT ARE YOU DOING...?
IT'S NO GOOD.
THEIR EYES ARE GLASSY.
I WONDER WHAT HAPPENED.
OH... MY LADY...
YOU'RE BLEEDING.
HUH?
OH...

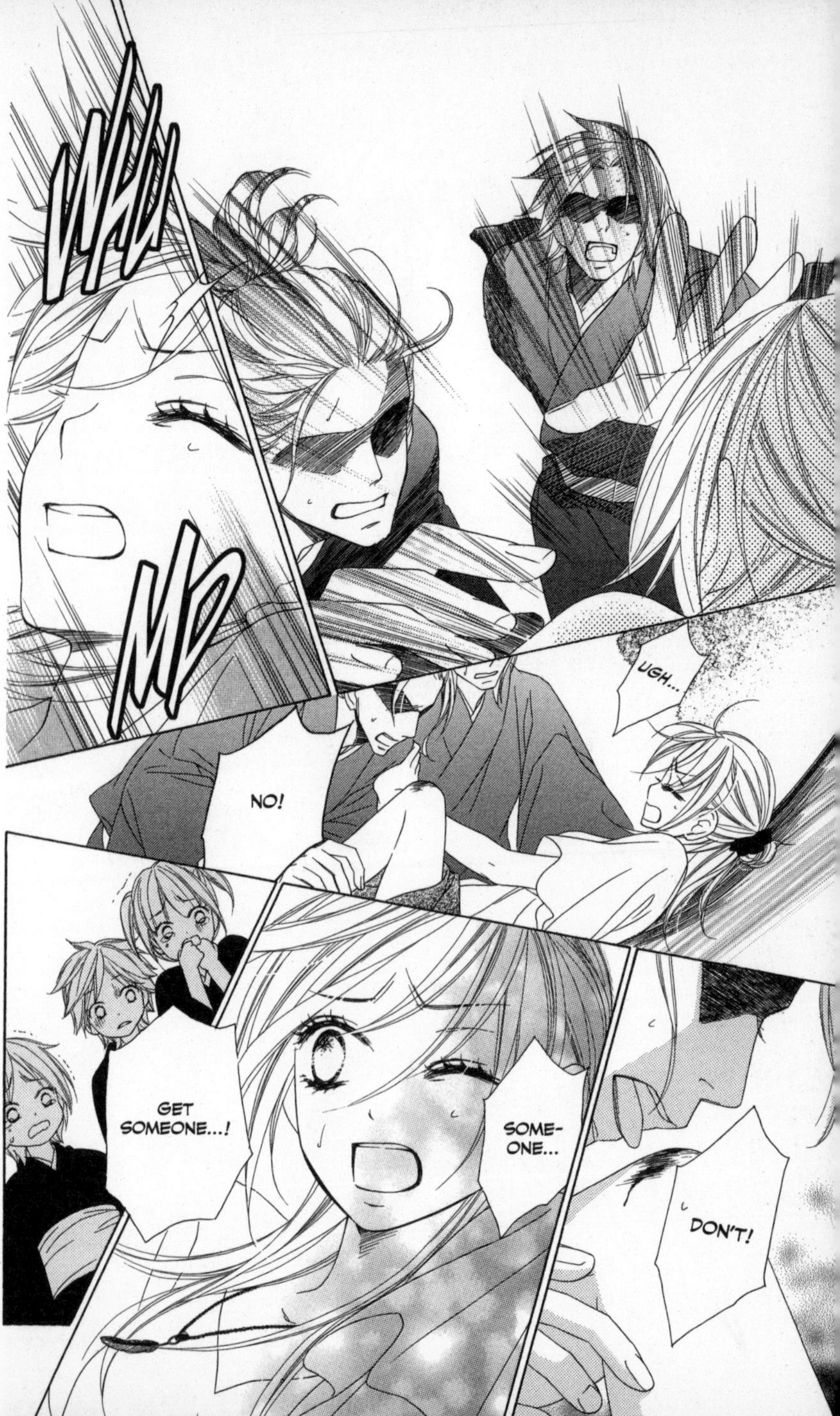
UGH...
NO!
DON'T!
SOME-ONE...
GET SOMEONE...!

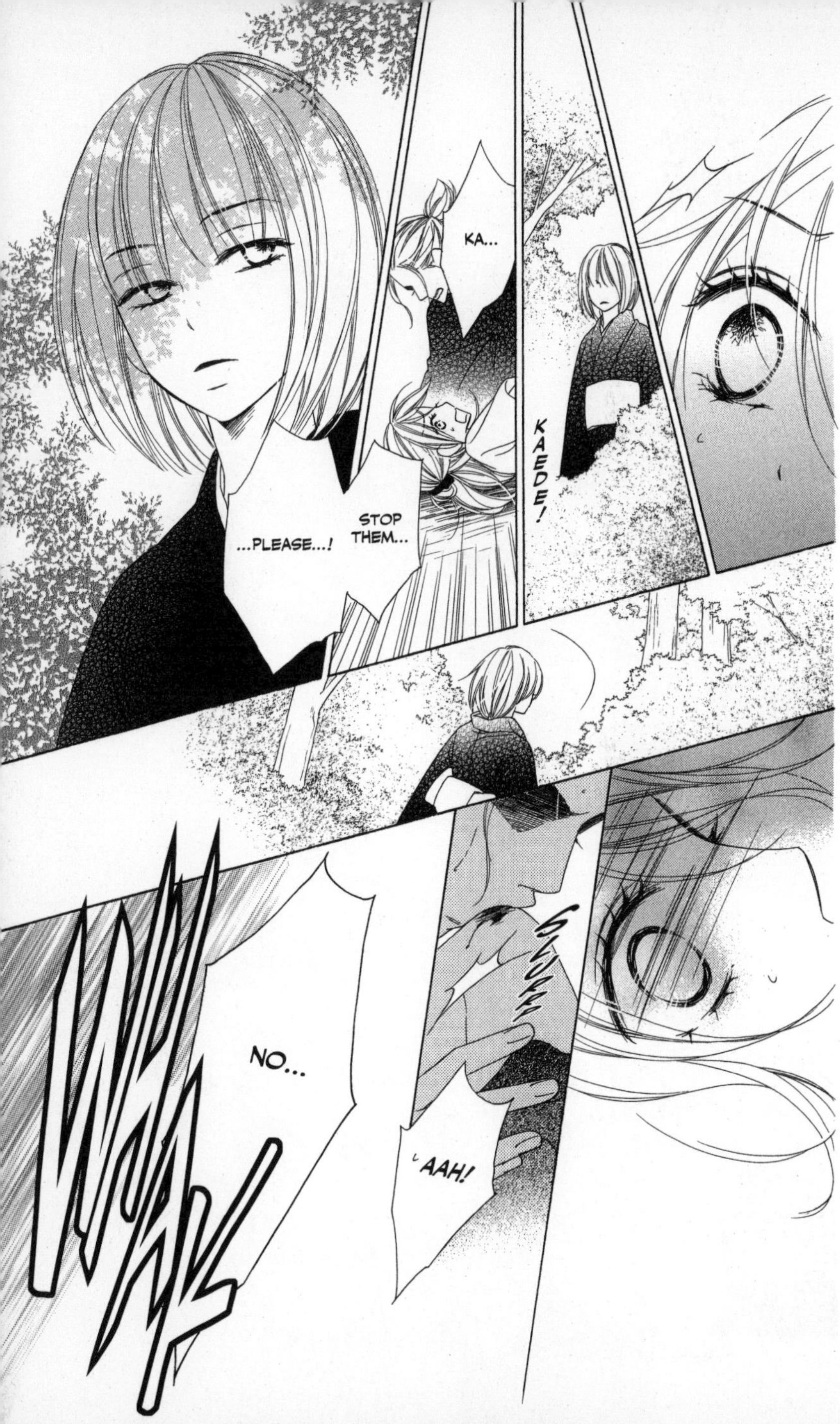
KAEDE!
KA...
STOP THEM...
...PLEASE...!
'AAH!
NO...

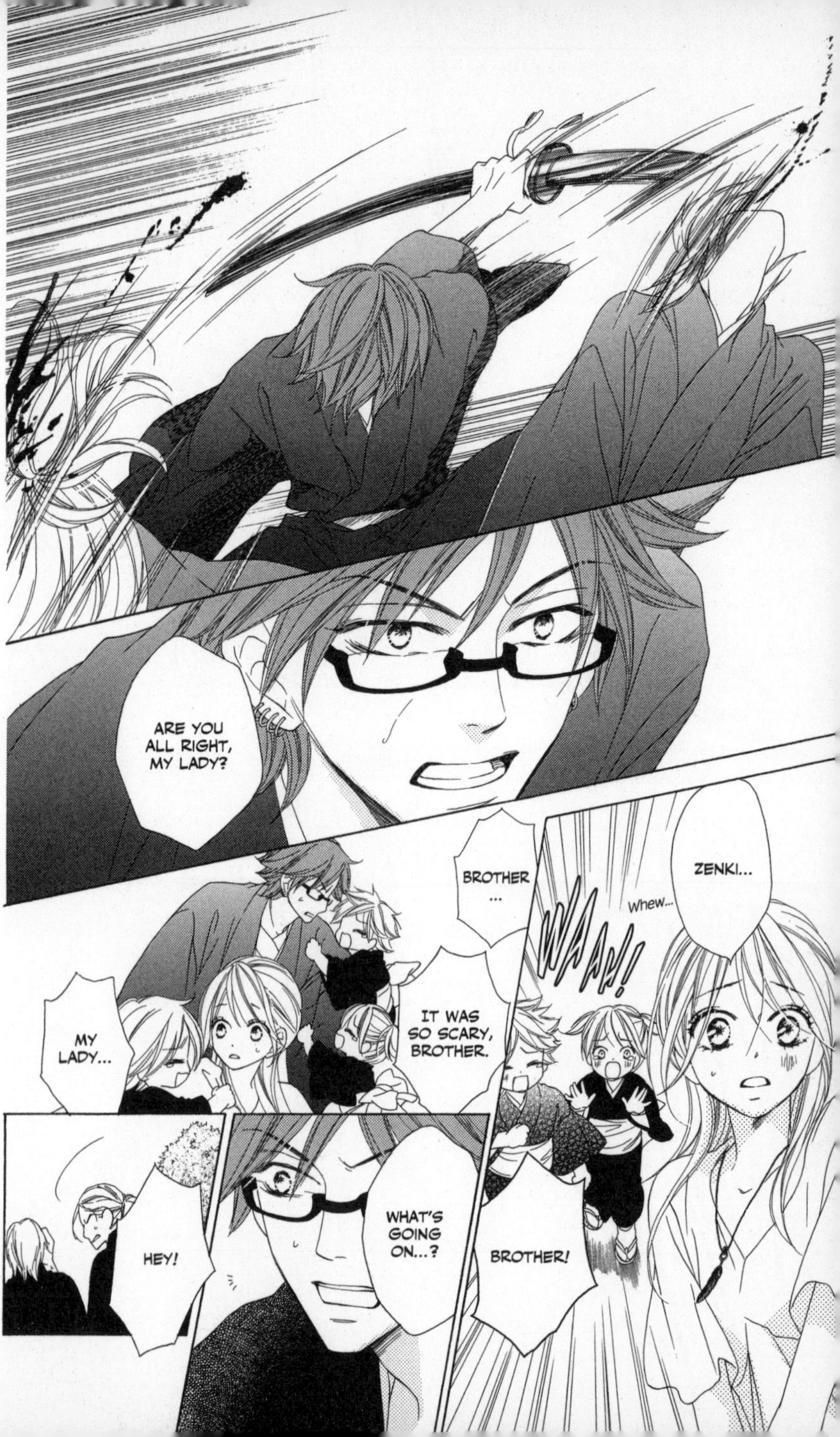
ARE YOU ALL RIGHT, MY LADY?
ZENKI...
Whew...
WAAH!
BROTHER!
BROTHER ...
IT WAS SO SCARY, BROTHER.
MY LADY...
WHAT'S GOING ON...?
HEY!

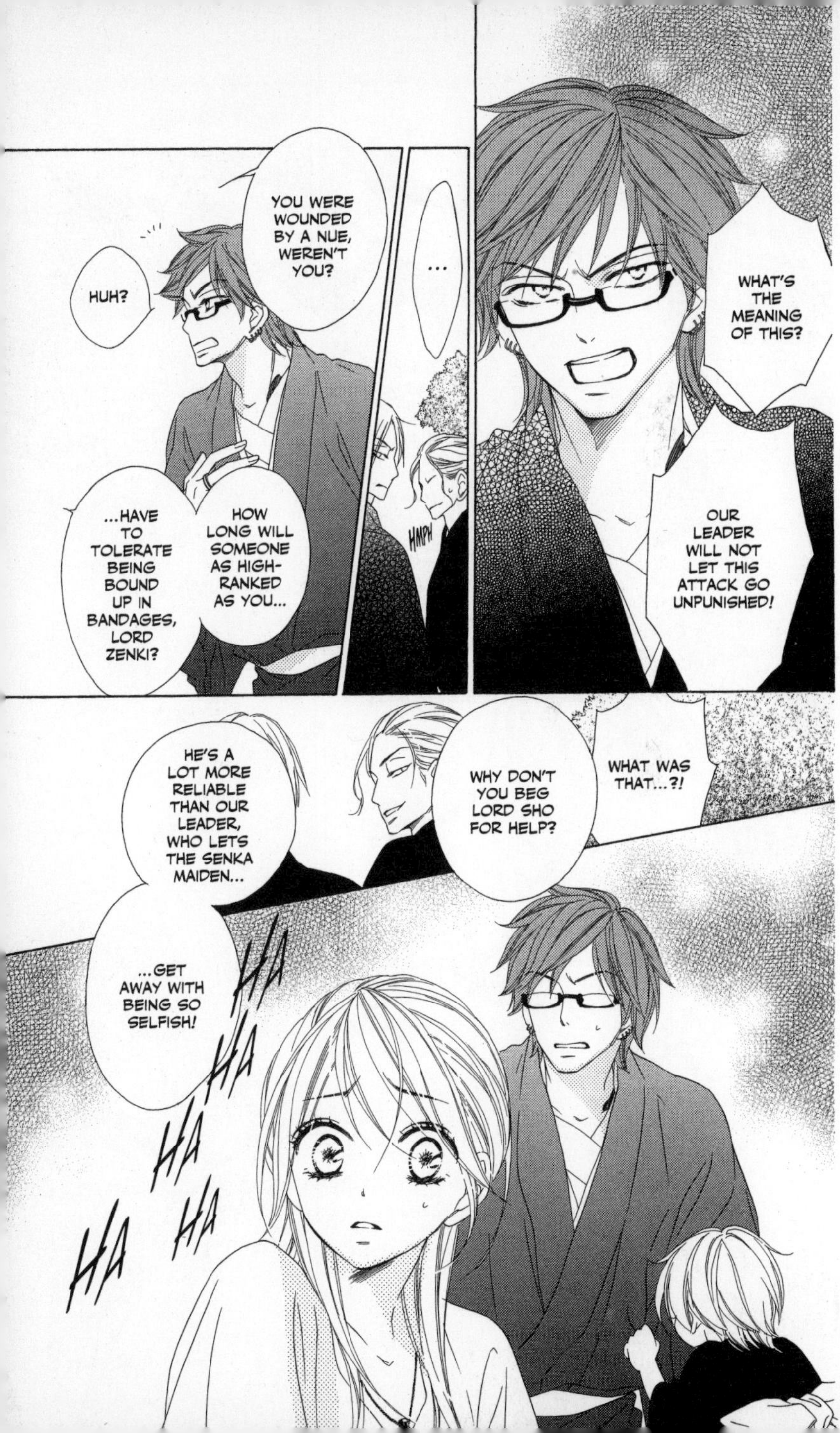
WHAT'S THE MEANING OF THIS?
OUR LEADER WILL NOT LET THIS ATTACK GO UNPUNISHED!
...
HMPH
YOU WERE WOUNDED BY A NUE, WEREN'T YOU?
HUH?
HOW LONG WILL SOMEONE AS HIGH-RANKED AS YOU...
...HAVE TO TOLERATE BEING BOUND UP IN BANDAGES, LORD ZENKI?
WHAT WAS THAT...?!
WHY DON'T YOU BEG LORD SHO FOR HELP?
HE'S A LOT MORE RELIABLE THAN OUR LEADER, WHO LETS THE SENKA MAIDEN...
...GET AWAY WITH BEING SO SELFISH!
HA HA HA HA HA HA HA

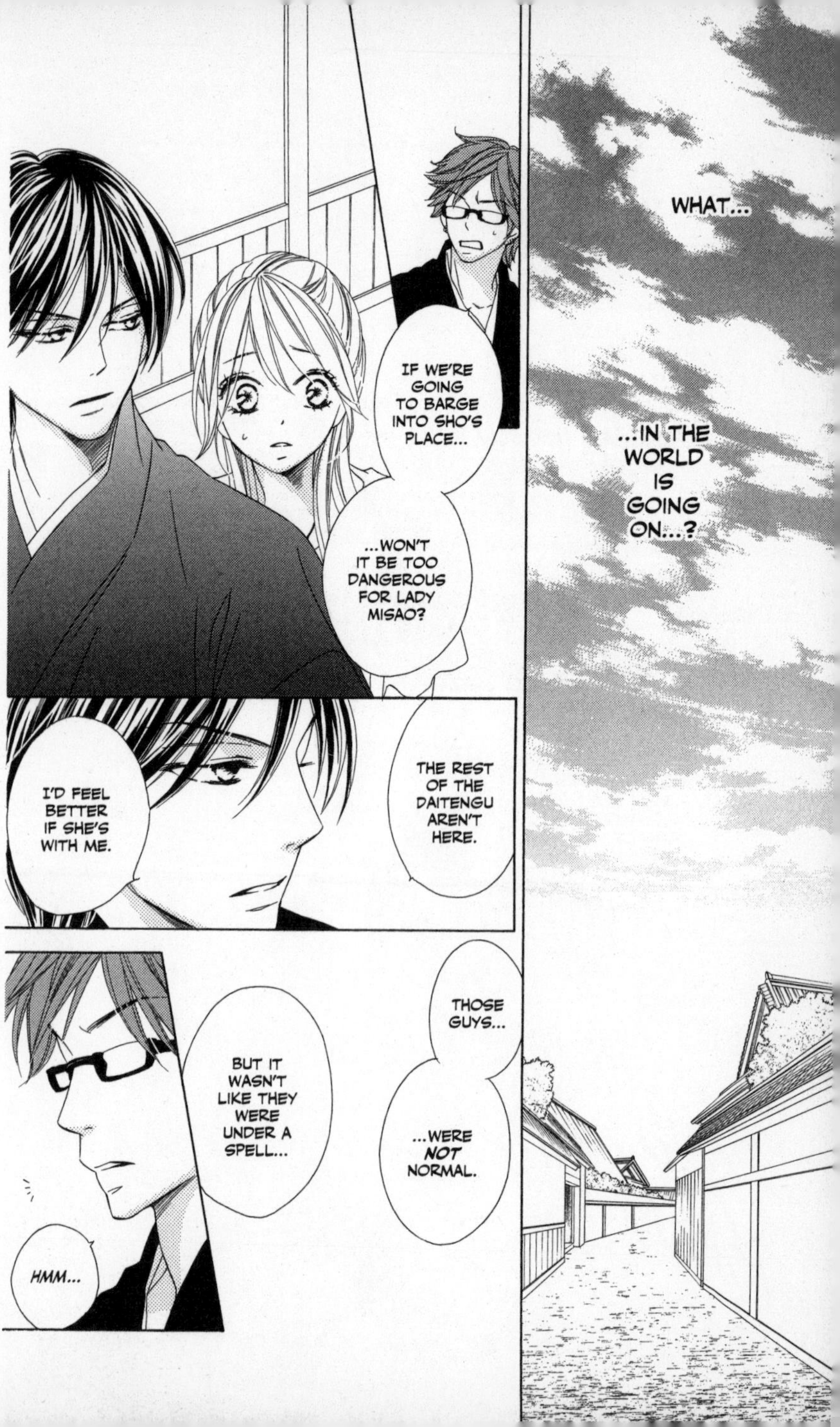
WHAT...
...IN THE WORLD IS GOING ON...?
IF WE'RE GOING TO BARGE INTO SHO'S PLACE...
...WON'T IT BE TOO DANGEROUS FOR LADY MISAO?
THE REST OF THE DAITENGU AREN'T HERE.
I'D FEEL BETTER IF SHE'S WITH ME.
THOSE GUYS...
...WERE *NOT* NORMAL.
BUT IT WASN'T LIKE THEY WERE UNDER A SPELL...
HMM...

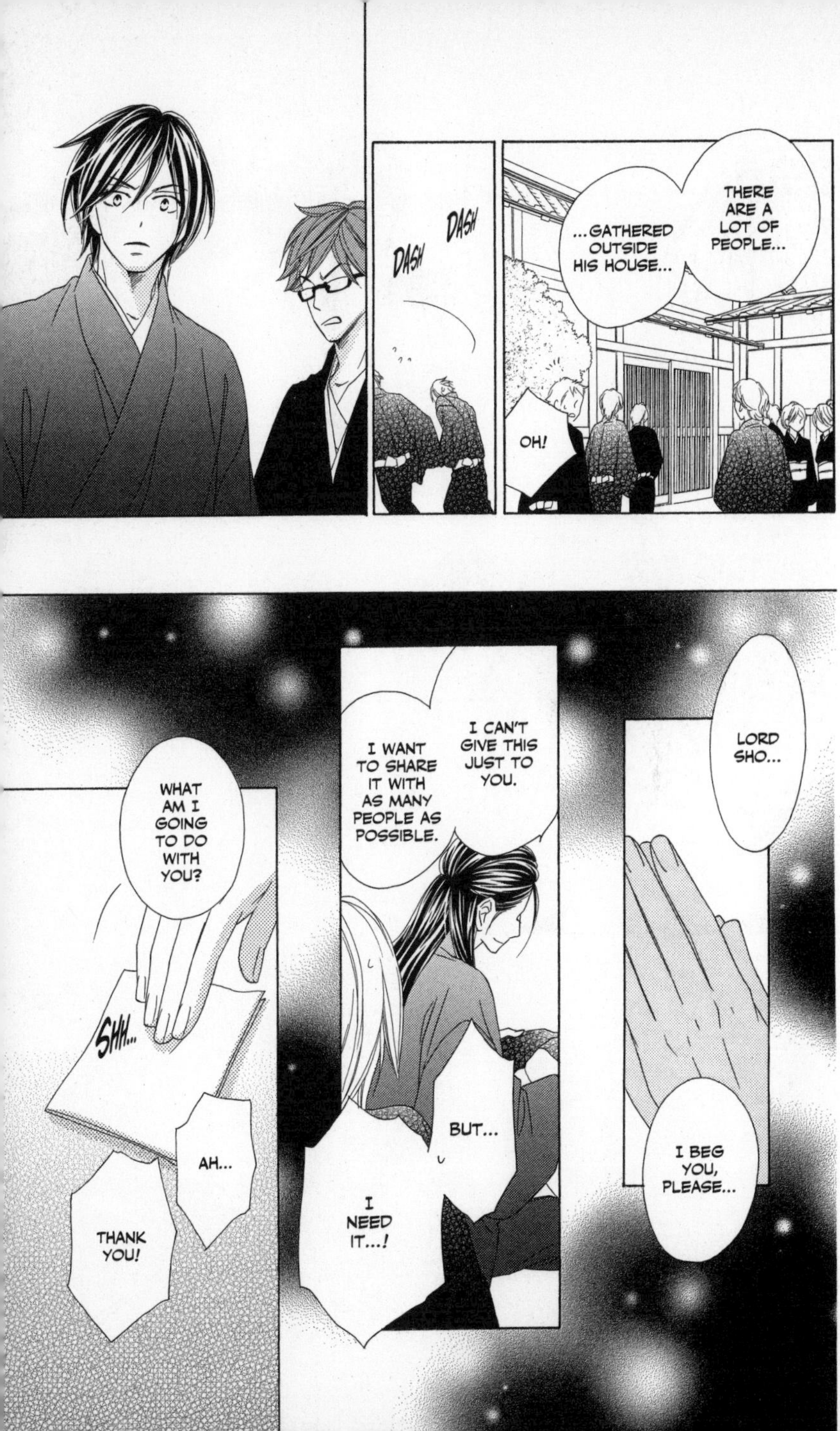

THERE ARE A LOT OF PEOPLE...
...GATHERED OUTSIDE HIS HOUSE...
OH!
DASH
DASH
LORD SHO...
I BEG YOU, PLEASE...
I CAN'T GIVE THIS JUST TO YOU.
I WANT TO SHARE IT WITH AS MANY PEOPLE AS POSSIBLE.
BUT...
I NEED IT...!
WHAT AM I GOING TO DO WITH YOU?
SHH...
AH...
THANK YOU!

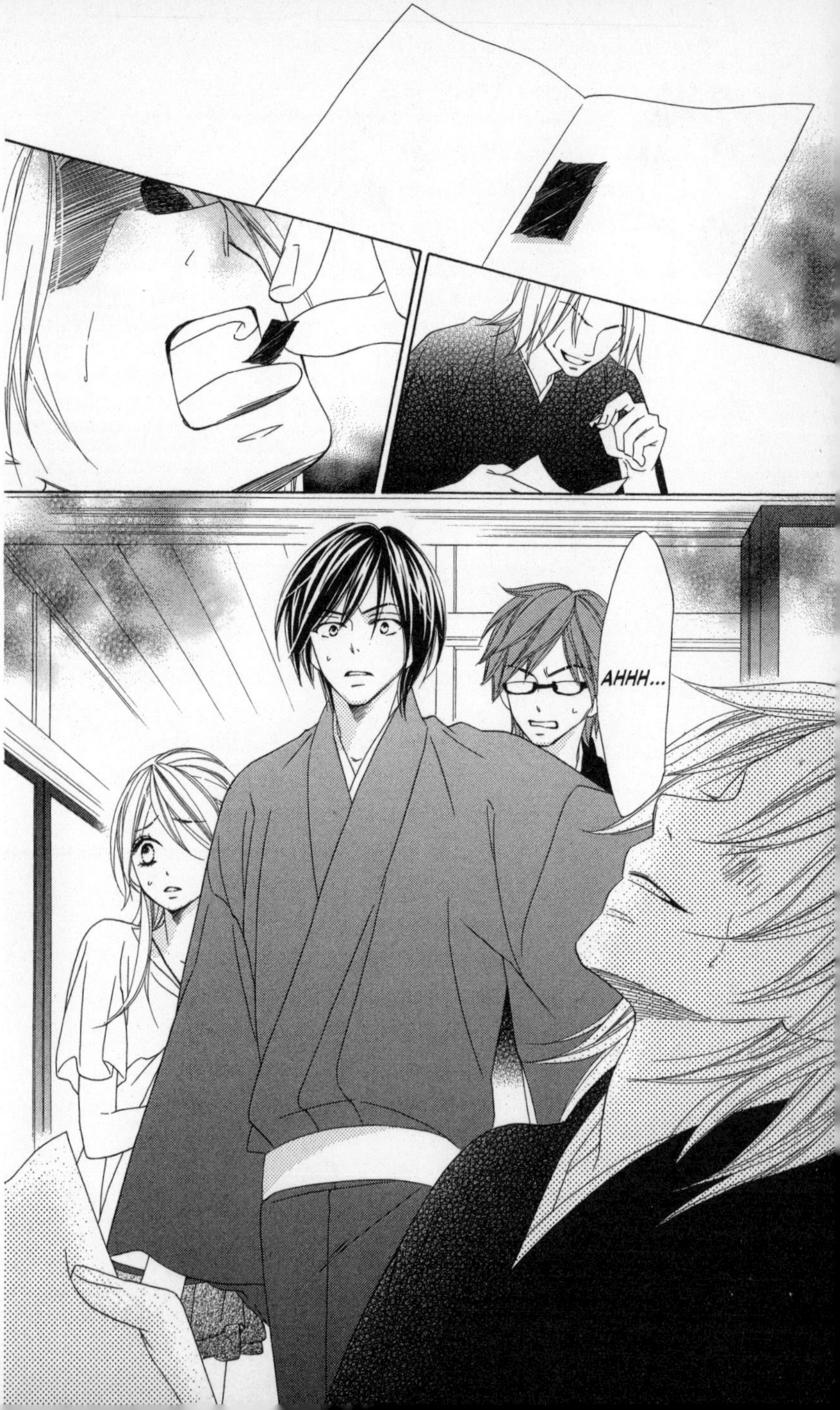
AHHH...

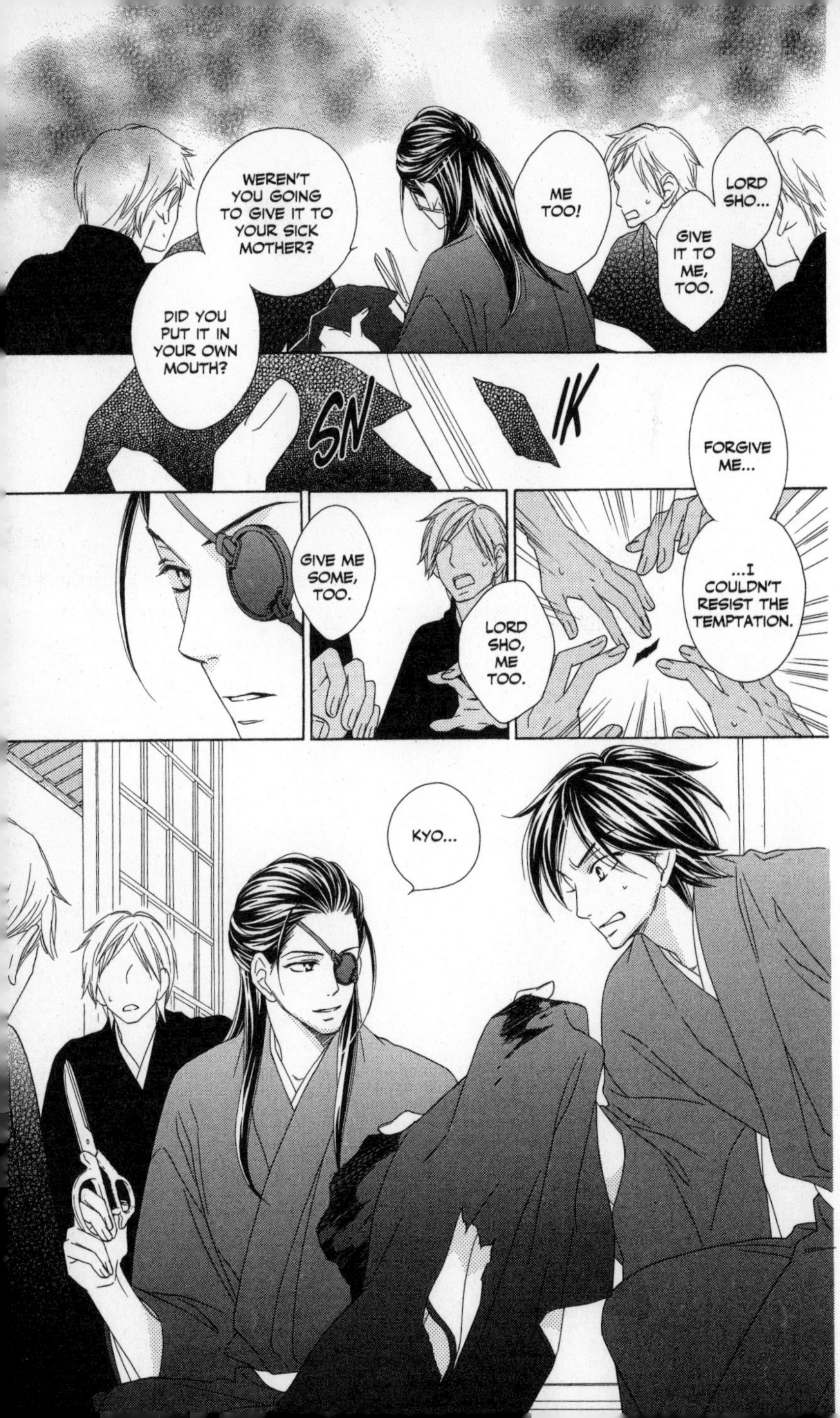

LORD SHO...
GIVE IT TO ME, TOO.
ME TOO!
WEREN'T YOU GOING TO GIVE IT TO YOUR SICK MOTHER?
DID YOU PUT IT IN YOUR OWN MOUTH?
SNIK
FORGIVE ME...
...I COULDN'T RESIST THE TEMPTATION.
GIVE ME SOME, TOO.
LORD SHO, ME TOO.
KYO...

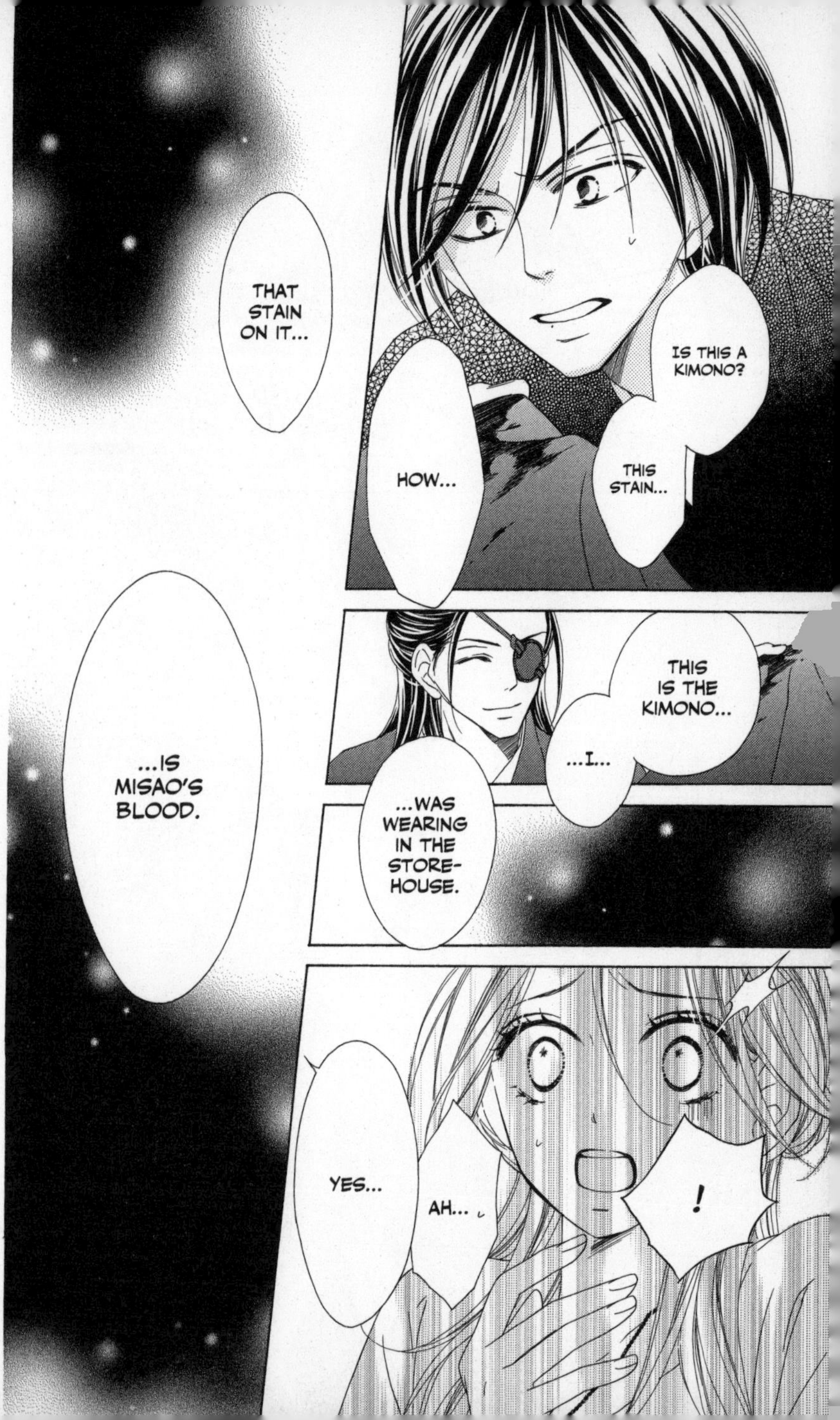
IS THIS A KIMONO?
THIS STAIN...
HOW...
THIS IS THE KIMONO...
...I...
...WAS WEARING IN THE STORE-HOUSE.
!
AH...
YES...
THAT STAIN ON IT...
...IS MISAO'S BLOOD.

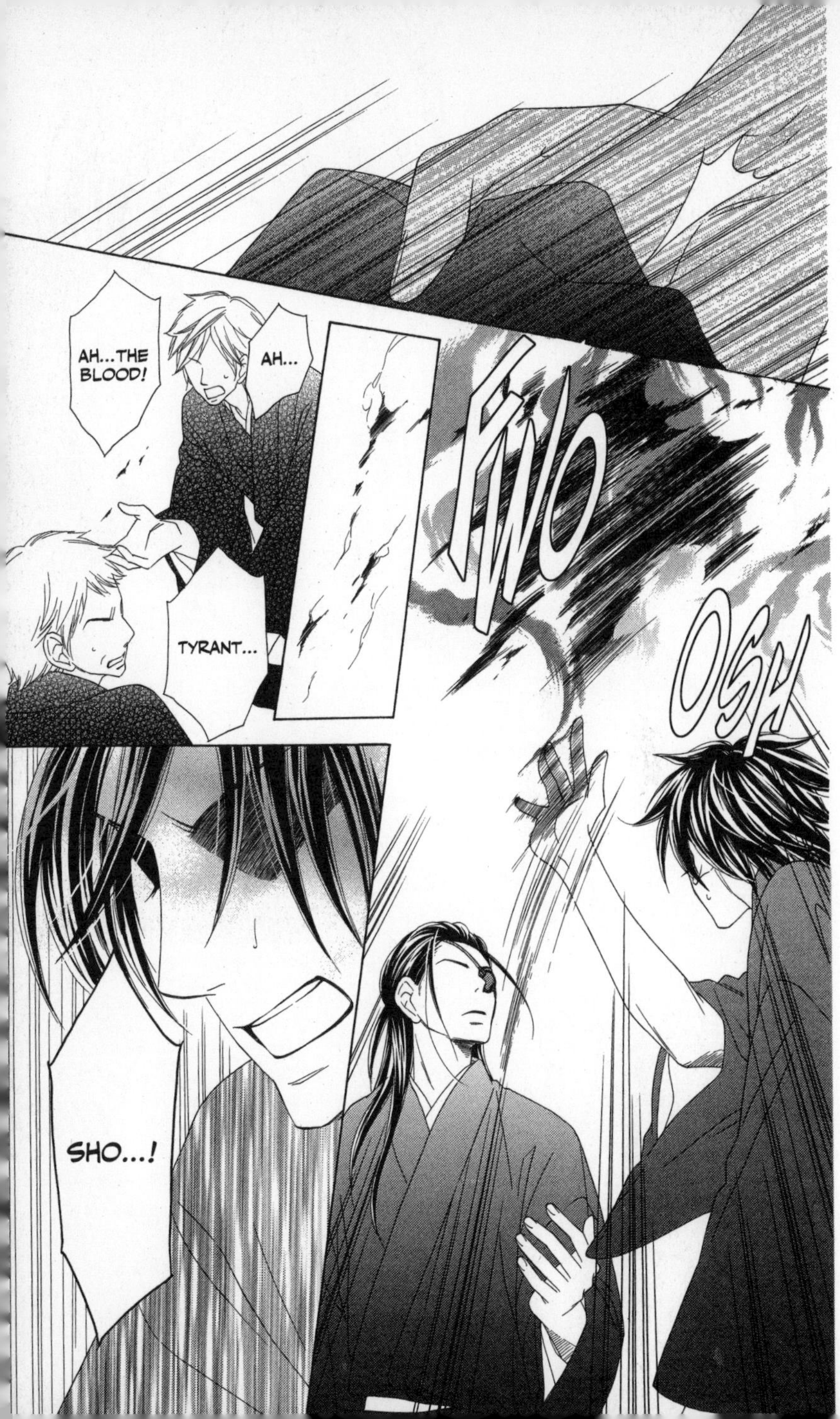
FWOOSH
AH...
AH...THE BLOOD!
TYRANT...
SHO...!

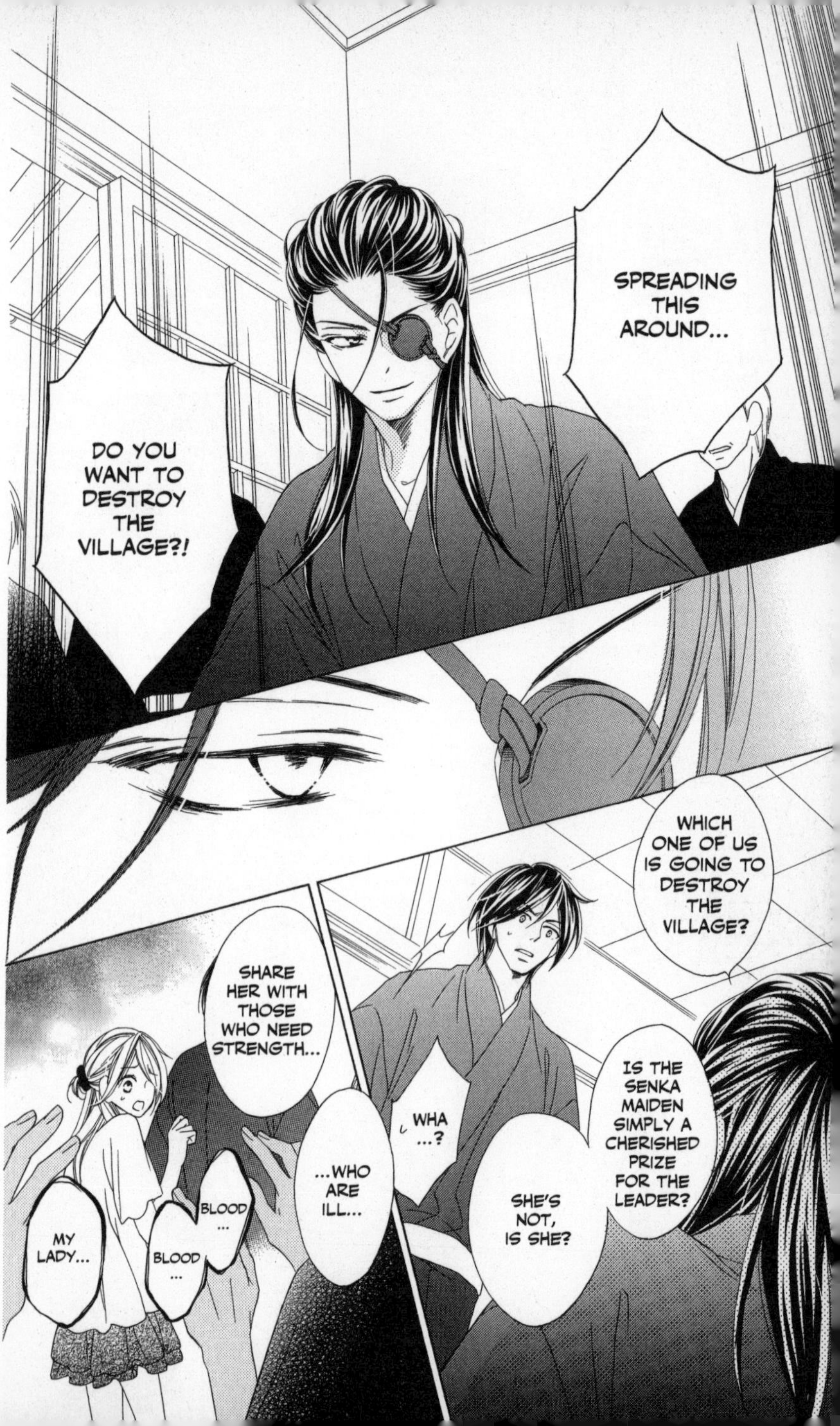
SPREADING THIS AROUND...
DO YOU WANT TO DESTROY THE VILLAGE?!
WHICH ONE OF US IS GOING TO DESTROY THE VILLAGE?
IS THE SENKA MAIDEN SIMPLY A CHERISHED PRIZE FOR THE LEADER?
SHE'S NOT, IS SHE?
WHA ...?
SHARE HER WITH THOSE WHO NEED STRENGTH...
...WHO ARE ILL...
BLOOD ...
BLOOD ...
MY LADY...

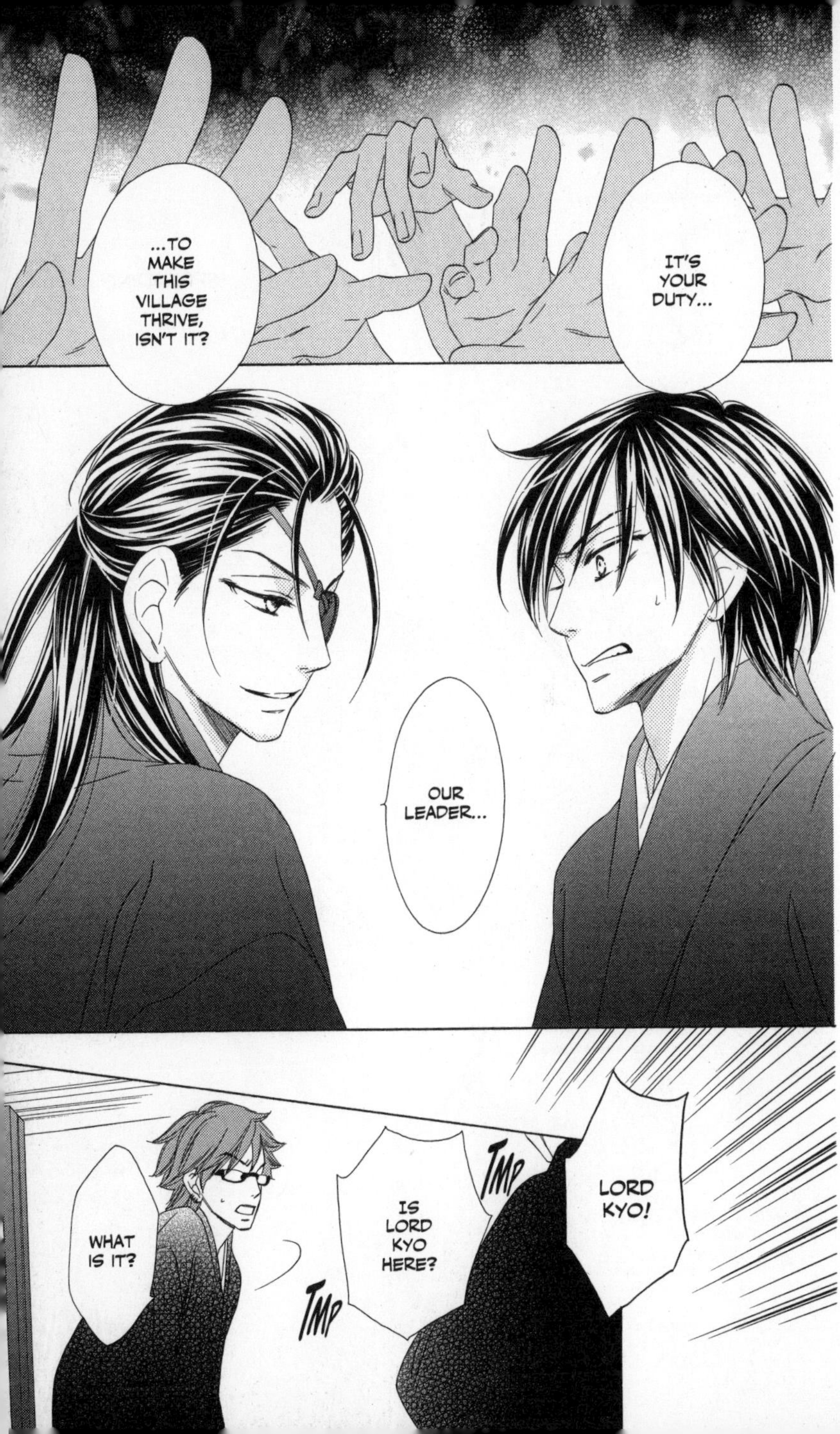
IT'S YOUR DUTY...
...TO MAKE THIS VILLAGE THRIVE, ISN'T IT?
OUR LEADER...
LORD KYO!
TMP
IS LORD KYO HERE?
TMP
WHAT IS IT?

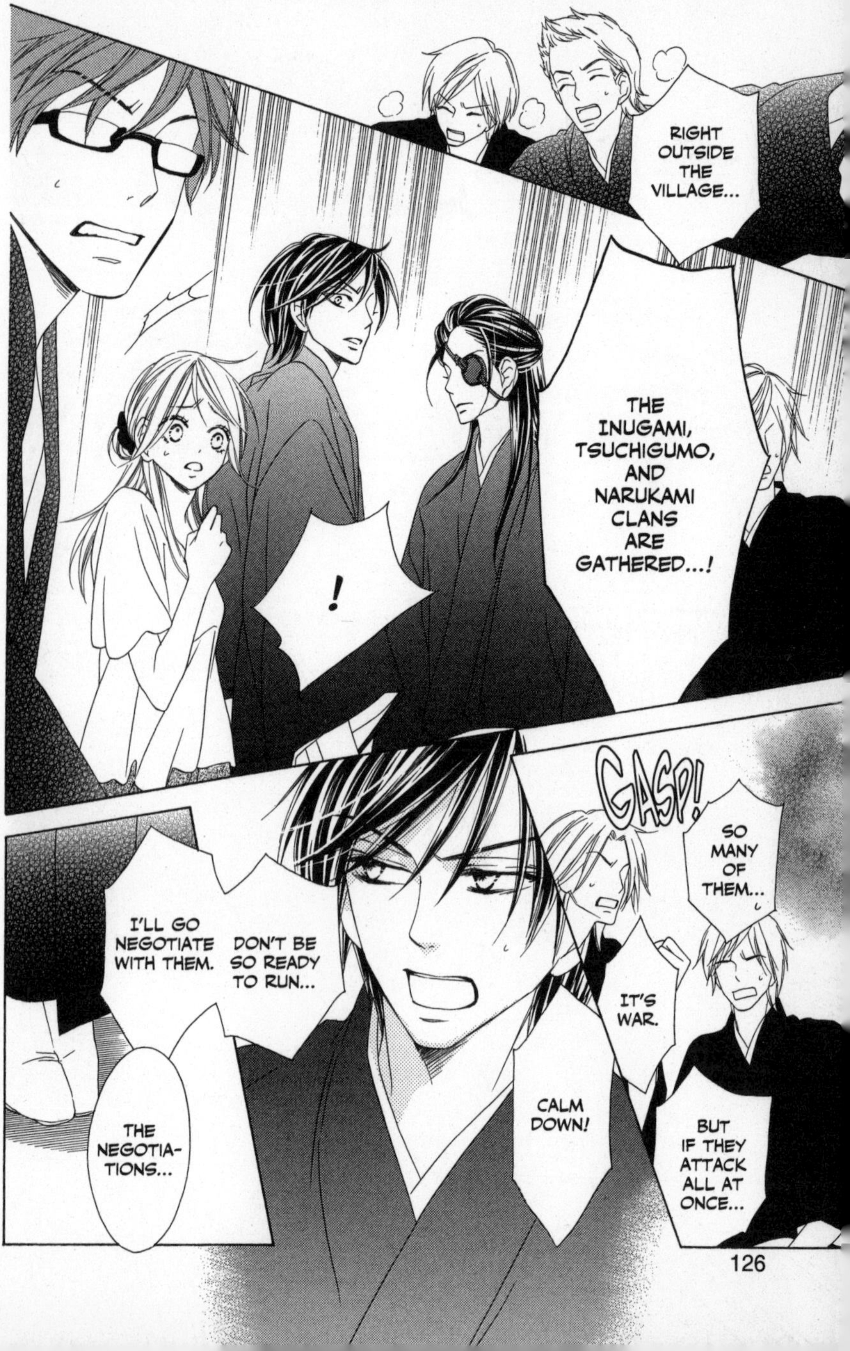
RIGHT OUTSIDE THE VILLAGE...
THE INUGAMI, TSUCHIGUMO, AND NARUKAMI CLANS ARE GATHERED...!
!
GASP!
SO MANY OF THEM...
IT'S WAR.
BUT IF THEY ATTACK ALL AT ONCE...
CALM DOWN!
DON'T BE SO READY TO RUN...
I'LL GO NEGOTIATE WITH THEM.
THE NEGOTIATIONS...

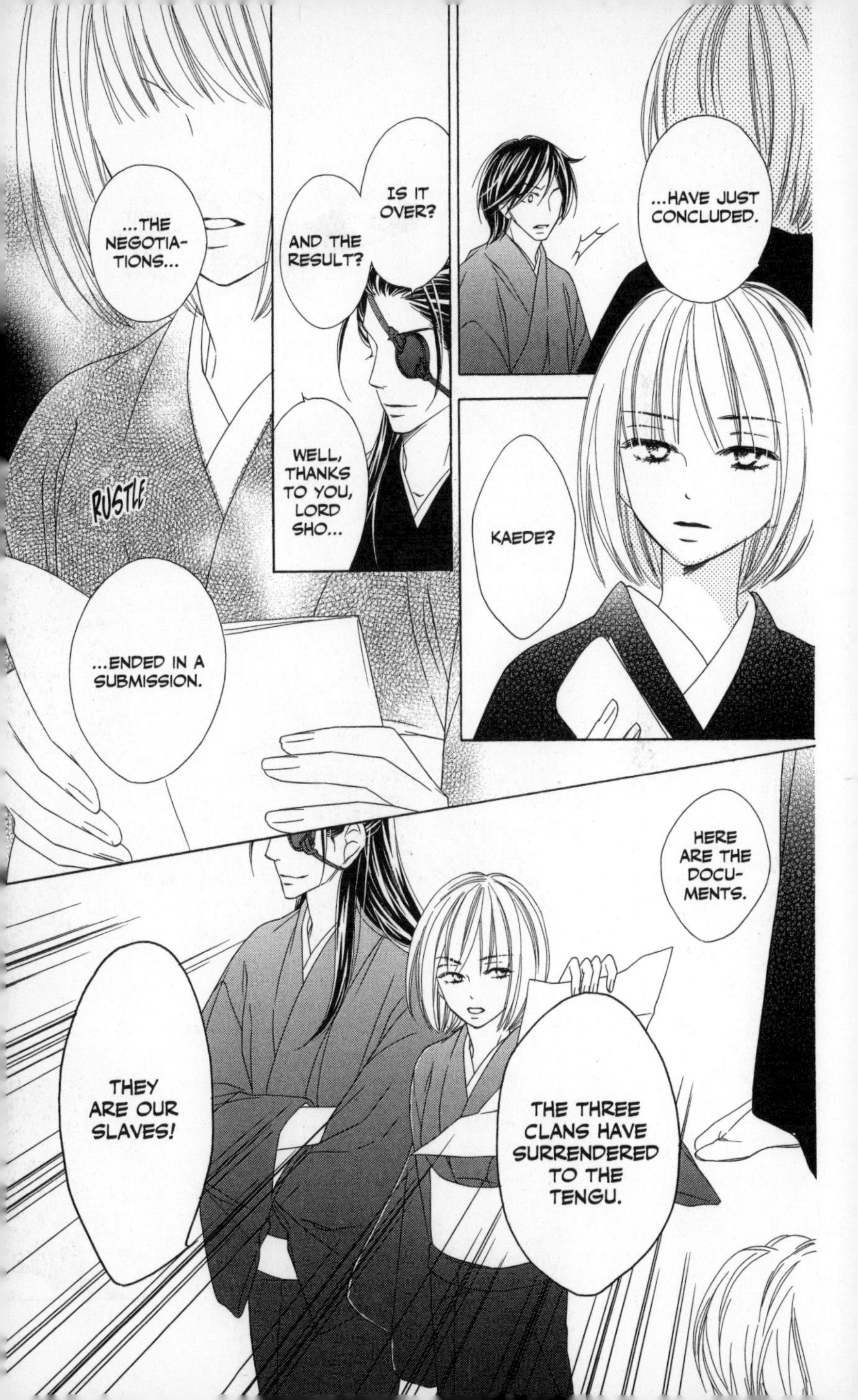
...HAVE JUST CONCLUDED.
KAEDE?
IS IT OVER?
AND THE RESULT?
WELL, THANKS TO YOU, LORD SHO...
...THE NEGOTIATIONS...
RUSTLE
...ENDED IN A SUBMISSION.
HERE ARE THE DOCUMENTS.
THE THREE CLANS HAVE SURRENDERED TO THE TENGU.
THEY ARE OUR SLAVES!

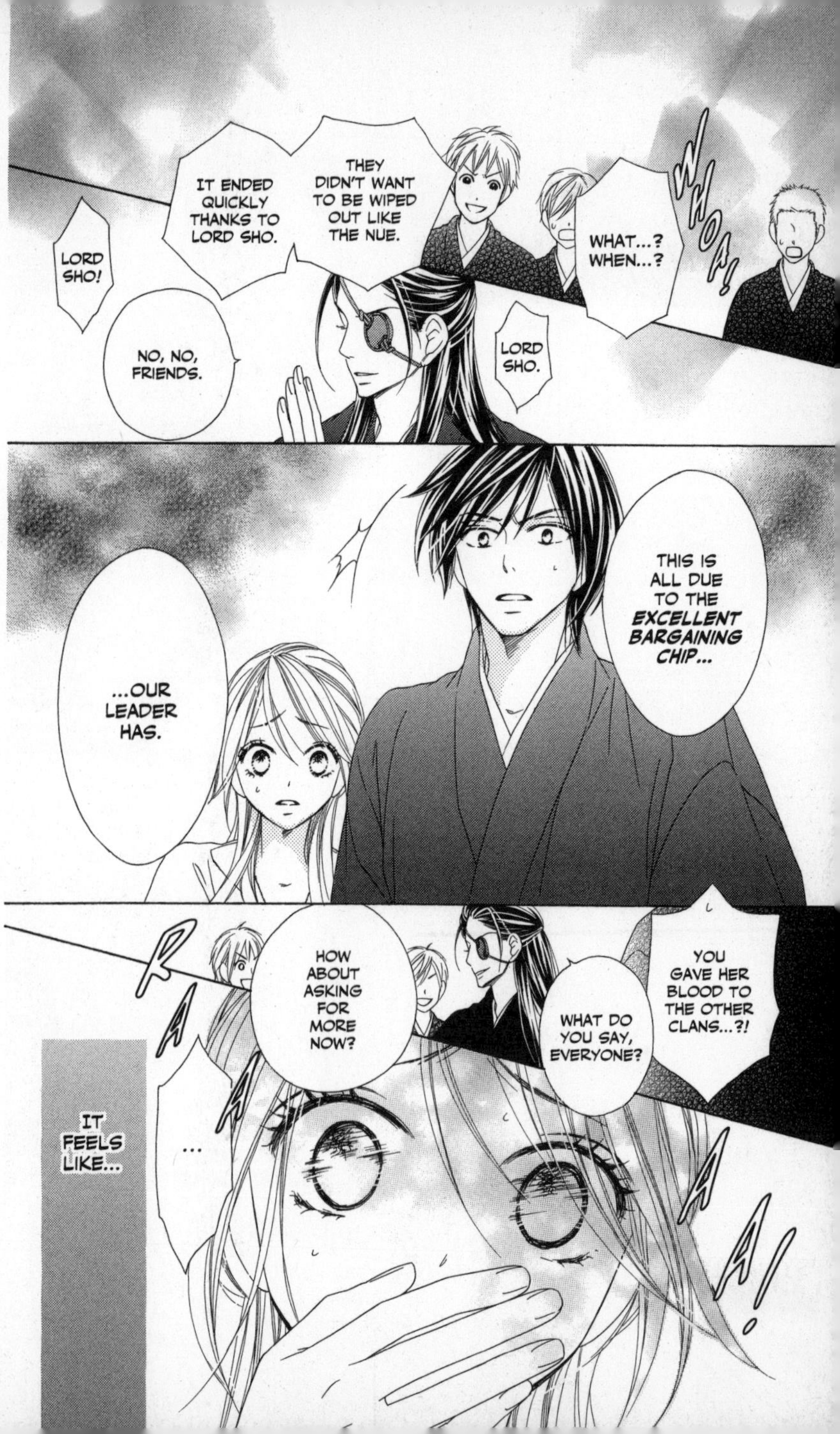
WHOA!
WHAT...? WHEN...?
LORD SHO.
THEY DIDN'T WANT TO BE WIPED OUT LIKE THE NUE.
IT ENDED QUICKLY THANKS TO LORD SHO.
LORD SHO!
NO, NO, FRIENDS.
THIS IS ALL DUE TO THE ***EXCELLENT BARGAINING CHIP...***
...OUR LEADER HAS.
YOU GAVE HER BLOOD TO THE OTHER CLANS...?!
WHAT DO YOU SAY, EVERYONE?
HOW ABOUT ASKING FOR MORE NOW?
RAAAAA!
...
IT FEELS LIKE...

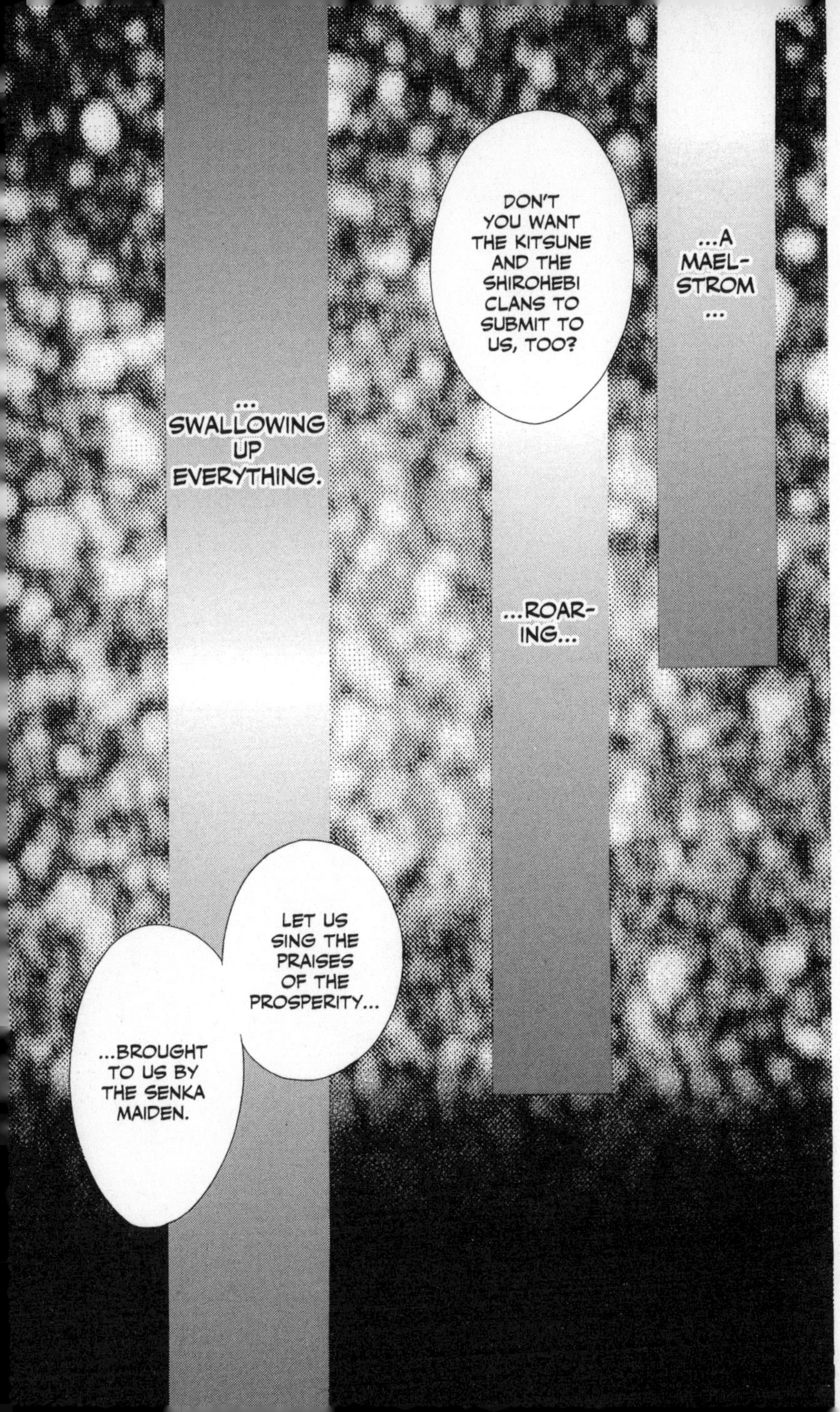
...A MAEL- STROM ...
DON'T YOU WANT THE KITSUNE AND THE SHIROHEBI CLANS TO SUBMIT TO US, TOO?
...ROAR- ING...
... SWALLOWING UP EVERYTHING.
LET US SING THE PRAISES OF THE PROSPERITY...
...BROUGHT TO US BY THE SENKA MAIDEN.

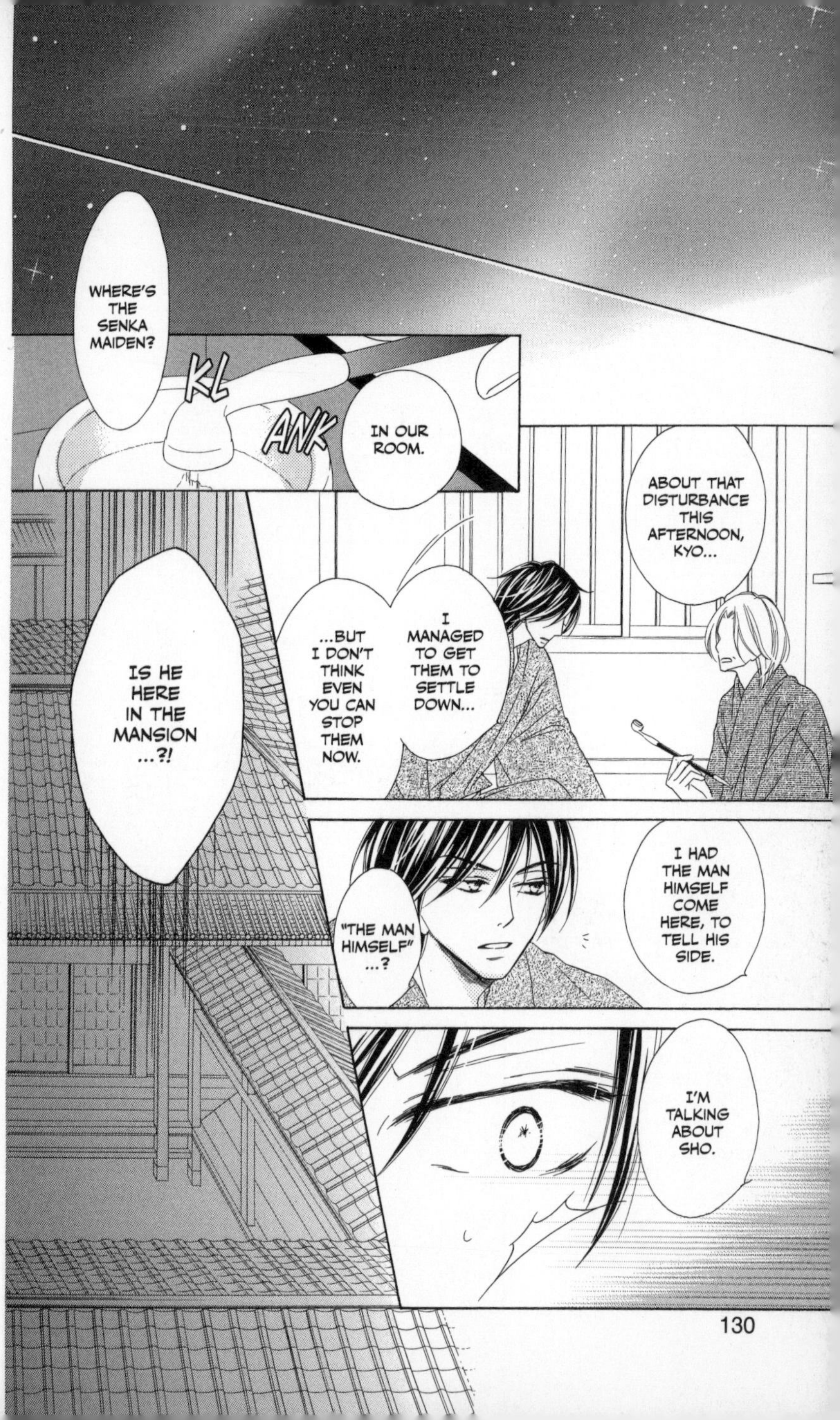
WHERE'S THE SENKA MAIDEN?
KLANK
IN OUR ROOM.
ABOUT THAT DISTURBANCE THIS AFTERNOON, KYO...
I MANAGED TO GET THEM TO SETTLE DOWN...
...BUT I DON'T THINK EVEN YOU CAN STOP THEM NOW.
I HAD THE MAN HIMSELF COME HERE, TO TELL HIS SIDE.
"THE MAN HIMSELF"...?
I'M TALKING ABOUT SHO.
IS HE HERE IN THE MANSION...?!

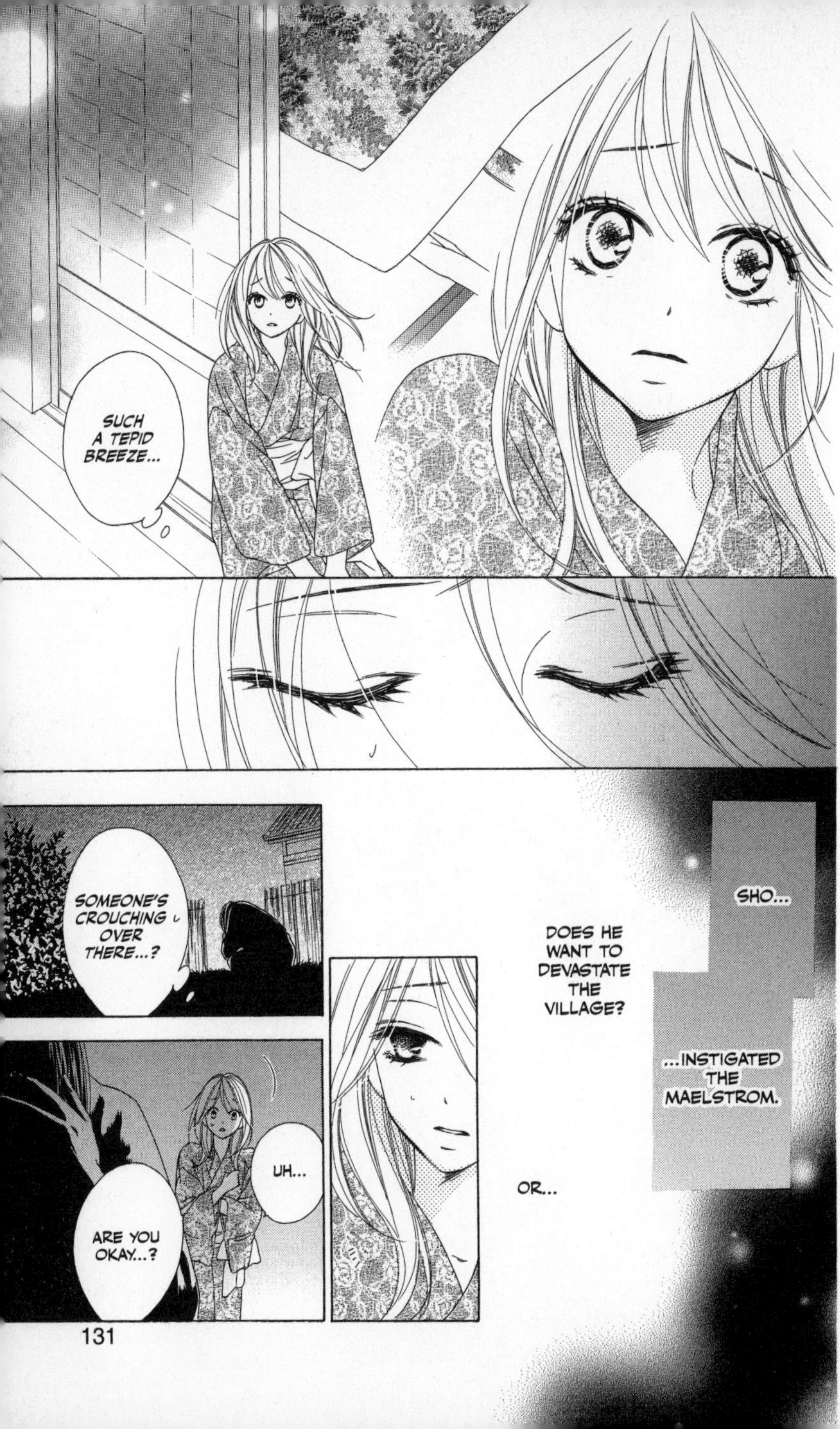
SUCH A TEPID BREEZE...
SHO...
...INSTIGATED THE MAELSTROM.
DOES HE WANT TO DEVASTATE THE VILLAGE?
OR...
SOMEONE'S CROUCHING OVER THERE...?
UH...
ARE YOU OKAY...?

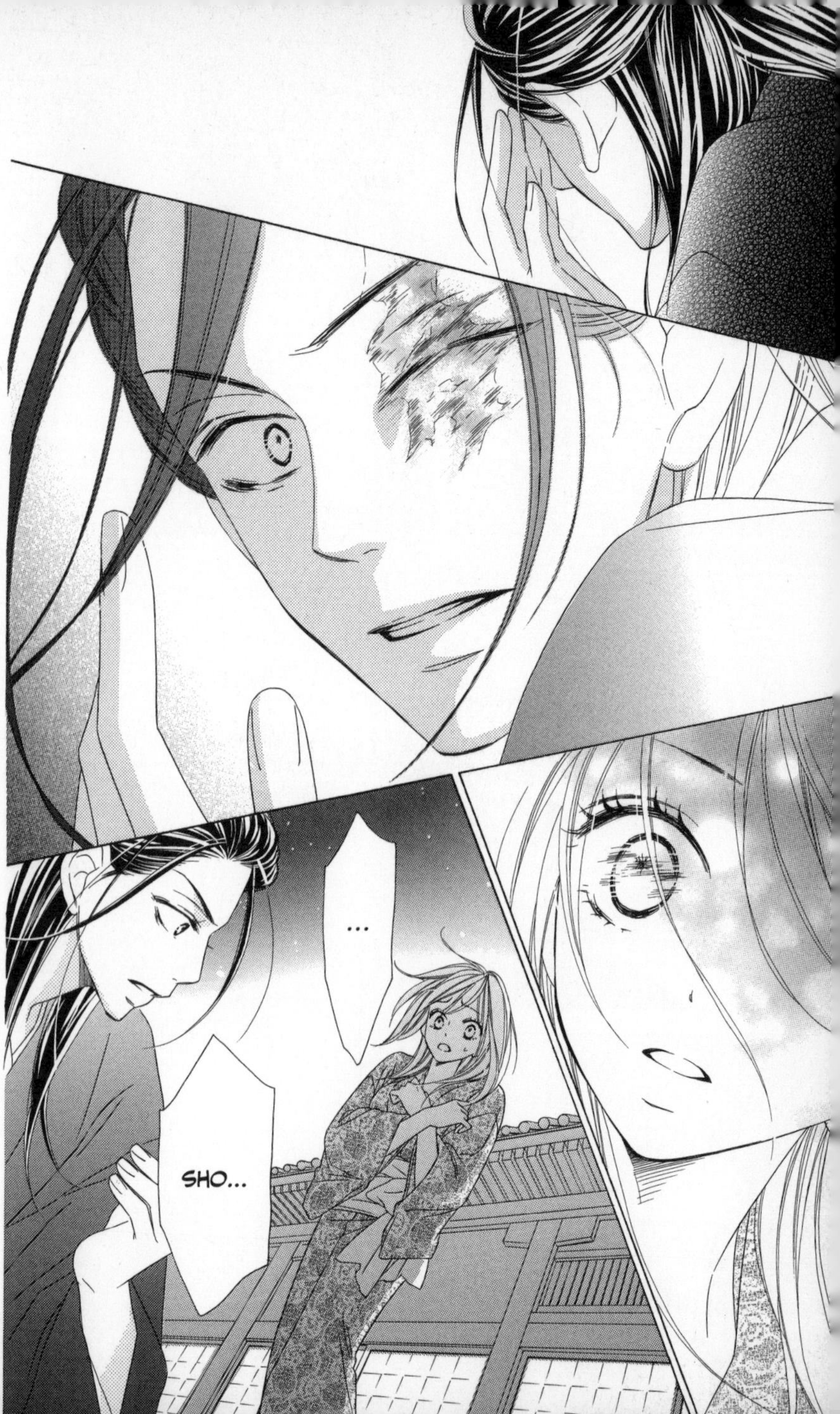
...
SHO...

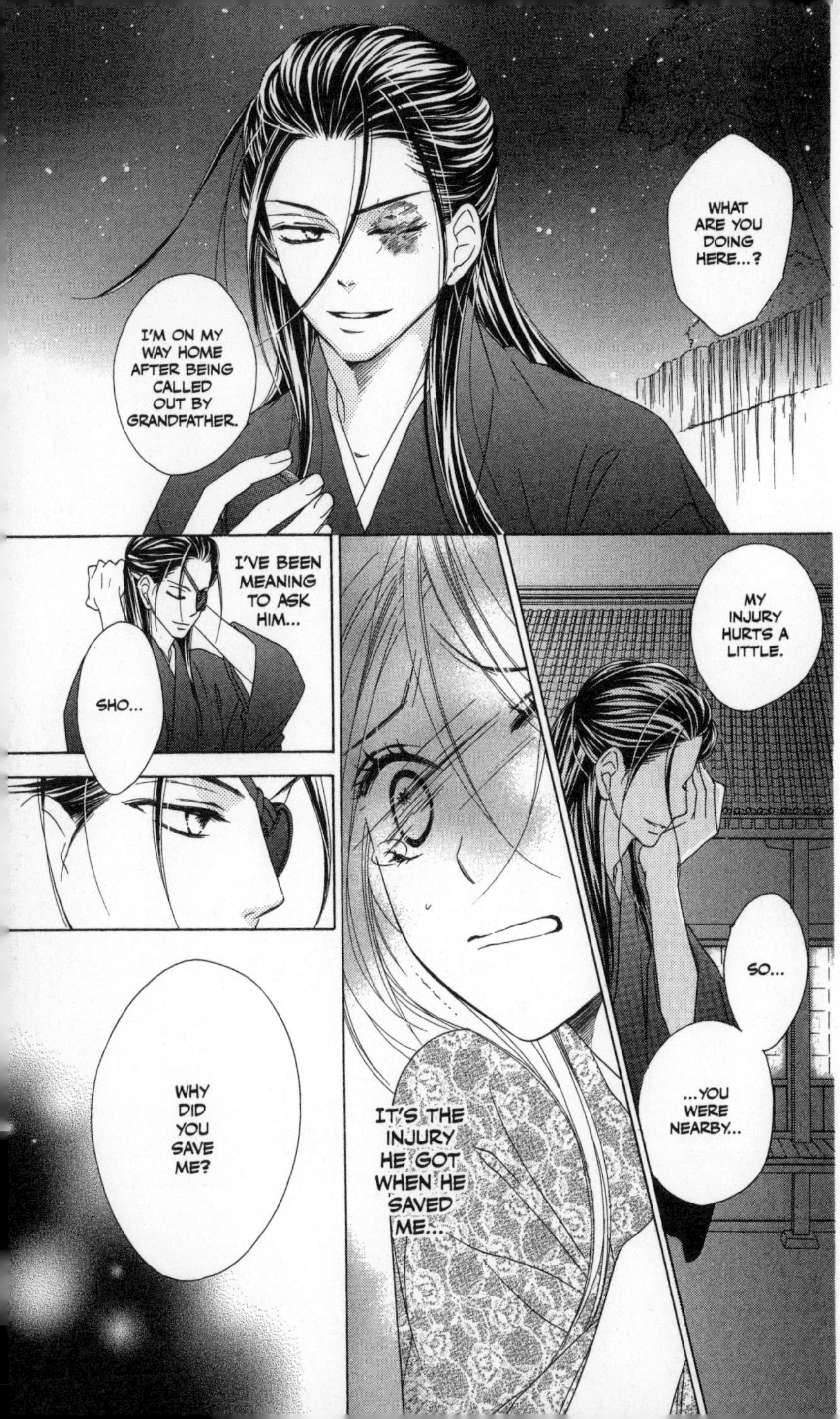
WHAT ARE YOU DOING HERE...?
I'M ON MY WAY HOME AFTER BEING CALLED OUT BY GRANDFATHER.
MY INJURY HURTS A LITTLE.
SO...
...YOU WERE NEARBY...
IT'S THE INJURY HE GOT WHEN HE SAVED ME...
I'VE BEEN MEANING TO ASK HIM...
SHO...
WHY DID YOU SAVE ME?

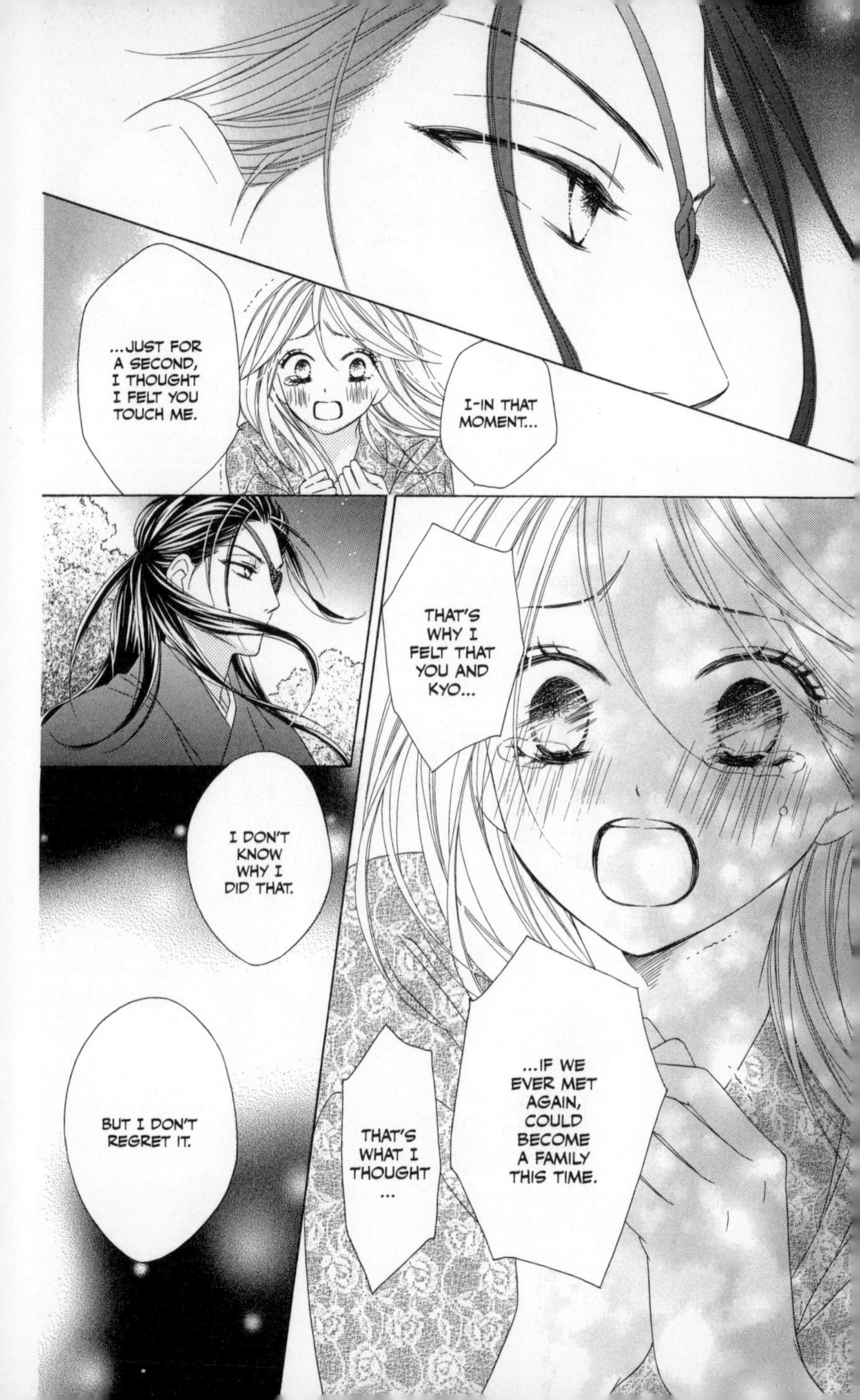
I-IN THAT MOMENT...
...JUST FOR A SECOND, I THOUGHT I FELT YOU TOUCH ME.
THAT'S WHY I FELT THAT YOU AND KYO...
...IF WE EVER MET AGAIN, COULD BECOME A FAMILY THIS TIME.
THAT'S WHAT I THOUGHT ...
I DON'T KNOW WHY I DID THAT.
BUT I DON'T REGRET IT.

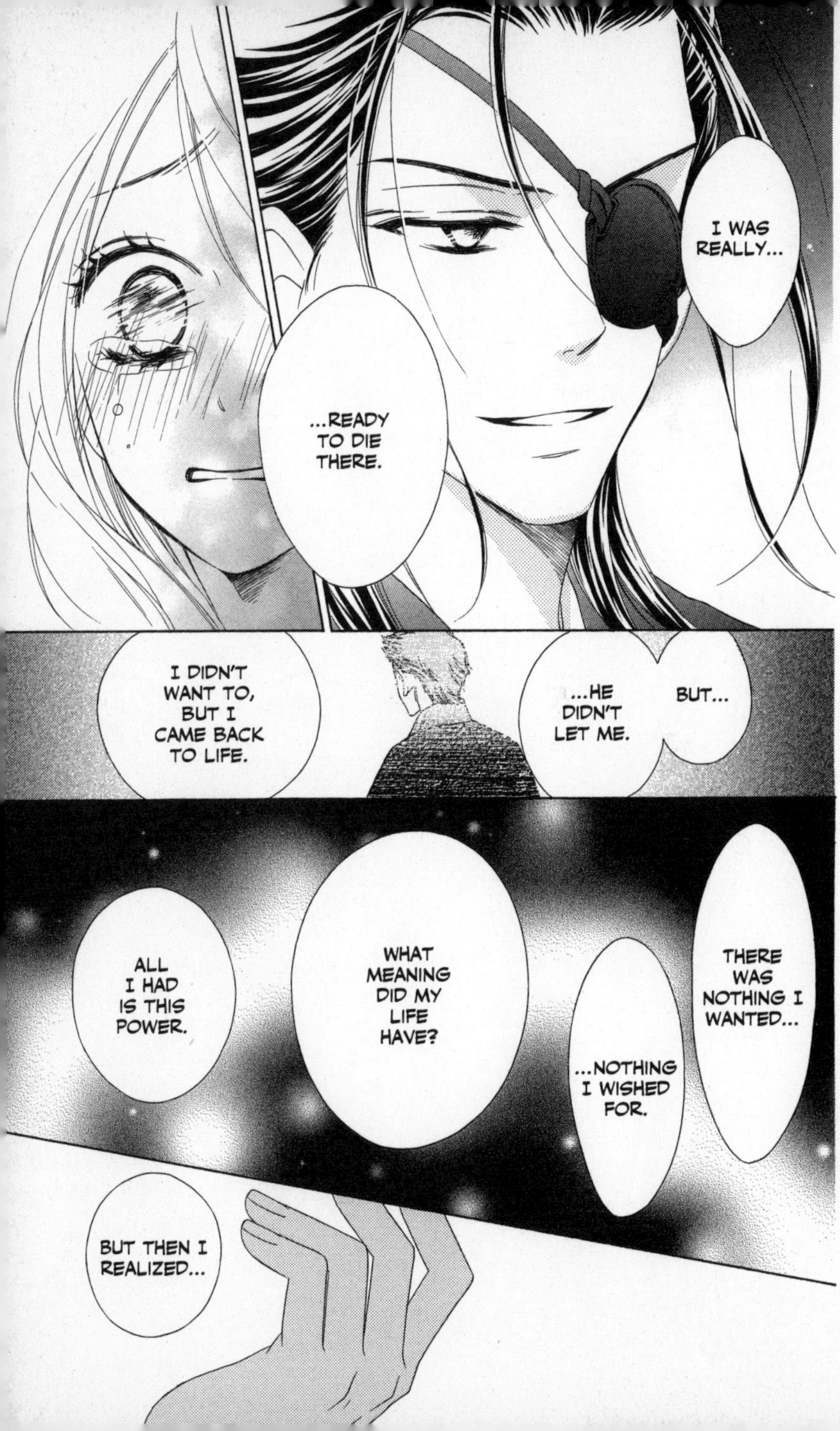
I WAS REALLY...
...READY TO DIE THERE.
BUT...
...HE DIDN'T LET ME.
I DIDN'T WANT TO, BUT I CAME BACK TO LIFE.
THERE WAS NOTHING I WANTED...
...NOTHING I WISHED FOR.
WHAT MEANING DID MY LIFE HAVE?
ALL I HAD IS THIS POWER.
BUT THEN I REALIZED...

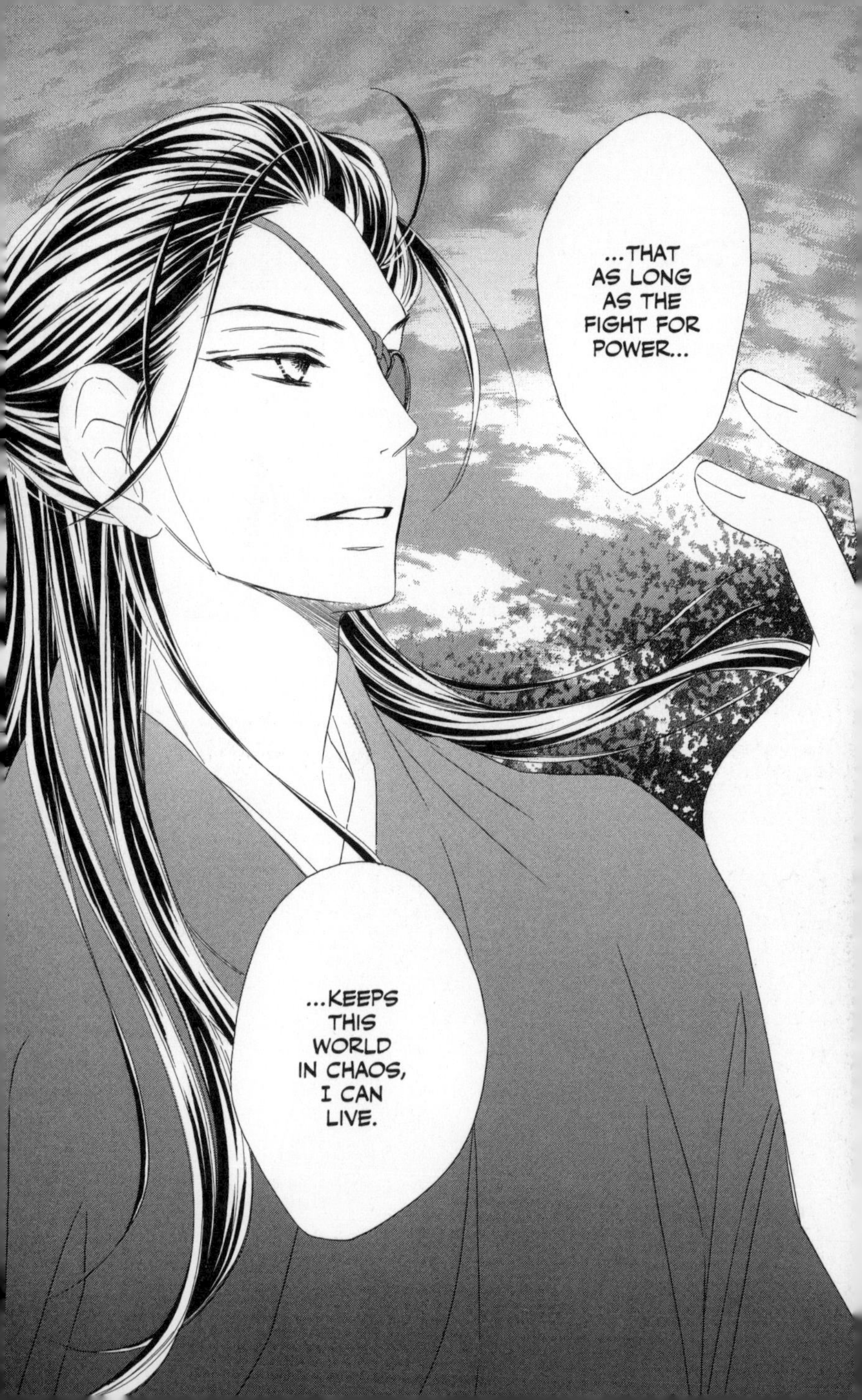
...THAT AS LONG AS THE FIGHT FOR POWER...
...KEEPS THIS WORLD IN CHAOS, I CAN LIVE.

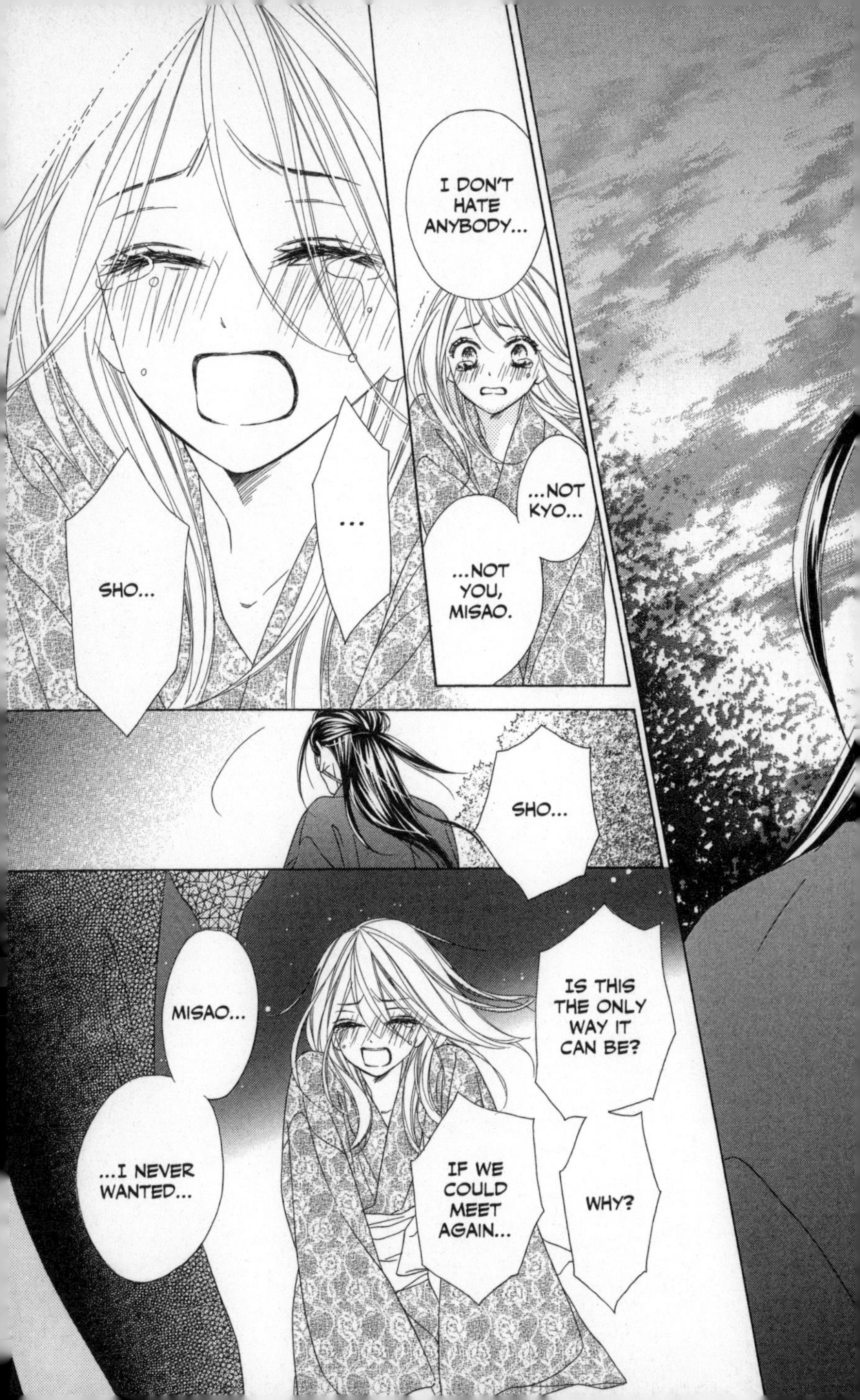
I DON'T HATE ANYBODY...
...NOT KYO...
...NOT YOU, MISAO.
...
SHO...
SHO...
IS THIS THE ONLY WAY IT CAN BE?
WHY?
IF WE COULD MEET AGAIN...
MISAO...
...I NEVER WANTED...

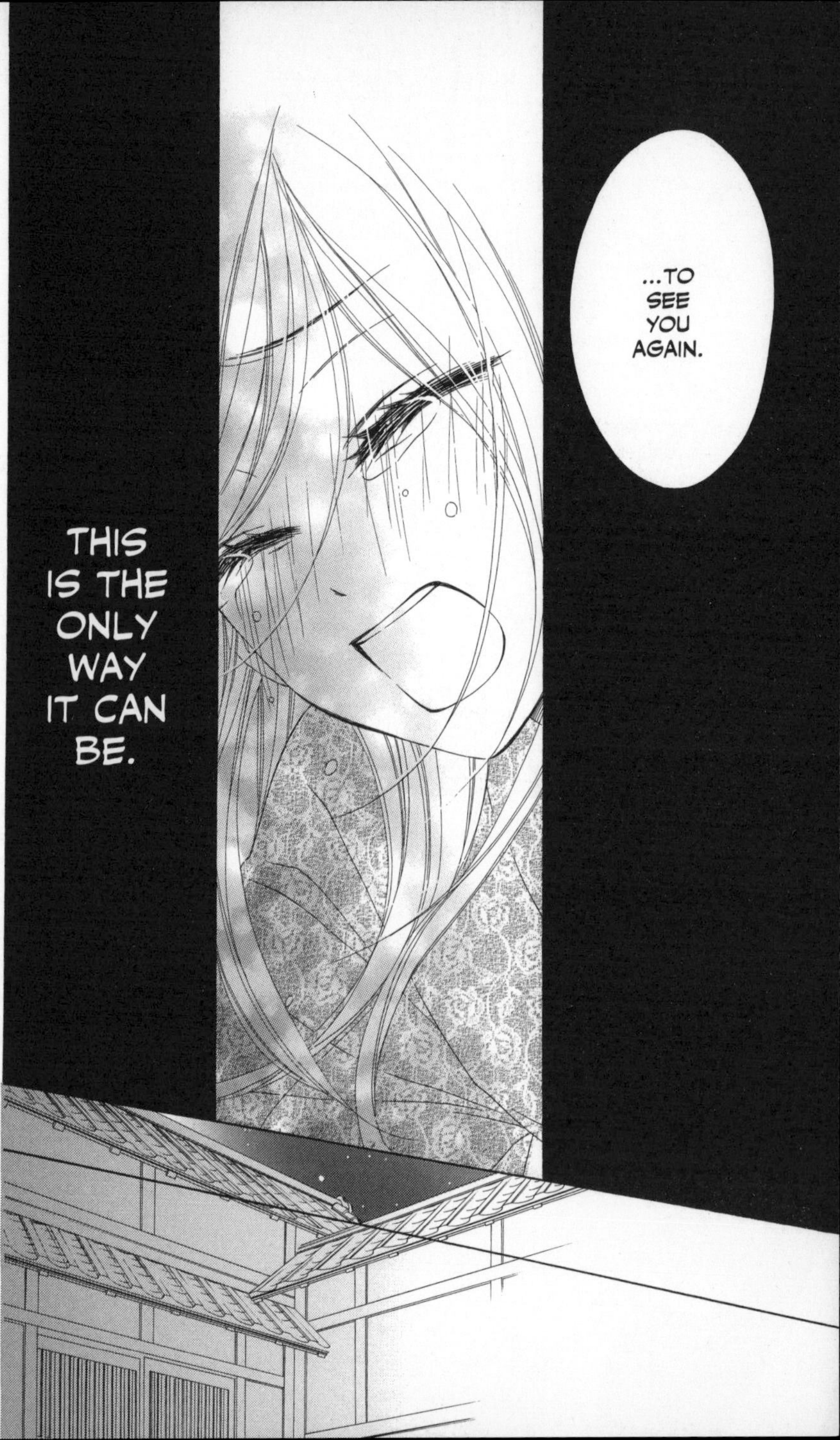
...TO SEE YOU AGAIN.
THIS IS THE ONLY WAY IT CAN BE.

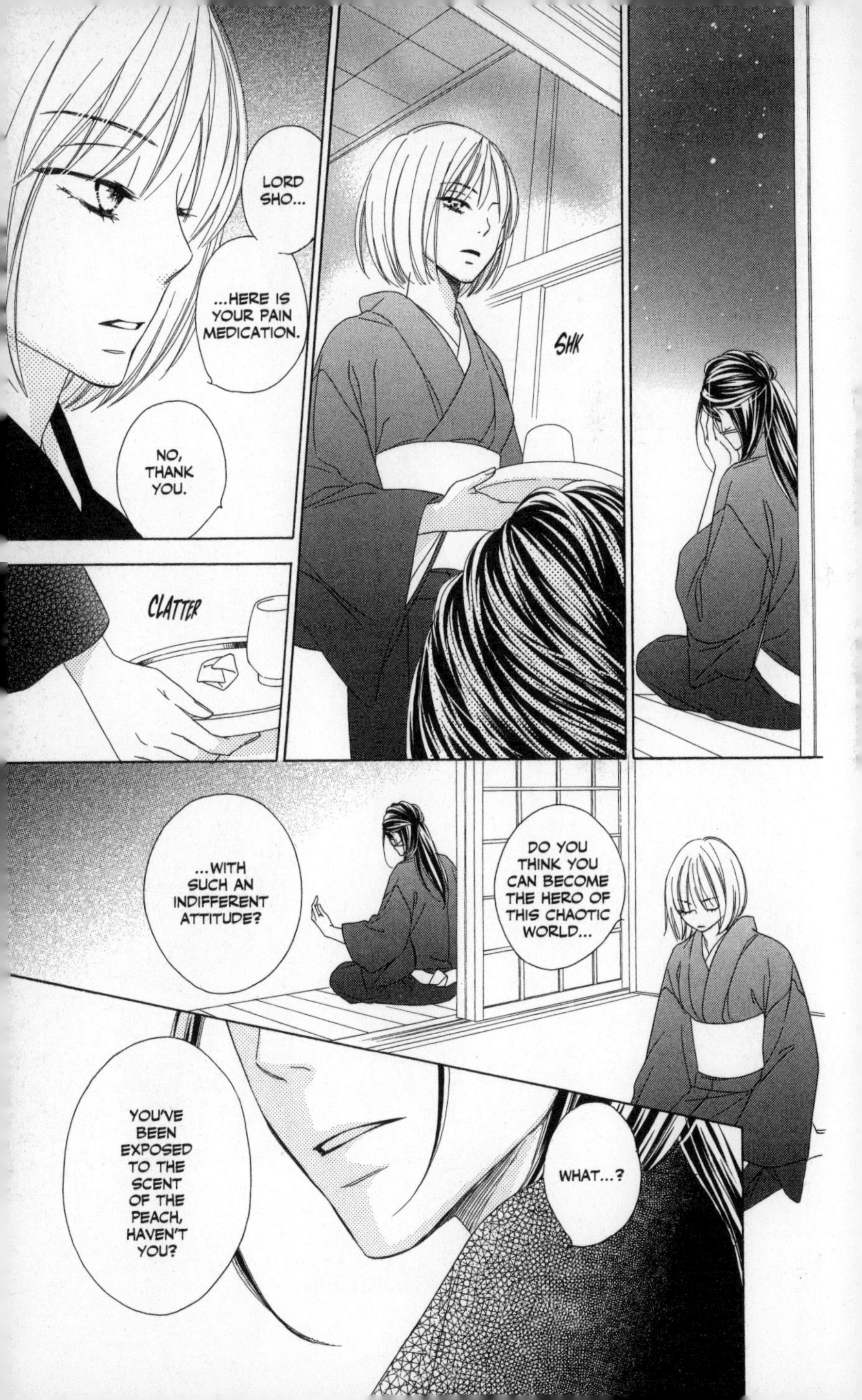
SHK
LORD SHO...
...HERE IS YOUR PAIN MEDICATION.
NO, THANK YOU.
CLATTER
DO YOU THINK YOU CAN BECOME THE HERO OF THIS CHAOTIC WORLD...
...WITH SUCH AN INDIFFERENT ATTITUDE?
WHAT...?
YOU'VE BEEN EXPOSED TO THE SCENT OF THE PEACH, HAVEN'T YOU?

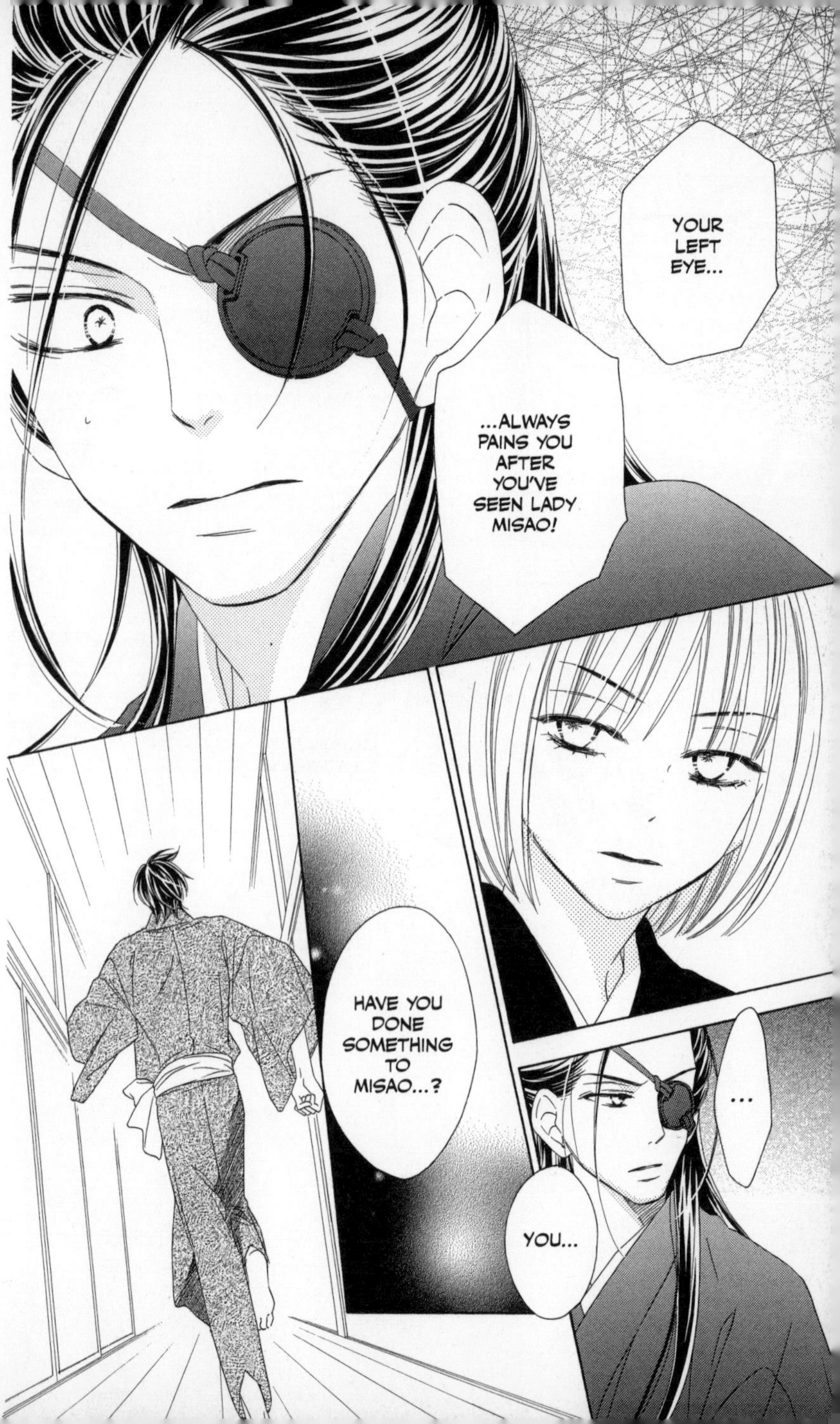
YOUR LEFT EYE...
...ALWAYS PAINS YOU AFTER YOU'VE SEEN LADY MISAO!
HAVE YOU DONE SOMETHING TO MISAO...?
...
YOU...

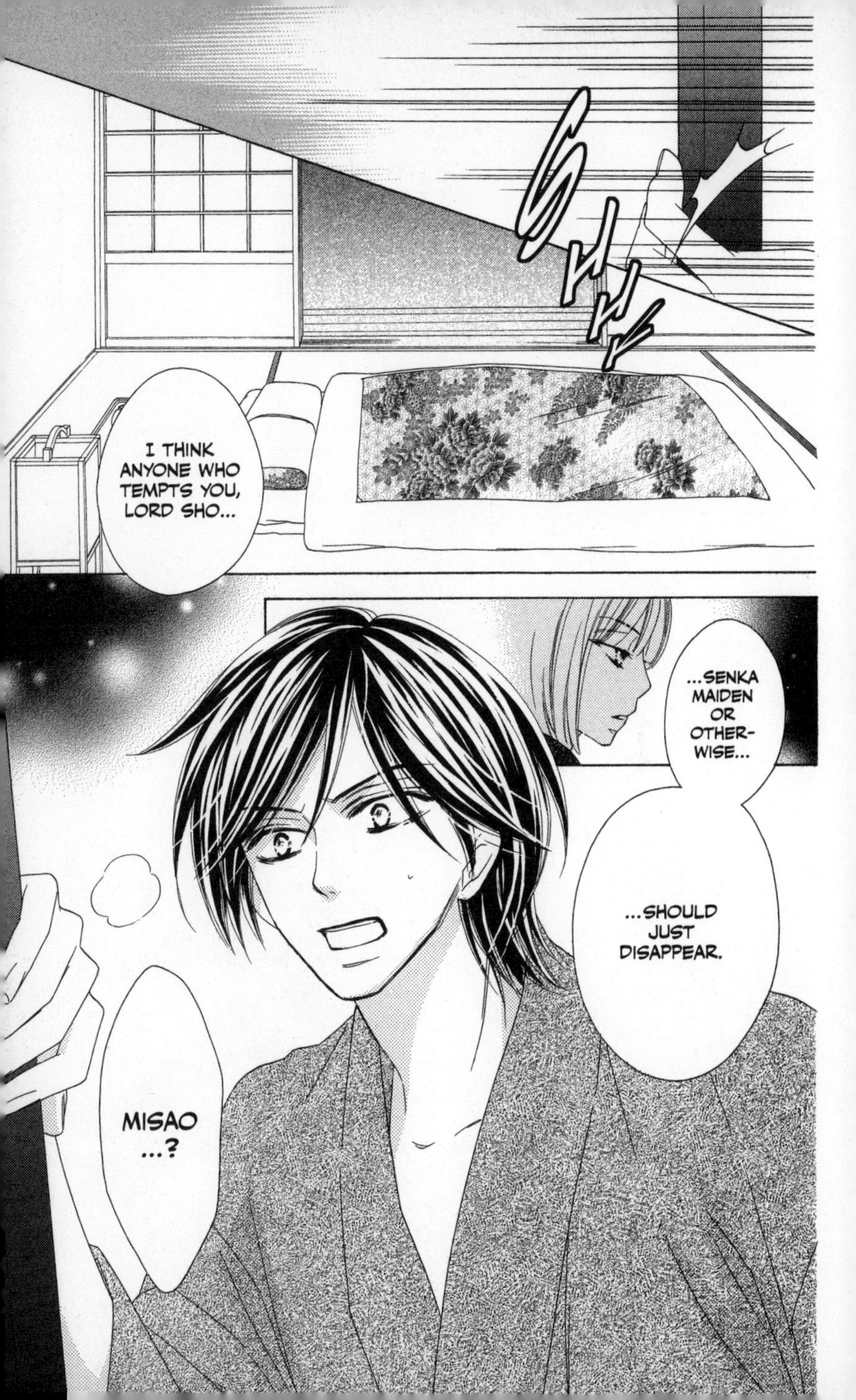
I THINK ANYONE WHO TEMPTS YOU, LORD SHO...
...SENKA MAIDEN OR OTHER-WISE...
...SHOULD JUST DISAPPEAR.
MISAO ...?

The
making of...

Just a
minute...

I think
I can
squeeze
them a
little more...

Great,
Misao-baby.
You're doing
great.

Why don't
you stretch
your legs
out a little
more, too.
♡

SQUEEZE

Taro,
I can see
everything!

This is the
photoshoot for
← the next title page...

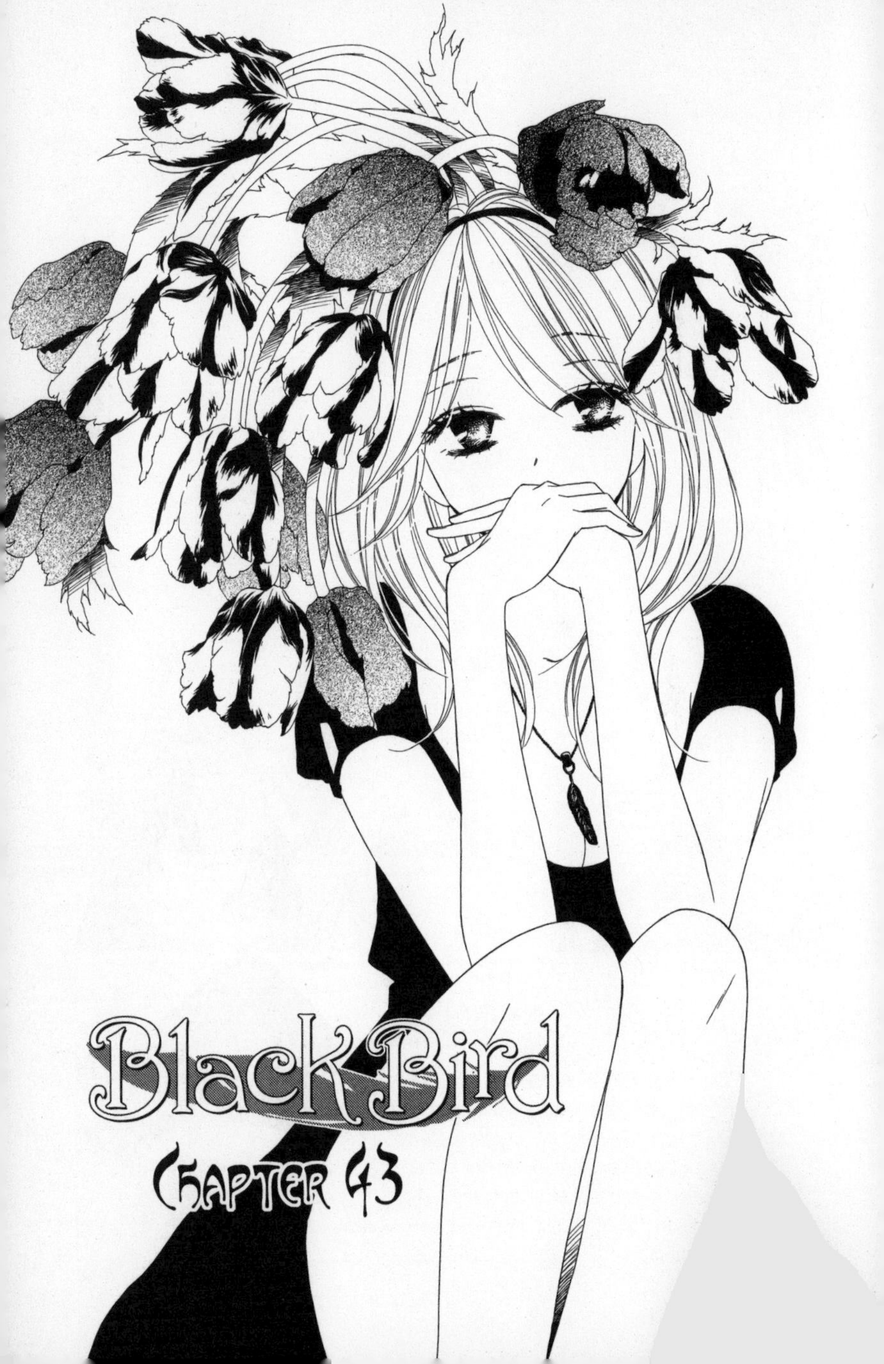
Black Bird
Chapter 43

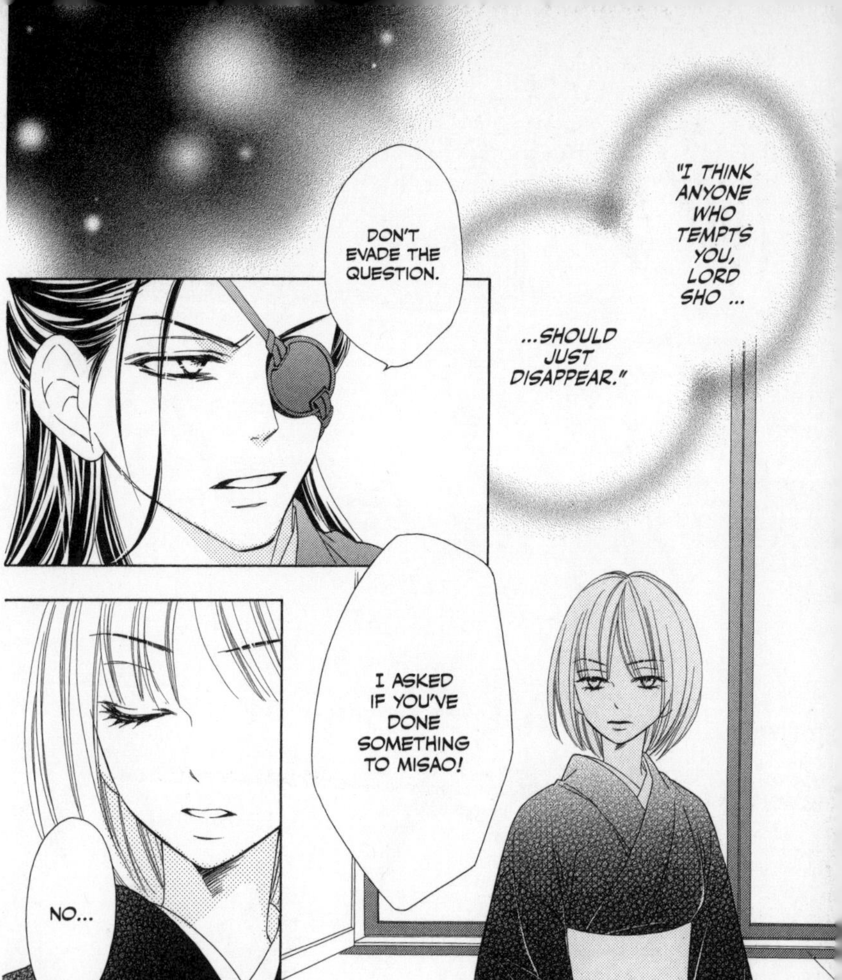
"I THINK ANYONE WHO TEMPTS YOU, LORD SHO ...
...SHOULD JUST DISAPPEAR."
DON'T EVADE THE QUESTION.
I ASKED IF YOU'VE DONE SOMETHING TO MISAO!
NO...

かえで
Kaede

age: 21
height: 5′ 3″

I love this kind of short bob (I've tried it myself several times, but it didn't work out...). She's no raving beauty, but there's something sexy about her. I modeled her after someone specific to capture that image. This is one person I wouldn't want for an enemy! I'd be no match for her!

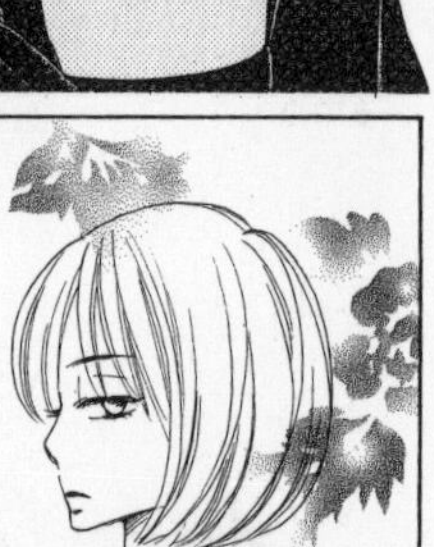

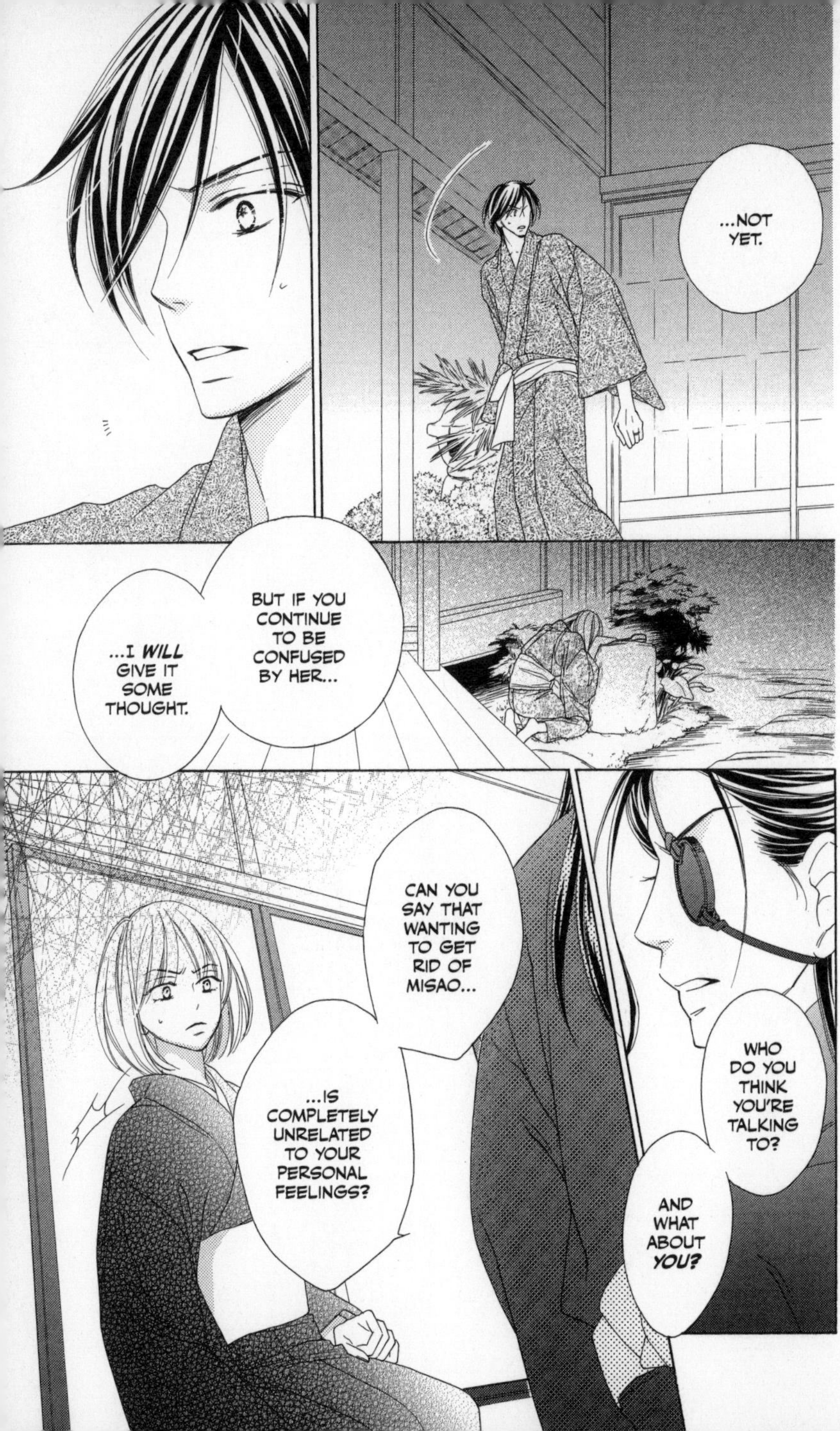
...NOT YET.
BUT IF YOU CONTINUE TO BE CONFUSED BY HER...
...I *WILL* GIVE IT SOME THOUGHT.
WHO DO YOU THINK YOU'RE TALKING TO?
AND WHAT ABOUT *YOU?*
CAN YOU SAY THAT WANTING TO GET RID OF MISAO...
...IS COMPLETELY UNRELATED TO YOUR PERSONAL FEELINGS?

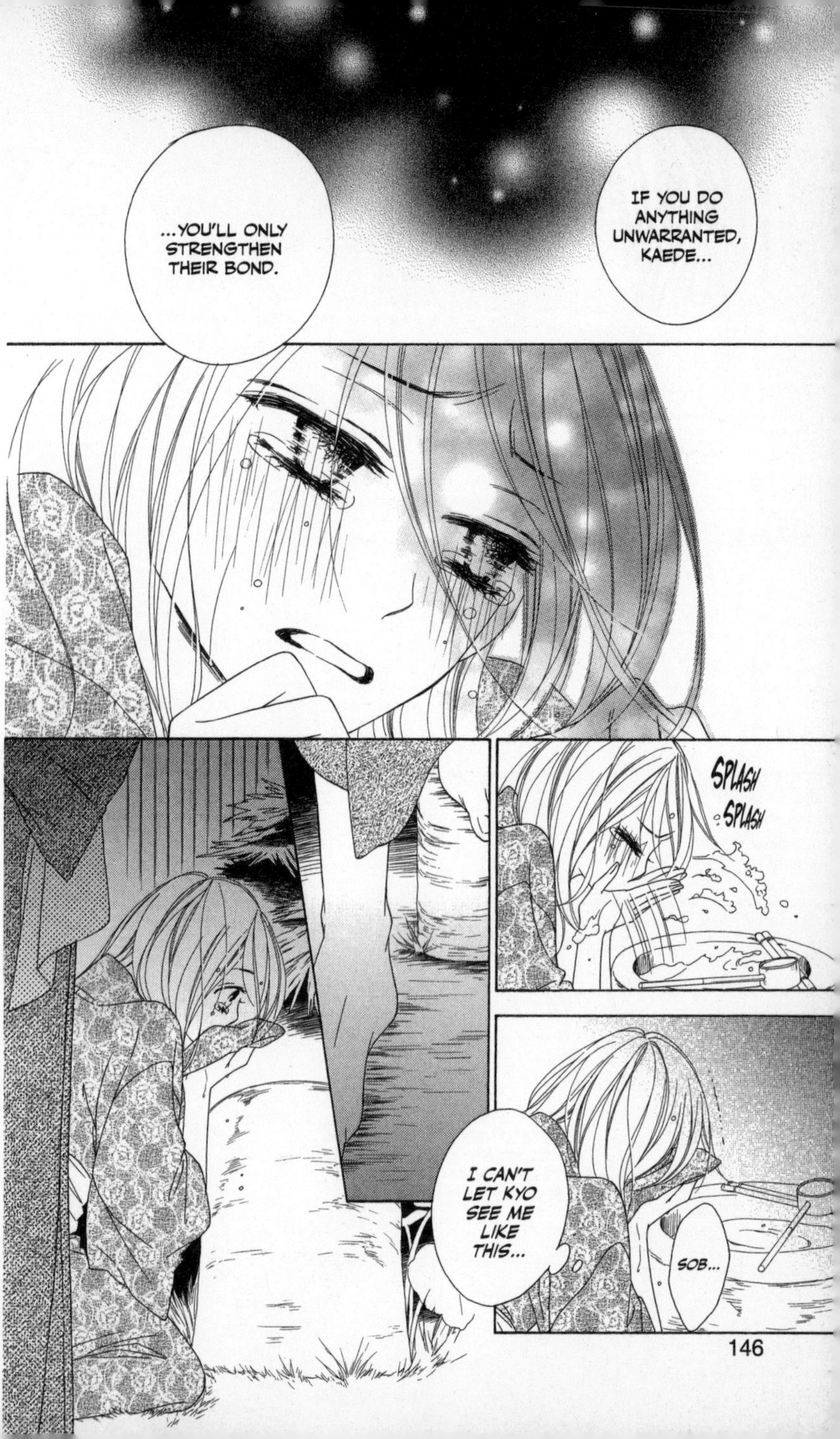
IF YOU DO ANYTHING UNWARRANTED, KAEDE...
...YOU'LL ONLY STRENGTHEN THEIR BOND.
SPLASH
SPLASH
SOB...
I CAN'T LET KYO SEE ME LIKE THIS...

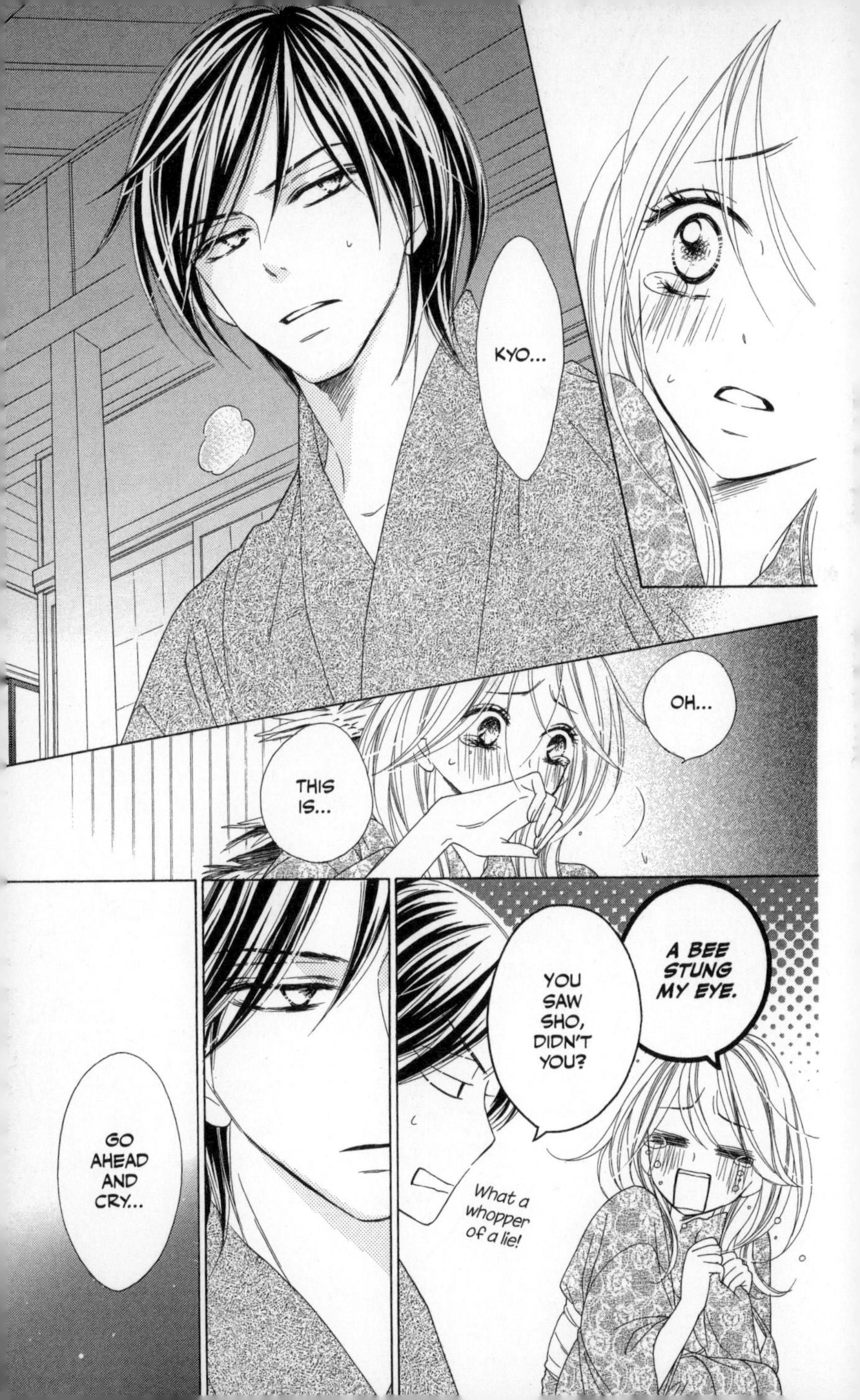
KYO...
OH...
THIS IS...
A BEE STUNG MY EYE.
YOU SAW SHO, DIDN'T YOU?
What a whopper of a lie!
GO AHEAD AND CRY...

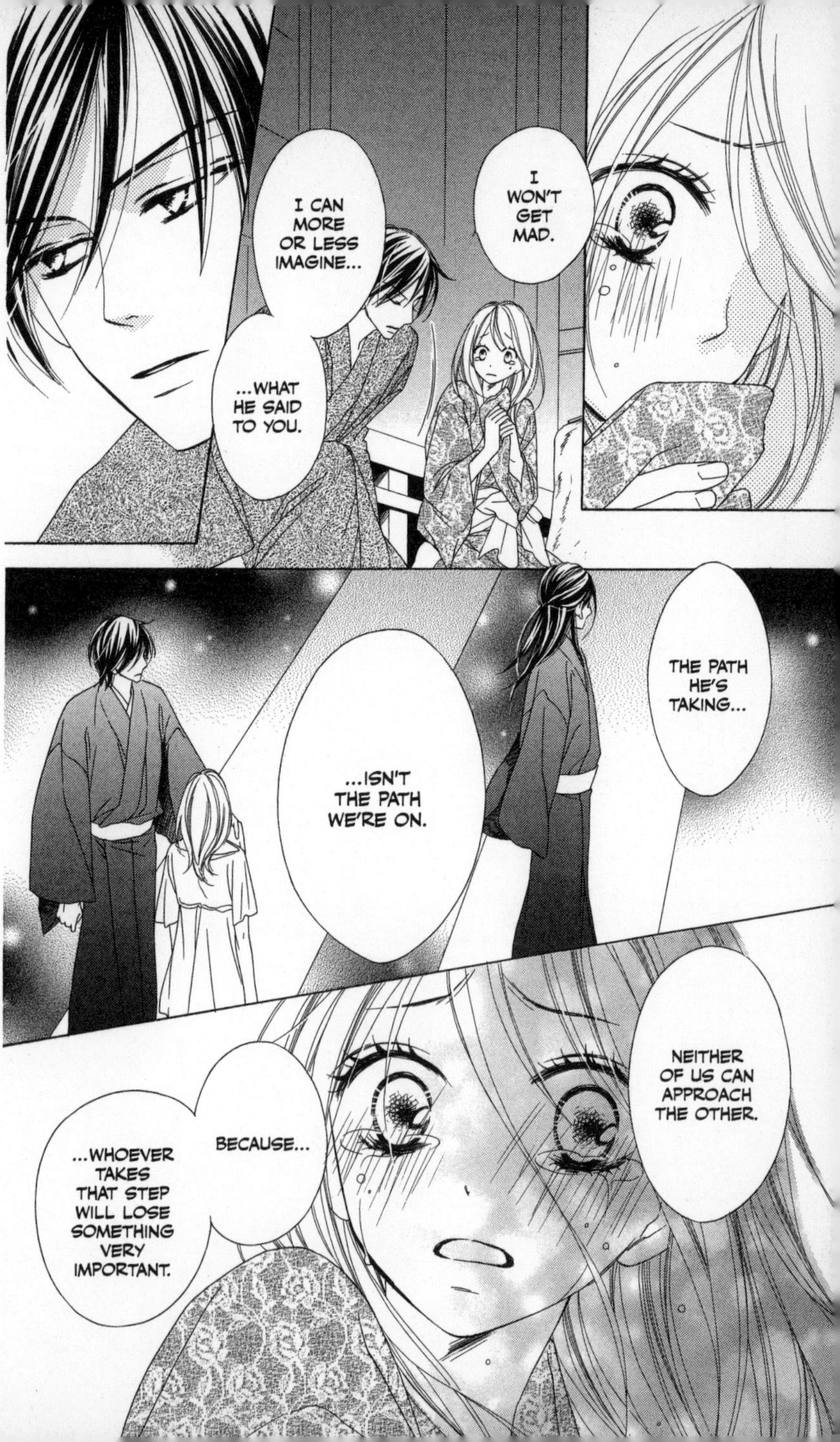
I WON'T GET MAD.
I CAN MORE OR LESS IMAGINE...
...WHAT HE SAID TO YOU.
THE PATH HE'S TAKING...
...ISN'T THE PATH WE'RE ON.
NEITHER OF US CAN APPROACH THE OTHER.
BECAUSE...
...WHOEVER TAKES THAT STEP WILL LOSE SOMETHING VERY IMPORTANT.

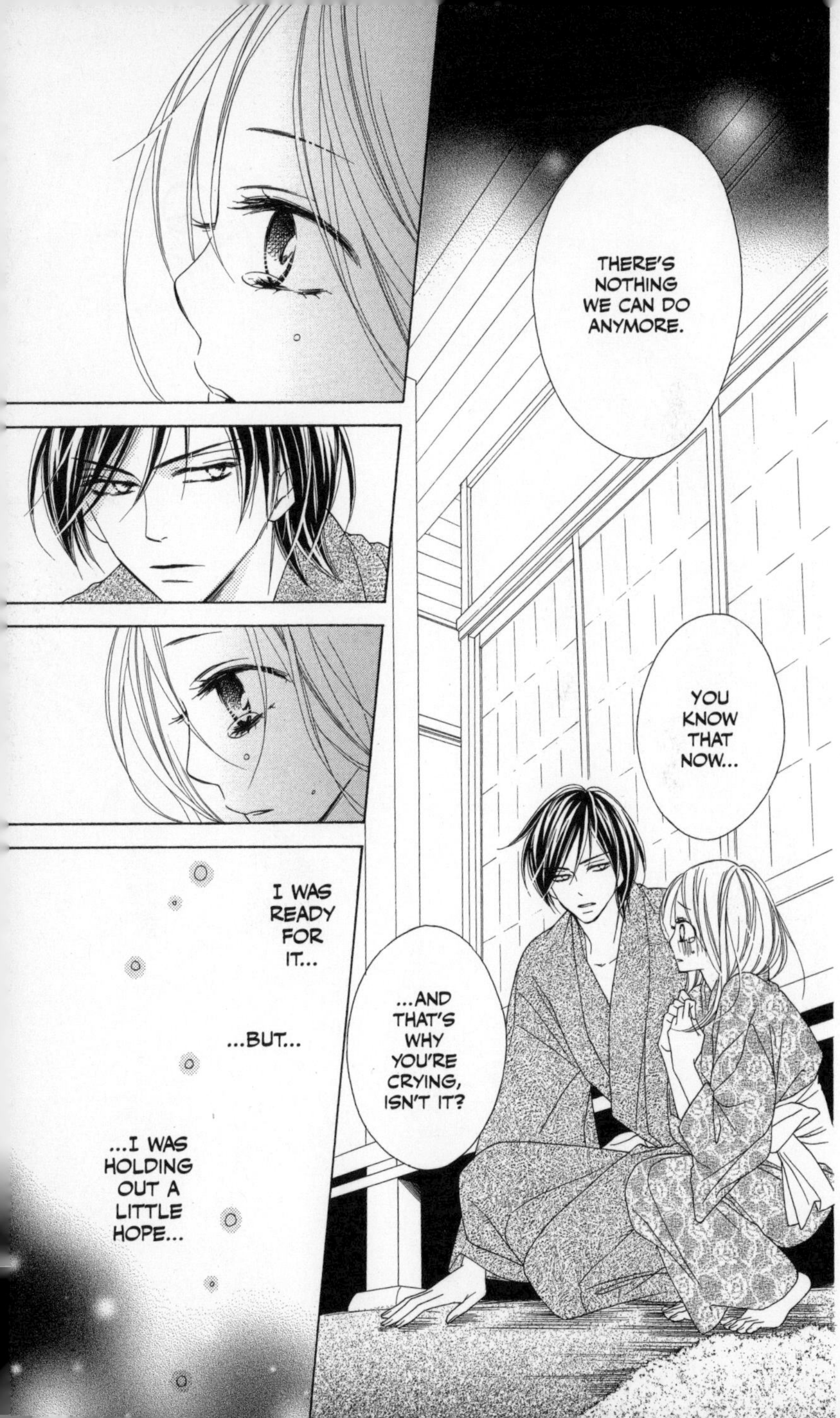
THERE'S NOTHING WE CAN DO ANYMORE.
YOU KNOW THAT NOW...
...AND THAT'S WHY YOU'RE CRYING, ISN'T IT?
I WAS READY FOR IT...
...BUT...
...I WAS HOLDING OUT A LITTLE HOPE...

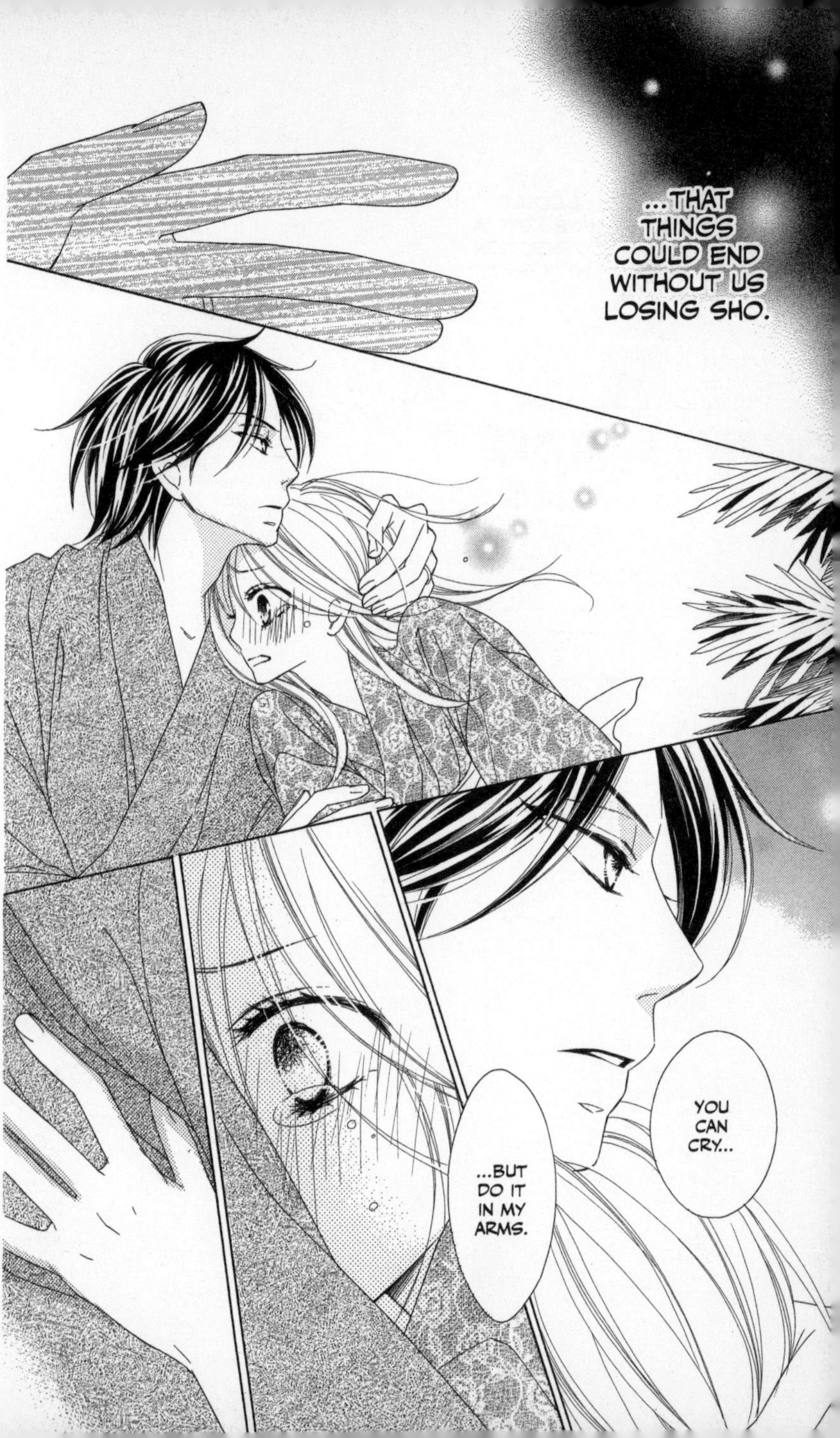
...THAT THINGS COULD END WITHOUT US LOSING SHO.
YOU CAN CRY...
...BUT DO IT IN MY ARMS.

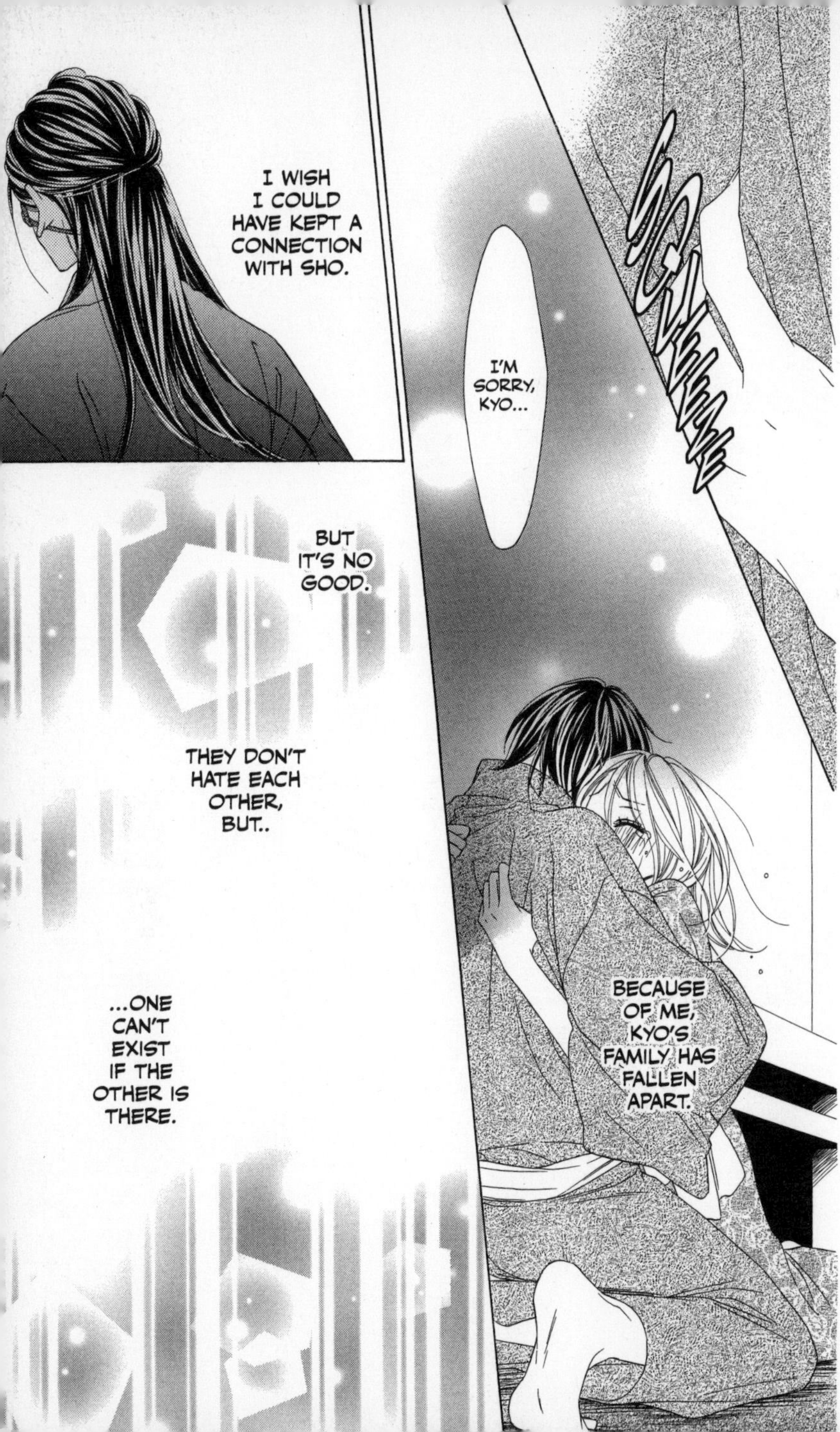
I'M SORRY, KYO...
BECAUSE OF ME, KYO'S FAMILY HAS FALLEN APART.
I WISH I COULD HAVE KEPT A CONNECTION WITH SHO.
BUT IT'S NO GOOD.
THEY DON'T HATE EACH OTHER, BUT..
...ONE CAN'T EXIST IF THE OTHER IS THERE.

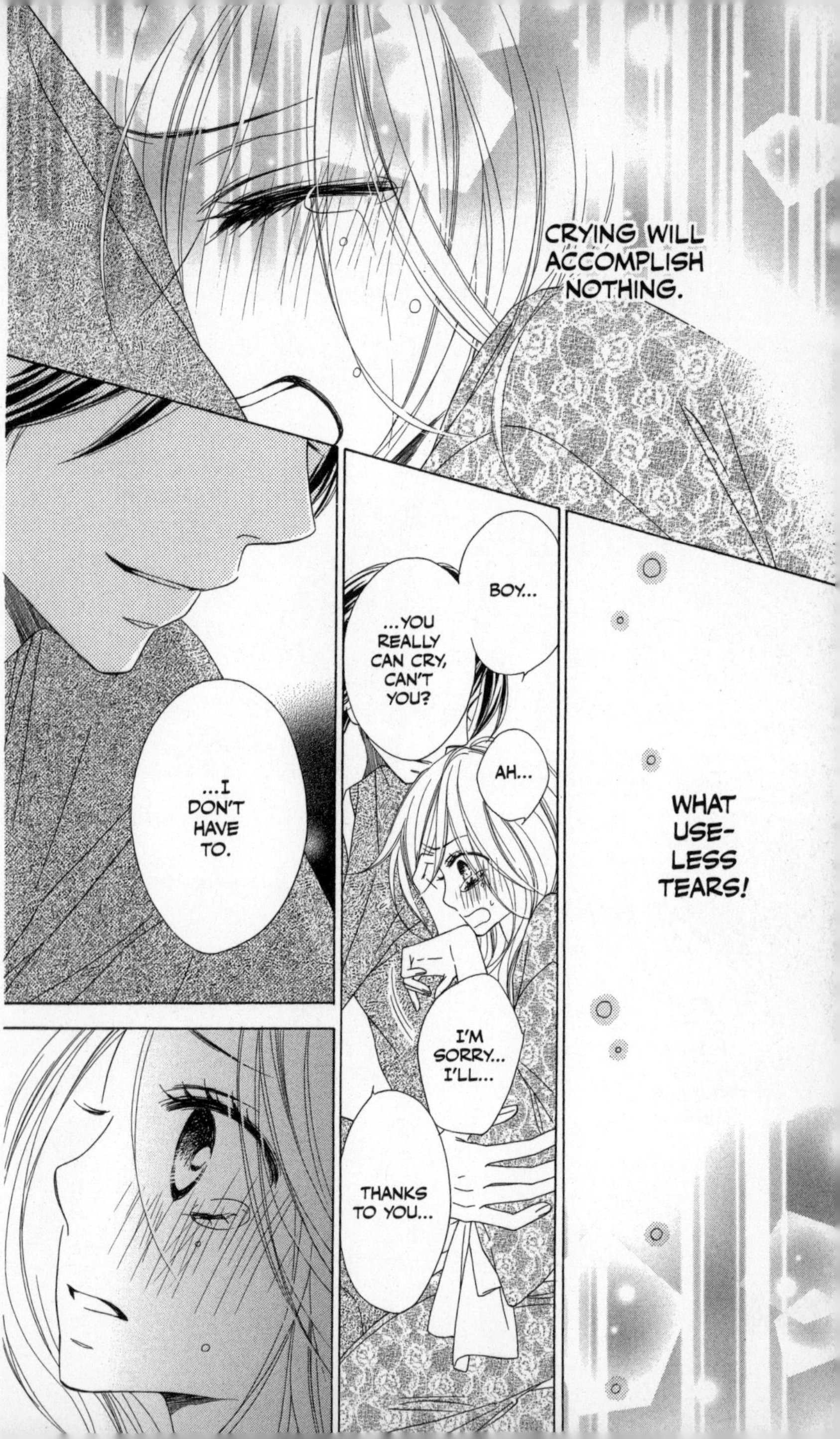
CRYING WILL ACCOMPLISH NOTHING.
WHAT USE-LESS TEARS!
BOY...
...YOU REALLY CAN CRY, CAN'T YOU?
AH...
I'M SORRY... I'LL...
THANKS TO YOU...
...I DON'T HAVE TO.

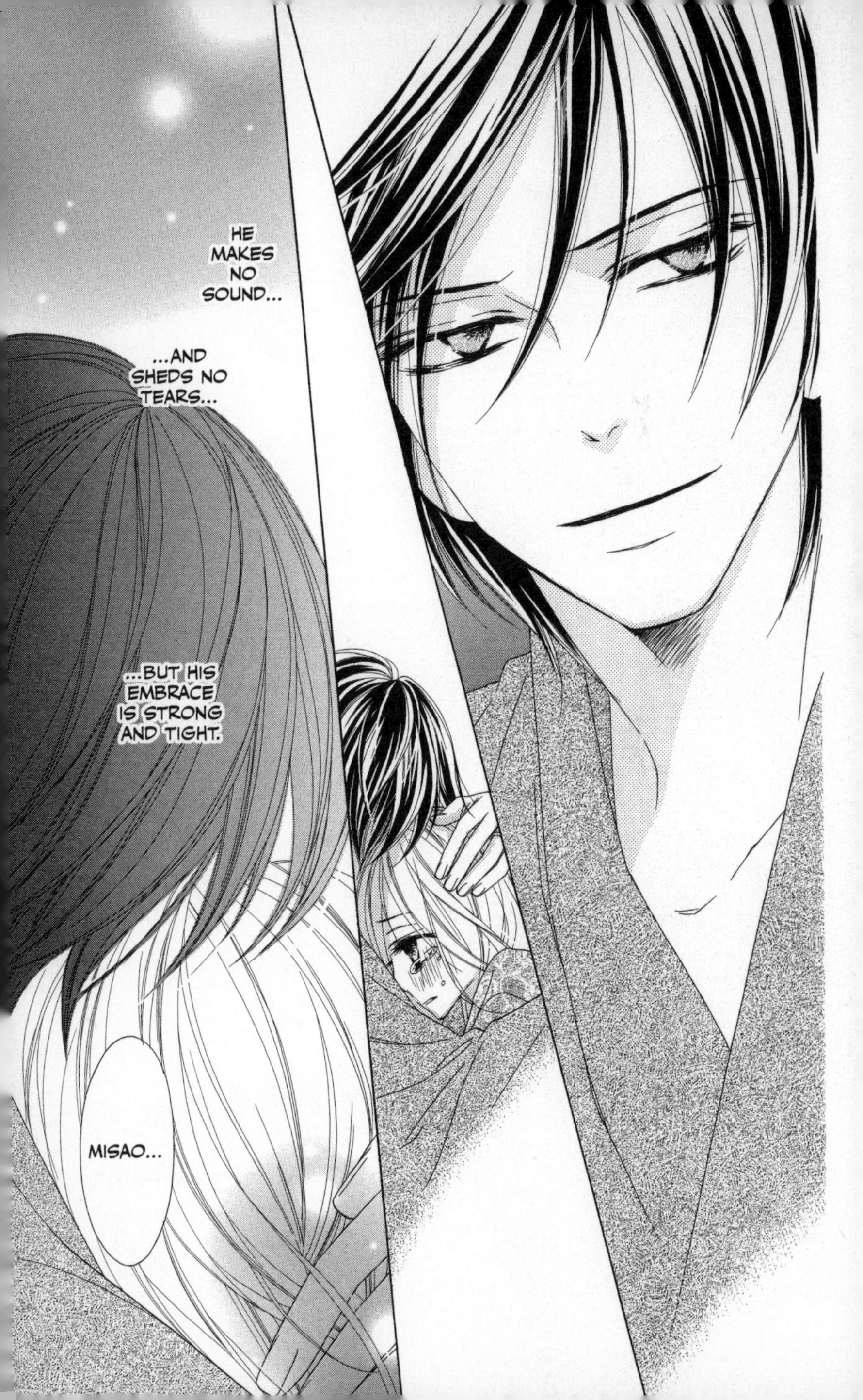
HE MAKES NO SOUND...
...AND SHEDS NO TEARS...
...BUT HIS EMBRACE IS STRONG AND TIGHT.
MISAO...

I'M GLAD THAT YOU'RE HERE...

...WITH ME...

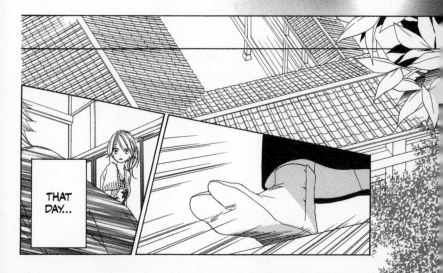

THAT DAY...

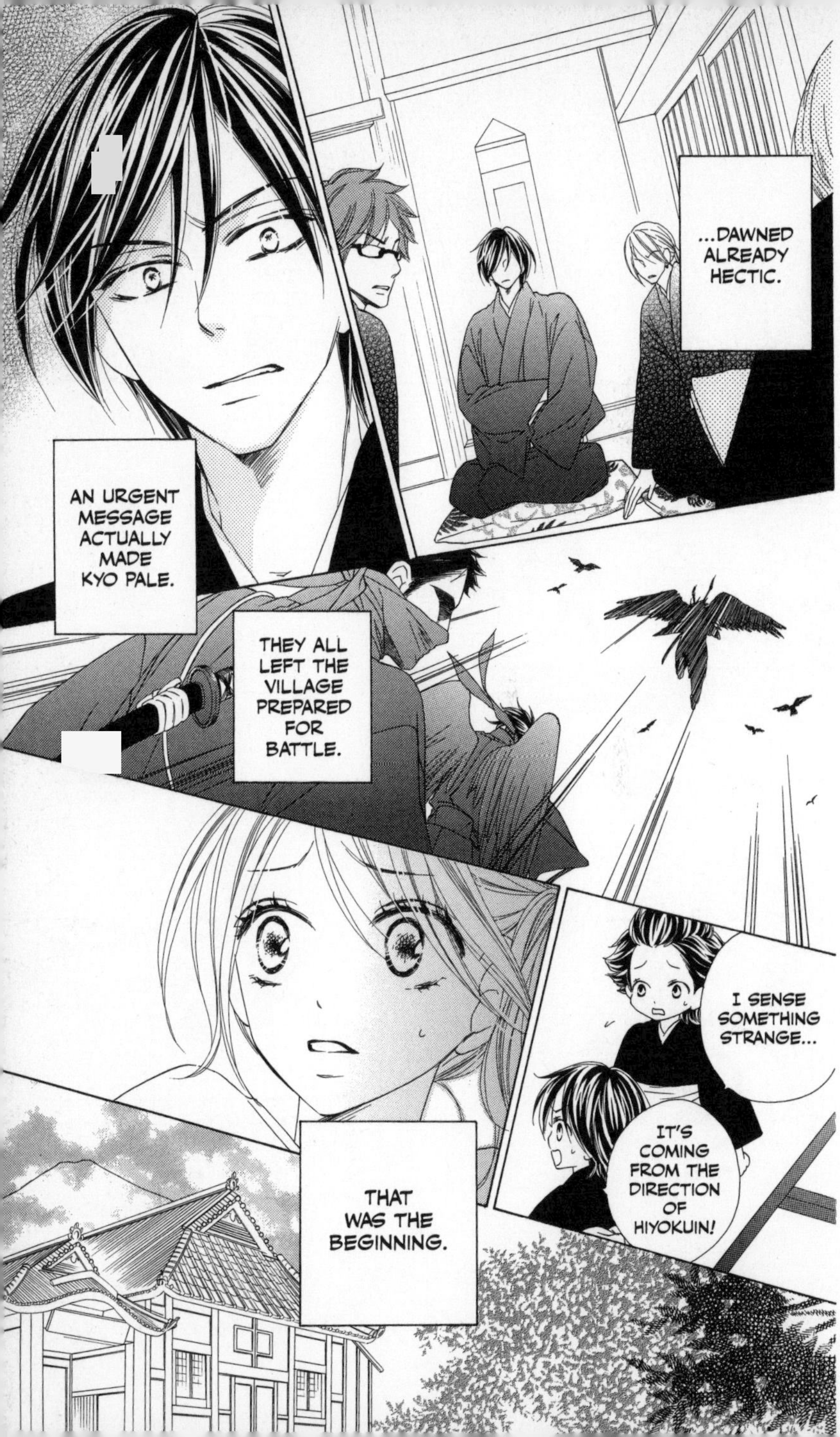
...DAWNED ALREADY HECTIC.
AN URGENT MESSAGE ACTUALLY MADE KYO PALE.
THEY ALL LEFT THE VILLAGE PREPARED FOR BATTLE.
I SENSE SOMETHING STRANGE...
IT'S COMING FROM THE DIRECTION OF HIYOKUIN!
THAT WAS THE BEGINNING.

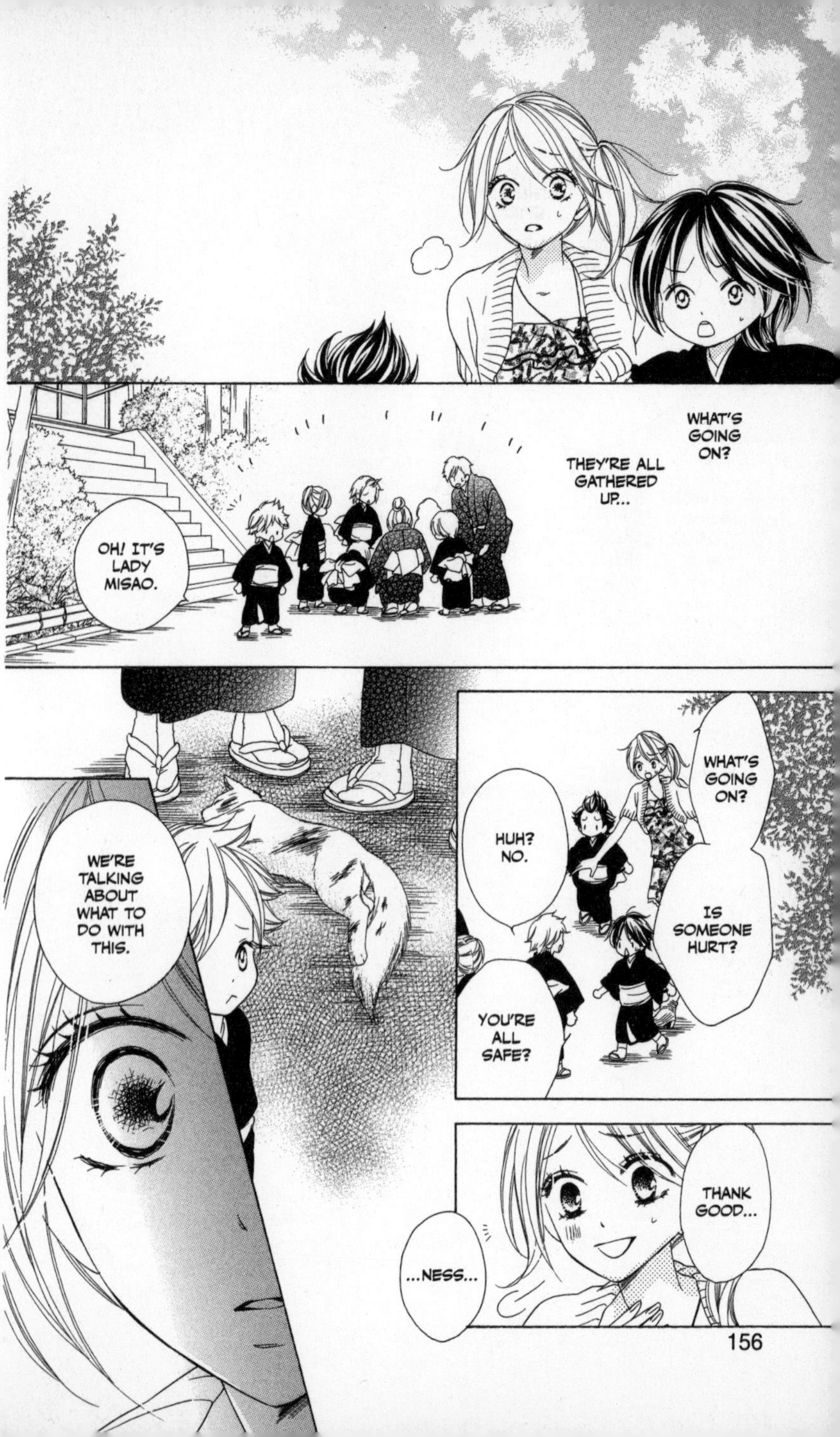
WHAT'S GOING ON?
THEY'RE ALL GATHERED UP...
OH! IT'S LADY MISAO.
WHAT'S GOING ON?
IS SOMEONE HURT?
HUH? NO.
YOU'RE ALL SAFE?
THANK GOOD...
...NESS...
WE'RE TALKING ABOUT WHAT TO DO WITH THIS.

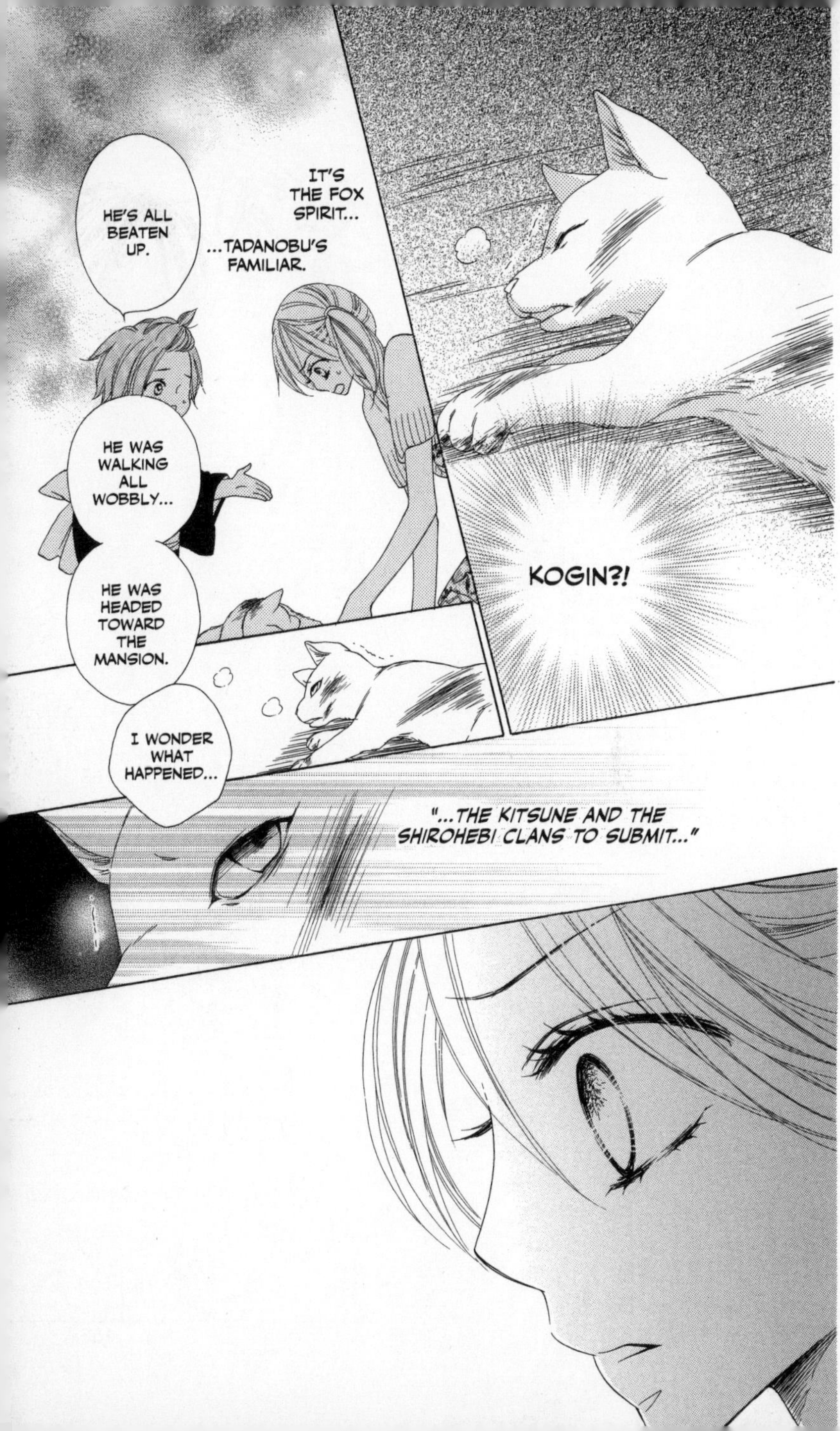
KOGIN?!
IT'S THE FOX SPIRIT...
...TADANOBU'S FAMILIAR.
HE'S ALL BEATEN UP.
HE WAS WALKING ALL WOBBLY...
HE WAS HEADED TOWARD THE MANSION.
I WONDER WHAT HAPPENED...
"...THE KITSUNE AND THE SHIROHEBI CLANS TO SUBMIT..."

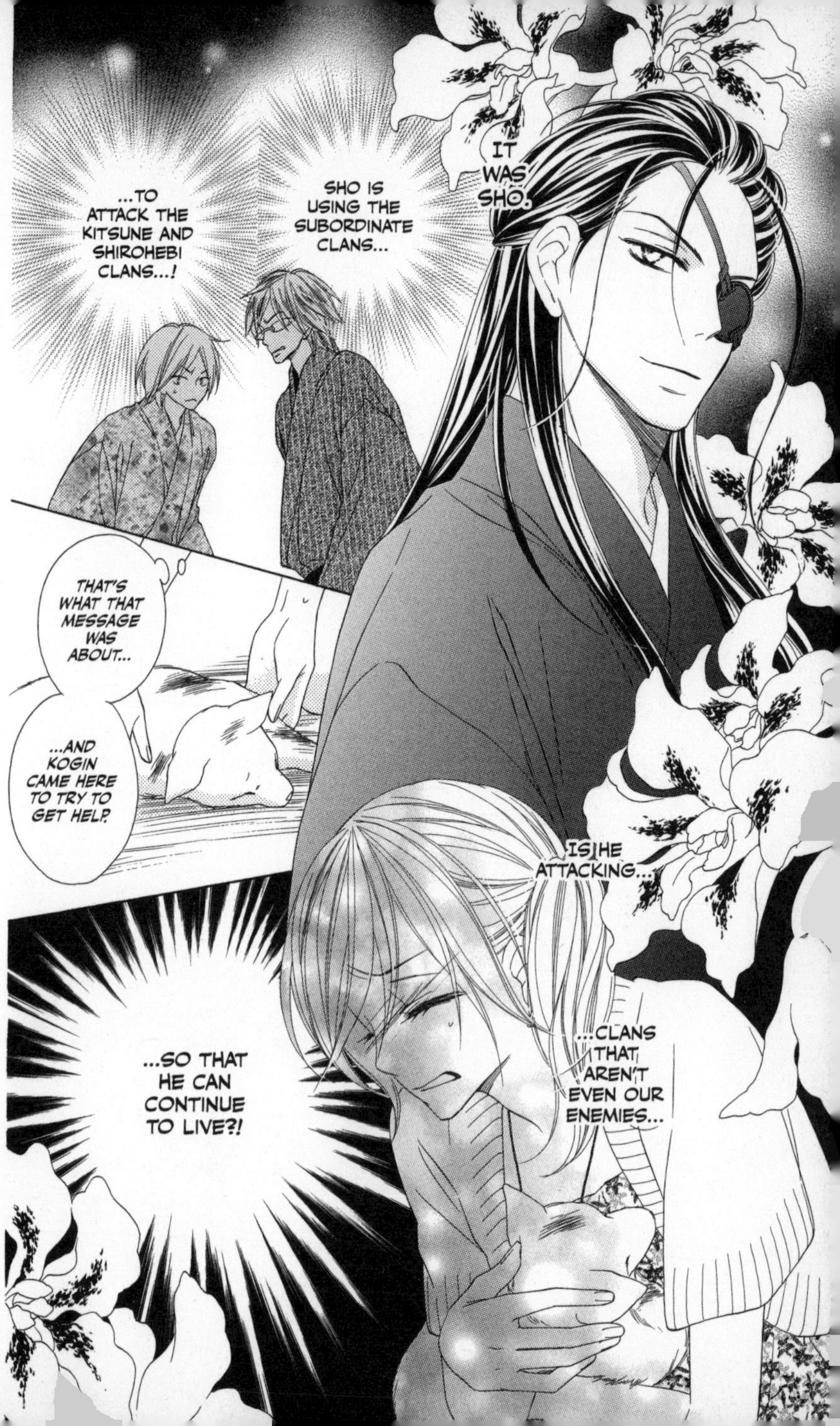
IT WAS SHO.
SHO IS USING THE SUBORDINATE CLANS...
...TO ATTACK THE KITSUNE AND SHIROHEBI CLANS...!
THAT'S WHAT THAT MESSAGE WAS ABOUT...
...AND KOGIN CAME HERE TO TRY TO GET HELP?
IS HE ATTACKING...
...CLANS THAT AREN'T EVEN OUR ENEMIES...
...SO THAT HE CAN CONTINUE TO LIVE?!

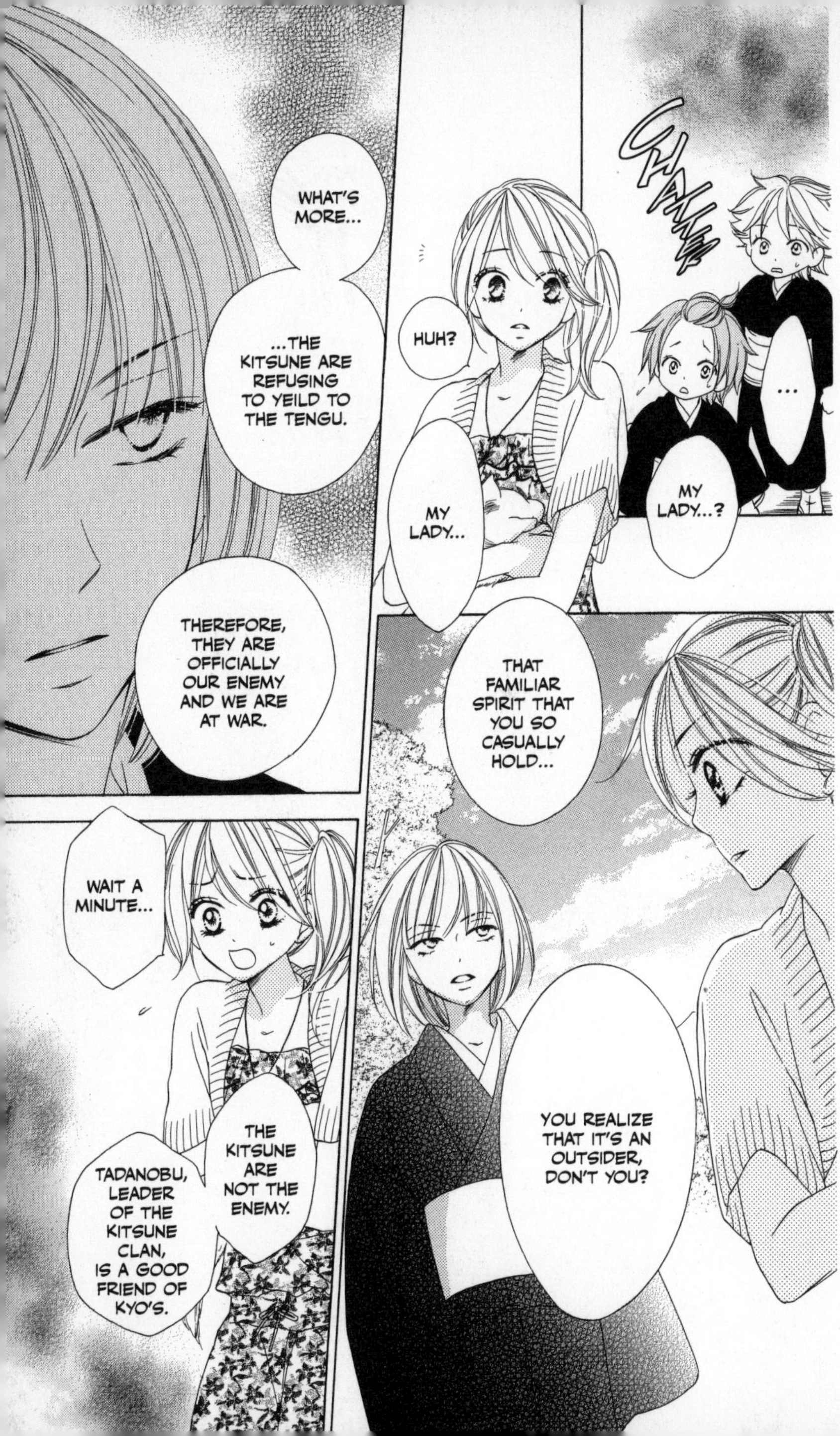
...
MY LADY...?
HUH?
MY LADY...
THAT FAMILIAR SPIRIT THAT YOU SO CASUALLY HOLD...
YOU REALIZE THAT IT'S AN OUTSIDER, DON'T YOU?
WHAT'S MORE...
...THE KITSUNE ARE REFUSING TO YEILD TO THE TENGU.
THEREFORE, THEY ARE OFFICIALLY OUR ENEMY AND WE ARE AT WAR.
WAIT A MINUTE...
THE KITSUNE ARE NOT THE ENEMY.
TADANOBU, LEADER OF THE KITSUNE CLAN, IS A GOOD FRIEND OF KYO'S.

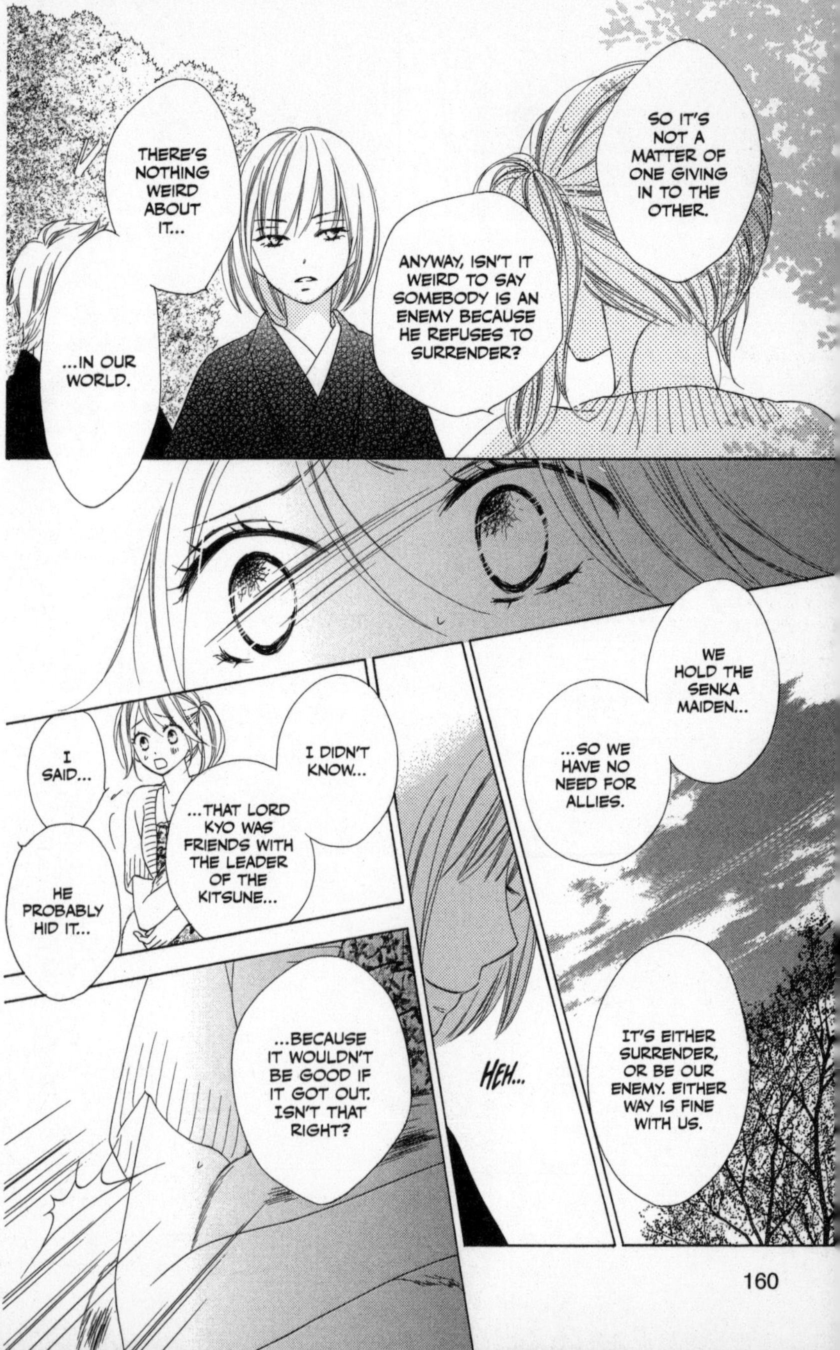
SO IT'S NOT A MATTER OF ONE GIVING IN TO THE OTHER.
ANYWAY, ISN'T IT WEIRD TO SAY SOMEBODY IS AN ENEMY BECAUSE HE REFUSES TO SURRENDER?
THERE'S NOTHING WEIRD ABOUT IT...
...IN OUR WORLD.
WE HOLD THE SENKA MAIDEN...
...SO WE HAVE NO NEED FOR ALLIES.
HEH...
IT'S EITHER SURRENDER, OR BE OUR ENEMY. EITHER WAY IS FINE WITH US.
I DIDN'T KNOW...
...THAT LORD KYO WAS FRIENDS WITH THE LEADER OF THE KITSUNE...
I SAID...
HE PROBABLY HID IT...
...BECAUSE IT WOULDN'T BE GOOD IF IT GOT OUT. ISN'T THAT RIGHT?

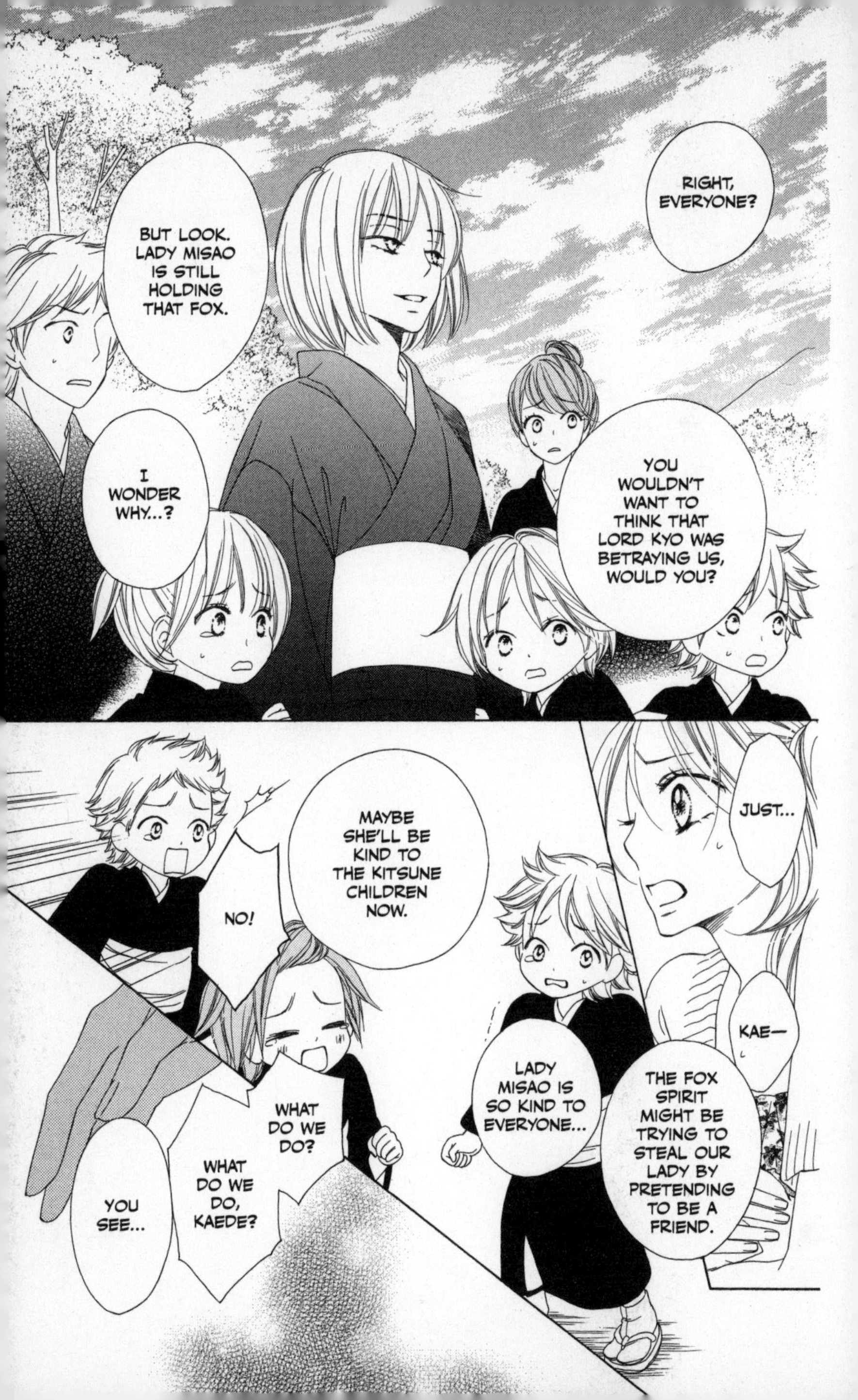
RIGHT, EVERYONE?
YOU WOULDN'T WANT TO THINK THAT LORD KYO WAS BETRAYING US, WOULD YOU?
BUT LOOK. LADY MISAO IS STILL HOLDING THAT FOX.
I WONDER WHY...?
JUST...
KAE—
THE FOX SPIRIT MIGHT BE TRYING TO STEAL OUR LADY BY PRETENDING TO BE A FRIEND.
LADY MISAO IS SO KIND TO EVERYONE...
MAYBE SHE'LL BE KIND TO THE KITSUNE CHILDREN NOW.
NO!
WHAT DO WE DO?
WHAT DO WE DO, KAEDE?
YOU SEE...

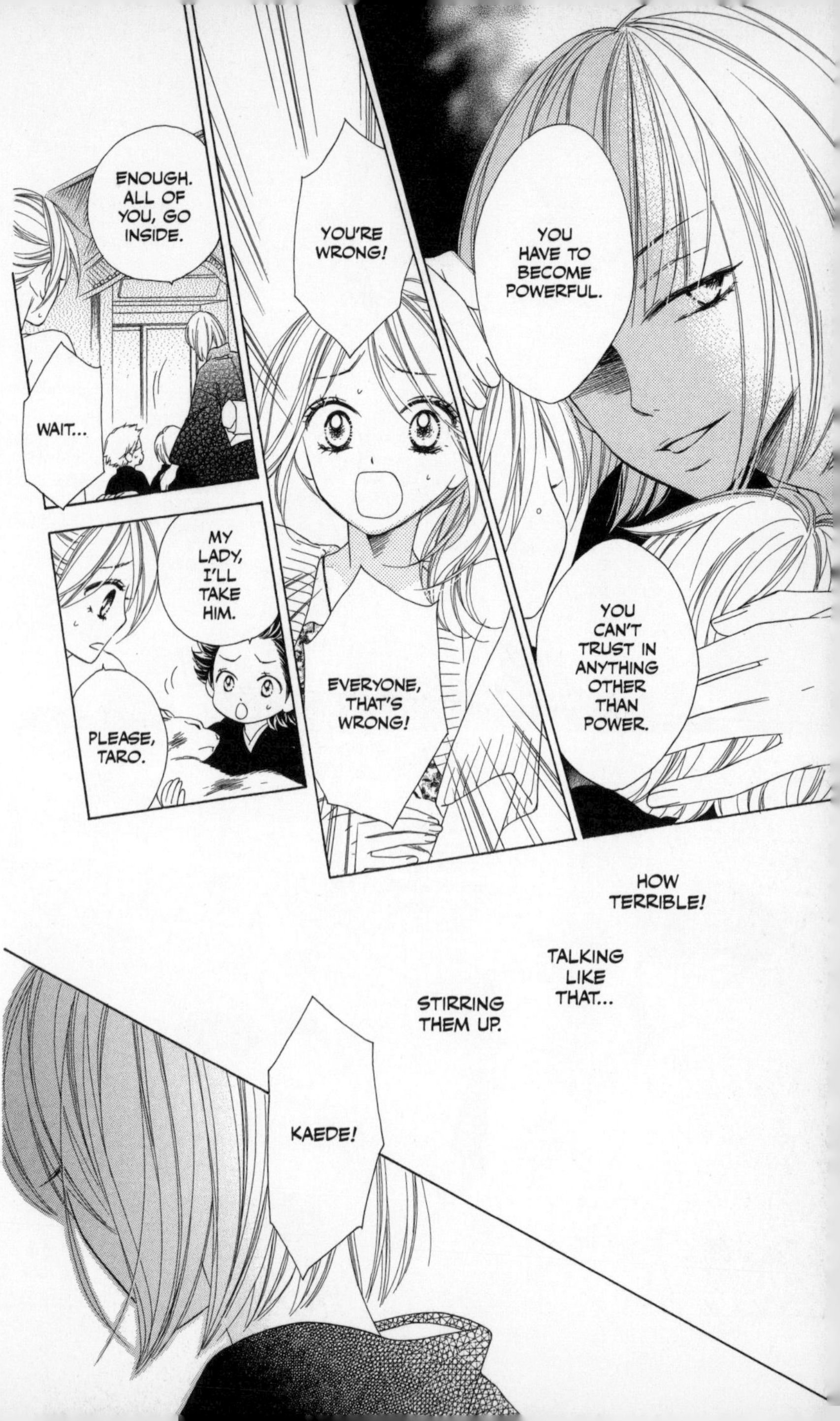
YOU HAVE TO BECOME POWERFUL.
YOU CAN'T TRUST IN ANYTHING OTHER THAN POWER.
YOU'RE WRONG!
EVERYONE, THAT'S WRONG!
ENOUGH. ALL OF YOU, GO INSIDE.
WAIT...
MY LADY, I'LL TAKE HIM.
PLEASE, TARO.
HOW TERRIBLE!
TALKING LIKE THAT...
STIRRING THEM UP.
KAEDE!

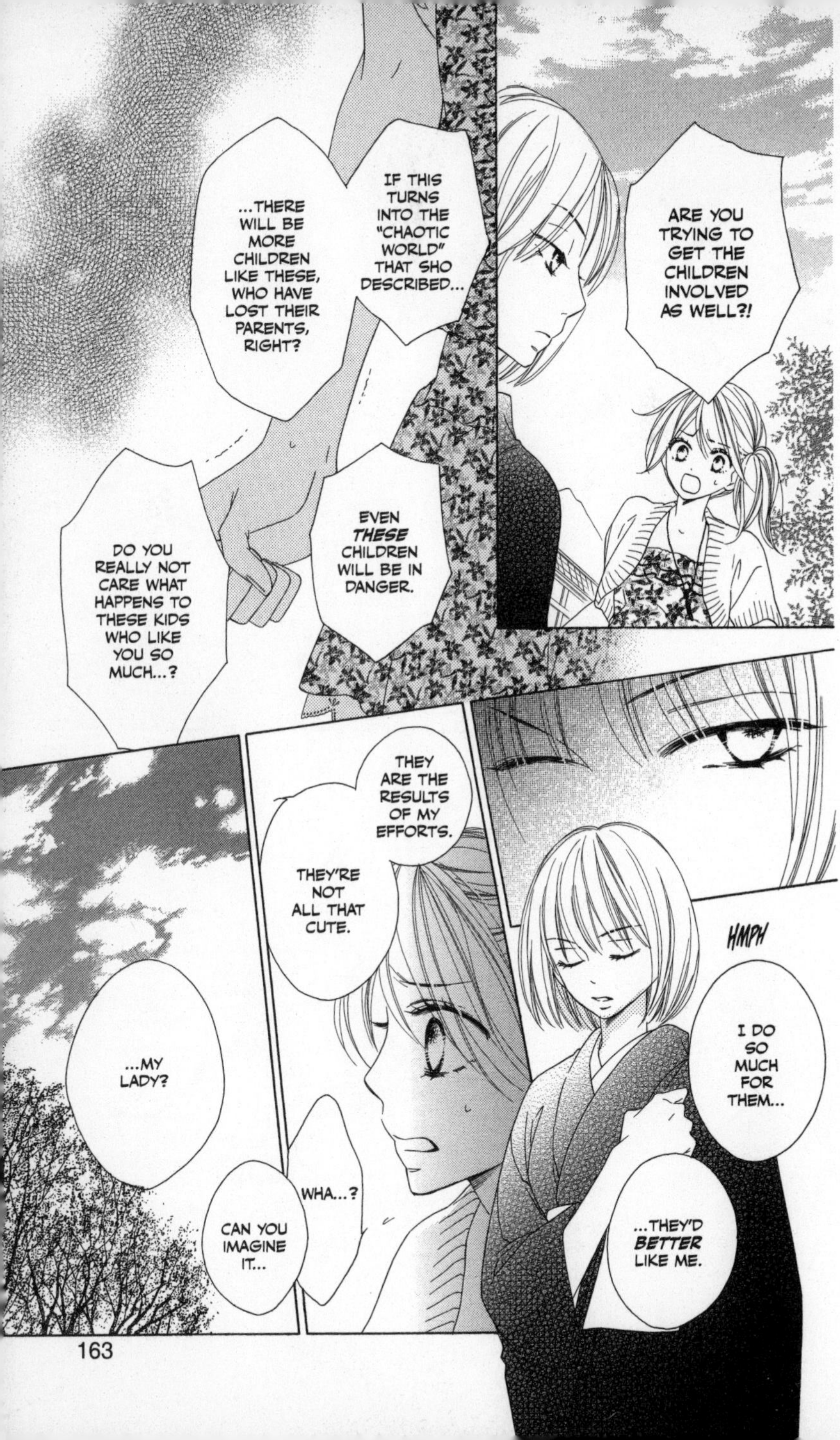
ARE YOU TRYING TO GET THE CHILDREN INVOLVED AS WELL?!
IF THIS TURNS INTO THE "CHAOTIC WORLD" THAT SHO DESCRIBED...
...THERE WILL BE MORE CHILDREN LIKE THESE, WHO HAVE LOST THEIR PARENTS, RIGHT?
EVEN *THESE* CHILDREN WILL BE IN DANGER.
DO YOU REALLY NOT CARE WHAT HAPPENS TO THESE KIDS WHO LIKE YOU SO MUCH...?
HMPH
I DO SO MUCH FOR THEM...
...THEY'D *BETTER* LIKE ME.
THEY ARE THE RESULTS OF MY EFFORTS.
THEY'RE NOT ALL THAT CUTE.
WHA...?
CAN YOU IMAGINE IT...
...MY LADY?

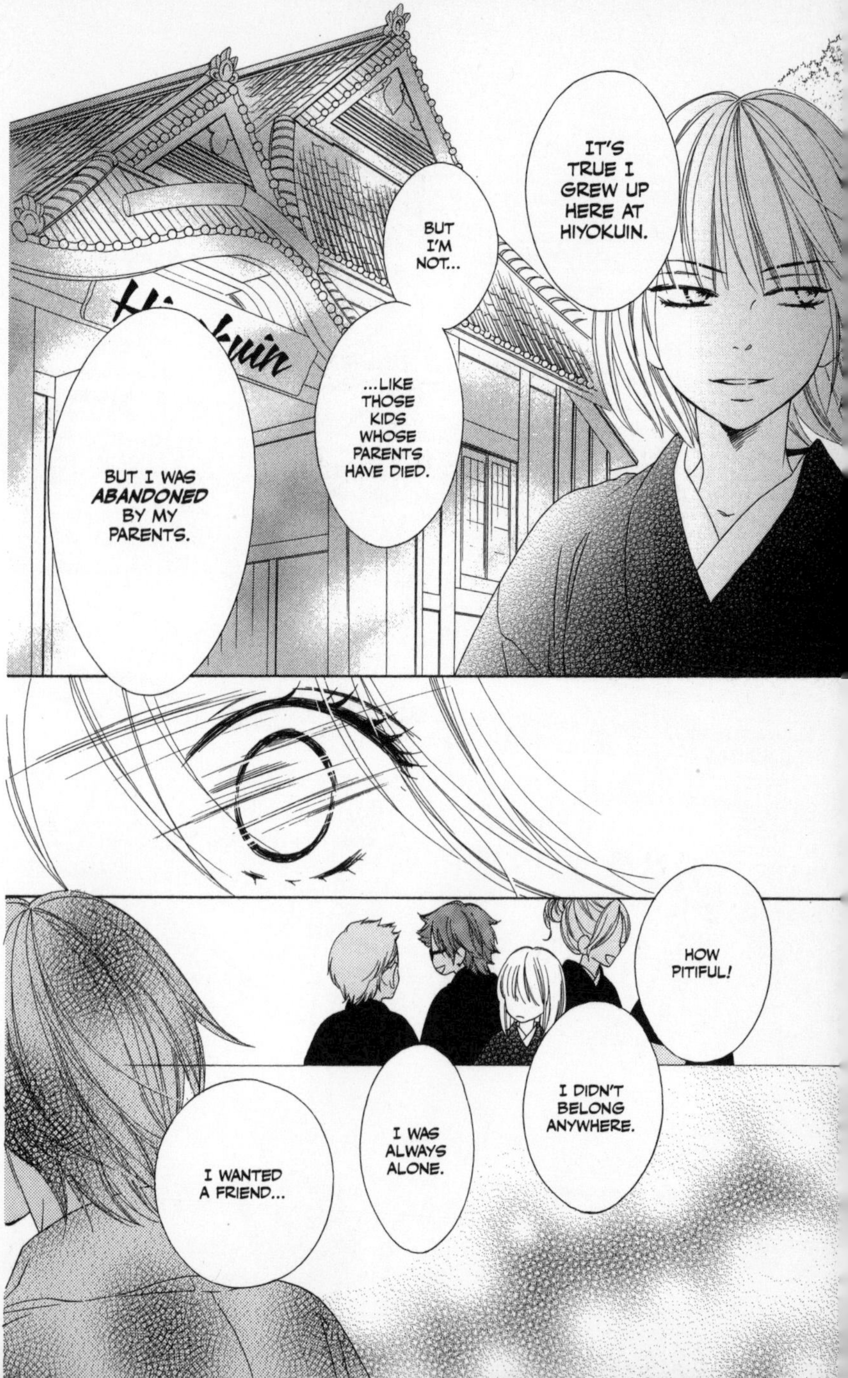
IT'S TRUE I GREW UP HERE AT HIYOKUIN.
BUT I'M NOT...
...LIKE THOSE KIDS WHOSE PARENTS HAVE DIED.
BUT I WAS *ABANDONED* BY MY PARENTS.
HOW PITIFUL!
I DIDN'T BELONG ANYWHERE.
I WAS ALWAYS ALONE.
I WANTED A FRIEND...

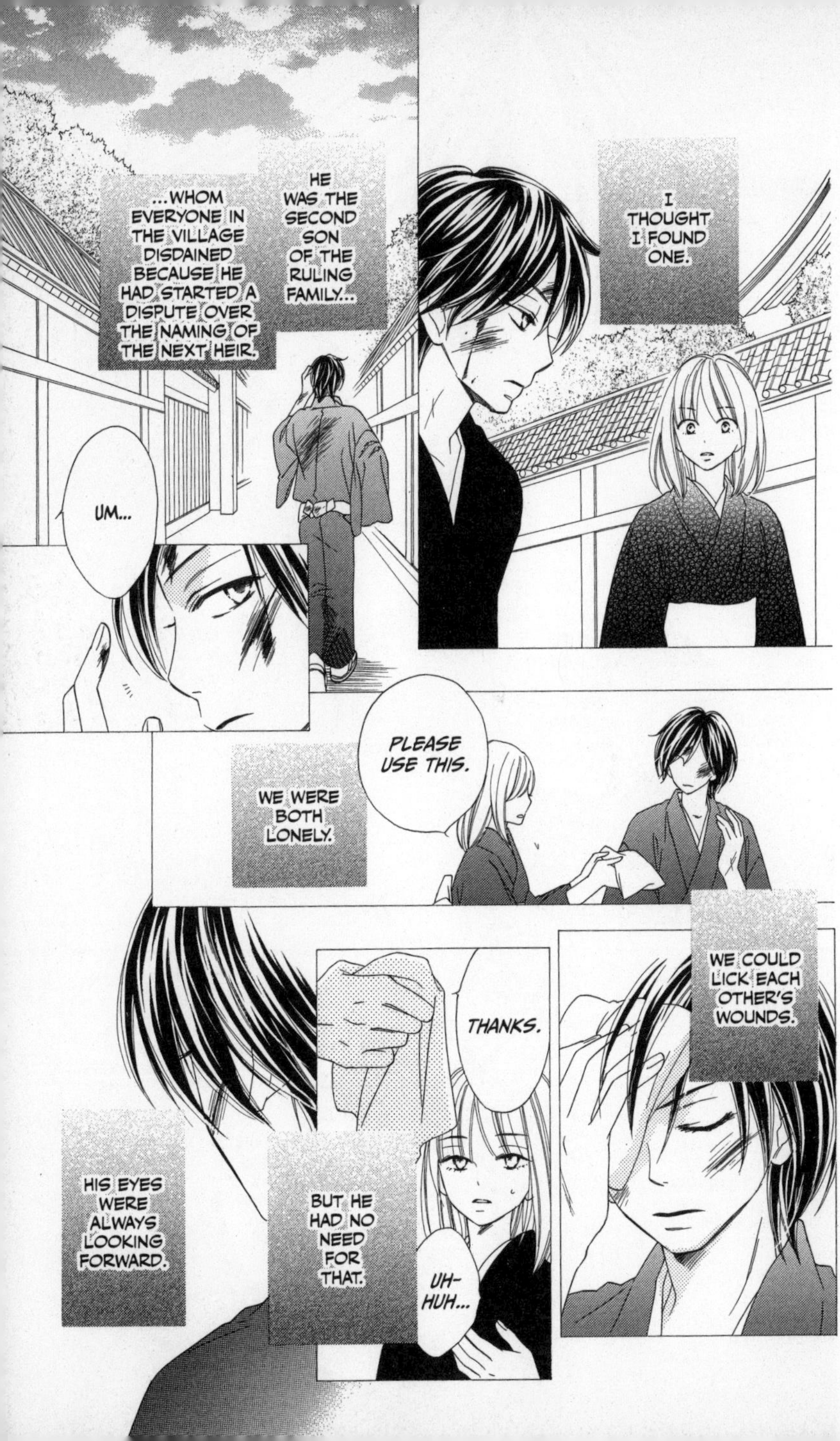
I THOUGHT I FOUND ONE.
HE WAS THE SECOND SON OF THE RULING FAMILY...
...WHOM EVERYONE IN THE VILLAGE DISDAINED BECAUSE HE HAD STARTED A DISPUTE OVER THE NAMING OF THE NEXT HEIR.
UM...
PLEASE USE THIS.
WE WERE BOTH LONELY.
WE COULD LICK EACH OTHER'S WOUNDS.
THANKS.
BUT HE HAD NO NEED FOR THAT.
UH-HUH...
HIS EYES WERE ALWAYS LOOKING FORWARD.

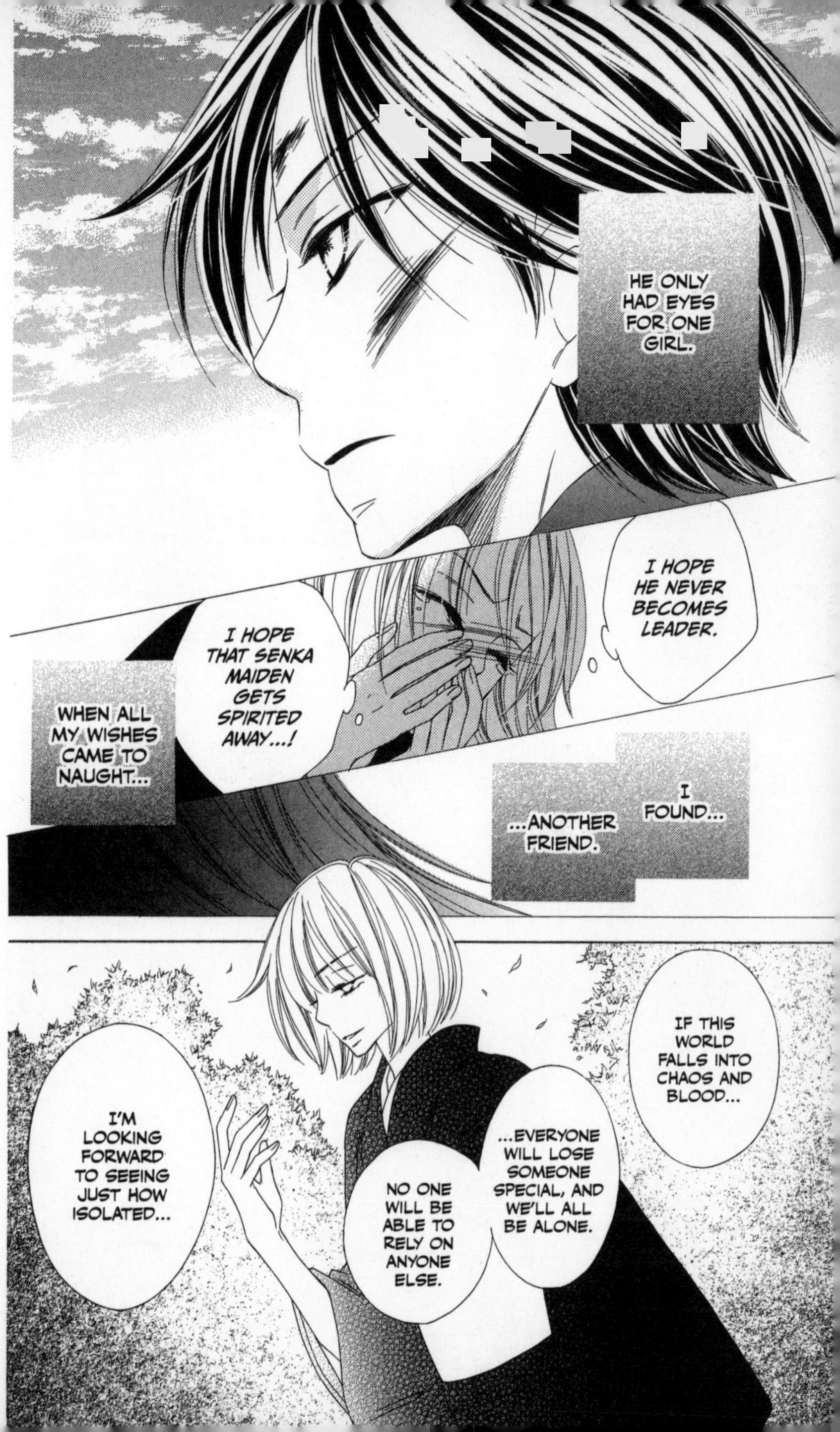
HE ONLY HAD EYES FOR ONE GIRL.
I HOPE HE NEVER BECOMES LEADER.
I HOPE THAT SENKA MAIDEN GETS SPIRITED AWAY...!
WHEN ALL MY WISHES CAME TO NAUGHT...
I FOUND...
...ANOTHER FRIEND.
IF THIS WORLD FALLS INTO CHAOS AND BLOOD...
...EVERYONE WILL LOSE SOMEONE SPECIAL, AND WE'LL ALL BE ALONE.
NO ONE WILL BE ABLE TO RELY ON ANYONE ELSE.
I'M LOOKING FORWARD TO SEEING JUST HOW ISOLATED...

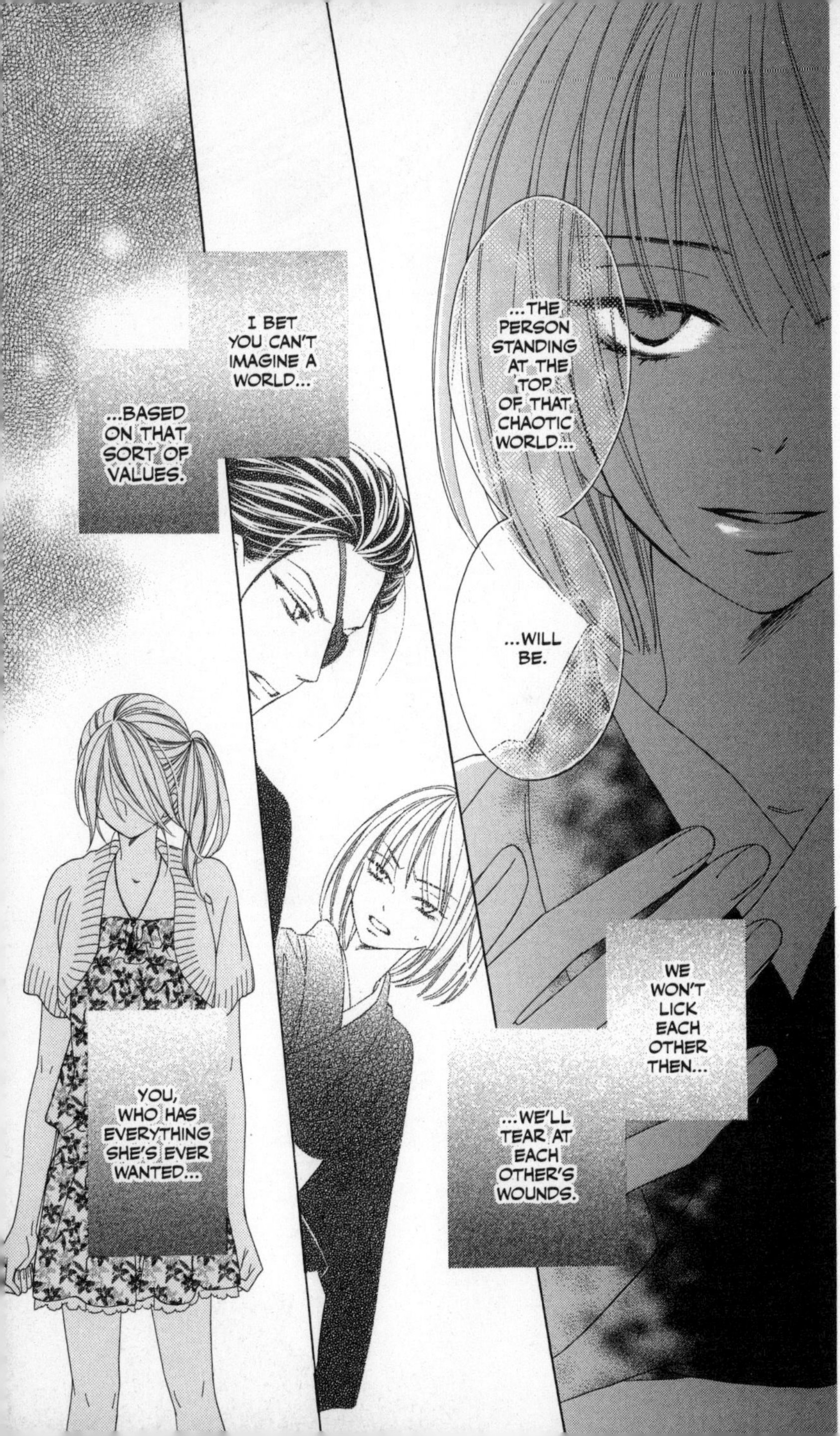
...THE PERSON STANDING AT THE TOP OF THAT CHAOTIC WORLD...
...WILL BE.
WE WON'T LICK EACH OTHER THEN...
...WE'LL TEAR AT EACH OTHER'S WOUNDS.
I BET YOU CAN'T IMAGINE A WORLD...
...BASED ON THAT SORT OF VALUES.
YOU, WHO HAS EVERYTHING SHE'S EVER WANTED...

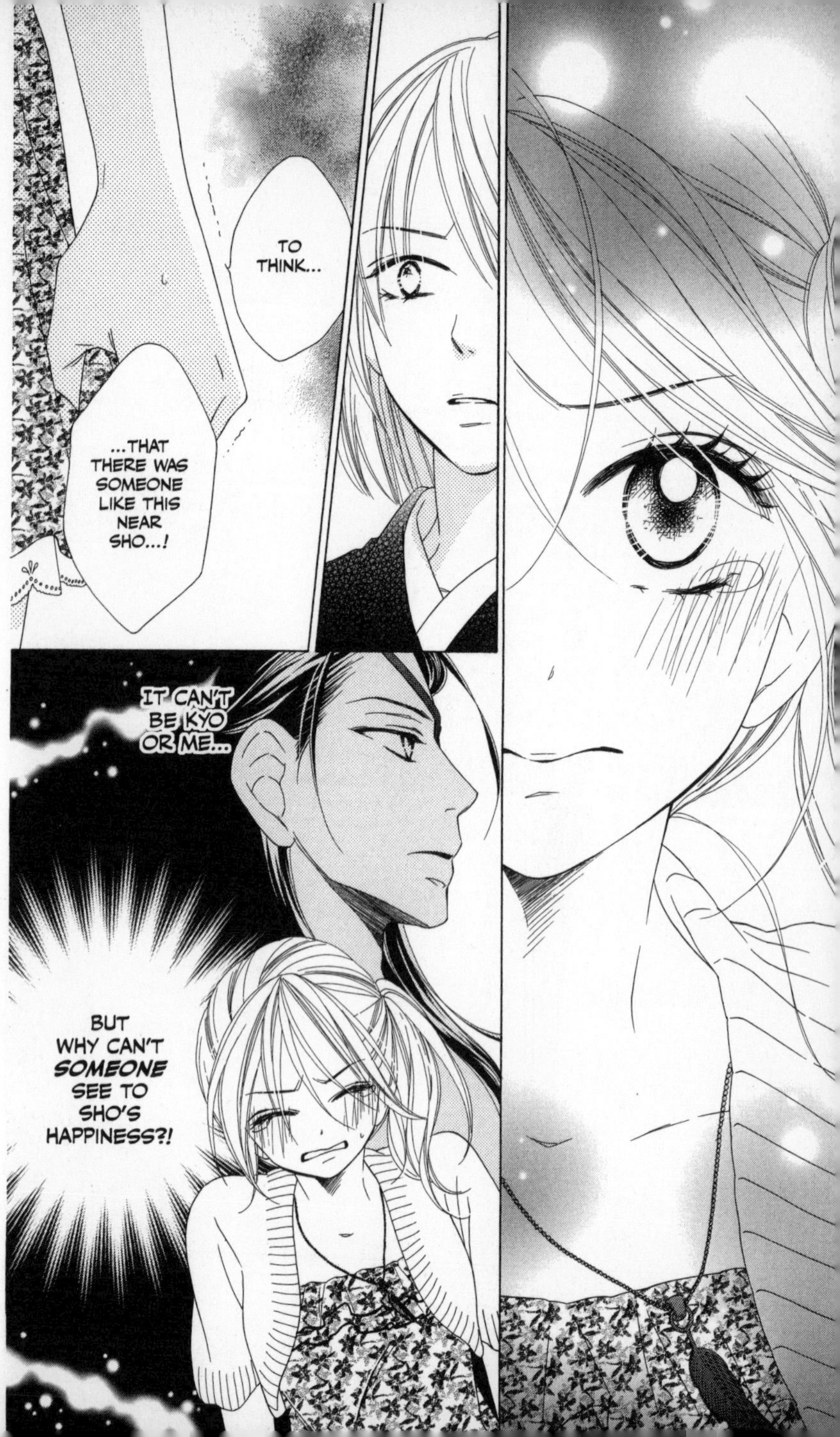
TO THINK...
...THAT THERE WAS SOMEONE LIKE THIS NEAR SHO...!
IT CAN'T BE KYO OR ME...
BUT WHY CAN'T *SOMEONE* SEE TO SHO'S HAPPINESS?!

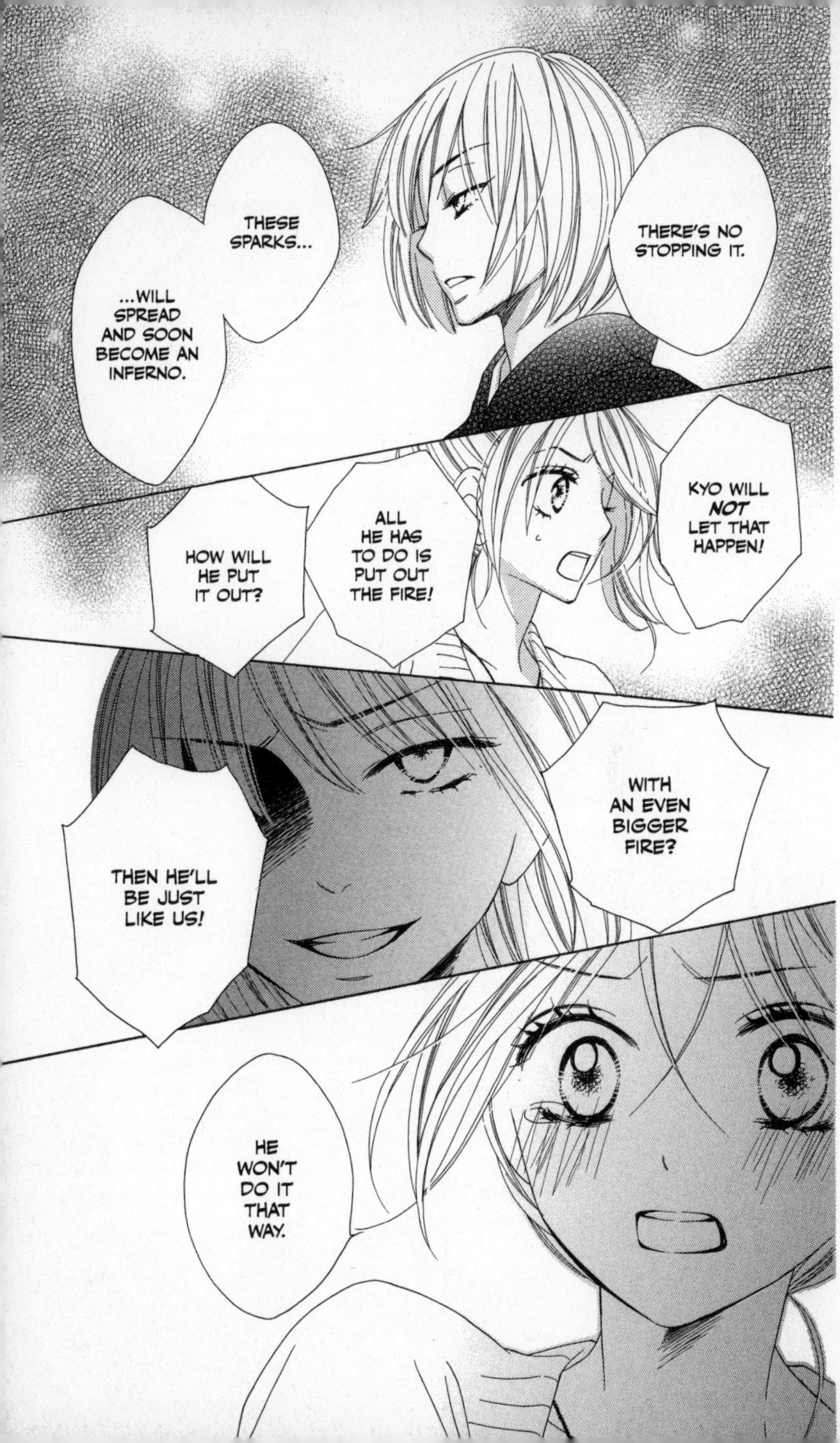
THERE'S NO STOPPING IT.
THESE SPARKS...
...WILL SPREAD AND SOON BECOME AN INFERNO.
KYO WILL ***NOT*** LET THAT HAPPEN!
ALL HE HAS TO DO IS PUT OUT THE FIRE!
HOW WILL HE PUT IT OUT?
WITH AN EVEN BIGGER FIRE?
THEN HE'LL BE JUST LIKE US!
HE WON'T DO IT THAT WAY.

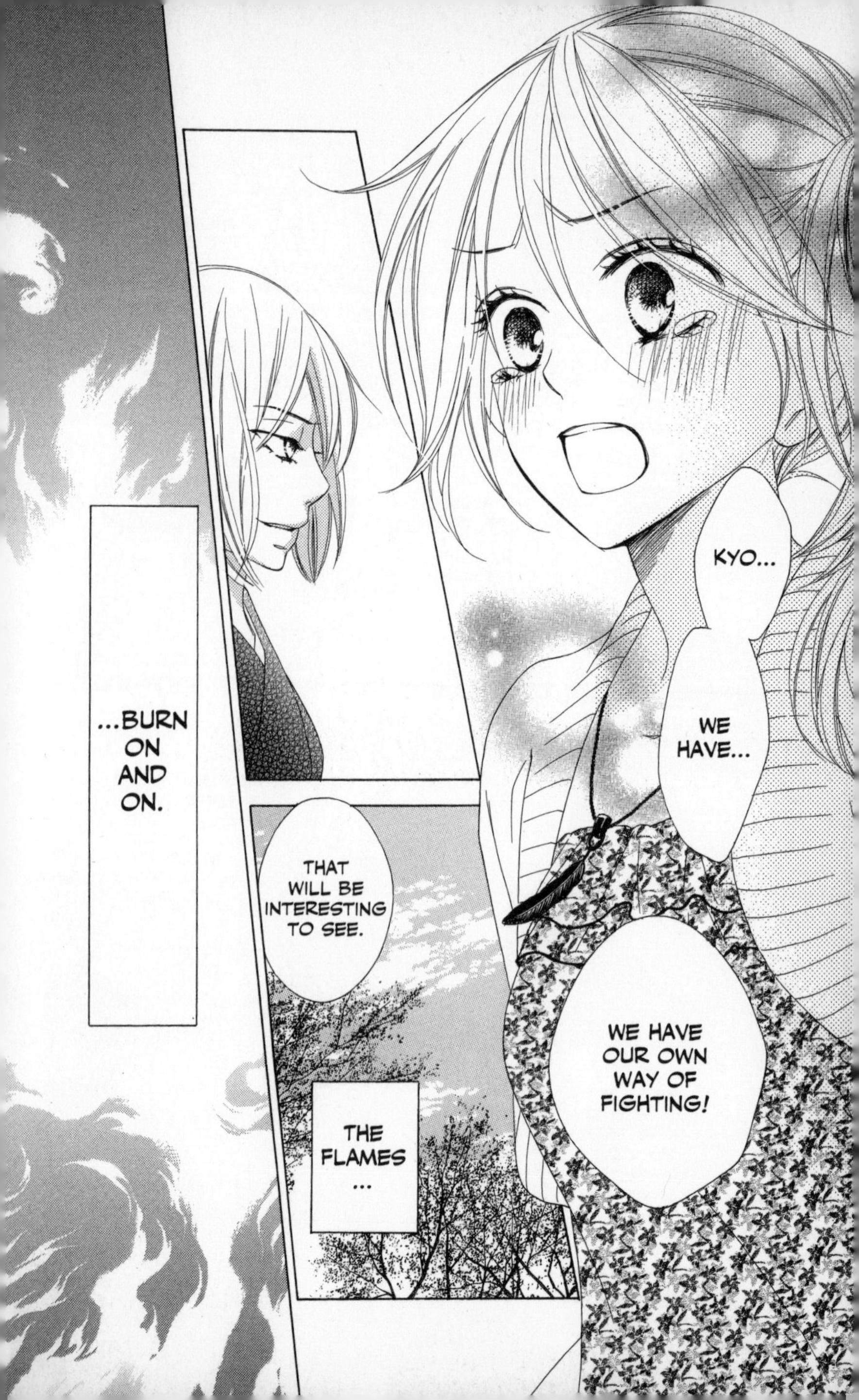
KYO...
WE HAVE...
WE HAVE OUR OWN WAY OF FIGHTING!
THAT WILL BE INTERESTING TO SEE.
THE FLAMES ...
...BURN ON AND ON.

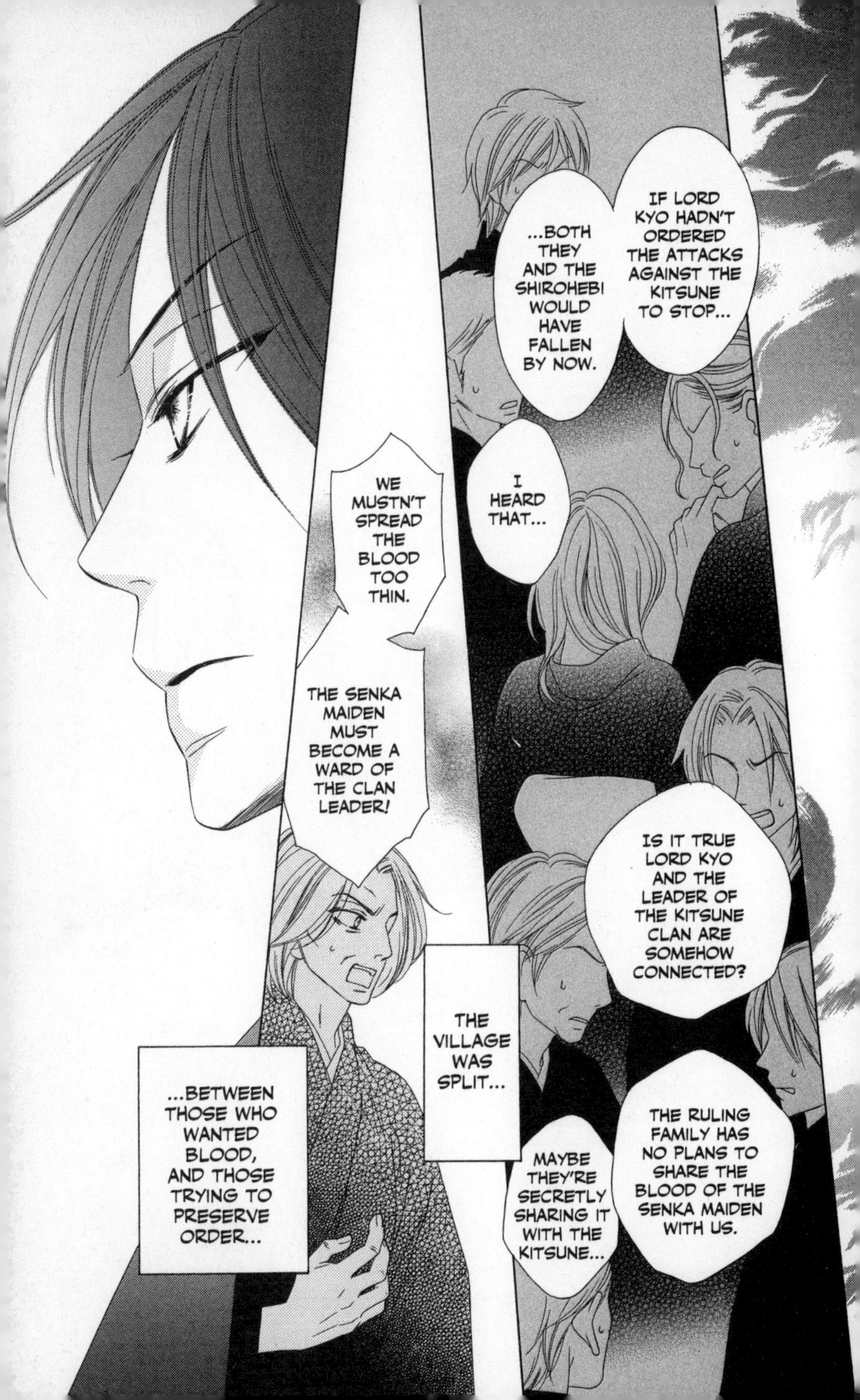
IF LORD KYO HADN'T ORDERED THE ATTACKS AGAINST THE KITSUNE TO STOP...
...BOTH THEY AND THE SHIROHEBI WOULD HAVE FALLEN BY NOW.
I HEARD THAT...
IS IT TRUE LORD KYO AND THE LEADER OF THE KITSUNE CLAN ARE SOMEHOW CONNECTED?
THE RULING FAMILY HAS NO PLANS TO SHARE THE BLOOD OF THE SENKA MAIDEN WITH US.
MAYBE THEY'RE SECRETLY SHARING IT WITH THE KITSUNE...
WE MUSTN'T SPREAD THE BLOOD TOO THIN.
THE SENKA MAIDEN MUST BECOME A WARD OF THE CLAN LEADER!
THE VILLAGE WAS SPLIT...
...BETWEEN THOSE WHO WANTED BLOOD, AND THOSE TRYING TO PRESERVE ORDER...

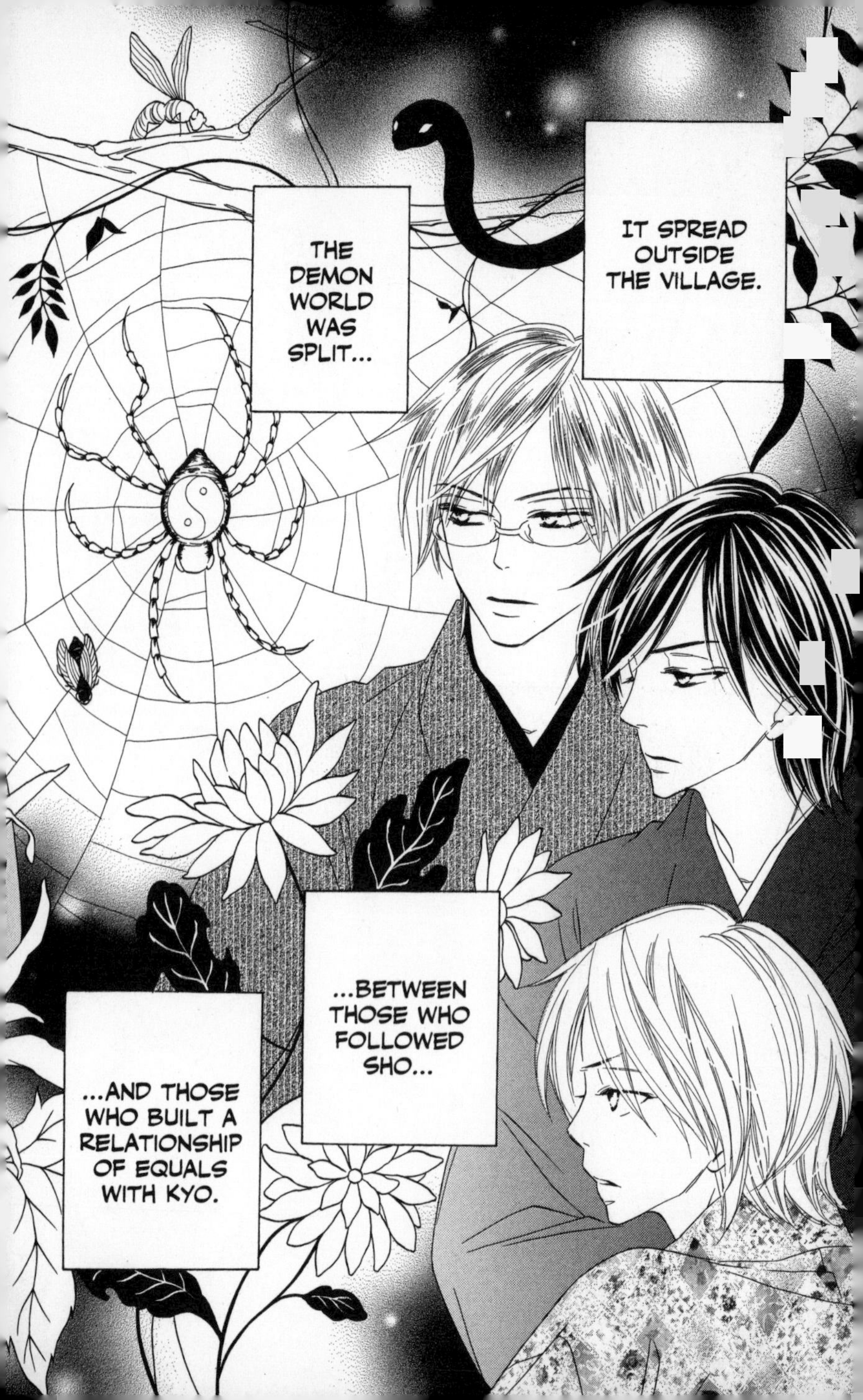
IT SPREAD OUTSIDE THE VILLAGE.
THE DEMON WORLD WAS SPLIT...
...BETWEEN THOSE WHO FOLLOWED SHO...
...AND THOSE WHO BUILT A RELATIONSHIP OF EQUALS WITH KYO.

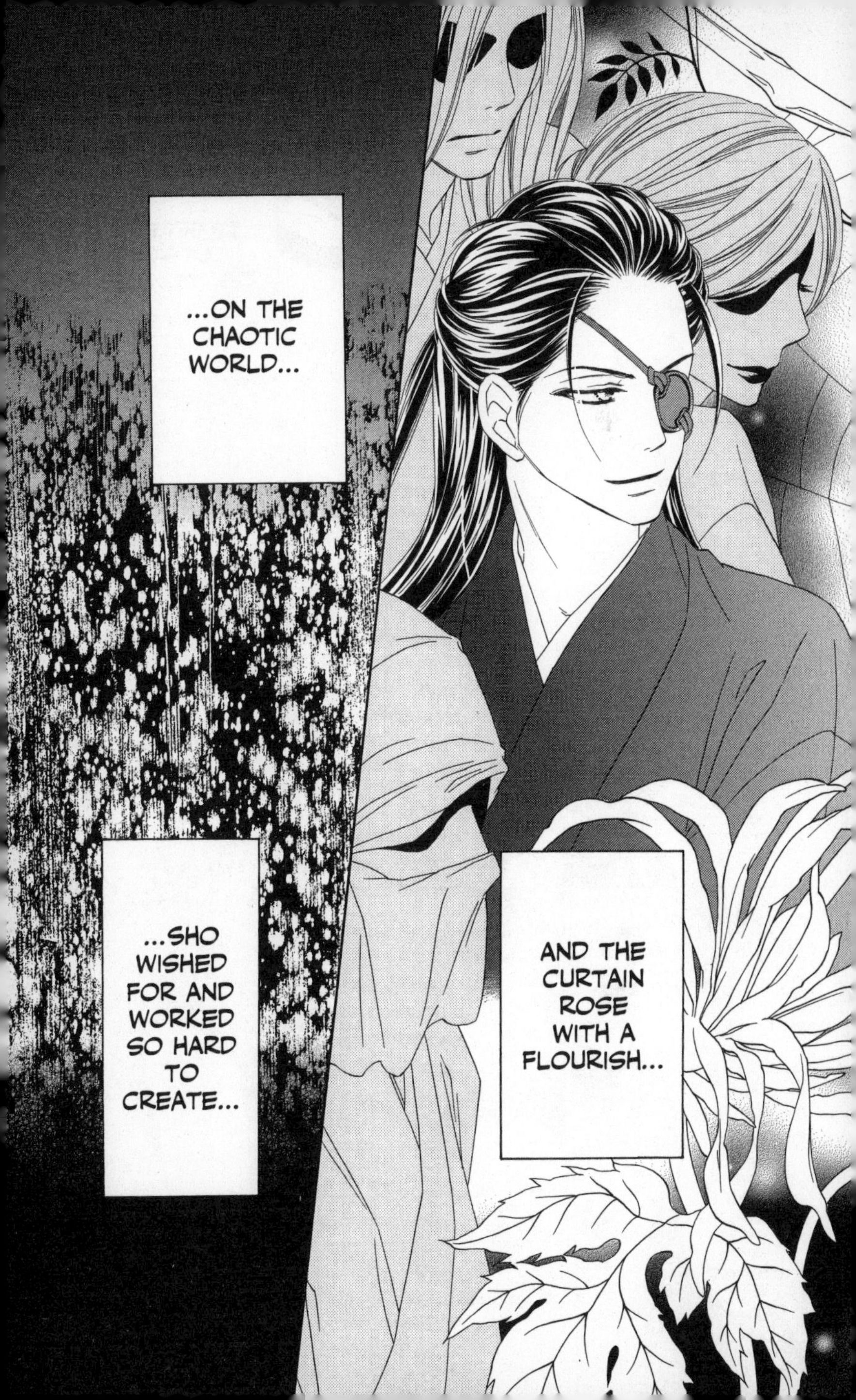
AND THE CURTAIN ROSE WITH A FLOURISH...
...ON THE CHAOTIC WORLD...
...SHO WISHED FOR AND WORKED SO HARD TO CREATE...

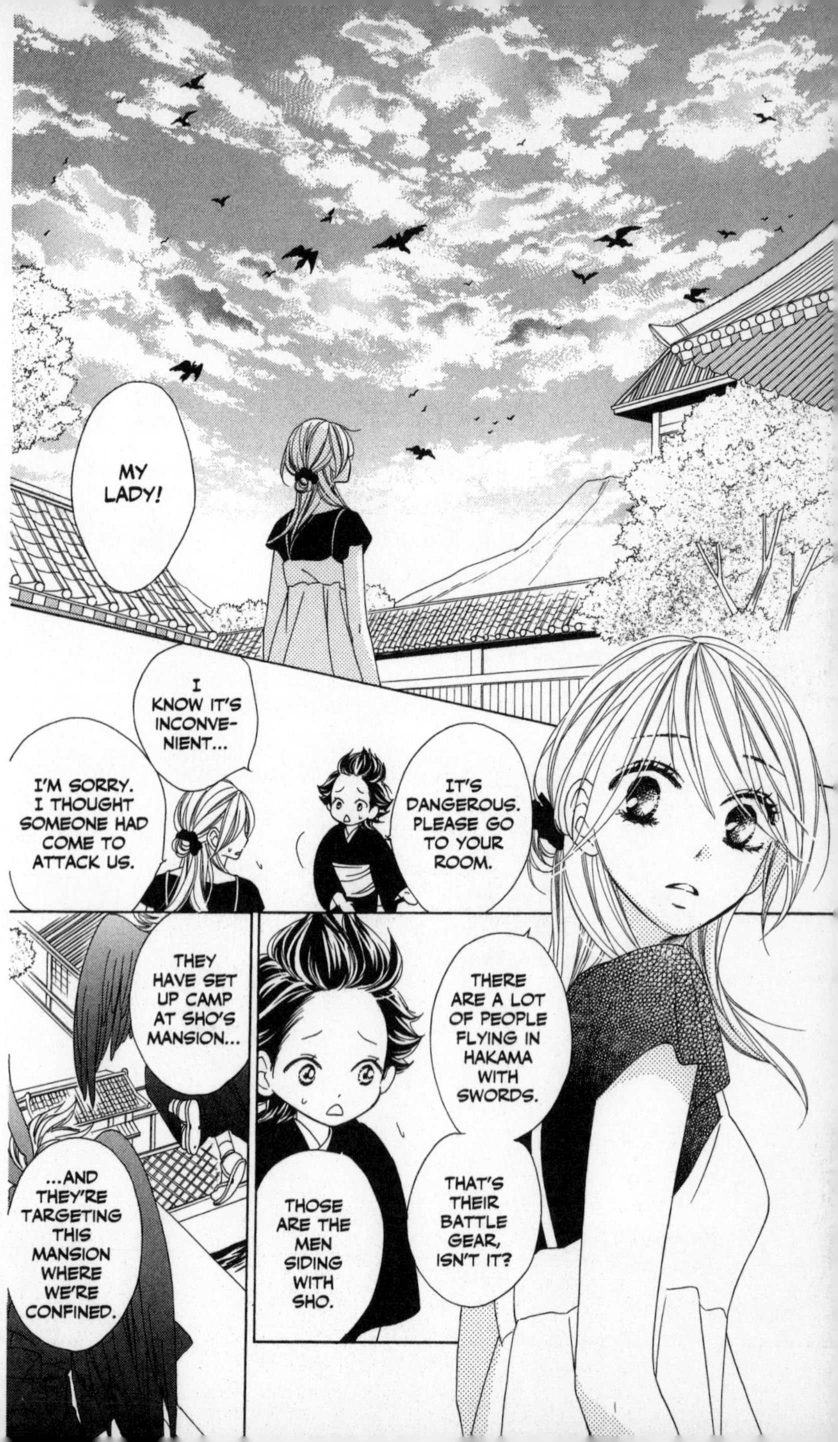
MY LADY!
IT'S DANGEROUS. PLEASE GO TO YOUR ROOM.
I KNOW IT'S INCONVE-NIENT...
I'M SORRY. I THOUGHT SOMEONE HAD COME TO ATTACK US.
THERE ARE A LOT OF PEOPLE FLYING IN HAKAMA WITH SWORDS.
THAT'S THEIR BATTLE GEAR, ISN'T IT?
THOSE ARE THE MEN SIDING WITH SHO.
THEY HAVE SET UP CAMP AT SHO'S MANSION...
...AND THEY'RE TARGETING THIS MANSION WHERE WE'RE CONFINED.

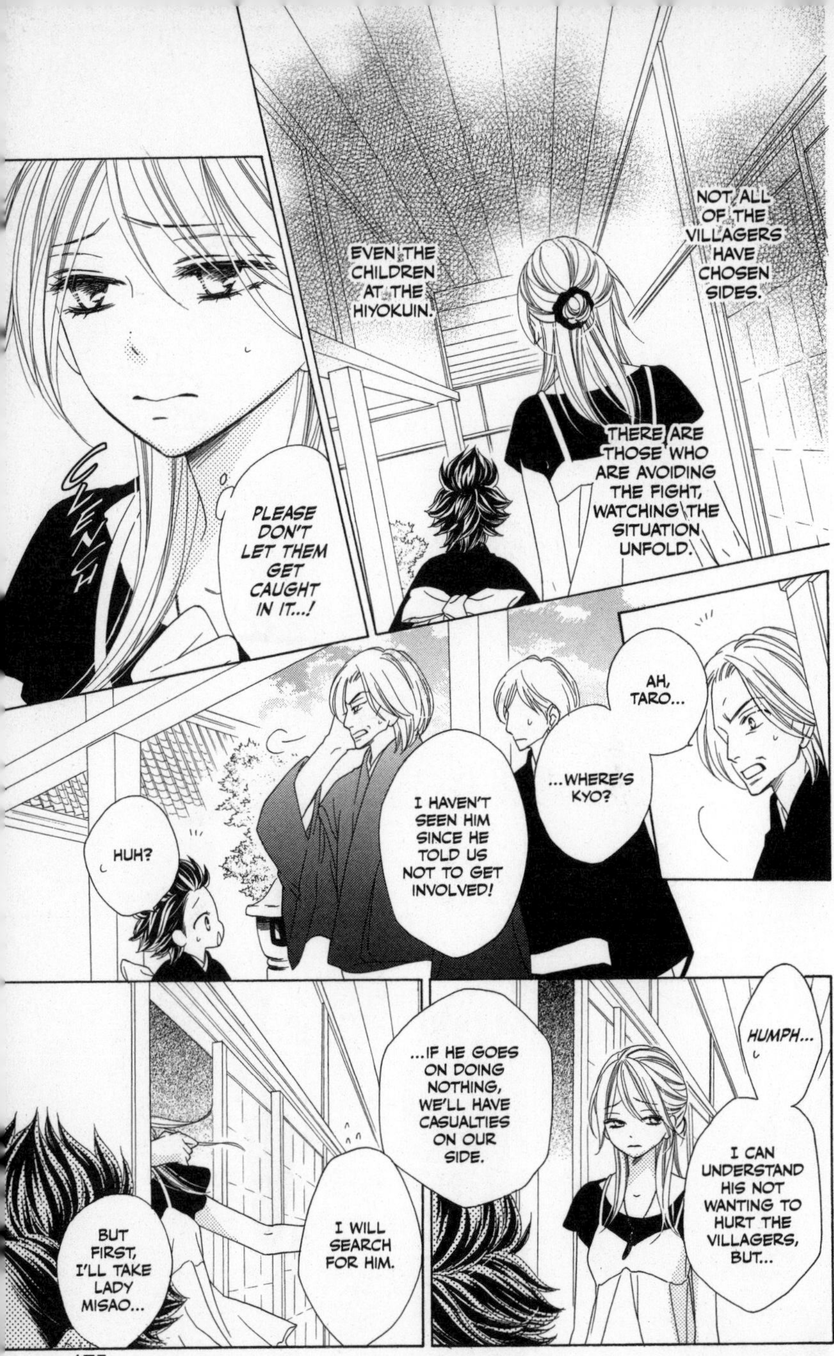
NOT ALL OF THE VILLAGERS HAVE CHOSEN SIDES.
EVEN THE CHILDREN AT THE HIYOKUIN.
THERE ARE THOSE WHO ARE AVOIDING THE FIGHT, WATCHING THE SITUATION UNFOLD.
CLENCH
PLEASE DON'T LET THEM GET CAUGHT IN IT...!
AH, TARO...
...WHERE'S KYO?
I HAVEN'T SEEN HIM SINCE HE TOLD US NOT TO GET INVOLVED!
HUH?
HUMPH...
I CAN UNDERSTAND HIS NOT WANTING TO HURT THE VILLAGERS, BUT...
...IF HE GOES ON DOING NOTHING, WE'LL HAVE CASUALTIES ON OUR SIDE.
I WILL SEARCH FOR HIM.
BUT FIRST, I'LL TAKE LADY MISAO...

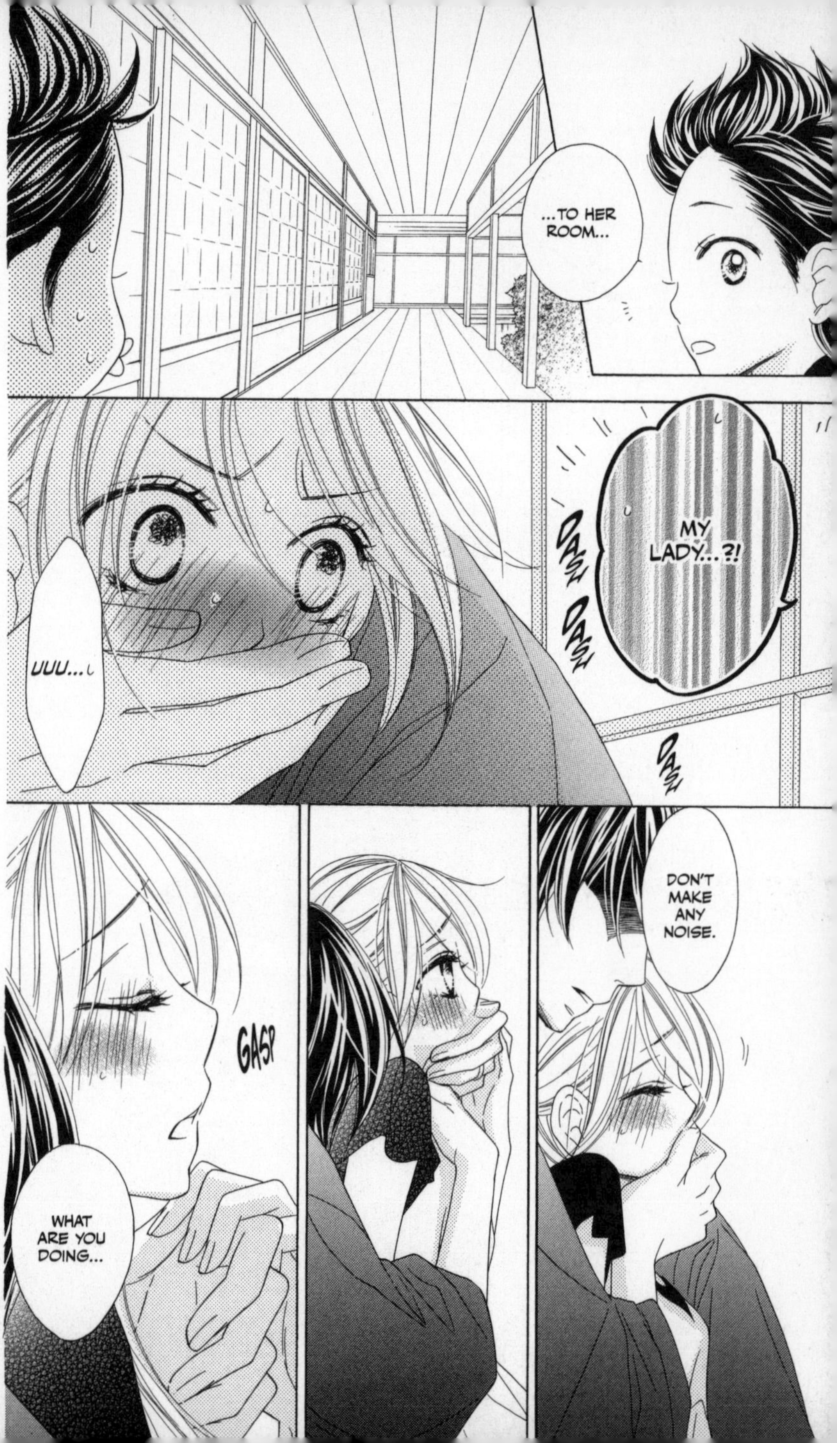
...TO HER ROOM...
MY LADY...?!
DASH DASH
DASH
UUU...
DON'T MAKE ANY NOISE.
GASP
WHAT ARE YOU DOING...

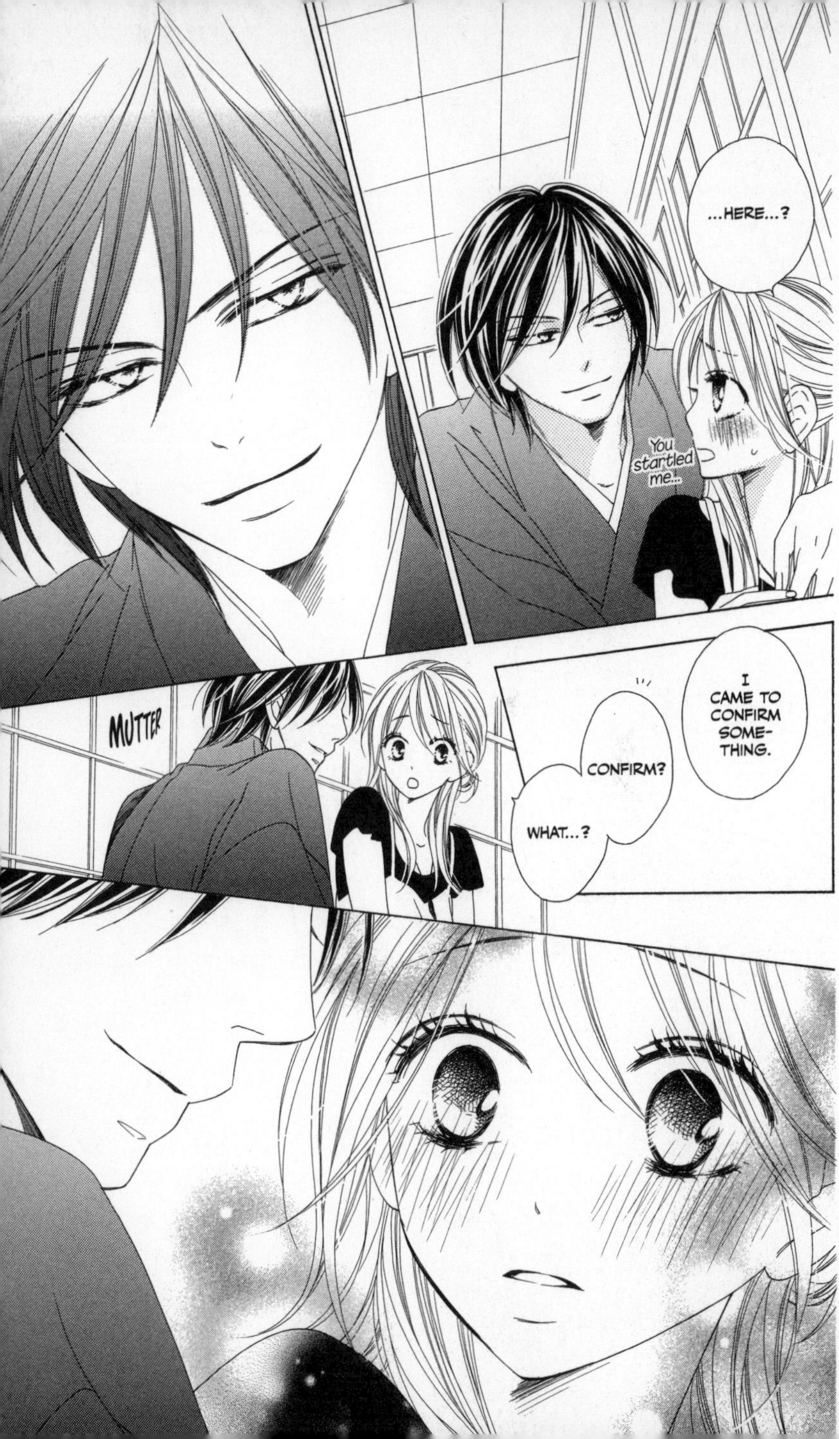
...HERE...?
You startled me...
I CAME TO CONFIRM SOME-THING.
CONFIRM?
WHAT...?
MUTTER

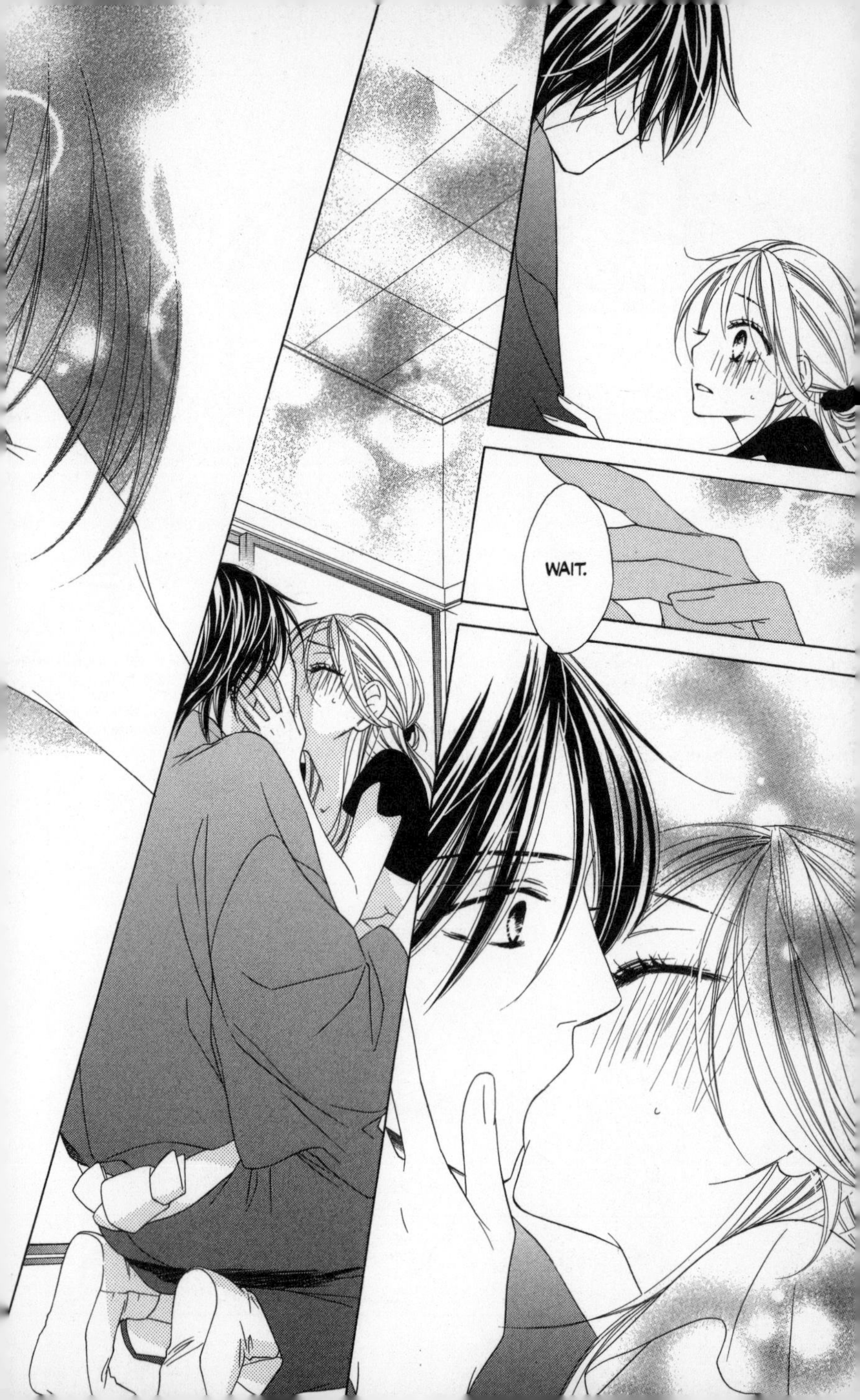
WAIT.

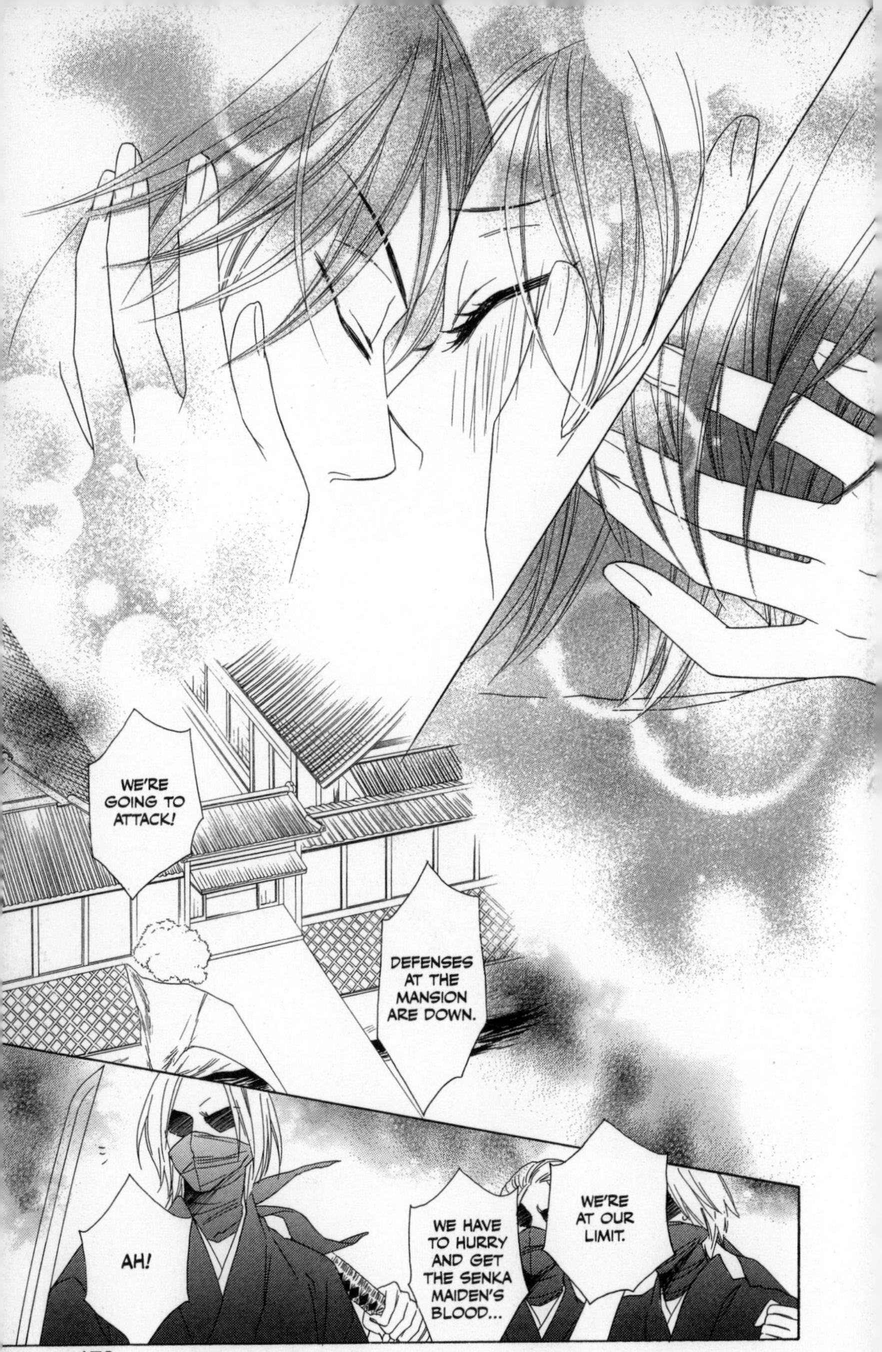
DEFENSES AT THE MANSION ARE DOWN.
WE'RE GOING TO ATTACK!
WE'RE AT OUR LIMIT.
WE HAVE TO HURRY AND GET THE SENKA MAIDEN'S BLOOD...
AH!

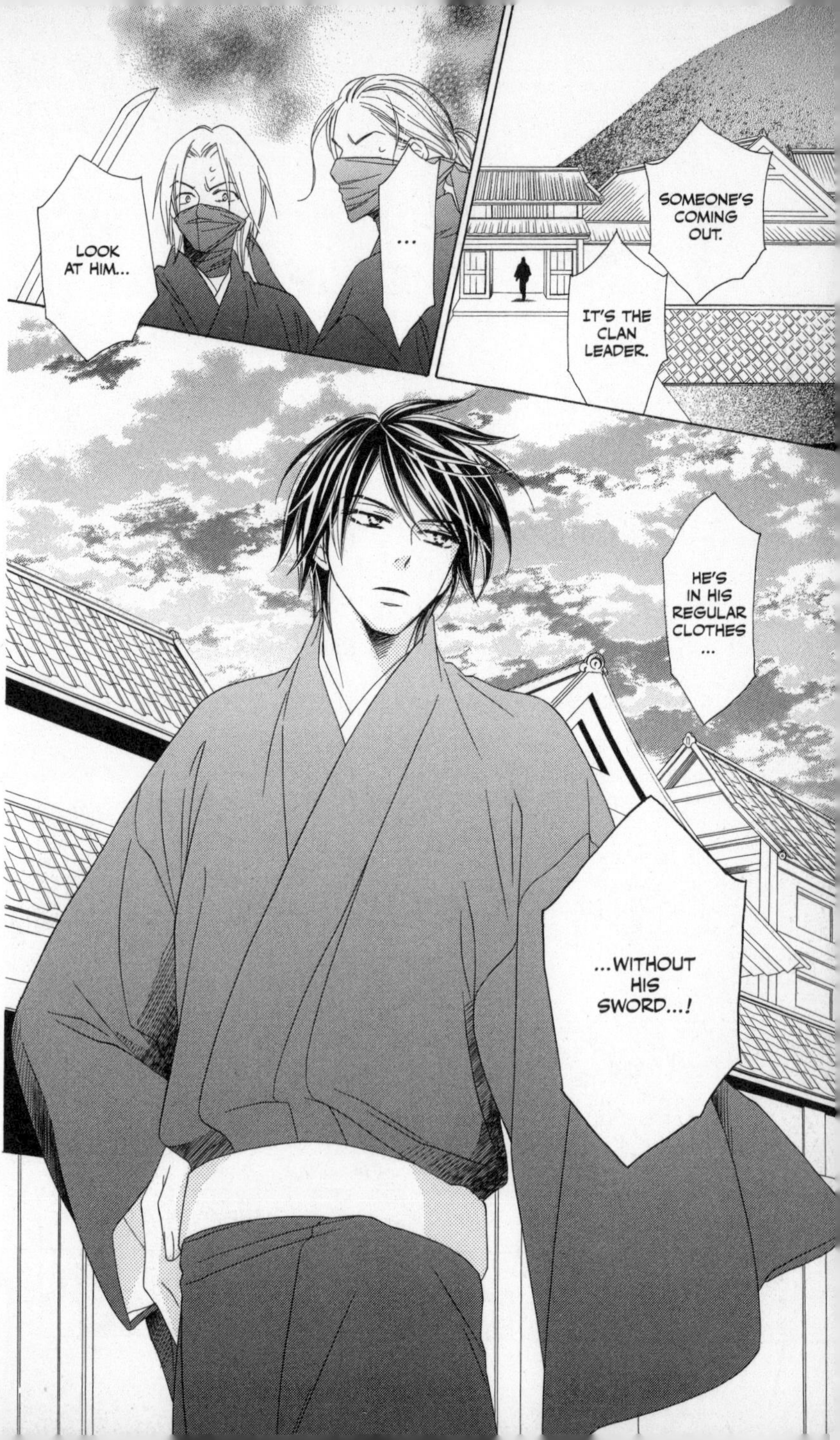
SOMEONE'S COMING OUT.
IT'S THE CLAN LEADER.
...
LOOK AT HIM...
HE'S IN HIS REGULAR CLOTHES...
...WITHOUT HIS SWORD...!

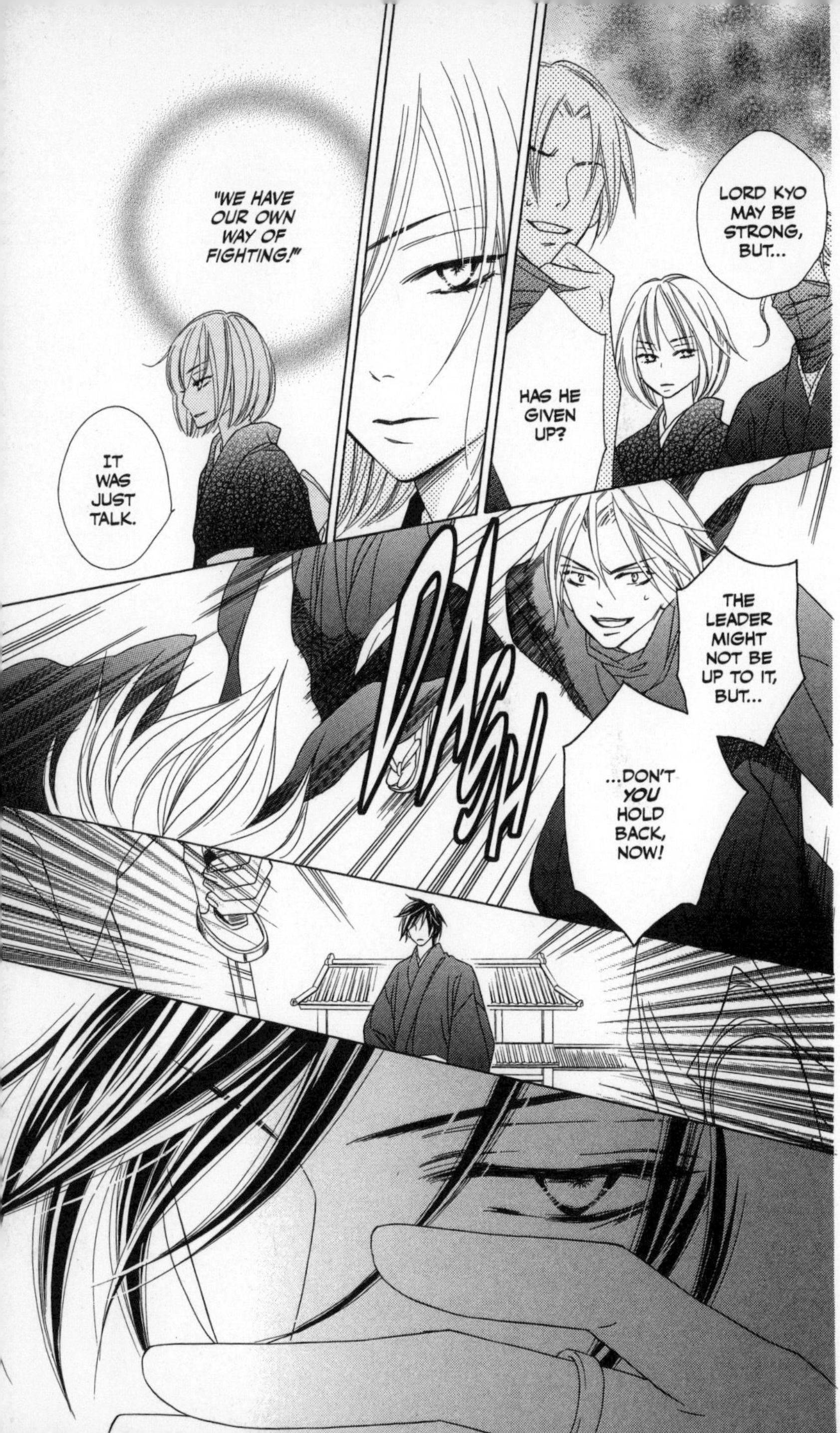
LORD KYO MAY BE STRONG, BUT...
HAS HE GIVEN UP?
"WE HAVE OUR OWN WAY OF FIGHTING!"
IT WAS JUST TALK.
THE LEADER MIGHT NOT BE UP TO IT, BUT...
...DON'T *YOU* HOLD BACK, NOW!

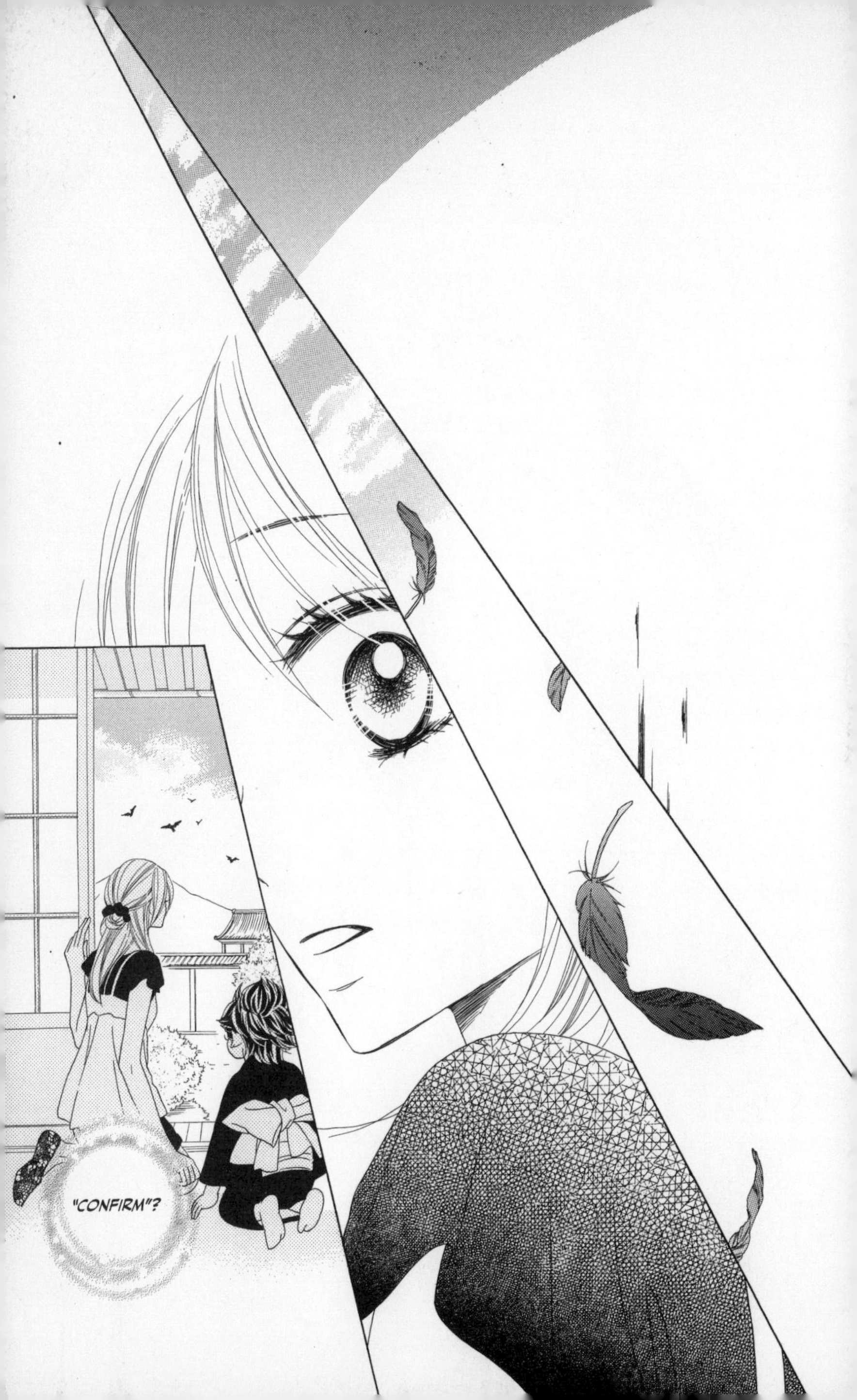
"CONFIRM"?

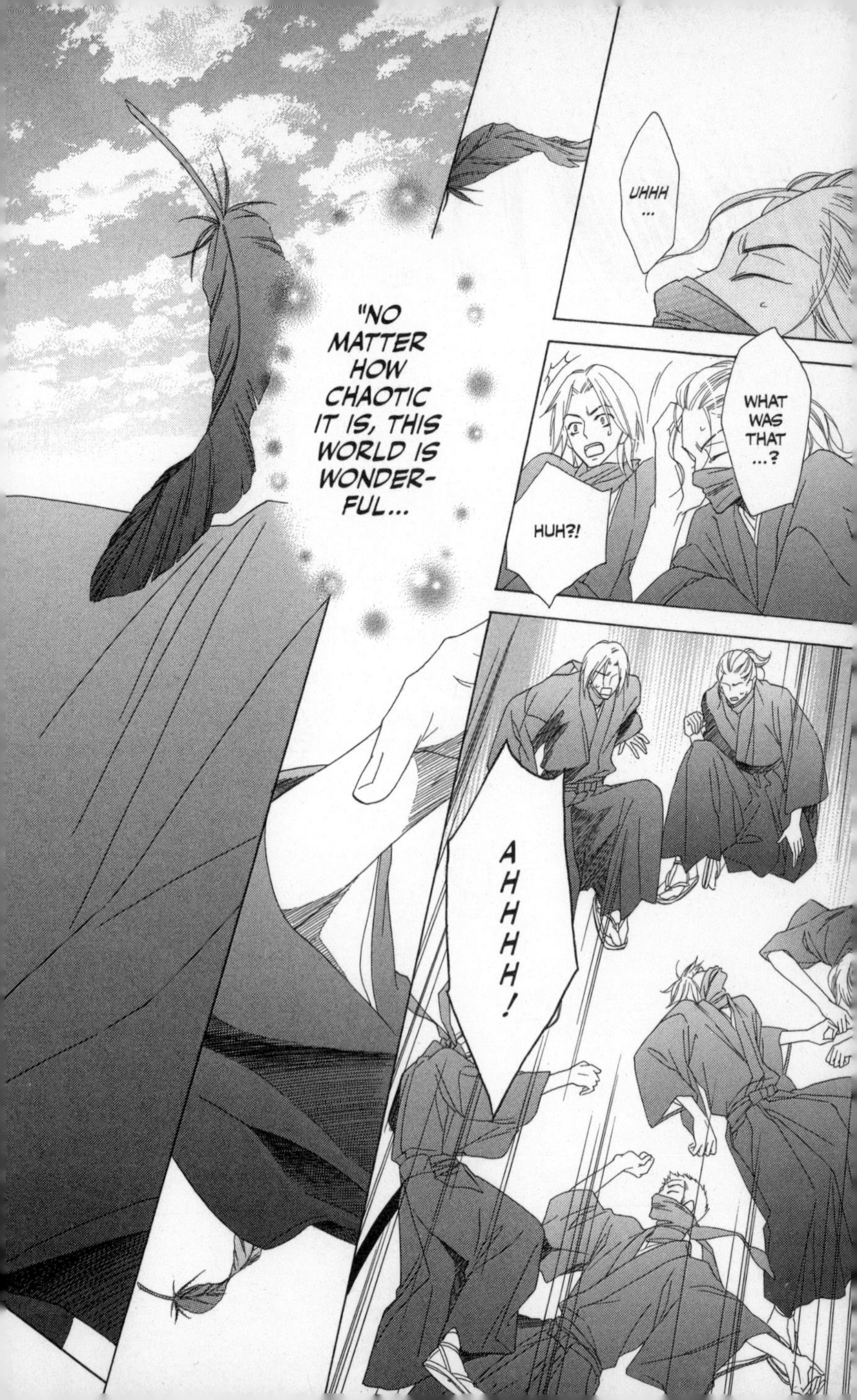
UHHH ...
WHAT WAS THAT ...?
HUH?!
AHHHHH!
"NO MATTER HOW CHAOTIC IT IS, THIS WORLD IS WONDERFUL...

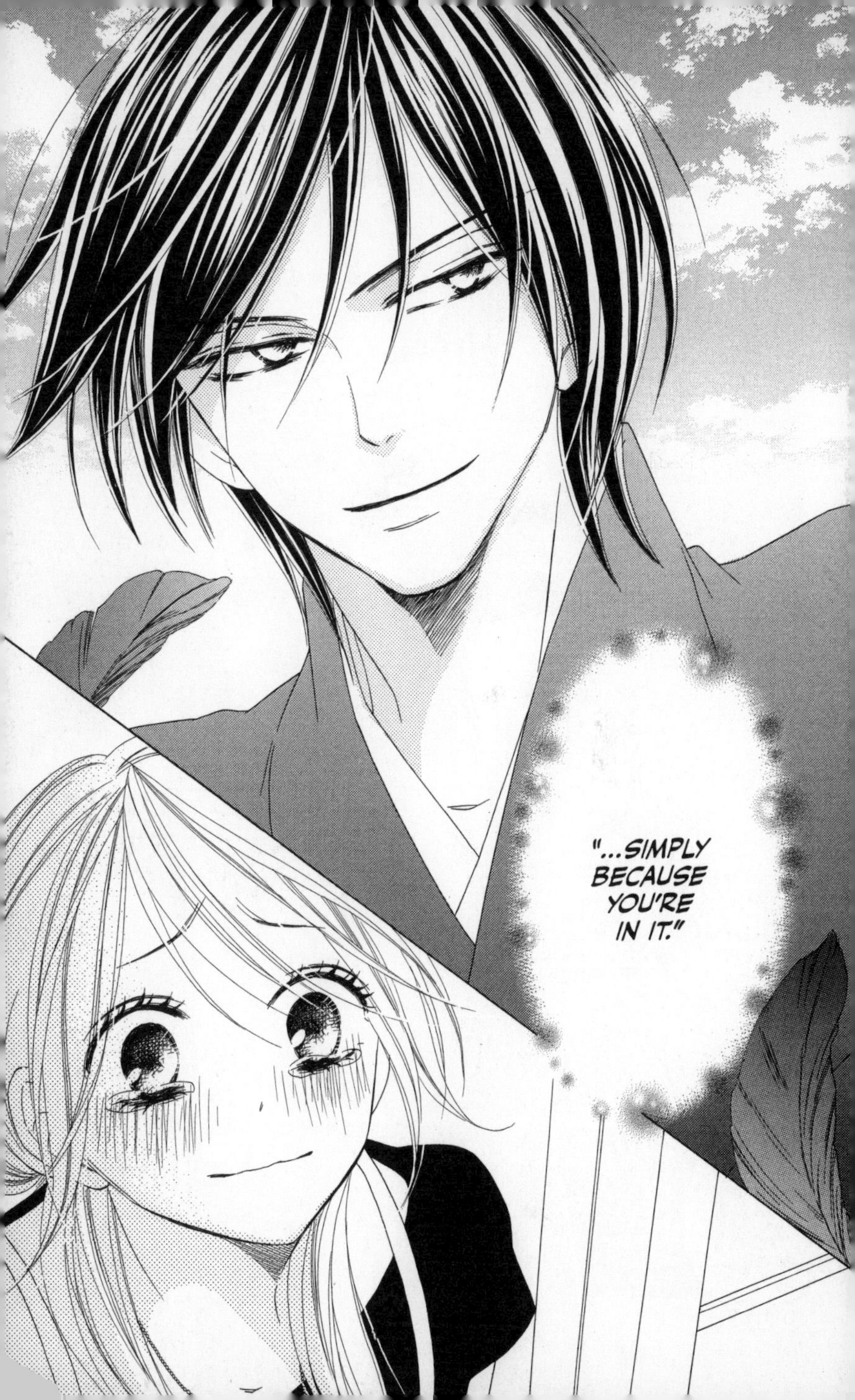
"...SIMPLY BECAUSE YOU'RE IN IT."

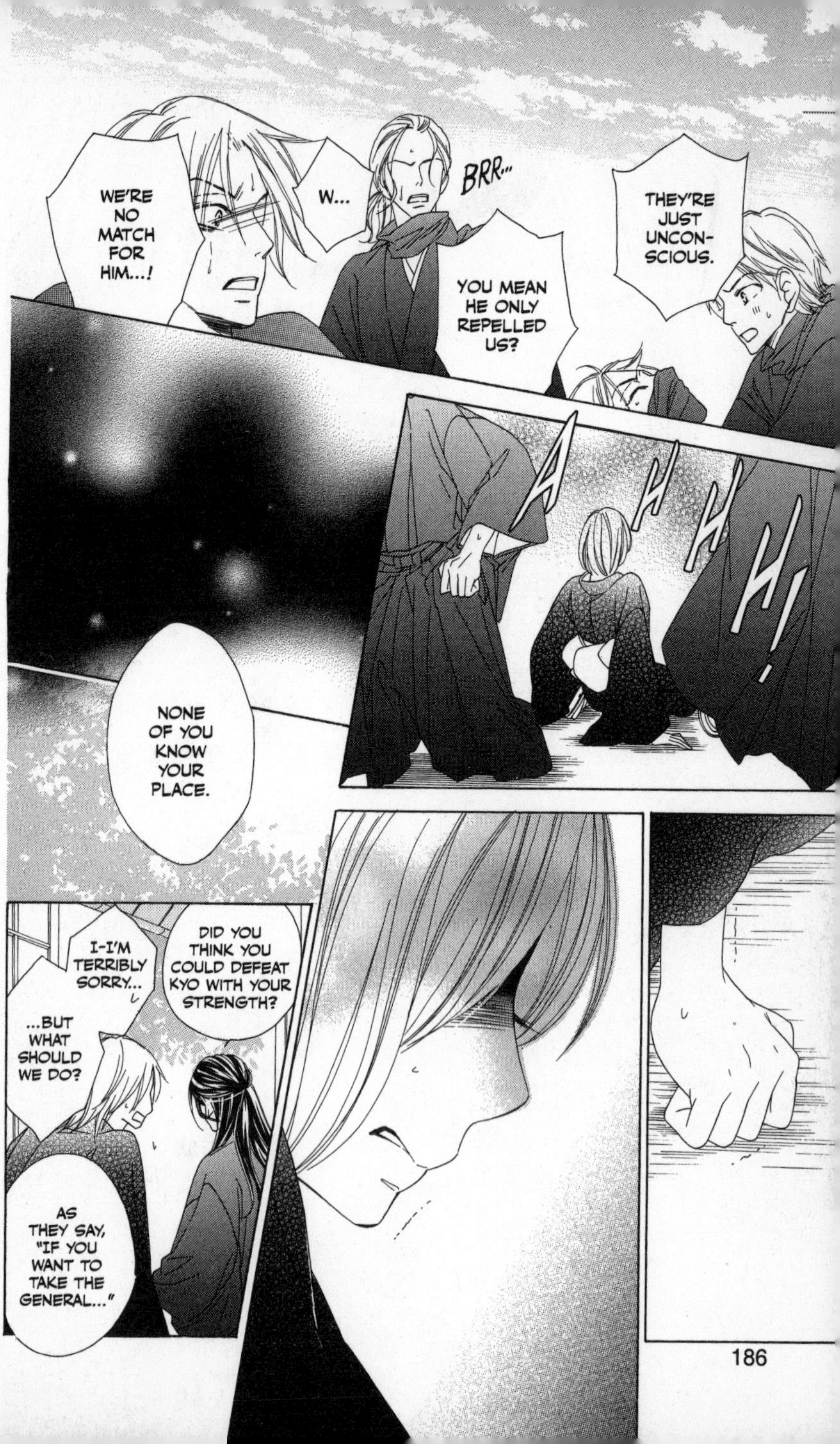
THEY'RE JUST UNCON-SCIOUS.
BRR...
W...
YOU MEAN HE ONLY REPELLED US?
WE'RE NO MATCH FOR HIM...!
AHHHHH!
NONE OF YOU KNOW YOUR PLACE.
DID YOU THINK YOU COULD DEFEAT KYO WITH YOUR STRENGTH?
I-I'M TERRIBLY SORRY...
...BUT WHAT SHOULD WE DO?
AS THEY SAY, "IF YOU WANT TO TAKE THE GENERAL..."

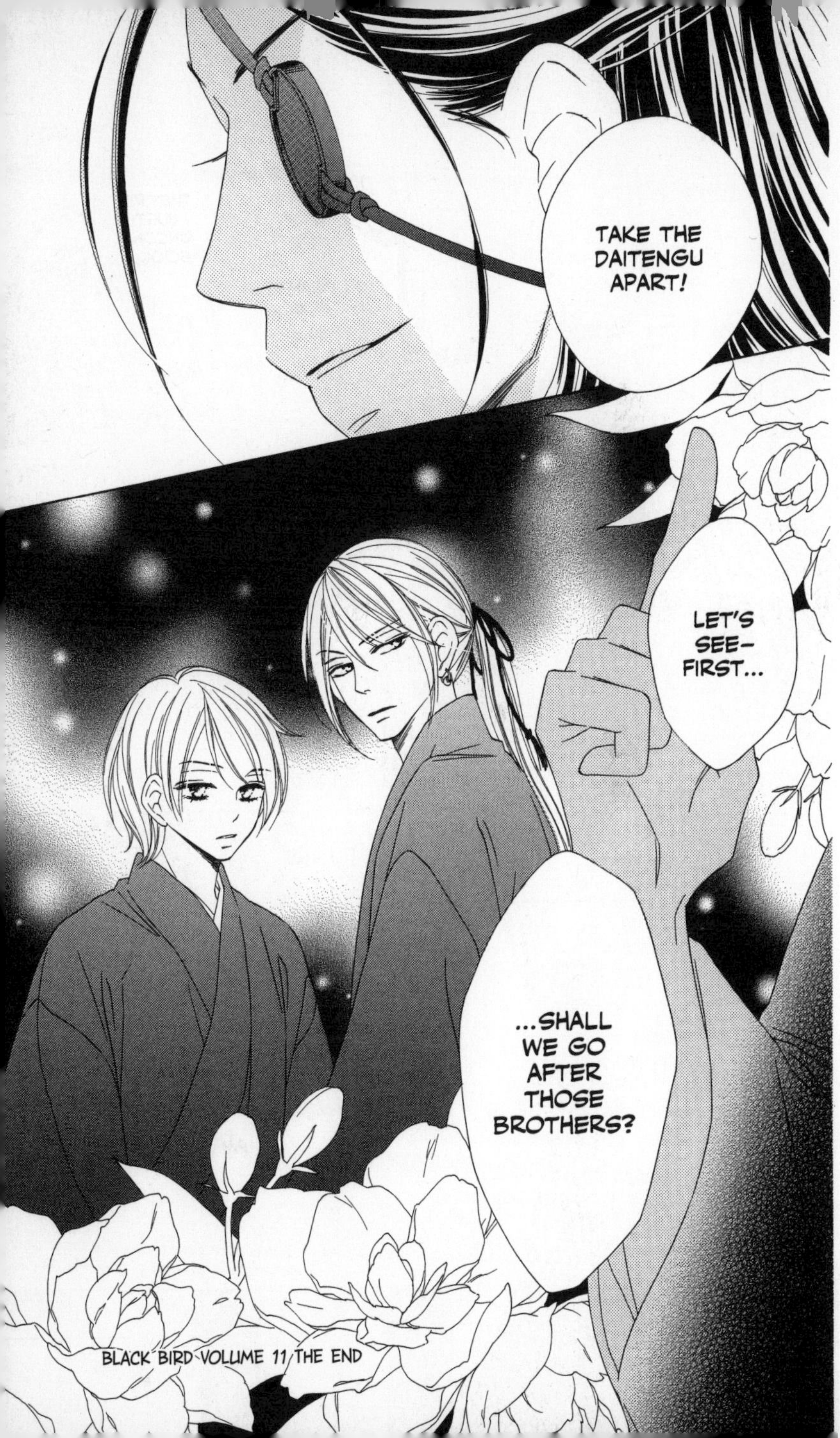
TAKE THE DAITENGU APART!
LET'S SEE—FIRST...
...SHALL WE GO AFTER THOSE BROTHERS?
BLACK BIRD VOLUME 11 THE END

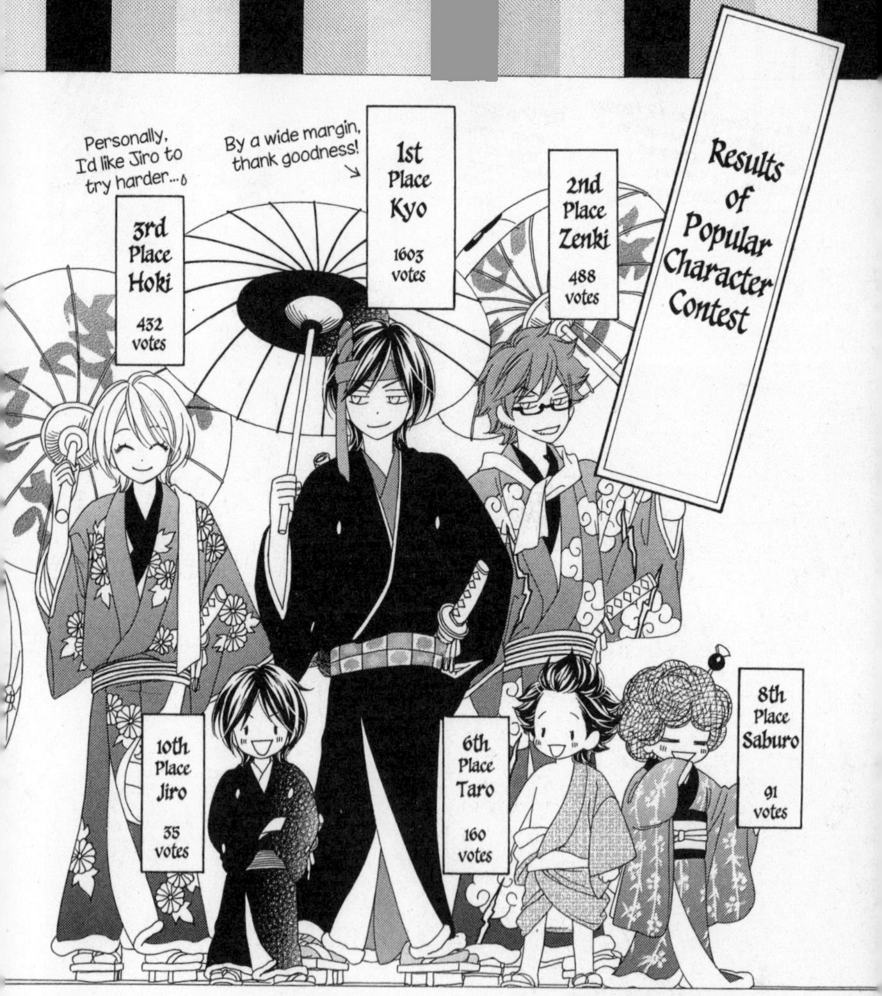
Results of Popular Character Contest
2nd Place Zenki 488 votes
1st Place Kyo 1603 votes
By a wide margin, thank goodness!
3rd Place Hoki 432 votes
Personally, I'd like Jiro to try harder...
8th Place Saburo 91 votes
6th Place Taro 160 votes
10th Place Jiro 35 votes

Great Demon Kabuki Plays

Afternoon Performances

1. Sannin Kichi Zatomoe no Shiranami
Taro - Jiro - Saburo
2. Kagami Jishi
Kensuke
3. Sukeroku Yukari no Edo Zakura
Kyo - Misao - Ayame

Evening Performances

1. Sonezaki Shinjuu
Yoh - Yuri
2. Benten Musume Meo no Shiranami
Zenki - Hoki - Sagami - Buzen - Sho

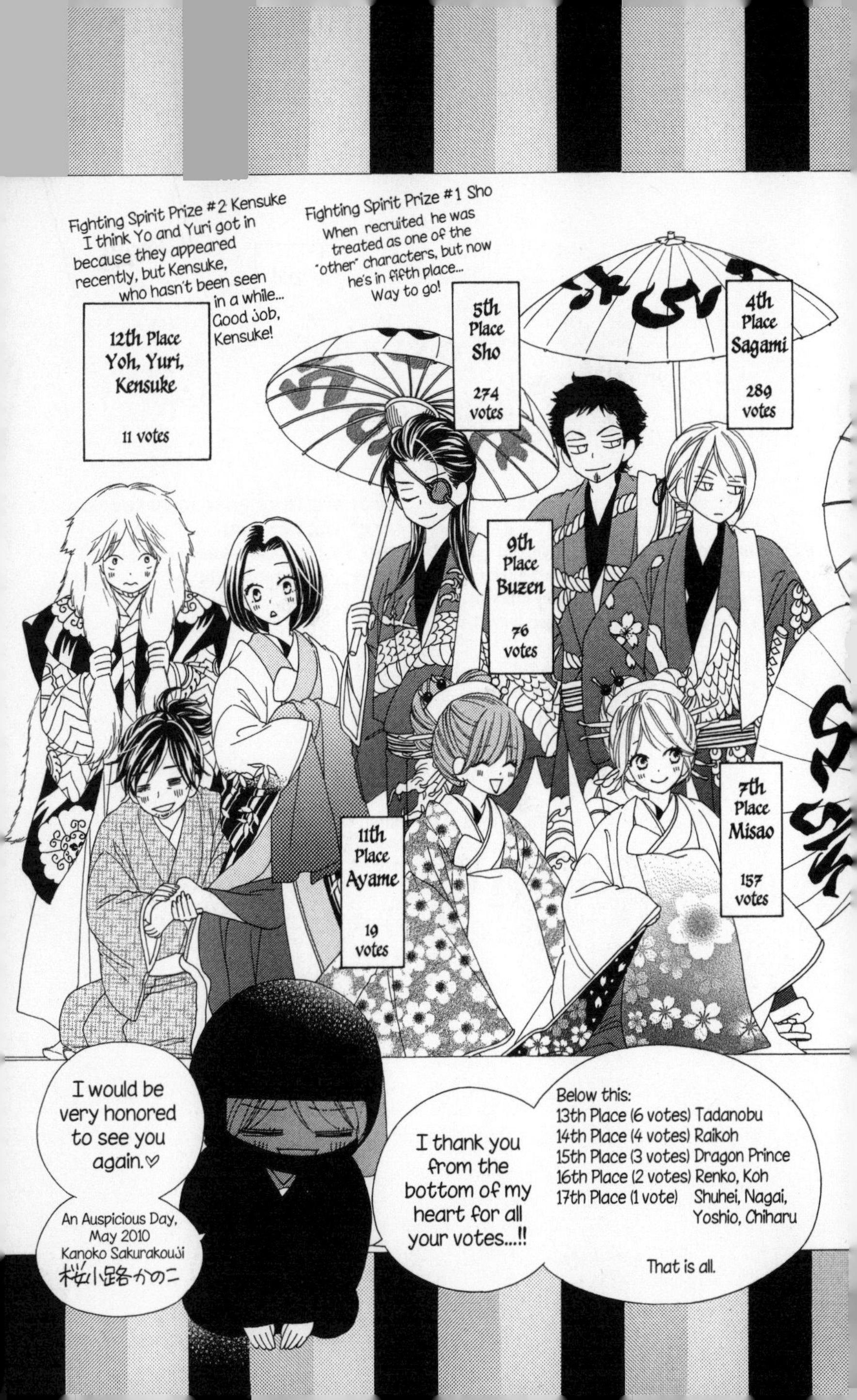
Fighting Spirit Prize #1 Sho
When recruited he was treated as one of the "other" characters, but now he's in fifth place... Way to go!
Fighting Spirit Prize #2 Kensuke
I think Yo and Yuri got in because they appeared recently, but Kensuke, who hasn't been seen in a while... Good job, Kensuke!
4th Place Sagami 289 votes
5th Place Sho 274 votes
12th Place Yoh, Yuri, Kensuke 11 votes
9th Place Buzen 76 votes
7th Place Misao 157 votes
11th Place Ayame 19 votes
Below this:
13th Place (6 votes) Tadanobu
14th Place (4 votes) Raikoh
15th Place (3 votes) Dragon Prince
16th Place (2 votes) Renko, Koh
17th Place (1 vote) Shuhei, Nagai, Yoshio, Chiharu
That is all.
I thank you from the bottom of my heart for all your votes...!!
I would be very honored to see you again.♡
An Auspicious Day, May 2010
Kanoko Sakurakouji
桜小路かのこ

GLOSSARY

PAGE 84, PANEL 1: KYO-CHAN
Chan is a type of honorific used to create diminutives. It is commonly used for and by young children and among friends. In this case, it can represent Misao's age and her close friendship with Kyo.

PAGE 174, PANEL 3: HAKAMA
A traditional Japanese garment worn with kimono. Hakama resemble pants or a skirt and are worn below the waist.

PAGE 186, PANEL 7: IF YOU WANT TO TAKE THE GENERAL...
Part of a Japanese saying. The rest goes "...first shoot his horse."

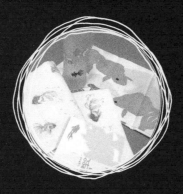

Kanoko Sakurakouji was born in downtown Tokyo, and her hobbies include reading, watching plays, traveling and shopping. Her debut title, *Raibu ga Hanetara*, ran in *Bessatsu Shojo Comic* (currently called *Bestucomi*) in 2000, and her 2004 *Bestucomi* title *Backstage Prince* was serialized in VIZ Media's *Shojo Beat* magazine. She won the 54th Shogakukan Manga Award for *Black Bird*.

BLACK BIRD
VOL. 11
Shojo Beat Edition

Story and Art by KANOKO SAKURAKOUJI

© 2007 Kanoko SAKURAKOUJI/Shogakukan
All rights reserved.
Original Japanese edition "BLACK BIRD" published by SHOGAKUKAN Inc.

TRANSLATION JN Productions
TOUCH-UP ART & LETTERING Gia Cam Luc
DESIGN Amy Martin
EDITOR Pancha Diaz

The rights of the author(s) of the work(s) in this publication
to be so identified have been asserted in accordance with
the Copyright, Designs and Patents Act 1988. A CIP catalogue
record for this book is available from the British Library.

Printed in the U.S.A.

Published by VIZ Media, LLC
P.O. Box 77010
San Francisco, CA 94107

10 9 8 7 6 5 4 3 2 1
First printing, November 2011

www.shojobeat.com   www.viz.com